The Two Horizons Old Testament Commentary

J. Gordon McConville and Craig Bartholomew, *General Editors*

Two features distinguish The Two Horizons Old Testament Commentary series: theological exegesis and theological reflection.

Exegesis since the Reformation era and especially in the past two hundred years emphasized careful attention to philology, grammar, syntax, and concerns of a historical nature. More recently, commentary has expanded to include social-scientific, political, or canonical questions and more.

Without slighting the significance of those sorts of questions, scholars in The Two Horizons Old Testament Commentary locate their primary interests on theological readings of texts, past and present. The result is a paragraph-by-paragraph engagement with the text that is deliberately theological in focus.

Theological reflection in The Two Horizons Old Testament Commentary takes many forms, including locating each Old Testament book in relation to the whole of Scripture—asking what the biblical book contributes to biblical theology—and in conversation with constructive theology of today. How commentators engage in the work of theological reflection will differ from book to book, depending on their particular theological tradition and how they perceive the work of biblical theology and theological hermeneutics. This heterogeneity derives as well from the relative infancy of the project of theological interpretation of Scripture in modern times and from the challenge of grappling with a book's message in Greco-Roman antiquity, in the canon of Scripture and history of interpretation, and for life in the admittedly diverse Western world at the beginning of the twenty-first century.

The Two Horizons Old Testament Commentary is written primarily for students, pastors, and other Christian leaders seeking to engage in theological interpretation of Scripture.

Judges

David J. H. Beldman

William B. Eerdmans Publishing Company
Grand Rapids, Michigan

Wm. B. Eerdmans Publishing Co.
4035 Park East Court SE, Grand Rapids, Michigan 49546
www.eerdmans.com

Published 2020
Printed in the United States of America

26 25 24 23 22 21 20 1 2 3 4 5 6 7

ISBN 978-0-8028-2701-2

Library of Congress Cataloging-in-Publication Data

A catalog record for this book is available from the Library of Congress.

To my parents, Simon and Mary Beldman,

my parents-in-law, Arend and Dianne Korvemaker,

and my Oma, Nellie Beldman

Contents

Acknowledgments

The roots of my academic interest in Judges go back to my doctoral research at the University of Bristol. Countless times since, I've been asked the question (usually posed with no attempt to veil the questioner's incredulity), "Why Judges?" The honest truth is that I had no intention of having anything to do with Judges when I entered my doctoral studies, but as is so often the case with research of this kind, it takes on a life of its own and develops in ways the researcher never expected. While Judges was not on my radar, it then began to emerge as a good case study (among others), and eventually consumed my doctoral dissertation. In short, my academic interest in Judges was an accident. However, I don't regret that for a moment. My understanding of Judges was solidified during those years and this commentary is indebted to the sustained focus on Judges at that time. I read widely and interacted with both dominant and obscure secondary sources on Judges. All those sources have certainly influenced my understanding of the book and, thus, I want to acknowledge my indebtedness to them here, even if they do not appear in the footnotes. This commentary includes a revised and expanded version of chapter four of my dissertation, which I did not include in the published version.[1] I'm grateful for the supervision of my research on Judges at that time that Gordon Wenham and Trent Butler provided.

I'm deeply grateful to the editors of The Two Horizons Old Testament Commentary series, Craig Bartholomew and Gordon McConville, for inviting me to contribute to the series and reserving the commentary for me until I had finished my PhD. Craig has been a mentor, a colleague, and a friend for many years now. We've often discussed how biblical scholars are rarely adequately

1. *The Completion of Judges: Strategies of Ending in Judges 17–21*, Siphrut 21 (Winona Lake, IN: Eisenbrauns, 2018).

trained for the task of theological interpretation of the kind that this series represents, and at the end of this project I feel that more strongly than ever before. Craig's input and encouragement, not to mention the inspiration of his own work, have been of inestimable value. Additionally, my gratitude goes out to Andrew Knapp and the whole editorial team at Eerdmans for their work in improving this volume and bringing it to publication.

The members of the committee of the Scripture and Hermeutics Seminar (Amber Bowen, A. J. Culp, Matthew Emerson, William Olhausen, Heath Thomas, and Luke Wisely) as well as the wider Scripture and Hermeutics Seminar community have also been a source of encouragement and inspiration for this project. I was grateful to present some of my ideas on Judges at the Scripture and Hermeutics Seminar annual meeting in Boston in 2017. Thanks as well go to my friends A. J. Culp and Daniel Lowery—our annual get togethers provided not only lots of laughs but encouragement for the task (I'm grateful to Daniel for helping me get hold of much needed sources at just the right time).

I'm thankful for my colleagues and students at Redeemer University College and at the Missional Training Centre in Phoenix for indulging my passion for Judges and providing good feedback. A generous grant from the Stanford and Priscilla Reid Trust afforded me some extra time to do research and writing for this project, for which I'm very grateful. I would be negligent if I did not acknowledge our good friends Brian and Holly for their gracious gift of a distraction-free space to write in the final stages—I'm grateful for such a productive writing retreat that they provided.

As always, I'm thankful for the unconditional love, encouragement, and support of my wife Elsie and our children. Thanks for enduring my periodic nattering about some discovery or other I made with regard to Judges. Thank you for your patience and the sacrifices you made so that I could work on this project. I'm also grateful for the support of my parents and parents-in-law, to whom, with my Oma who in the year that I finished this commentary turned one hundred years old, I dedicate this book. Their commitment to passing on a love for God and a knowledge of his great redemptive deeds on behalf of his people has impacted subsequent generations.

Dave Beldman
September, 2018

Abbreviations

AB	Anchor Bible
ABRL	Anchor Bible Reference Library
ANEM	Ancient Near East Monographs
Ant.	Josephus, *Jewish Antiquities*
Apos. Con.	Apostolic Constitutions
BDB	Brown, Francis , S. R. Driver, and Charles A. Briggs, *A Hebrew and English Lexicon of the Old Testament*
Bib	*Biblica*
BibInt	*Biblical Interpretation*
BibInt	Biblical Interpretation Series
BR	*Bible Review*
BSac	*Bibliotheca sacra*
BT	*Bible Translator*
CBQ	*Catholic Biblical Quarterly*
Cels.	Origen, *Against Celsus*
CTJ	*Calvin Theological Journal*
CurBR	*Currents in Biblical Research*
ErIsr	*Eretz-Israel*
EvQ	*Evangelical Quarterly*
FOTL	Forms of the Old Testament Literature
Haer.	Irenaeus *Against Heresies*
IBC	Interpretation: A Bible Commentary for Teaching and Preaching
ICC	International Critical Commentary
Int	*Interpretation*
ISBL	Indiana Studies in Biblical Literature
JBL	*Journal of Biblical Literature*
JETS	*Journal of the Evangelical Theological Society*

Jov.	Jerome, *Treatise Against Jovinianus*
JPT	*Journal of Pentecostal Theology*
JPTSup	Journal of Pentecostal Theology Supplement
JSOT	*Journal for the Study of the Old Testament*
JSOTSup	Journal for the Study of the Old Testament: Supplement Series
LAB	Liber antiquitatum biblicarum
LCC	Library of Christian Classics
LHBOTS	Library of Hebrew Bible/Old Testament Studies
Marc.	Tertullian *Against Marcion*
NAB	New American Bible
NAC	The New American Commentary
NASB	New American Standard Bible
NICOT	New International Commentary on the Old Testament
NIV	New International Version
NIVAC	New International Version Application Commentary
NJB	New Jerusalem Bible
NJPS	New Jewish Publication Society
NLT	New Living Translation
NRSV	New Revised Standard Version
OTL	Old Testament Library
OTR	Old Testament Readings
Proof	*Prooftexts: A Journal of Jewish Literary History*
PRSt	*Perspectives in Religious Studies*
REB	Revised English Bible
RTR	*Reformed Theological Review*
Scorp.	Tertullian, *Antidote for the Scorpion's Sting*
SJOT	*Scandinavian Journal of the Old Testament*
Spir.	Ambrose, *The Holy Spirit*
STJHC	Studies and Texts in Jewish History and Culture
Strom.	Clement of Alexandria, *Miscellanies*
Symp.	Methodius, *The Banquet of the Ten Virgins or Concerning Chastity*
TBN	Themes in Biblical Narrative
Test.	Cyprian, *To Quirinius: Testimonies against the Jews*
THOTC	Two Horizons Old Testament Commentary
TOTC	Tyndale Old Testament Commentaries
TynBul	*Tyndale Bulletin*
Vid.	Ambrose, *Concerning Widows*
VT	*Vetus Testamentum*
VTSup	Supplements to Vetus Testamentum
WBC	Word Biblical Commentary

Theological Introduction

Introduction to Judges

Murder, warfare, state and economic terrorism, sexual exploitation, child abuse, political assassination, nepotism, perversion of justice, authoritarianism, populism, tribalism, revolution—one might see this list and suppose that it was drawn from today's newspaper headlines and social media newsfeeds. In fact, the list is just some of the topics and situations that readers encounter on the pages of Judges. As I am writing this introduction troubling stories are breaking from around the world. To name just one, the Saudi Arabian government literally just (in the last twenty-four hours) released a statement that the assassination at the Saudi consulate in Turkey of *Washington Post* journalist Jamal Khashoggi (who it seems was tortured, killed, and whose slain body was cut into pieces and hidden in the consulate gardens) was premeditated. The media outlets will not allow us easily to ignore this and other troubling current events, but somehow we often ignore the equally troubling events we find in Judges. Christians today have reasons for and ways of ignoring the geopolitical, economic, and social dimensions of the book of Judges. A pervasive dualism often prevents us from seeing the connection between faith and matters of a public nature (politics, etc.). Judges forces us to confront the reality that faith has *everything* to do with these matters; in fact, it paints for us a disturbing picture of what happens when social order is not oriented toward God and his purposes for the world.

Judges is a book about God's covenant people whose witness and way of being in the world had been deeply compromised by the religion and culture of the surrounding nations. A seemingly insignificant nation among the powerful empires all around them, they could have experienced and influenced widespread and profound blessing in allegiance to Yahweh and his kingdom, but instead divided their allegiance, which only brought violence, misery, and chaos. Judges marks a pivotal moment in Israel's history as the people were settling into the promised land and forging a society in their new location. However, as they were settling into Canaan, "Canaan" was settling into them. The results are shocking. The puzzling behavior of God's people in this time and the resulting violence have caused contemporary readers of Judges to shy away from the book and its message. However, these things should make the book more relevant and not less so for God's people today. Judges offers a profound message about the calling of God's people and the power of idolatry that prevents them from being the salt and light they are called to be.

The crisis of Israel in the settlement period is a good example of what Andy Crouch discusses as institutional failure.[1] Crouch charts the general patterns in the initiation, growth, and establishment of institutions. All institutions, according to Crouch, emerge out of some creational good (what he refers to as an image-bearing quality), but also contain in their inception seeds of sin (what he identifies as patterns of idolatry and injustice). He observes that by the third generation every institution experiences failure.[2] Key to the enduring success and flourishing of an institution beyond failure is the exposure and rooting out of idolatry and injustice and a more consistent rooting in God's design and order for the world. Thus, "Some institutions, by the common or special grace of God, plant themselves deeply enough in the soil of image bearing that they sustain creativity and flourish in spite of their failures. But others not only fail but die—or worse."[3] The "worse" that Crouch refers to is a kind of zombie-like existence in which the institution continues to limp along, neither fully alive nor fully dead.

This precisely describes the situation of Israel during the period of the judges. Three generations from those foundational, identity-forming events of the exodus from Egypt and the Sinai covenant, God's people are in crisis. They have arrived in the promised land and are emerging as a nation, but the seeds of idolatry and injustice are in full bloom, strangling the image-bearing quality of the covenant people. The response to failure does not result in rooting out idolatry and injustice—in fact the people wrongly diagnose the problem (i.e., unstable political governance) and consequently propose the wrong solution (i.e., strong, perpetual leadership). We witness a seemingly unending cycle, in which the people of God are not dead, but they are by no means thriving and flourishing. Israel is a zombie nation!

In this way, Judges stands as a prophetic clarion call for the people of God today. To what extent have the seeds of idolatry taken root and choked out

1. Crouch, *Playing God*, 195–206.
2. Crouch, *Playing God*, 197.
3. Crouch, *Playing God*, 197.

our call to bear the image of Christ in the context of the twenty-first century? Is our commitment to the idols of our day compromising our calling to be faithful witnesses to Jesus and his countercultural kingdom for the sake of the flourishing of all people? Are we looking for solutions in all the wrong places, retreating into pietistic isolationism, or putting our trust in the wrong things (e.g., authoritarian government)? Is it possible that the church has become a community of zombies?

Judges is a book for our time. My sincere hope is that this commentary helps readers draw inspiration and instruction from the timely message of Judges.

The Title

A word about the title is necessary at the outset. Why is the book called Judges? In a book shrouded by confusion and chaos, perhaps it shouldn't be surprising that the title is somewhat puzzling. From our modern western perspective, a judge is someone involved in passing judgment in criminal cases and settling legal disputes—it's a judicial role. We don't really find the major characters of Judges engaged in that kind of activity. We get our English title from the Latin title of the book (*Liber Judicum*), which, like the Greek title in the Septuagint (*kritai*), is a literal translation of the traditional Hebrew title *šōpeṭîm* (שׁפטים).[4] The Hebrew word *šōpēṭ* ("judge") and its related verbal root are not limited to judicial roles but more broadly connote "the exercise of some form of government, political or sociological, depending on the context."[5] Perhaps "governor" might be a more appropriate term for this role.

To add to the confusion, while it is true that the title is a nod to the central individuals in the book (e.g., Ehud, Gideon, and Samson), it may come as a surprise that not one of the human figures in the book is actually given the title "judge" individually. Four of the six so-called major judges (3:10; 4:4; 12:7; 15:20; 16:31) and five of the six so-called minor judges (10:2, 3; 12:8, 9, 11, 13) are the subject of the verb "to judge/govern," but their importance in the book of Judges is not in their role as judges/governors. In fact, Judges provides virtually no information about the actual governance of the judges.[6] The introduction to the book does refer collectively to the judges as such, and then immediately

4. Boling, *Judges*, 5; Younger, *Judges and Ruth*, 21.

5. Soggin, *Judges*, 2. See, e.g., 2 Kgs 15:5; Isa 40:23; Amos 2:3; Pss. 2:10; 94:2; 96:13; 148:11.

6. The one exception may be the ending of the Gideon cycle, which recounts that Gideon set up the idolatrous shrine in his home town, acquired a substantial harem, and fathered seventy sons (8:22–32); however, these are the actions more in keeping with kingship than judgeship.

specifies the significance of their role: "Then Yahweh raised up judges, *who saved them* out of the hand of those who plundered them" (2:16, emphasis added). The judges, therefore, are saviors, deliverers who emerged at a time of crisis, brought relief from foreign oppression, and then apparently ruled for a time. The role of judge in the settlement period was for times of crisis and brought periods of temporary peace.

It is customary to distinguish between the major judges and the minor judges. The difference between the two groups has to do primarily with the amount of space devoted to each in the book. None of the so-called minor judges (Shamgar, Tola, Jair, Ibzan, Elon, and Abdon) has more than three verses devoted to him—Shamgar is covered in a single verse. The length and detail of the accounts of the so-called major judges vary, but on the whole, they are much more in-depth. These accounts are also structured, with some variation, according to a cyclical pattern, which also sets them apart from the accounts of the minor judges. This highlights another puzzling feature of the book—what function do the minor judges play in the book and why do they appear where they do, peppered as they are among the cycles of the major judges?[7]

Finally, in correctly identifying and understanding the judges in Judges, we should not ignore the divine Judge, Ruler, and King who features as the main character of Judges. In the book of Judges, the title "judge" only applies individually to Yahweh. Jephthah refers to God as "Yahweh, the Judge" (11:27)—whether or not he was being genuine, he was right. In the book of Judges kingdoms rise and fall by the will of Yahweh, Yahweh's Spirit moves, incredible miracles take place by the hand of Yahweh, and Yahweh speaks, listens, and responds (though perhaps not always in the ways we or the human characters expect). In the messiness that we encounter in Judges we need to be attentive to the activity and purpose of Yahweh, the Judge.

Hearing the Book of Judges

The fundamental conviction that drives the practice of theological interpretation is that in and through Scripture God speaks. It follows, therefore, that the principal task of theological interpreters is to situate ourselves in the very best position to hear the divine address. In this introduction we want to keep this principal task in clear focus. The tradition of commentary writing is long and varied, and there is no shortage of commentaries on Judges. Especially in the last century or two commentary introductions have been dominated by

7. We will consider this question in the commentary section.

questions of a historical nature: authorship and audience, date, religious and cultural background, chronology, compositional prehistory of the text, textual transmission, and so on. More recent commentaries expand beyond historical concerns in their introductions to include a panoply of interests including reception history, ideological concerns (e.g., feminist), literary criticism and poetics, and in some cases matters of a theological nature (e.g., place in the canon, theological significance).

With the goal of hearing the divine address in and through Judges, we have a keen interest in all of these matters. Theological interpretation by no means short-circuits academic rigor but ought rather to utilize every tool available in service of attuning our ears to listen to Scripture. For example, whatever knowledge we can gain about the author, occasion, and audience will help us hear the message of Judges. Moreover, listening to others in the history of the interpretation of Judges and from a variety of perspectives will help us to hear those aspects of the book that we may be deaf to because of our own limited perspectives. Of course, we should acknowledge that the practice of historical, literary, and ideological approaches is not always directed toward hearing and understanding the biblical texts and they do not always yield helpful interpretations of the texts. In some cases, they may distort or even silence the message of Judges. Theological interpretation will at times involve redirecting these approaches for the task at hand.

In keeping with the distinctives of this commentary series, I have tried to keep this introduction focused on those things that help us hear the divine address in Judges.[8] In the sections that follow we will fine-tune our hearing. To get ourselves in the best position to hear Judges we will (1) hear Judges in its broad and narrow literary contexts; (2) hear Judges as Hebrew narrative, highlighting those features of composition that define it as such; (3) hear Judges in its historical context, foregrounding the social, religious, and cultural dimensions of the book; and (4) hear Judges as it resonates in the history of interpretation and from a variety of perspectives.

Hearing Judges in Its Literary Context

Texts always assume a context. Knowing something about the author, the audience, the occasion, as well as the cultural environment deepens our understanding of a text. The next section will focus on these aspects of Judges. The context

8. Interested readers can consult the major commentaries for the typical matters that occupy commentary introductions.

that this section explores is the literary context. Something happens to a text when it is set in the context of other texts. Layers of meaning and significance emerge as the text resonates with its "cotexts." Even an anthology of literature, say an anthology of nineteenth-century British fiction, invites readers to compare and contrast how the texts of various authors dealt with the realities of nineteenth-century life in Britain.

The Bible is by no means an anthology. It is more like a rich tapestry. Its main character is God, the creator of the cosmos, the covenant partner of Israel, and the father of Jesus the Messiah. The various books and sections of the Bible combine so that a single narrative—from creation to new creation—emerges. Judges stands out as an important chapter in this grand, cosmic narrative, filling the gap between Israel's conquest narratives in Joshua and the rise of the united kingdom in 1 Samuel. The section in this commentary on Judges and biblical theology examines in detail how Judges functions in the broad context of the biblical narrative and also in the contexts of the Old and New Testaments. I will briefly summarize some of that here, but it may be worthwhile to read that section for a fuller understanding of the broader context in which we encounter Judges before tackling the details of the section-by-section commentary.

The Broad Context of Judges

The opening line of Judges sets the context for the book: "After the death of Joshua" (1:1). Before his death, Joshua addressed a gathering of all the Israelite people, indicating the significance of the moment—with the gift of the land, all the promises that Yahweh made to the patriarchs Abraham, Isaac, and Jacob have been fulfilled (Josh 23:14). The people respond with great enthusiasm and a three-fold affirmation that they will be loyal to their divine king Yahweh and be the distinct royal subjects that he called them to be (Josh 24). Judges demonstrates in reality Israel's rejection of Yahweh as king and loyalty to the Canaanite gods, which results in a society and nation that is governed by the practices and principles of Canaanite culture. Subsequent to Judges, the Israelites continue to spiral out of control, incurring the curses of the covenant (Deut 28) until they are finally divided, conquered, and exiled (the exile of the north is specifically alluded to in Judg 18:30). Jesus emerges on the scene as the Messiah and as the embodiment of the kingdom of God, a perfect demonstration of what Israel was called and yet failed to be. Through his death and resurrection, he initiates a new exodus and recommissions the people of God, the new Israel (including Jews and gentiles), to continue his kingdom mission until he returns again to establish his kingdom in its fullness.[9]

Various passages of Judges draw on the preceding covenantal history. The whole book assumes the conquest narrative of the book of Joshua, with countless references to the nations the Israelites conquered and the places they possessed. At various points in the book, the narrator, Yahweh (through his messenger), and specific individuals recall Yahweh's mighty act of redemption in the exodus and his covenant with their ancestors (2:1–2, 12, 20; 3:4; 5:5; 6:8–10, 13; 10:11; 11:13, 16; 19:30). Jephthah recounts in some detail the Israelites' dealing with the Ammonites during their wilderness journey (11:14–27; cf. Num 20–21; Deut 2). Moreover, customs and practices stipulated in the Sinai covenant feature on the pages of Judges, like Samson's Nazarite status (13:7; cf. Num 6:1–8) and the yearly pilgrimage festivals (21:19; cf. Exod 23:14–17; 34:18–23; Deut 16:1–17). The ancestry of two characters of Judges draws an unmistakable line between them and Israel's preeminent political and priestly leaders Moses and Aaron (18:30 and 20:28 respectively).

All of these specific references (and more besides) to names, places, events, and customs place Judges firmly in the literary (and, by virtue of the historical nature of this literature, historical) context of Genesis–Joshua. With regard to its literary context, perhaps even more significant than these specific references are all the subtler ways that the situations and actions of God's people in Judges undermine the normative standards established in the Pentateuch and Joshua.[10] The literary background of Genesis–Joshua brings into full relief the thorough corruption of Israel on a multiplicity of levels. Again, the section on Judges and Biblical Theology provides more detail in this regard.

Finally, Judges anticipates and shapes the unfolding covenantal history. The seeds of rebellion and corruption that take root in Judges grow and bear fruit (albeit rotten fruit) in the subsequent narratives of the books of Samuel and Kings. Although I interpret the "no king in Israel" refrain running through Judg 17–21 (17:6; 18:1; 19:1; 21:25) as ultimately a statement about Israel's rejection of Yahweh's kingship, it does at a certain level anticipate the rise of monarchy in Israel. By and large, the idolatry that gives rise to Israel's religious, moral, and social corruption becomes institutionalized under the leadership of Israel's (and Judah's) kings. We witness how all the great promises that Yahweh made to the

9. Again, the story of Israel leading up to and following Judges can be found in much more detail in the section of this commentary on Judges and biblical theology.

10. In her detailed examination of allusions to the Pentateuch in Judges, Ross concludes that the rhetorical strategy of pentateuchal allusions is to highlight the dire consequences of disobeying Yahweh's commandments and breaking his covenant; see Ross, "People Heeds Not Scripture," 344.

patriarchs and were fulfilled in Joshua (becoming a great nation, experiencing a relationship of mutual blessing, and possessing land) slowly erode in the period of monarchy until first the Northern Kingdom and then the Southern Kingdom are defeated and sent into exile, with the latter eventually returning as foreign subjects of the Persian Empire. Judges, therefore, stands as an important linchpin in the literary context of Genesis through Nehemiah.

The Immediate Context of Judges

Judges is, in my opinion, a literary composition in its own right. Doubtless, the one responsible for composing Judges drew on sources (almost certainly oral history but possibly also written historical records) but has carefully selected, arranged, and crafted the events of Judges into a sophisticated and integrated literary masterpiece.[11] The book divides clearly into three sections: the introduction or what I refer to as the exposition (1:1–3:6), the body, which is made up of the cycle of Judges as well as the accounts of the minor judges (3:7–16:31), and the end section (17:1–21:25).

The exposition consists of two parts. The first (ch. 1) narrates "mop-up" campaigns of the various tribes against the remaining Canaanite peoples and highlights the progressive failure of each tribe (starting with Judah/Simeon and ending with Dan) as they battle for possession of the land. The remaining Canaanite residents in the promised land as a result of the tribes' failure provide the "complication" with which the book will deal. The second part of the exposition (2:1–3:6) clarifies the complication and provides the interpretive framework for understanding the events of the settlement period as narrated in the rest of the book. The Israelites failed to drive out the Canaanites as Yahweh commanded them, they made covenants with them, and worshiped their gods (2:1–5); moreover, they failed to pass on the stories and traditions of Yahweh's mighty works on behalf of the Israelites so that generations emerged after the death of Joshua who were ignorant of Yahweh's special relationship with them (2:6–10). Then the exposition announces in advance (2:11–23) the cyclical pattern that characterizes the events of the core section of the book: (1) Israel does evil in the sight of Yahweh, (2) Yahweh's anger is aroused and he delivers them into the hand of foreign oppressors, (3) the Israelites cry out to Yahweh for relief, (4) Yahweh raises up deliverers who bring relief from the foreign op-

11. Since the late 1960s, countless essays, books, and commentaries have explored the book of Judges as an integrated literary whole. I have surveyed the scholarly literature in this vein in Beldman, *Completion of Judges*, 14–50.

pression, and (5) the land experiences a period of rest until the cycle starts all over again. The exposition ends with a list of Canaanite peoples that remained in the land and became a snare to Israel (3:1–6).

The bulk of the core section of the book consists of the cycles of six major judges: Othniel (3:7–11), Ehud (3:12–30), Deborah/Barak/Jael (4:1–5:31), Gideon and Abimelech (6:1–9:57), Jephthah (10:6–12:8), and Samson (13:1–16:31). A few observations about the organization and design of the cycle of judges is in order. It would be wrong to assume that chronology is the organizing principle behind the ordering of the six accounts. In fact, the author provides scant data for fixing the events of the cycle of judges to specific points in history, which makes reconstructing the sequence of events in the cycle difficult.

If these events do not follow in sequence, what is the organizational principle behind their ordering? Here, the author does provide clear clues that all point in the same direction. First, as we read from one cycle to the next we notice that the narratives get longer and more detailed—from the basic summary of the Othniel cycle (a mere five verses) to the detailed account of the prenatal announcement of Samson's birth to his death and burial—ninety-six verses all told. Second, as the narratives of each cycle get longer and more detailed, the behavior (of the Israelites and the judges) we encounter in each cycle gets more sordid and corrupt. For this reason, interpreters of Judges often point out that this section displays not just a cycle, but a downward spiral.

Finally, the extent to which each of the six narratives conforms to the five-part cyclical framework reinforces the pattern of degeneration. In the first two cycles (Othniel and Ehud) all five elements of the cycle appear. In the next two (Deborah/Barak/Jael and Gideon) all the elements appear except the formulaic language of Yahweh raising up the judge. The missing element is more or less assumed in the Deborah/Barak/Jael cycle, but in that cycle the absent formulaic phrase adds to the confusion over who the narrator thinks is the real deliverer. In place of the phrase "Yahweh raised up" in the Gideon cycle we encounter a long drawn out call narrative in which Yahweh has to convince fearful Gideon with signs and assurances before he will take up the call. In the final two cycles, it's as though the cyclical pattern breaks apart under the force and speed of the downward spiral. The list of gods that the Israelites served in the Jephthah cycle drastically inflates the first element of the cycle, which in turn causes the most terrible description of foreign oppression in the book to that point (the second element of the cycle). This in turn induces Israelites' crying out, which is accompanied with their very first expression of repentance in the core section of the book, along with a purging of idols. Thus, the cycle in the Jephthah narrative is top-heavy, the first three elements being drastically inflated. If that's not enough, the fourth and fifth elements are missing altogether—Yahweh determines not to save them (Jephthah is a deliverer of the people's choice) and it is no surprise that according to these circumstances the land does not experience rest. In the Samson cycle, the first two elements are present but for the first time the people do not cry out (element three). The formulaic language of Yahweh raising up does not appear, but it is implied with the extensive birth announcement of Samson; however, there is a caveat: Samson will only *begin* to deliver Israel from the Philistines (13:5). This implies that Samson will not bring deliverance in its fullness and thus it comes as no surprise that the fifth element of the cycle is absent—there is no rest in the land.

The following chart demonstrates the elements of the cycle and the extent to which they appear in the six cycles:

	Element #1	Element #2	Element #3	Element #4	Element #5
Othniel	present	present	present	present	present
Ehud	present	present	present	present	present
Deborah/ Barak/Jael	present	present	present	absent (but implied)	present
Gideon	present	present	present	absent (but implied)	present
Jephthah	present	present	present (but more extensive)	absent	absent
Samson	present	present	absent	absent (implied but limited)	absent

This overview of the core section of the book shows the great care and sophistication that the author put into the telling of these events. In addition to the six cycles of the major judges, we also encounter the brief notices about the minor judges scattered throughout this core section: Shamgar (3:31), Tola and Jair (10:1–5), and Ibzan, Elon, and Abdon (12:8–15). The placement of the minor judges and their purpose in the design of the core section is not as clear as that of the major judges, and we will explore these issues in the commentary section.

Finally, the end section (chs. 17–21), like the exposition, consists of two parts, namely, the story of Micah's shrine and the Danite migration to the north (chs. 17–18) and the account of the Levite and his concubine that sparks a pan-Israelite civil war against Benjamin (chs. 19–21). On multiple levels (spiritual, moral, and social), the worst behavior in the whole book appears in these chapters. The cyclical framework is nowhere to be found but is replaced with a new refrain: "In those days there was no king in Israel; everyone did what was right in his own eyes." This refrain appears in full at the beginning and conclusion of the end section (17:6 and 21:25) and in a truncated form in 18:1 and 19:1, putting an indelible stamp on this part of the book. As I argue in the commentary, this refrain is referring to the rejection of Yahweh as king and its basic message is this: when the people rebel against king Yahweh, chaos and anarchy rule the day.

In the final section, attention to chronology does become rhetorically significant. Two carefully placed references to a certain generation (18:30 and 20:28) situate these events very early in the period that Judges covers—only two generations from Moses and Aaron. Just as we thought that these terrible events happened at the end of a consistent downward spiral, the narrator jolts us with the reality that the worst behavior in the book happened at the very beginning of the period, in fact, the moment they rejected Yahweh as king and pledged their allegiance to the Canaanite gods. The ending is circular, and the effect is to produce a profound sense of aimlessness and futility in the period of the judges—more on this in the commentary section.

The immediate literary context and design of the book emerge only from a close reading of the book itself. This overview is meant to guide readers as they navigate the twists and turns of Judges, so that they might carefully scrutinize the book for clues to the author's design. An outline of the structure of the book appears below.

Outline of Judges

- Exposition (1:1–3:6)
  - Israel's Unsuccessful Mop-Up Campaign (1:1–2:5)
  - Israel's Rebellion and the Announcement of the Cycle (2:6–3:6)
- The Cycle of Judges (3:7–16:31)
  - The Othniel Cycle (3:7–11)
  - The Ehud Cycle (3:12–30)
  - Shamgar (3:31)
  - The Deborah/Barak/Jael Cycle (4:1–5:31)
    - The Deborah/Barak/Jael Narrative (4:1–24)
    - The Song of Deborah (5:1–31)
  - The Gideon Cycle (6:1–8:35)
    - The Reign of Abimelech (9:1–57)

Tola and Jair (10:1–5)
The Jephthah Cycle (10:6–12:7)
Ibzan, Elon, and Abdon (12:8–15)
The Samson Cycle (13:1–16:31)
The End Section (17:1–21:25)
Micah's Idol and the Danite Migration (17:1–18:31)
The Atrocity at Gibeah and the Pan-Israelite War against Benjamin (19:1–21:25)

Hearing Judges as Hebrew Narrative

In the preceding section on the immediate context of Judges, I provided a general overview of the careful design of the whole of Judges. The focus there is specific to Judges and aims at uncovering how the deliberate composition of the book mediates the message of Judges. In this section the view is more general—we want to focus on Judges as a type of Hebrew (biblical) narrative.[12] The aim here is to describe those general characteristics of Hebrew narrative that Judges exhibits so as to further refine our hearing and understanding of it. I will not be covering characteristics of narrative in general that Judges shares by virtue of the fact that it is narrative, but only those that are specific to Hebrew (biblical) narrative. So, for example, the notion of narrative plot common to all narratives will not receive attention. However, there are peculiarities of Hebrew narrative that may strike readers of other kinds of narratives as unusual, foreign, and (at times) perplexing. It is these features of Hebrew narrative to which we need to give attention.

A word about the relationship between history, literature, and inspired Scripture may be in order, anticipating at least two objections to the notable literary sensibilities that motivate the approach to Judges in this commentary. The first objection concerns the nature of Holy Scripture and its relationship to literary art. Should we really use tools from literary criticism when the object of our interpretation is the word of God and not "mere" literature? The Bible, after all, is unlike any other kind of writing by virtue of its divine inspiration. This concern is understandable, but it assumes, in my opinion, a faulty notion of inspiration. God has inspired the biblical texts and, therefore, does speak through them, but these texts were written and composed over thousands of years, by human authors, writing to real audiences, in response to concrete life

12. Judges reflects those features of Hebrew narrative most exemplified in the earlier biblical narratives, namely, the Pentateuch and the books that in the Hebrew Bible make up the Former Prophets (Joshua through Kings).

situations. The biblical literature was written in ancient languages and by means of the conventions of ancient literary composition. Some of the most troubling interpretations of the Bible in the past are the products of well-intentioned readers who have circumvented careful exegetical work, with a deep conviction that God has spoken directly to them through the texts. Hearing God's address in Scripture should drive us deeper into the texts, their contexts, and the pattern of meaning that emerges from their literary artistry. In this way, we should acknowledge that the text's message is mediated through its form.

The second objection concerns the relationship between history and literature, and the nature of truth. Judges (and much of the biblical material) is a text of history, recounting events of Israel's past—doesn't literature embellish and distort events and thereby falsify or at least call into question the historical veracity of the events and by implication undermine the truth of Scripture? Again, this is a valid concern, but it assumes a deficient view of history writing in general and biblical history in particular. On the one hand, history-writing, including modern historiography, involves studying, selecting, arranging, and interpreting historical events. Postmodernism rightly critiques the modern notion of history-writing as an objective portrayal of events as they truly happened. The telling of history is always subjective, a telling of events from the perspective of the historian.

On the other hand, the biblical accounts of the history of Israel or of the events in the first century about Jesus and the church were not written solely for the sake of historical interest.[13] Although there is nothing intrinsically wrong with the many attempts to reconstruct the chronology of the period of the judges, we need not regard it as a problem to be solved (at least not a historical problem). The arrangement of Judges out of chronological order serves a purpose that transcends historical interests. Judges is history, but like all biblical history, it is not history for history's sake but rather history *with a purpose*. I would even go a step further. The biblical authors' careful and deliberate shaping of the events of the past does not carry us further away from the truth but actually helps us understand the past as it truly is. The original audience of Judges may have had some knowledge of the events and figures of the settlement period, but not until they read (or more likely heard) the divinely inspired book of Judges did they comprehend the true nature of this chapter in their

13. Consider John's sentiments at the close of his gospel. He notes, with hyperbole, that there are so many other events of Jesus's life that if he were to write them all down the whole world could not contain all the books about him (John 21:25). Rather, John studied, selected, and arranged all the events of his account for this purpose: "that you may believe that Jesus is the Messiah, the Son of God, and that by believing you may have life in his name" (20:30).

history—one that is characterized by Israel's persistent rebellion and Yahweh's long-suffering patience.

With those clarifications aside, the following will sketch some of the key characteristics of Hebrew narrative that will help attune our ears to hear Judges.

Narrator

By means of the narrator we hear the voice of the storyteller, and the narrator's perspective and manner of storytelling is what gives Hebrew narrative its distinctiveness. Old Testament narrative almost always narrates the events in the third person.[14] This does not mean that the narrators are detached (although at times it may seem so)—they have a deep interest in the events they recount.

Three characteristics of Old Testament narrators are key for understanding the stories they tell. The narrators are (1) omniscient, (2) reliable, and (3) reticent (i.e., restrained)—we will explore these in turn.[15] First, the overwhelming evidence from Old Testament narrative is that the narrators are omniscient, having insight and knowing details that are sometimes beyond the capacity of human perception. For example, the narrator of Judges tells details of events that happened between Ehud and Eglon in the intimacy of the upper chamber of King Eglon's palace (3:20–22) and between Jael and Sisera in the privacy of Jael's tent (4:18–21). The narrator tells of Gideon all alone, beating out wheat in a winepress (6:11). The best evidence for the narrators' all-knowingness is when they express the inner intentions or emotions of people in the stories. We see this at work in Judges when the narrator indicates that Eglon's attendants thought he was relieving himself, which accounted for his delay in returning (3:24), that Gideon's fear motivated him to tear down his father's altar at night (6:27), that Gideon's explanation cooled the anger of the Ephraimites (8:3), that Jephthah's motivation for doing battle with the Ephraimites was their insulting him (12:4), that Samson returned home in a state of extreme anger (14:19), and that Samson thought to himself after his hair was cut that he would break free as on previous occasions but was ignorant of the departure of Yahweh's Spirit (16:20). The narrator even knows of the inner thoughts and emotions of God, as in the many expressions of Yahweh's anger burning against Israel in Judges. Moreover, we also read of Yahweh's

14. The one exception to this rule is Nehemiah, which is narrated in the first person by Nehemiah, a cupbearer to the Persian king Artaxerxes.

15. See Beldman, "Literary Approaches," 79–81. On the art of reticence see Alter, *Art of Biblical Narrative*, 114–30.

impatience over the misery of Israel (10:16), and Yahweh's unexpressed desire for an opportunity to move against the Philistines (14:4).

Second, Old Testament narrators are reliable and trustworthy. In some forms of storytelling, the author's perspective is at odds with the narrator's perspective (e.g., satire), but this is not so in Old Testament narrative. While it is true that for a variety of reasons "they may choose to withhold information, they never deceive."[16] The reliability of the narrator undergirds the authority with which the narrators speak. Yaira Amit makes this point when she writes, "Doubting the narrator of the Pentateuch . . . means doubting the Pentateuch's authority and its laws, which is tantamount to breaking the contract."[17] By virtue of Old Testament narrative's status as divinely inspired Scripture, through the voice of the narrator we hear the voice of God. Meir Sternberg draws a connection between the omniscience of the biblical narrators and the reality of an omniscient God, and we could draw the same connection with regard to the narrator's trustworthiness.[18] In Old Testament narrative (including Judges), the narrator's interpretation and evaluation of historical events is authoritative for theological interpretation. Although this is the case, the manner of Old Testament narration is complex, and the narrator's evaluation of events can seem difficult to discern. This characteristic of Hebrew narrative foregrounds the third distinctive of Old Testament narrators.

Third, Old Testament narrators are reticent, generally reserving overt evaluative statements.[19] Explicit statements of judgment do at times appear in Old Testament narrative (e.g., after David commits adultery with Bathsheba and kills her husband the narrator notes "But the thing that David had done was evil in Yahweh's eyes" [2 Sam 11:27b]; or after Solomon asks Yahweh for wisdom the narrator says, "It was good in Yahweh's eyes that Solomon requested this thing" [1 Kgs 3:10]). Evaluations of this kind appear in Judges, particularly in the book's exposition (2:6–3:6), but also in the framework of the cycle (3:7, 12; 4:1; 6:1; 10:6; 13:1) and in the end section by means of the "no king in Israel" refrain (17:6; 18:1; 19:1; 21:25).

However, on the whole we do not often encounter these kinds of statements in Old Testament narrative or in Judges. The mode of narration functions such that the way the events unfold, and the actions and words of the characters speak for themselves. This can be frustrating and confusing for readers not used

16. Beldman, "Literary Approaches," 80.

17. Amit, *Reading Biblical Narrative*, 95.

18. Sternberg, *Poetics of Biblical Narrative*, 84–128.

19. The groundbreaking work on the art of reticence in biblical narrative appears in Alter, *Art of Biblical Narrative*, 114–30.

to this kind of storytelling. In Judges we read about the deceptive acts of assassination by Ehud and Jael, about Gideon's cold-blooded murder of residents of the Israelite cities of Succoth and Penuel and the two Midianite kings, about Jephthah's human sacrifice of his own daughter (and slaughter of forty-two thousand Ephraimites), about Samson's sexual exploits with Philistine women, about the Levite's "sacrifice" of his concubine and dismemberment of her lifeless body, and the list could go on and on. However, we look in vain for *explicit expressions* of evaluation (e.g., "But the thing that Gideon, Samson, etc., did was evil in the eyes of Yahweh") that might help us make sense of the behavior we encounter in the book. That is not to say that Old Testament narrators are detached or provide no evaluation. When reading Judges, we do need to take seriously those overt evaluative statements, but more often we need to attend carefully to the words, actions, and situations of the characters to discern all those subtler clues to the narrator's evaluation.

Foolproof Composition

Being sensitive to these subtleties and to the careful way that the narrator portrays events rarely leaves readers confused about how they ought to evaluate events and figures in Old Testament narrative. In his magisterial work *The Poetics of Biblical Narrative*, Sternberg describes the "foolproof composition" of Hebrew narrative.[20] According to foolproof composition, readers are able to follow the narrative's clues to discern the narrator's evaluation of events and characters, even if the narrator does not provide overt evaluation.

Take the ambiguous character of Jacob in Genesis, for example. In the narratives about Jacob, the great patriarch of the Israelites comes across as a spoiled deceiver who manipulates everyone around him, including those closest to him, to get what he wants (ultimately the covenantal blessing). When he deceives blind Isaac, securing his father's blessing that by rights would have gone to Esau (Gen 27), the narrator is eerily silent. However, as Robert Alter notes, "the judgment that Jacob has done wrong in taking what is, in a sense, his, is later confirmed in the narrative . . . Jacob becomes the victim of symmetrical poetic justice, deceived in the blindness of the night by having Leah passed off on him as Rachel, and rebuked in the morning by the deceiver, his father-in-law Laban" (ch. 29).[21] In this case, the pattern of Jacob's deception returns on his own head and, thereby, we have a clue to the narrator's displeasure regarding

20. Sternberg, *Poetics of Biblical Narrative*, 114–30.

21. Alter, *Art of Biblical Narrative*, 45.

Jacob's earlier actions. Alter's notion of "symmetrical poetic justice" seems to be at work in the narrative of Micah in Judg 17–18 such that the thieving Micah himself becomes the victim of the Danites' thievery, but this is only one of many ways the narrators provide clues of foolproof composition.

The narrator's characterization of Gideon is detailed and complex. Over the course of the cycle, Gideon's fear and doubt transform to over-confidence and power-hungriness, and this transformation seems to pivot on the verse where Gideon instructs his puny army to shout at the beginning of the battle "For Yahweh *and for Gideon*" (7:18b, emphasis added). The narrator's inclusion of Gideon's words "and for Gideon" (in fact all one word in the Hebrew) prepares readers for Gideon's significant evolution. At the end of his narrative, when the Israelites want to crown him as a dynastic king (8:22), he says the right words (essentially, "Yahweh is your king") but the narrator's portrayal of Gideon in this context (8:18–32) contradicts his words—he acts in all sorts of kingly ways and in a manner that contravenes Yahweh's kingship. Gideon's character may on the surface seem ambiguous, but read as a whole and with attention to the careful nuances of the text, the narrator's negative evaluation of Gideon is clear and is another example of the foolproof composition of Old Testament narrative.

Indications of the narrator's evaluation of situations may emerge from comparing/contrasting similar events within Old Testament narrative books (e.g., the pan-Israelite battles against the Canaanites in Judg 1 and the pan-Israelite battles against Benjamin in ch. 20) or from comparing/contrasting similar events from other places in the Old Testament (e.g., the circumstances surrounding the events in Gibeah in Judg 19 and those of Sodom in Gen 19). We ought not doubt the narrator's disapproval of Samson's romantic desire of the Timnite woman—his stated justification (in spite of the warnings of his parents) is that "she is right in my eyes," a phrase which within Judges and according to many Old Testament passages indicates a blatant disregard for what is right in Yahweh's eyes. Even though the narrator juxtaposes the Spirit's empowering of Jephthah (11:29) and his tragic vow (11:30–31), and despite the fact that the narrator casts no expressed evaluation on the sacrifice of his daughter, we know from the Old Testament witness that Yahweh detests child sacrifice and would not be implicated in or condone such a practice (Lev 18:21; 20:1–5; Deut 12:31; 18:10; 2 Kgs 3:27; 16:3; 17:17; 21:6; 2 Chr 28:3; 33:6, etc.). A comparison of the Song of Deborah (Judg 5) and the Song of Moses (Exod 15:1–18) reveals that the anthropocentric tenor of the former pales in comparison to the theocentric poetry of the latter.

Thus, although the narrators in the Old Testament are often reticent in providing expressions of evaluation, they have many means of communicating their appraisal of events and characters. This does not mean that we will never encounter ambiguity. However, generally speaking through careful, nuanced, and holistic reading of Old Testament narrative, readers can discern clues for understanding and evaluating the situations and characters in Old Testament narrative.

Much more could be said about the distinctiveness of Old Testament narrative. This section has hinted at other important aspects of this kind of literature, like characterization and repetition. I trust that the preceding has provided tools for careful attention to the mode of communication that we find in Old Testament narrative so that we can better hear Judges, with all of its texture and nuance.

Hearing Judges in Its Historical Context

Setting Judges within the context of the traditions and literature of the Old Testament, as well as in its more immediate literary context, helps us attune our ears to the book's teaching, and it should be clear that there is a historic dimension to the literary (broad and narrow) context of Judges. In Judges, the people of God are in a time of great change. The book provides a picture of the settlement period in Israel's history—that period that stands between the conquest of Canaan and the rise of monarchy. The people are settling into a new territory and encountering new cultures. As such, the book assumes a wider cultural, religious, and social environment that is key to understanding the book. Cultural context is foundational for responsible exegesis and theological interpretation; however, it is all the more important for Judges. Many scholars and commentators have argued that in Judges the Israelites take on the characteristics, practices, thought patterns, and such of the surrounding Canaanite nations (Daniel Block helpfully refers to the "canaanization" of Israel). If this is true (as I think it is), then the more composite and nuanced portrait of Canaanite culture we can grasp the better.

The aim in this section, therefore, is to sketch the broad contours of the ancient Near Eastern context of Judges. It will answer key questions like: What was the social and economic structure of Israel in the settlement period? What was the political context of the Fertile Crescent, into which Israel was settling? What is the character of Canaanite culture that was so alluring to Israel? How did the Canaanites view the gods, the world, and human nature? What were the religious practices of the Canaanites and how did they translate into an order for society? These key questions and more regarding the ancient Near Eastern cultural and historical context of Judges will occupy the following pages. Beyond this cultural environment, knowing something of the author, audience, and occasion of Judges is helpful for understanding the book's teaching; we will discuss these matters at the end of this section, with the acknowledgement that the evidence for them is limited and subject to interpretation.

The Social Structure and Economy of Israel in Canaan

The implicit social structure of Israel in Judges, which at points in the book is made explicit, reflects a hierarchy of kinship relationships. This hierarchy is structured as such (in descending order): the nation of Israel → the twelve tribes → tribal clans → patriarchal households (note Gideon's reference to tribe, clan, and household in 6:15).[22] Evidence of this structure goes back at least as far as the exodus and wilderness wandering, as the census in Numbers is structured according to tribe, clan, and father's household (Num 1:1–46).

The closest social (and geographical) relationship, therefore, is the household, which consists of the patriarch and his wife/wives, his children, and their families (including grandchildren), all living communally in proximity to one another.[23] We can see social relationships of this kind reflected in the interaction between Achsah/Othniel and Achsah's father Caleb (Judg 1:11–15), in Gideon's status and actions regarding his father's household (6:15, 25–32) and his establishment of his own household (8:29–32), in Samson's relationship with his parents in adulthood (ch. 14), in the anticipated complaint of the brothers/fathers of the Shiloh virgins who would be "married off" without their consent (21:22), and in other places. In Judg 17–18, Micah makes "household gods" (17:5) which, with the Levite, come to reside "in the house" of Micah (vv. 4, 12), and yet the Danites can speak of Micah's "houses" (18:14) which contain household gods.

Groups of multigenerational patriarchal households, united by common descent, combined together to form clans.[24] Block notes that they settled "in their own villages and/or settlements and [used] communal land. Every member of the clan knows everyone else. Unrelated or distantly related clans may be interlocked by exogamous marriage (i.e., marriage outside one's clan)."[25] Lawson Younger notes that Israel's laws concerning the גאל/*gōʾēl* (kinsmen-redeemer) functioned in the social orb of the clan.[26] The social structure of

22. Block, *Judges*, 32; Younger, *Judges and Ruth*, 25–26.
23. Block, *Judges*, 32; Younger, *Judges and Ruth*, 25–26.
24. Younger, *Judges and Ruth*, 27.
25. Block, *Judges*, 33.
26. Younger, *Judges and Ruth*, 27.

clans is evident at various places in Judges, most notably in Abimelech's appeal to the loyalty of his mother's Shechemite clan for support (9:1–2), and in the Danite warriors who reason with Micah's Levite that to be a priest for a whole Israelite tribe and clan would be far superior than to be the priest of a mere household (18:19). Moreover, the men who want to kill Gideon are likely his clansmen, perceiving his breaking down of the idolatrous altar as an act of betrayal (6:28–30). These examples indicate that clan members expected a degree of loyalty and solidarity at the clan level.

Next in the structure is the level of the tribes, which in the case of Israel are rooted in the twelve patriarchs. According to Block, "A series of clans combine to form a tribe, though all still claimed descent from a common ancestor many generations removed. The population spreads over a large tract of land, and the members no longer know everyone. Internal endogamous marriage is common."[27] Thus, common descent, geographical boundaries, and, in some cases, dialect (see Judg 12:6) were unifying factors at the tribal level.[28] The significance of the tribal unit and tribal identity is a dominating motif throughout Judges. The opening chapter recounts the success/failure of specific tribes in order: Judah, Simeon, Benjamin, Joseph (i.e., Manasseh and Ephraim), Zebulun, Asher, Naphtali, and Dan (Judg 1). In the cycle of judges, the perspective is regional, often highlighting the participation of specific tribes. Barak summons Zebulun and Naphtali (4:10), though the Song of Deborah also lauds the tribes of Benjamin and Issachar for their participation and chides the tribes of Reuben and Dan for their lack of involvement (Judg 5). Gideon summons Manasseh, Asher, Zebulun, and Naphtali, and later Ephraim to battle against the Midianites (6:35; 7:24). Tribal concerns dominate the end section, with the Danite migration north dominating chapter 18 and the coordinated pan-Israelite campaign against Benjamin coming to the foreground in chapters 20–21.

At the top of the social structure of Israel is the nation. Thus, the tribes "combine to form the ethnic group, the 'am, 'people.' This social structure determined the shape of Israel's religious, economic, and political life until the time of Solomon (1 Kings 4)."[29] There can be no doubt that the author of Judges has a keen interest in highlighting the unity of Israel. Block identifies five stylistic features that contribute to this sense of unity:

1. The numerous references to "Israel," more so than in any other Old Testament book.

27. Block, *Judges*, 33.
28. Younger, *Judges and Ruth*, 27.
29. Block, *Judges*, 33.

2. The countless occurrences of pan-Israelite expressions (e.g., "all Israel," "all the sons of Israel," "the men of Israel," "the sons of Israel").
3. The many references to an individual judging Israel, ruling over Israel, saving Israel, and so on.
4. The regular expressions involving Israel as a collective.
5. Several references to the "tribes of Israel" in the end section.[30]

This distinctly "pan-Israel perspective" combined with the frequency with which Judges features tribal affairs exposes a tension in the book.[31] Will God's people in the land emerge as a nation marked by unity and solidarity, or will self-seeking tribal interests fragment and set them at odds with one another? The second half of the book demonstrates increasing fragmentation and intertribal squabbling, such that they become their own worst enemies.

Of course, governing the whole of this hierarchical socio-political structure is the divine king. In this way, Israel was fashioned to be a theocracy. Surveying the ancient Canaanite literature, Robert Boling notes the significant information it has yielded for understanding socio-economic structures. He notes,

> Especially significant for elucidation of the Book of Judges is the access now gained to the pre-Yahwist history of poetic idiom, mythological imagery, and rhetoric in Canaan itself. See especially the beginning of the Song of Deborah (5:4–5), which harks back to the original arrival of the Yahweh-army in Canaan. What is presupposed there is that Yahweh has already defeated the hosts of Egypt and thus legitimated his claim to kingship in Israel. Moreover, Israelites have already built his movable palace, the venerable Tabernacle. These are the two great organizing themes—mighty victory and splendid new abode—in the mythological recounting of Baal's victory in Canaan. The difference is that Yahweh's victories are historical; they are the kind of victories that liberate and order the well-being of his people.[32]

Indeed, the people are liberated but also unified under the kingship of Yahweh, and in the organization of Yahweh's kingdom, tribal self-interest has no place.

Younger provides two pieces of information that are vital for understanding the social structure in Judges. First, he notes, "The covenant or treaty (*berît*) functioned not only as a moral and religious document but also as a basis for

30. See Block, *Judges*, 30, which includes the textual references.

31. See the section in Chisholm, *Commentary on Judges and Ruth*, 29–34.

32. Boling, *Judges*, 18.

tribal alliances within the confederacy or league."[33] In other words, in Israel the covenant had a unifying function. Second, he notes that according to clan or tribal ideology in general (not necessarily limited to Israel's conception of tribal identity), "the concept of abstract justice is lacking. All actions are based on specific loyalties, the lines of which are structurally determined. One supports one's fellow clansman in a dispute, regardless of moral questions."[34] The example Younger provides from Judges is the Benjamites' loyalty to Gibeah, in spite of the blatant immorality of the offence and in spite of the pressure from the other tribes. This is most illuminating because it again exposes the tension of Israel in the land—will they live according to the practices and principles of a priestly kingdom and a holy nation or will they capitulate to the ways of the world and the culture in which they find themselves? According to the former, there is freedom to flourish and develop tribal distinctiveness within the boundaries of a fixed and unified social and moral order; according to the latter, tribal interests trump everything, and moral boundaries are fluid. In Judges, the Israelites choose the way of "the world."

The settlement of Israel in Canaan brought about a change in Israel's economic life. No longer tent-dwelling, wandering nomads, the Israelites became sedentary, dwelling in houses surrounded by arable land. Central to security and economic prosperity was land, which was divided equitably by lot after the conquest according to tribe and clan (see Josh 13–21). The economic value of land is evident in the Mosaic laws that protect land "ownership" and make economic provisions for the landless (widows, foreigners, etc.), like the Jubilee laws (Lev 25) and the gleaning laws (Lev 19:9; 23:22).

Canaan is regularly referred to as the land "flowing/gushing with milk and honey" (Exod 3:8, 17; 13:5; 33:3; Lev 20:24; Num 13:27; 14:8; 16:13, 14; Deut 6:3; 11:9; 26:9, 15; 27:3; 31:20; Josh 5:6). This way of speaking of the promised land indicates (albeit hyperbolically) its abundant fertility ("flowing/gushing"). Milk and honey are renewable resources, one the product of human agriculture (milk) and the other the product of nature (honey).[35] Moreover, "milk and honey" may also function as a merism, in which case the force of the phrase would be: this is a land abundant in the products of human labor, in the products of nature, and in everything in between. Samson's discovery of a colony of honeybees in the carcass of the lion he killed is literal evidence of rapid and abundant honey production in Canaanite territory (14:8–9).

In a subsistence-based agricultural economy such as this, wheat, barley,

33. Younger, *Judges and Ruth*, 27–28.

34. Younger, *Judges and Ruth*, 28.

35. Merrill, *Deuteronomy*, 161.

and other grain fields, vineyards, olive groves, and fruit orchards, as well as animal husbandry were the primary means by which the Israelites would eat and feed their families, and provided the bedrock of economic capital. Even though Canaan was well suited for agricultural prosperity, famines and other natural disasters (locusts, hail, etc.) could spell disaster for land-dwellers there. The loss of a single grain crop meant not only loss of food for human consumption, but also the loss of animal feed, valuable seed for the planting of future crops, and commodities for trade. In the case of multiple crop failures, the situation becomes even more perilous—the incursion and accumulation of debt, voluntary slavery, and/or the loss of land.

We do not encounter these kinds of natural disasters in the settlement period. However, the cycle of foreign oppression that the Israelites experience creates a similar situation. The foreign domination brought with it economic destitution. In the Ehud cycle, the Moabites took possession of Israelite territory (3:12–13) and King Eglon demanded the Israelites pay tribute to him (vv. 15, 18). In the Gideon cycle, the nature of economic hardship is vividly described: the Israelites are forced into hiding (6:2), the Midianites (along with their livestock)—described in terms of locust swarms—devoured their crops, laid waste the land, and appropriated their sheep, oxen, and donkeys (vv. 3–6). This is nothing short of economic devastation and it lasted seven years (6:1). Gideon himself is pictured beating out grain in hiding (6:11), it becomes clear that his father's household somehow held onto livestock (vv. 25–26), and the "fleecing" incident implies wool production at that time (vv. 36–40). When Samson sets the paired foxes loose among the Philistines' standing grain, the stacked (i.e., harvested) grain, and the olive orchards with blazing torches attached to them, he shows a shrewd understanding of economic terrorism.

Of course, Israel's economy in the settlement period must also have included the trade of not only goods, but also services and precious metals, though evidence in the book for this is scarce. We know that the Israelites emerged from Egypt with Egyptian plunder. In the case of Gideon's defeat of the Midianites, Gideon and the Israelite armies acquired the spoils of war—the gold earrings alone amounted to 1700 shekels of gold (8:24–25). Micah stole 1100 shekels of silver, and his mother hires a local silversmith with an amount of this silver to craft a molten image (17:4). Similarly, we may assume the hiring of a goldsmith in Gideon's case, though there the narrator simply states that Gideon made an ephod (8:27). Perhaps Ehud was also a skilled tradesman, given that he crafted for himself a double-edged sword (3:16), though whether or not he ever hired himself out as a metalsmith we can only guess.

The significance of Israel's changed status from seminomadic herdspeople to sedentary farmers should not be missed—a transition that Bernhard Anderson considers "fateful and far-reaching."[36] Anderson notes:

> Previously, Yahweh had been the God of the wanderers, but now Israel's relationship was to the soil, which had to be tilled. The human problem increasingly came to center around man's relation to nature: the need of rainfall for crops, the dependence upon the rotation of the seasons, and the concern for fertility which pervaded the whole Fertile Crescent. In the past, Yahweh had shown his power to control history; the new question was whether he could win out in the rivalry with the gods who controlled the cycles of nature.[37]

Of course, Yahweh had shown his power over nature in the past—most vividly in miracles of the ten plagues in the context of the exodus. Yet, there is no question that as the Israelites settled into an agrarian existence among the Canaanite peoples and their cultures, the powerful allure of the local fertility cults became irresistible in their new reality. Just like Israel's approach to tribal interests, so too their approach to economic life—will they choose the way of the world (i.e., the Canaanites) or choose the countercultural way of Yahweh and his covenant principles?

We must return to this all-important religious and cultural environment into which Israel moved, but first we turn to the lay of the political landscape of Canaan.

The Land of Canaan

Canaan is situated at the heart of the Fertile Crescent, a geographical band of territory with the Mediterranean Sea to the west and the great Eastern Desert to the east and including the region of Syria to the north, Assyria to the east, and Babylonia to the southeast.[38] As the name suggests, this region is marked by its agricultural fruitfulness, but it is also significant as a vital trade and military thoroughfare. The major route from Egypt to Mesopotamia traces along

36. Anderson, *Understanding the Old Testament*, 94.

37. Anderson, *Understanding the Old Testament*, 94.

38. "The Fertile Crescent," in *Lexham Bible Dictionary*. For the geographical, political, and historical description of Canaan, I am indebted to the work of Anderson, *Understanding the Old Testament*, 72–78. Unless otherwise stated, the information in this section derives from that source.

the Mediterranean Sea, veers east through the hill country via the Jezreel Valley (Canaanite territory), and then heads north to Damascus.[39]

The strategic location of Canaan along this commercial and military route contributed to its political importance. Before Israel arrived in Canaan, Egypt had long since maintained control of this part of the Fertile Crescent. Canaan was by no means a unified empire with centralized rule but consisted rather of a number of autonomous city-states concentrated in the areas that had the best farmland and/or were ideally suited for military defense. Egyptian outposts in Canaan housed troops that maintained Egyptian control, inspectors that collected tribute and enlisted laborers, and officers that "policed and exploited the country under the authority of the pharaoh."[40]

Political upheaval in the so-called Amarna Age (roughly 1400–1350 BC) and beyond, including the expansion southward into the Fertile Crescent of the Hittite Empire in the north and migration into the area of the Aegean "People of the Sea" (most significantly, the Philistines), radically diminished Egyptian dominance in Canaan. In the context of this political uncertainty and instability, the Israelites made their journey to Canaan. A debate exists over the precise dating of the exodus and subsequent conquest, with some scholars holding to an earlier fifteenth century dating and others for a later mid-thirteenth century dating.[41] If the earlier date is correct, then the arrival of Israel in Canaan contributed to Egypt's slipping grasp in the Fertile Crescent; if the later date is accurate then Israel benefited from the weakening of Egyptian hegemony in the area.[42] Regardless, this general picture of political and military contestation in the heart of the Fertile Crescent provides the backdrop of Israel in the land of Canaan.

Although it is common to refer to the Canaanites almost as though they are a monolithic and unified entity, the reality is much more complex. In fact, to refer to the foreign nations in Judges as Canaanites is not quite accurate, as the nations that Israel encounters are not limited to the Canaanites. According to the table of nations in Gen 10, Canaan (descended from Noah's son Ham; 10:6) spawned a number of nations, including some of those mentioned in Judges:

39. Anderson, *Understanding the Old Testament*, 94.

40. Anderson, *Understanding the Old Testament*, 73.

41. See the discussion in Webb, *Book of Judges*, 10–12.

42. Anderson notes that in 1220 BC, the Egyptian pharaoh Merenptah commissioned a stele, celebrating his victory over Asiatic nations that contains this line: "Israel is laid waste, his seed is not. Hurru is become a widow for Egypt." Anderson notes the hyperbolic nature of the statement, but whatever the historical veracity of the stele, "Merneptah was in no position to follow up whatever victory he achieved, for his energies were soon diverted by the greater problem of other invaders"; Anderson, *Understanding the Old Testament*, 77–78.

the Sidonians (descended from Sidon), the Hittites (descended from Heth), the Jebusites, the Amorites, and the Hivites (vv. 15–18).[43] The specifically Canaanite nations that the various tribes battle in Judg 1 also include the Perezites, whose origins are uncertain.[44] The nations that Judg 3:1–6 lists as those that Yahweh left in Canaan to test the Israelites include many of the known Canaanite nations but also the Philistines, whose origins are not Canaanite. Moreover, nations from outside Canaan feature in the cycle of judges as foreign oppressors, including the Moabites (descended from Lot and thus a Semitic people) who resided in the area southeast of the Dead Sea, the Ammonites (neighbors to the north of Moab), the Amalekites (also a Semitic people descended from Esau residing in the region of Edom south of Moab but a seminomadic people), and the Midianites (raiders from the Arabian desert).[45]

By and large, the culture and religion that are irresistible to Israel in the settlement period are those of the Cannanites.[46] As Anderson notes, "In that ancient period, the most divisive and destructive threat that Israel faced was Canaanite religion."[47] Thus, we turn our attention to the contours of Canaanite religion and culture.

The Religious and Cultural Environment of Israel in Canaan

Israel's succumbing to Canaanite religion is expressed in Judges as service to the Baals (2:11; 8:33; 10:10), the Baals and the Ashtaroth (2:13; 10:6), or the Baals and Asheroth (3:7); the shrine in the household of Gideon's father contains an altar to Baal and an Asherah pole for the worship of the goddess Asherah, not to be confused with the goddess Astarte. Most often they are said to have "served" the foreign gods (2:11, 13, 19; 3:6, 7; 10:6, 10, 13), but the language also includes "going after" these gods (2:12, 19; 10:14), "bowing down to/worshiping" them (2:12, 17, 19), "fearing" them (implied in 6:10), and "whoring after" them (2:17; 8:27, 33). What was the nature of the Canaanite gods and what did it mean to commit oneself to them?

43. For the Sidonians, see Wenham, *Genesis 1–15*, 225.

44. Boling, *Judges*, 54.

45. For the Amalekites, see Butler, *Judges*, 69. For the Midianites, see Anderson, *Understanding the Old Testament*, 108–9.

46. The exception that is worth noting appears in the Jephthah cycle. There the Canaanite gods Baal and Ashtaroth do appear, but the story also includes a litany of gods that the Israelites serve: the gods of the Syrians, the Sidonians, the Moabites, the Ammonites, and the Philistines (see 10:6).

47. Anderson, *Understanding the Old Testament*, 96.

Canaanite religion was of course polytheistic, a common feature of the ancient Near Eastern religions in the second millennium BC (Assyro-Babylonian, Hurrian, Hittite, Achaean, and Egyptian).[48] The high god at the head of the Canaanite pantheon of gods was El, the divine king and father of the gods.[49] W. F. Albright notes that El was considered distant from and basically uninvolved in the affairs of humans; he was inaccessible even to the gods except by means of immense effort.[50] Although El does not figure in Judges, the Shechemites had a temple of El-berith ("Covenant God/El"; 9:46), though this seems to be the same temple of Baal-berith ("Covenant Baal") referred to in 8:33 and 9:4. That the temple is in the location of great covenantal significance for Israel (Josh 24) and signifies a covenant bond between the Shechemites and not one but two Canaanite deities is shocking. Webb notes, "This strange conjunction of terms is testimony to the corrupt, syncretistic Israelite-Canaanite religion practiced by the Shechemites in Abimelech's day."[51]

El's female partner was the goddess Asherah, the "queen mother of the gods," who is connected with fertility.[52] Together El and Asherah spawned the other gods.[53] Asherah was worshiped alongside Baal at the shrine of Gideon's father (6:25–26). Yahweh's instruction to Gideon to "cut down the Asherah" refers to the wooden pole or tree that symbolizes the goddess, a typical way of representing/worshiping Asherah. Other goddesses worshiped in ancient Canaan alongside Asherah include Anat and Astarte—Jonathan Golden notes that it can be difficult to distinguish the three.[54] In Judges, the Israelites worship the goddess Astarte (i.e., the various "Ashteroth," the plural images or worship places of Astarte). She was the "Canaanite goddess of love, fertility, and war, [and] the consort of Baal."[55]

By far the Canaanite god that looms largest in biblical literature and features prominently in Judges is the "storm king and warrior," the "Rider of the Clouds" and "Storm Bringer," Baal.[56] If El was the titular head of the Canaanite pantheon, Baal was the de facto head, the lord par excellence.[57] Hadad was his proper name and Baal is a title ("master"), though the latter took on the function

48. Albright, "Ancient Near East," 102.
49. See Holland, *Gods in the Desert*, 202–3.
50. Albright, "Ancient Near East," 106.
51. Webb, *Judges*, 291.
52. Walton, *Ancient Near Eastern Thought*, 339.
53. Albright, "Ancient Near East," 106–7.
54. Golden, *Ancient Canaan and Israel*, 182.
55. Golden, *Ancient Canaan and Israel*, 281.
56. Golden, *Ancient Canaan and Israel*, 182. See also Holland, *Gods in the Desert*, 203–6.
57. Albright, "Ancient Near East," 107.

of a proper name, as is evident in the biblical literature. The significant role and identity of Baal is captured well by Albright: "Baal was the lord of heaven, the giver of all life, the ruler of gods and of men, to whom it is said . . . 'thou shalt take thy eternal kingdom, thy dominion for ever and ever.' The throne of Baal is on a lofty mythical mountain in the far north."[58] Baal is not only the master of gods and humans but is also acclaimed as the creator of humankind.[59]

Baal was particularly associated with fertility. As "master" he "owns the land and controls its fertility."[60] The Ras Shamra tablets from the Amarna Age (1400–1350 BC) contain fragments of a Baal epic. There Baal is victorious over a water dragon. Moreover, in a battle with Mot, the deity of summer drought, Mot kills Baal and drags him to the underworld. His goddess sister Anath sets out to rescue him. The result is that Mot is defeated, Baal conquers death and takes up his divine throne, and great rejoicing ensues. A hymn marks the glorious occasion:

> In a dream, O Kindly One, God of Mercy (?),
> In a vision, Creator of Creatures,
> The heavens rained oil,
> The dry valleys flowed with honey;
> So I know
> That Triumphant Baal lives,
> That the Prince, Lord of Earth, is alive![61]

Anderson notes the significance of Baal's death and resurrection for fertility: "the myth of Baal's death and resurrection represents the conflict waged in nature as the seasons come and go. Baal personifies the fertilizing powers of springtime; Mot personifies the destructive powers that bring death to vegetation and life. There is a rhythm in nature: springtime and summer, fertility and drought, life and death."[62]

Already from this brief sketch of the Canaanite gods, we should be impressed by the affront they represent to the identity, character, and function of Yahweh. There cannot be two divine and merciful kings, whose kingdoms are eternal and dominions are everlasting. There cannot be two divine creators of humans and all creatures. There cannot be two divine lords of heaven, givers of

58. Albright, "Ancient Near East," 107.

59. Anderson, *Understanding the Old Testament*, 99.

60. Anderson, *Understanding the Old Testament*, 97.

61. Cited in Anderson, *Understanding the Old Testament*, 100.

62. Anderson, *Understanding the Old Testament*, 100.

life, and rulers of gods and men. There cannot be two divine sustainers of life who govern the changing of the seasons, who hold summer drought at bay, and who provide vital rain to produce abundant fertility. It is a trustworthy saying and true: "No one can serve two masters, for either he will hate the one and love the other, or he will be devoted to the one and despise the other" (Matt 6:24).

Service of or allegiance to these Canaanite gods required various cultic practices and rituals. Worship of the Canaanite deities took place at local shrines and at temples, the earthly dwelling places of the gods from which they extended their rule and issued their blessings. John Walton notes,

> Temples were constructed to be a place of "rest" for the deity. Though the concept of relaxation (or even indolence) is not lacking, rest concerns most importantly the achievement of stability, security, and order. The deity can rest in his/her temple because the threat of chaos had been dispelled. The deity then takes his/her place in the ordered, controlled cosmos with the leisure of enjoying his/her estate.[63]

Often fashioned after the cosmos, temples were a symbol of cosmic rule. Customary at Baal temples was human ritual reenactment of the mighty deeds of Baal.

Because temples were the seat of divine authority and thus social and natural order, humans had a keen interest in temple worship. A temple was not only the anchor for social order, it was also the hub of human activity.[64] With regard to the function of temples in Mesopotamia, John Robertson notes, "To the members of any Mesopotamian urban community, the vast economic resources and complex administrative apparatus of its temple existed in order to minister to the needs and comfort of the city's patron god or goddess, for his or her numinous presence therein was believed to be the fundamental prerequisite for success in all human endeavors."[65] Sacrificial rituals were, therefore, key for the balance of order. Offerings in the form of animals, grains, dairy, fruit, wine, and so on (including child sacrifice) would provide for the well-being and contentment of the deity, which in turn would result in the deity's well-ordering of society, including abundant crops, healthy and vital herds, large families, and so on.[66]

This is a precarious system, especially given that the only ways of determining the will of the gods are subjective (omens, dreams/visions, and primarily

63. Walton, *Ancient Near Eastern Thought*, 114.

64. Walton, *Ancient Near Eastern Thought*, 87.

65. Robertson, "The Social and Economic Organization of Ancient Mesopotamian Temples," 1:444, cited in Walton, *Ancient Near Eastern Thought*, 128.

66. See the helpful chapter on temples and rituals in Walton, *Ancient Near Eastern Thought*, 113–34.

the material circumstances, either prosperity or poverty, of the devotee)—the Canaanite gods did not speak to their worshipers.[67] In fact, the Canaanite gods had no special interest in humans beyond their capacity to serve the immediate needs of the gods themselves. Canaanite anthropology in this way is of a kind with the conceptions of anthropology across the spectrum of ancient Near Eastern cultures, and radically at odds with Israelite anthropology, which affords a level of human dignity (by virtue of their divine image-bearing nature) unparalleled in the ancient Near East.[68] For this reason, Anderson maintains that Canaanite religion and Mosaic faith were incompatible: "Since both understood man's relationship to the deity in radically different terms, they found expression in diametrically different world outlooks."[69] According to Canaanite religion, humans were created and exist to serve the needs of the gods.

In Judges, the Israelites "serve" the Canaanite gods, and by implication engage in all the practices and rituals associated with the Canaanite cult. We should not think for a moment, however, that their apostasy was somehow limited to a realm we might call religious or spiritual. For simplicity's sake I have regularly referred to Canaanite "religion," but it must be noted that not a single culture or civilization in the ancient Near East conceived of a dichotomy between the religious realm and nonreligious realms (politics, economy, agriculture, etc.). Walton makes this point emphatically:

> There is no such word as "religion" in the languages of the ancient Near East. Likewise, there is no dichotomy between sacred and secular, or even between natural and supernatural. . . . In the end, there is a distinction between the heavenly realm and the earthly one, but events in the two were often intertwined or parallel. It would be difficult to discuss with ancients the concept of divine intervention, because in their worldview deity was too integrated into the cosmos to intervene in it. For the most part, deity is on the inside, not the outside. All experience was religious experience, all law was spiritual in nature, all duties were duties to the gods, all events had deity as their cause. Life was religion and religion could not be compartmentalized within life.[70]

Thus, the worldviews of the ancient Near East assume a fusion between the affairs of the gods and the affairs of humans, on all levels of society. This is key

67. Walton, *Ancient Near Eastern Thought*, 137.
68. Walton, *Ancient Near Eastern Thought*, 333.
69. Anderson, *Understanding the Old Testament*, 101–2.
70. Walton, *Ancient Near Eastern Thought*, 87.

for understanding Israel's attraction to Canaanite religion, the implications of which are worth exploring further.

Speaking about the universal human activity of culture-making, the sociologist Philip Rieff makes an intriguing and profound claim. He maintains that the inevitable human task of making culture involves the translation of a sacred order into an order for society.[71] In other words, the particularities of a given society's social order (government, justice system, family structure, economy, urban planning, foreign relations, etc.) are outworking of that society's conception of the divine and the whole system of derivative beliefs (ontology, anthropology, cosmology, epistemology, etc.).

Contextualizing this to the situation of Israel in the settlement period, we might rightly say that the Sinai covenant and its explanation and expansion on the plains of Moab provide the contours of a social order for Israel in the land that reflects the reality and character of Yahweh and the derivative conceptions of what it means to be human, what the nature of reality is, and so on. Boling expresses this reality, though using different language, when he notes, "Israel is the nucleus of the earthly half of the kingdom of Yahweh."[72] The kind of society that we expect Israel to develop would, for example, care for the most vulnerable (widows, orphans, and foreigners), prize justice and mercy, cultivate and care for the land in sustainable ways, encourage equitable and responsible economic practice, promote hard work and revitalizing rest, and so on—all of these as tangible manifestations of Yahweh's kingdom and his royal character. The result and ultimate aim of such a society would be blessing: the blessing of God's people, the blessing of the land, and even the blessing of the foreign nations.

The reality on the ground, or more appropriately in the promised land, is something altogether different. The tragedy of Israel forsaking Yahweh and serving the Canaanite gods is not merely that they violated the first and second commandments, but rather that in so doing they constructed an order for society that was founded on and reflected the sacred order of Canaanite religion. Kingship provides a good example of this dynamic at play. According to ancient Near Eastern thought, kings were either divine or at least closely associated with the gods and certainly mediators of the divine and human realms.[73] Kings had distinct cultic duties, especially revolving around the *image* of the god, often situated in a temple in the king's city. It seems entirely appropriate according to the

71. Rieff, *My Life Among the Deathworks*, 2. Rieff thinks that for the first time modern secular society is attempting to engage in culture-making without reference to any kind of transcendent order.

72. Boling, *Judges*, 24.

73. Walton, *Ancient Near Eastern Thought*, 281.

sacred order of Canaanite religion that Gideon the king de facto should build a shrine in his home city, that he should act capriciously and in self-interest after the manner of the gods, that he should accumulate a vast royal treasure and sizable harem (8:18–35), and so on.[74] Moreover, it would seem in keeping with Canaanite values that King Abimelech should kill his seventy brothers to eliminate any threat to his "rightful" claim to the throne. The sacred order of Canaanite religion prompted Jephthah to sacrifice his daughter to secure divine favor, Micah to construct an idolatrous shrine and hire a priest to secure divine blessing, and the Benjamites to value tribal interest above the norms of law and morality. It is not too much of an exaggeration to say that Judges is one example after another of what happens when the people of Yahweh choose to translate the sacred order of Canaan into an order (disorder?) for society.

The results? The Canaanite sacred order yields a society marked by devastation, division, self-destruction, fear, exploitation, injustice, and chaos. The sacred order of the kingdom of Yahweh could have yielded peace, prosperity, and blessing not only for Israel but for the surrounding nations as well. An interesting irony in the study of Judges is that the cultural background of Judges comes to the foreground again and again and again as we journey through the book. We see the values and character of Canaanite culture through the situations, characters, and events we encounter in Judges, and the picture stands in stark contrast to the distinct society that Yahweh envisioned for his people and the world.

The Author, Audience, and Occasion of Judges

The author of Judges does not identify himself, and it seems unlikely that we will ever know who wrote the book.[75] In his commentary, Younger includes a section on authorship and date of composition, which consists of two short paragraphs. With the reams of material written on this subject and the many

74. This tendency to mimic Canaanite monarchy may account for the ambivalence toward monarchy that we find in the teachings and narratives in Israel's tradition. Monarchy as such is not evil according to the Torah or Old Testament narratives, but its tendency toward absolutism, self-interest, and self-sufficiency is at odds with the principles of the kingdom of Yahweh. This is most evident in Deuteronomy's teaching on kingship (17:14–20)—all those things that the nations regard as providing stability and strength, namely, military might (horses), prosperity (silver and gold), and political alliances (wives), are regarded as worthless and out of bounds for Israel's king. A king immersed in Yahweh's Torah is the necessary condition for stability and prosperity.

75. The author was most likely male, hence my use of the masculine pronoun. Cf. Block, *Judges*, 49 n. 127, who notes "the historico-cultural fact that in the ANE female scribes were extremely rare" (he references Baker, "Scribes as Transmitters of Tradition," 65–77).

different and conflicting opinions, the temptation to keep it simple is appealing. The problem is that the evidence for dating the composition of Judges (and thus understanding something of the audience and occasion) is limited, in some cases seems contradictory, and subject to interpretation. In addition, in many cases one's interpretation of the book's message will influence one's understanding of its date of composition. A further challenge is to what extent we can discern sources from earlier than the time of final composition. As a result of these complexities, Gordon Wenham notes, "Much of the evidence is compatible with the book's composition at a wide variety of dates in Israel's history from the early monarchy to the postexilic era."[76]

The approach I will take to these matters is simple, though I hope not simplistic. First, we need to give attention to those places in Judges that provide hints regarding the historical setting of the book's composition. Second, I will propose hypothetical scenarios in the history of Israel and how the message of Judges may have been heard in those contexts, without necessarily judging which one was *the* historical setting.

The note in 18:30 indicates that Moses's grandson Jonathan and his descendants ministered at the Danite shrine in the north "until the captivity of the land." Although this phrase is unusual, it seems to be referring to the Assyrian victory over and exile of the northern kingdom in 722 BC.[77] If this is correct, then the author of Judges had an awareness of the Assyrian exile and the final composition of Judges took place no earlier than 722. However, when 1:21 notes that the Jebusites dwelt with the Benjamites in Jerusalem "to this day" it suggests a time of writing no later than David's conquest of Jerusalem sometime in the tenth century BC. Similarly, the note in 1:29 indicates that Canaanites continued to dwell in Gezer; however, 1 Kgs 9:16 says that the Egyptian Pharaoh killed the Canaanite inhabitants of Gezer and bequeathed the city to Solomon, which suggests a date for the writing of 1:29 prior to Solomon's reign (also early tenth century BC).[78] My own opinion is that 18:30 is a reference to the northern exile and, therefore, the final composition of Judges occurred sometime after 722 BC. The references in 1:21 and 29 do present a challenge, but perhaps, as Robert Chisholm suggests, they reflect earlier sources that were incorporated into the exposition.[79]

76. Wenham, *Story as Torah*, 70.

77. Although some scholars amend the text to read הארון/*hā'ārôn* ("the ark") instead of הארץ/*hā'āreṣ* ("the land"), in which case this could be a reference to the Philistine capture of the ark in 1 Sam 4:21. Wenham maintains that the emendation is motivated by the conviction that a reference here to the Assyrian exile is out of place; see Wenham, *Story as Torah*, 70 n. 40.

78. Chisholm, *Commentary on Judges and Ruth*, 53–54.

79. Chisholm, *Commentary on Judges and Ruth*, 54.

Another challenge to the dating of Judges regards the perceived north versus south polemic in the book. According to this now common theory, Judges displays an implied but distinct critique of the north (represented especially by Benjamites) and endorsement of the south (represented by Judahites). For many proponents of this theory, the book purposely portrays the north/Benjamin negatively and the south/Judah positively to serve as a polemic against Saul and his dynastic claim and as a support for David and his dynasty.[80] This would suggest a setting of the composition of Judges either in the time of rivalry between Saul/Ishbosheth and David or in the context of the division of the kingdom and the resulting dispute between Rehoboam and Jeroboam.[81] Of course, both of these proposed settings require explaining away the note in 18:30 about the captivity of the land. Alternatively, the antinorthern/prosouthern perspective serves to explain the fall of the northern kingdom in 722 BC and the survival of the southern kingdom, a theory proposed by Amit who situates the composition of the book during the time of Hezekiah.[82]

I am not at all convinced by the view that sees an overarching anti-Saul/pro-David political interest as the driving force of Judges. Admittedly, the tribe of Benjamin comes off very poorly in Judges and that is hard to ignore. However, the Judahites are hardly paragons of virtue and moral leaders in Judges. They are chosen by Yahweh twice to lead in battle—in the exposition they seem to circumvent this divine appointment by forming a coalition with Simeon and are not completely successful in battle (though they do fare better than any other tribe), and in the end section they are soundly defeated twice as leaders in the battle against Benjamin. It is true that Othniel is apparently a Judahite and is portrayed positively. If the author of Judges was motivated to portray Judah in the most positive light, the actions of Judahites in the Samson cycle (15:9–13) would have been best left on the editorial chopping block. There the men of Judah express their resignation to Philistine rule and actually tie up their would-be deliverer and hand him over to the Philistines! The negative actions of Benjamin (and Ephraim) in Judges are noteworthy, but need there be hidden political polemics behind these events, or is it just a reflection of history that some of these northern tribes displayed some very bad behavior? Thus, the north/south dynamics in Judges are, in my mind, not helpful in determining the date of the composition of Judges.

Granting that it is extremely difficult to determine the date of the composition of Judges, let us consider some hypothetical settings for Judges and how its message might be heard in those settings. We will attempt to hear Judges

80. See, most notably, O'Connell, *Rhetoric*.

81. See Butler, *Judges*, lxxiv.

82. Amit, *Book of Judges*, 375.

in the context of (1) the rise of monarchy in Israel, (2) the fall of the northern and then southern kingdoms, (3) the exilic experience, and (4) the postexilic return to the land.

The Message of Judges to Israel on the Eve of Monarchy

If Judges was delivered to the twelve tribes of Israel on the verge of uniting under the leadership of a king, how would they hear the message it has to offer? The events of the settlement period would be their immediate history. Intriguingly, they would no doubt recognize that they are still in the terrible cycle of sin/oppression/deliverance. They are suffering under the oppression of the Philistines, the priesthood under the leadership of Eli's sons is corrupt, and the ark of the covenant, the symbol of Yahweh's presence among the Israelites, has been captured and taken to Philistia. The Israelites' request for a king reveals that a certain searching of hearts is taking place. No doubt they are wondering, what can break us out of this cycle? What can unite us as a great nation? What can bring peace and stability to our nation? The message the people of God would hear in the midst of this introspection would be something like this:

Your parents, grandparents, and great-grandparents deserted King Yahweh and pledged allegiance to the gods of the nations. You have inherited the social (dis)order that was the logical outworking of their service to the foreign gods. Don't think for a moment that a change in the political order will solve your problems. What is needed for a time such as this is a radical reorientation, because you don't know just how immersed you are in Canaanite culture. Repent. Abandon the foreign gods and tear down their temples and shrines. Tell the old stories of Yahweh's mighty deeds, ponder them, teach them to your children, sing songs about them, relive them by means of ritual activity. And then live before the face of Yahweh as his kingdom of priests and holy nation, allowing the principles and practices of Yahweh's kingdom to permeate every aspect of your lives. Make no mistake, this will be hard, but it is the way of great blessing! Regarding those foreign nations: they have been a terrible scourge, but Yahweh has a plan for them too. By living out Yahweh's kingdom on earth you will display to them what great things are possible and they too might come to taste and see Yahweh's goodness—not as enemies but as partners.

The Message of Judges to Israel/Judah on the Eve of Exile

If Judges was delivered to Israel and/or Judah in anticipation of their defeat and exile, centuries would have passed since the events which the book recounts.

The audiences would have known of the relative prosperity in Israel under the leadership of David and Solomon, but they would also be keenly aware of the string of bad kings that ruled Israel and Judah after the kingdom divided. Here is how the message of Judges may have resonated in those contexts:

Your ancestors thought that a king like the kings of the foreign nations would bring peace, stability, and prosperity that they were so longing after. A king could have been instrumental in changing the fortunes of your forebears, but not any old king. A king that was completely devoted to King Yahweh and immersed in his Torah could have made the all-important difference. Instead, the kings not only did not abandon the practices of the people in the settlement period, they actually institutionalized them on a national level. You've seen kings set up temples and shrines to foreign gods, not tear them down; you've seen them wage war against your fellow countrymen, not bring peace; you've seen them exploit the vulnerable, perpetrate injustice, enslave the people, not bring justice, peace, and rest. You yourselves are implicated in their covenant rebellion. You heard the warnings of the prophets, just as your ancestors did in the settlement period, and just like your ancestors you persist in your self-destructive behavior. You have not remembered Yahweh and all that he has done for you in the past. Repent. Leave this path that only leads to curse, misery, and death. Those things you hold so dear like being a great nation and possessing the land and the temple are only means by which you are to live out your calling as a kingdom of priests and a holy nation. If you can't carry out your calling with those things, you may have the opportunity to recenter on your calling without those things. It's not too late to learn from the mistakes of your predecessors in the settlement period. The roots of their rebellion run deep and are producing a society of rotten fruit. Root out the idolatrous foundation of your society. Time is running out.

The Message of Judges to the Exiles

If Judges was received by those experiencing exile, the settlement period would have been a distant memory. They would have seen their cities and countryside ravaged by foreign armies, their houses destroyed or taken away, and their fellow citizens and family members raped, murdered, or taken captive. To make matters worse, the Judean exiles may have witnessed firsthand the looting and destruction of the temple, the locus of Yahweh's presence and the symbol of his special relationship with the people. Their ruthless foe then carried the most educated and influential citizens to live in a foreign land, with a foreign language and with foreign customs, where they were forced to do the bidding of their imperial overlords. Feelings of humiliation, pain, abandonment, loneliness, and deep longing for revenge and vindication characterize the people (see Ps 137). The situation seems hopeless. The message of Judges would speak to the exiles something like the following:

You are feeling abandoned and humiliated and that is understandable. Never forget that Yahweh is the God who hears the cry of his people in distress—he always has been. Remember how many times he heard the cries of his people in distress in the settlement and responded with mighty acts of deliverance. He still hears, he sees, he knows your plight; and make no mistake, he is at work even right now through these terrible circumstances. If we could only turn back time to that moment of great potential and excitement as your ancestors were settling into Canaan—Israel was such a great and powerful nation, they were finally in the promised land, and they were set on serving Yahweh just as Yahweh was set on a life of abundant flourishing for your ancestors. All the promises that Yahweh made to father Abraham were finally fulfilled and the people were poised to be that channel of blessing to all nations that Yahweh called them to be! But your predecessors squandered that moment filled with so much potential. Instead of being a distinct nation for the sake of the nations, they deserted King Yahweh and became more and more like the foreign nations, which resulted in no good for anyone. And now look at you: no longer a great nation but divided and conquered, no longer dwelling in the land but in exile, and no longer in a relationship of mutual blessing but questioning your status before Yahweh and his care for you.

All hope is not lost. King Yahweh is on his throne, and his Spirit is at work, just as it was in the settlement period. Yahweh used foreign nations at that time to fulfill his ultimate purposes and he is using Assyria and Babylon now to achieve his ultimate purposes. The Israel of old didn't fulfill their calling to bless all nations with all the promises in place, and now you have the more difficult summons to fulfill that calling without those promises in place. This is going to be hard to hear in this moment, but you need to pursue the blessing of the nations that took away everything you hold dear. Jeremiah gave you a similar message by the mouth of Yahweh himself—seek the shalom of Babylon because their shalom and your shalom are mutually bound up together. Exile is not the end. A time of reestablishing those promises Yahweh made to Abraham is coming. But for now, repent (that's what was lacking in your ancestors' repeated cries of distress back in the settlement period) and start living out that countercultural way of life, which will result in great blessing for you and even for Babylon. Reports of the activities of Daniel and his three friends indicate that they are modeling this way of being in the very courts of emperors—that requires courage and nerves of steel, but praise Yahweh for what is at work there! Because of Daniel's witness even the Babylonian and Persian emperors are praising the name of King Yahweh and sending out decrees throughout the empire (indeed the world) about Yahweh's eternal kingdom (Dan 4:1–3, 34–37; 6:25–27)! Yahweh will one day reunite the twelve tribes, reestablish his throne on Mount Zion, and from there his blessings will stream like living waters that will flow to all nations. Give those foreign nations a taste of Yahweh's eternal kingdom of blessing right where he has placed you now.

The Message of Judges to the Returnees

If Judges was written to those returning from exile, its audience may be disappointed and overwhelmed at their arrival in a devastated land. Waves of returnees journeyed back to Palestine (now a province of the Persian Empire) to pick up the pieces and etch out some semblance of the glory days of Israel. The exilic experience purged their desire to engage in idol worship but, as is too true today, idols come in many forms, not just wood, stone, and metal. There are some covenantal highlights in this period like the rebuilding of the temple, the reinstitution of the Passover, the reading and teaching of Torah, and other reforms. Moreover, the faithfulness of the young Jewess Esther, who did not return to the land, averts what seems like an inevitable and comprehensive Jewish genocide. But immorality and injustice also exist in this context. In the ensuing centuries the Jews developed an intense longing for Yahweh to return, to establish his kingdom of peace and to liberate them from their foreign overlords. A number of Jewish sects or groups emerged to respond to this new reality (Pharisees, Sadducees, Essenes, and Zealots). This is how Judges may have been heard in such a context:

It took great courage and faith to leave the stability and security of your life in Persia and to start over in the land of your ancestors. No doubt you have had moments of doubt—the return has hardly been what you expected from the many prophecies, which spoke of liberation, peace, and abundance. Even the rebuilding of the temple, a wonderful achievement, filled some of you with disappointment not merely because it pales in comparison with Solomon's great temple, but because there has been no sign of Yahweh's return to dwell there. As you are settling back into the land of your ancestors, don't forget the lessons of the time when they originally settled there, and especially recall their foundational calling to be a people set apart from the nations but for the sake of the nations—after all, your calling is the same. There are encouraging signs in this regard. You rebuilt the temple, reinstituted the sacrificial system and festivals, you are learning the Torah, and striving for ethical reform. Idol worship is no longer the snare that it was to your forbears—great news! However, idolatry comes in many forms. What's more is that the idolatry of the Israelites in the settlement period was so devastating not because of mere words (prayers to the Canaanite gods or verbal pledges of allegiance) or cultic actions (burning of incense or sacrifices); the devastation resulted as a logical outworking of Canaanite religion in an order for society marked by fear, oppression, self/tribal-interest, and injustice. There are already signs among you of moral behavior, economic practices, and judicial procedures that display the character and principles of foreign religious systems and that are at odds with the kingdom of Yahweh—in this way you are falling back into the old patterns of your ancestors in the settlement period.

You might ask: Where is Yahweh's kingdom and when will Yahweh establish his kingship here—when will he return and liberate us? Answer: Yahweh is on his throne and the fact that you are being ruled by the great world empires (Persia, Greece, Rome) does not mitigate his sovereign reign. As always, he urges you to display his kingdom, even as a province of the world superpowers. In accordance with the visions that Daniel received, Yahweh will return, he will topple the kingdoms of the earth and establish his everlasting kingdom, but you are called to be faithful in the here and now. Some of you might be tempted to quicken his return, but know this: his kingdom is present wherever his people do his will. Don't think for a moment that political compromise is the best approach to your present situation—the Israelites in the settlement period should warn you against that. That is a sure way to keep Yahweh's kingdom at bay. Isolating yourself from your pagan context won't do either because Yahweh's kingdom should shine forth in every area of society and exists for the sake of the surrounding culture too. Some of you think that strict *external* adherence to the Torah is the way to bring about Yahweh's kingdom, but Torah adherence must flow from renewed hearts and transformed lives. Still others of you think that Yahweh's kingdom will come at the tip of a sword and through brutish acts of political terrorism—put away your swords! Don't you know that Yahweh could send legions of angels to fight on his behalf, but that is not how his kingdom will come. No, his kingdom will emerge as it could have done in the settlement period by means of undivided loyalty to Yahweh and communities committed to living out the practices and principles of that kingdom. By providing a taste of Yahweh's kingdom in this way, the pagan nations will observe your good works and glorify King Yahweh on the day of his visitation.

The hope in the preceding is that examining hypothetical settings in Israel's history we might imagine how the message of Judges would have been heard and received. As a vital part of the word of God, Judges resonates through the centuries and speaks powerfully to a variety of contexts and situations. This exercise may also provide an added advantage of getting us to think through how the message of Judges might speak into our own twenty-first century contexts. To be sure, the people of God today are distant (historically, culturally, and in other ways) from the people of Yahweh in the Old Testament, but the book has the potential to speak powerfully and relevantly to us too, as we strive to follow God and display his kingdom in the midst of "the nations." We will explore some of these contemporary implications of the message of Judges in the final section of this commentary.

Hearing Others Hearing Judges

Interpretation never takes place objectively or in isolation. The situation and perspective of every reader and a host of other factors particular to a reader (historical situatedness, gender, race, class, religious conviction, etc.) influence how he/she reads and understands texts. Our perspectives sometimes cause us to be in tune with aspects of the text, hearing the nuances with crystal clarity. However, our limited perspectives may dampen our hearing or make us altogether deaf to certain frequencies of a text. The best way to hear the full range of a text with all of its subtle nuances is to do so with a broad range of listeners. In this section, I offer a broad sketch of the history of the interpretation of Judges. In this way we will attempt to hear how others have heard and understood Judges. This survey is by no means exhaustive and does not even attempt to convey all the results of the vast secondary literature on Judges.[83] Rather I have tried to offer a sampling of various readings and identify trends in the approaches to its interpretation.

Early Christian/Jewish and Medieval Interpretation of Judges

J. Alan Groves maintains that "among the historical books in the OT, Judges has perhaps received the least attention in the history of interpretation, except in the modern period"; further, he notes, "Jewish interpretation in the Second Temple period and Christian interpretation in the NT (and early church period) also show relatively little use of the book, especially in light of much more substantial treatment of other portions of the OT."[84] I have identified and commented on the places in the Old and New Testaments that reference the book of Judges

83. The most comprehensive source in this regard is Gunn, *Judges*.

84. Groves, "Judges," 410.

in the section on Judges and biblical theology below and I will not repeat that here. Apart from the somewhat idiosyncratic and selective reading of some of the Judges in Heb 11:32–40, the few references to Judges/the settlement period tend to evaluate negatively this chapter in Israel's history. This is not generally the case in sources from the early Jewish and Christian interpretation of Judges, in which Groves observes an apologetic tendency to idealize figures and events from this part of Israel's history.[85] Similarly, according to Jack Sasson, "To assess from its citation in the New Testament, Apocrypha, and Pseudepigrapha, Judges was a source of modest inspiration."[86]

Ben Sirach (175 BC) provides an early (if brief) example of this idealizing tendency:

> The judges, each one of them,
> whose hearts were not deceived,
> Who did not abandon God—
> may their memory be ever blessed!
> May their bones flourish with new life where they lie,
> and their names receive fresh luster in their children! (Sir 46:11–12 NAB [revised ed.])

Book 5 in Josephus's *Jewish Antiquities* (late first century AD) includes substantial explanations of parts of Judges. Clearly, Josephus had a copy of Judges in front of him to inform his telling of the events of the settlement period, but it is equally clear that he felt at liberty to reorganize, gloss over, and embellish his source. In his account, the Israelites are more or less portrayed as the incorrigible people we encounter in the book of Judges; however, the judges/deliverers feature as distortions of the figures we encounter in Judges. Gideon, according to Josephus, is a "paragon of Jewish leadership," who, in the follow-up to his deliverance (an act of faith), ruled with justice and was revered by all (*Ant.* 5.vii.7).[87] Josephus makes no mention of Gideon's idolatrous shrine. Jephthah comes across as a virtuous and able warrior, one who piously entreats God for victory, though Josephus clearly condemns the sacrifice of his daughter as "neither conformable to the law, nor acceptable to God" and as an affront to subsequent hearers of his actions (*Ant.* 5.vii.8–10). Josephus certainly exaggerates the portrayal of Samson (and his parents). In the final analysis, he notes, "indeed this man deserves to be admired for his courage, strength, and

85. Groves, "Judges," 410–11.

86. Sasson, *Judges 1–12*, 15.

87. Quotation from Sasson, *Judges 1–12*, 17.

magnanimity at his death: and that his wrath against his enemies went so far as to die himself with them. But as for his being ensnared by a woman, that is to be ascribed to human nature; which is too weak to resist the temptation to that sin. But we ought to bear him witness, that in all other respects he was one of extraordinary virtue" (*Ant.* 5.vii.12).[88] Embellishments aside, Josephus does at times offer intriguing insights into the events he recounts. We must also bear in mind that he is writing to a non-Jewish Roman audience to explain (apologetically) the customs and traditions of Jewish history and draw lessons from them.

Also from the first century AD, Liber antiquitatum biblicarum (LAB), whose anonymous author is customarily referred to as Pseudo-Philo, deals at length with parts of Judges. It is difficult to characterize generally the author's approach to the interpretation of Judges. At points the work follows closely and faithfully the biblical text of Judges, at other points it embellishes slightly on events and figures, filling in blanks, and at still other points it wildly expands on Judges with elaborate midrashic bravado.[89] The tendency to idealize is present in some passage (e.g., Deborah [LAB 32–33]) but in other cases some characters are unjustifiably demonized (e.g., Ehud/Eod who features as an evil magician and priest of the Midianites [LAB 34], and Jair who is a zealous Baal follower who incites the people to Baal worship [LAB 38]). The importance of Pseudo-Philo's Liber antiquitatum biblicarum is that in spite of some significant embellishment, the interpretation of Israel in the settlement period in general follows closely the negative evaluation reflected in Judges itself. For example, Pseudo-Philo portrays God himself expressing judgment against Samson for letting his eyes lead him astray, forgetting God's mighty work through him, and liaising with Philistine women (LAB 43.5).[90]

Other early Jewish sources are similarly mixed in their evaluation of events and figures from Judges.[91] Groves notes that an incidental comment in *The Lives of the Prophets* (early first century AD) refers pejoratively to the period of the judges as "days of the anarchy."[92] The tractate Rosh Hashanah (ch. 2) in the Babylonian Talmud compares Gideon, Jephthah, and Samson, "the three commonest people" in their generation to Moses, Aaron, and Samuel,

88. For an analysis of Josephus's portrayal of Samson compared to the biblical account see Jonquière, "Of Valour and Strength, 119–28.

89. Sasson, *Judges 1–12*, 18.

90. See Crawford, "Reading Samson with the Dead," 228.

91. For an account of the evolution of the interpretation of the Samson narratives in the rabbinic literature see Nikolsky, "Rabbinic Discourse about Samson," 101–18.

92. Groves, "Judges," 411.

"the three noblest" in their generation. On account of the leadership and acts of deliverance these three judges ought to be held in high esteem. However, in the tractate Taahnith (ch. 1) Jephthah is listed as one of three men who made unsuitable requests of God, and in the case of Jephthah, God answered the prayer. In the tractate Pesachim (ch. 4), Deborah is criticized for being an example of a sage who lost her wisdom. The tractate Nazir includes a long discussion about Samson's Nazirite status and to what extent Samson violated and/or was responsible for the Nazirite vow. Timothy Crawford notes, "The rabbis seemed to have found no satisfactory answer to this problem. It appears that they are not willing to sanction Samson for violating the Nazarite vow, but neither are they able to find a way to excuse him."[93] Crawford also notes that in various places in the tractates of the Babylonian Talmud Samson's propensity to do what seems good "in his eyes" (14:3) is synonymous with sin, and the eventual plucking out of his eyes amounts to retribution for Samson's following his eyes.[94] For one rabbi (Midrash Numbers Rabbah 9.24), Samson's final prayer (16:28) represents Samson's confession of his loss of sight in the world, a confession for which God rewards Samson in the afterlife.[95]

Apart from a dozen or two passing references to passages in Judges, the ten-volume compendium of all the extant works of the early church fathers down to the first General Council of Nicea (AD 325) contains little sustained commentary on Judges.[96] The idealizing tendency is not as prevalent in early Christian literature as we find in much premodern interpretation of Judges. Irenaeus, for example, notes that although the Holy Spirit was active in the mighty feats of Samson, the Scriptures no longer associate the Spirit with Samson after he committed fornication because "the sin of fornication is perpetrated against the body, as involving also sin against the temple of God" (*Haer.* V.xl). In the same book, however, Irenaeus provides a fanciful allegory on the narrative of Samson's death in which the boy who led Samson prefigures John the Baptist, the Dagon temple represents the world, and the two pillars are the two covenants (*Haer.* V.xxvii). Clement of Alexandria provides a matter of fact and rather detailed account of the events covered in Judges, including references to most of the usual suspects (*Strom.* I.xxi). This telling of the events of Judges does not airbrush Israel's rebellion but honestly reflects the framework of Judges, as does the similar summary (albeit less detailed) by Tertullian (*Scorp.* III). *Against Marcion*, attributed to Tertullian, includes odes to Gideon, Deborah, Jephthah,

93. Crawford, "Reading Samson with the Dead," 230.

94. Crawford, "Reading Samson with the Dead," 230–31.

95. See Crawford, "Reading Samson with the Dead," 234.

96. Roberts and Donaldson, eds., *Ante-Nicene Fathers.*

and Samson with a christological bent—although there are hints of critique, these accounts paint a more positive picture than their antecedents in Judges (*Marc.* III.93–162).[97] Origen has a passing reference to the wickedness of the men of Gibeah (*Cels.* VI.xliii), and Cyprian specifically quotes Judges to explain in part why the wrath of God came against the Jews (*Test.* I.1). Methodius has a relatively lengthy allegorical interpretation of Jotham's parable (Judg 9:7–15) that encourages his audience to forsake the wiles of the devil and promotes chastity and faithful devotion to God (*Symp.* X.ii–v). A prayer in the Apostolic Constitutions draws on figures from Judges as trustworthy examples of God's hearing of and answering prayer (notice the hints of negative evaluation): "O Lord God accept the prayers as thou did respect the prayers/sacrifices of . . . Gideon at the rock, and the fleeces, before his sin; of Manoah and his wife in the field; of Samson in his thirst before the transgression; of Jephthah in the war before his rash vow; of Barak and Deborah in the days of Sisera" (Apos. Con. VII.ii.37). Finally, in the second of *Two Epistles Concerning Virginity*, attributed to Clement of Rome, Samson is held out as an example of someone consecrated and especially gifted by God who was brought to ruin by a woman. Samson shows how Christians ought not to live in the midst of a pagan nation (Second Epistle, IX).

A survey of the fourteen volumes of texts from the Nicene and post-Nicene fathers reveals similar trends after the General Council of Nicea (AD 325) that we observe in the interpretation of Judges before the great council, with some exceptions. Judges is seldom referred to in the works of the church fathers from the fourth to the eighth century, and they are often unsubstantial passing references. The tendency, as with the ante-Nicene fathers, was to draw contemporary application from the lives and events of judges, or to show enduring patterns of God's behavior or character. In most of these cases a figure or event from Judges is used as a prooftext, but Ambrose wrote quite a detailed example of Deborah, who he thinks should stir up women; according to Ambrose, women have "no excuse because of your nature" and widows have "no excuse because of the weakness of your sex" (*Vid.* VIII.42–51). An apologetic purpose is discernable at times; for example, both John Chrystostom (*Homilies on the Statutes*, XIV.7) and Jerome (*Jov.* I.23) justify God in condoning the sacrifice of Jephthah's daughter. According to John Thompson, Ambrose is unique in blaming not Jephthah but his daughter—something in her character prevented God from sparing her from sacrifice the way he did for Isaac (Gen

97. See Thompson's discussion of Origen's interpretation of Jephthah's daughter whom Origen sees as prefiguring Jesus, her sacrifice contributing to the defeat of evil. This interpretation, Thompson notes, is shared by, among other early interpreters, Pseudo-Philo, Josephus, and Ambrosiaster; see Thompson, "Preaching Texts of Terror," 55.

22); though in other places Ambrose is more favorable in his assessment of Jephthah's daughter.[98]

Allegorical interpretations also continue to appear after the ante-Nicene interpreters. Augustine supposed the rock upon which Gideon placed his offering was a figure of the body of Jesus (*Doctr. chr.* IV.21), Jerome considered Samson a type of Christ because he loved a harlot and slew more enemies in his death than his life (*Jov.* I.23), and Ambrose produced an elaborate and detailed allegorical interpretation of Gideon, who prefigures Jesus (*Spir.* I.i.1–6). Apart from these fanciful allegorical interpretations, the patristic writings by and large draw sensible lessons from Judges even if they ignore the overall purpose and message of the book. David Gunn notes,

> For a large part of the book's history, from late antiquity, the predominant way of reading Judges by Christians has been typologically. . . . While sometimes seeming arbitrary, such interpretation is usually anchored in some textual detail and metaphorical possibility. . . . To Judges, then, as elsewhere in the Bible, readers looked for religious inspiration and moral guidance. The stories taught lessons for life.[99]

Groves holds that Judges was rarely treated as a whole in the period between the ancient church and the present day (or more accurately the early modern period).[100] According to Gunn, the idealizing and allegorizing of the judges continued in this time: "Official patristic and medieval Christian interpretation, whether written commentary or spoken homily, tended to bypass the heroes' human qualities in favor of the spiritual codes their actions generated."[101] Sasson summarizes the interpretation of Judges in this time as such:

> Since late antiquity and through the Middle Ages, Judges has gathered its share of exegetical attention from leaders of individual confessions. With opportunity to derive devotional instruction from Judges remaining scarce, allegorical, typological, and mystical readings stoked piety and inspired homilies. Jewish sages annotated Judges, explicating individual words or phrases rather than commenting on the book's construction. Midrash readily buttressed their readings, and their pedagogic goal was moral rather than historical or anthropological. Many of these commentators are gath-

98. Thompson, *Reading the Bible with the Dead*, 37.
99. Gunn, "Judges," 90.
100. Groves, "Judges," 411.
101. Gunn, "Judges," 9.

ered in the *Miqra'ot gedolot*. Beyond finding inspiration in the occasional sermon, Christians could turn to decoration (mostly paintings) at monumental buildings for nicely prescribed interpretation. As far as I know, Judges did not inspire any medieval mystery plays.[102]

Renaissance and Reformation Interpretation of Judges

The Renaissance and Reformation brought about a "fuller treatment of Judges," which was buttressed by the desire to go back to the sources (the Hebrew text in the case of Judges), the invention of the printing press, and a more global perspective (the European expeditions to "lost" worlds).[103] Although neither Luther nor Calvin wrote a commentary on Judges, Jordan holds that the political and ecclesiastical context was such that "Protestant Reformers were much taken with the book of Judges."[104] Reformers found resources in Judges to combat the absolutism in both the papacy and northern European monarchies; for the Reformers, the teachings of Judges resisted centralized government and bolstered faithful resistance movements.[105] For example, Scottish Reformer John Knox (ca. 1513–1572) wrestled with the issue of the rightful rule of women in affairs of the state, trying to come to terms both with his reading of the story of Deborah and his frustration with the royal rule of (Catholic) Mary Queen of Scots and Mary Tudor of England.[106] Martin Bucer's commentary on Judges (1554) and Peter Martyr Vermigli's published lectures on the book (1564) drew out the political teachings of

102. Sasson, *Judges 1–12*, 19–20. Moore, *Judges*, xlviii–xlix, offers a helpful roundup and evaluation of early and medieval Jewish interpreters of Judges, as well as a list of "Catholic" commentators of the late Middle Ages. Also helpful in this regard is Cassel, *Book of Judges*, 16, which includes sources for getting acquainted with Talmudic interpretation of Judges. Cassel also refers to the general introductions to the Old Testament by Jerome, Theodoret, Rhabanus Maurus, and Rupert von Deutz, for valuable insights into Judges during this time period.

103. Sasson, *Judges 1–12*, 20. Moore, *Judges*, xlix, lists among the early Protestant commentators Sebastian Münster (1489–1552) and Drusius (1550–1616), and the published work of Sebastian Schmid (1684) and Clericus (1708). In addition to these, Cassel, *Book of Judges*, 16 notes that the Protestant expositions by Brentius, Bucer, P. Martyr, Chyträus, Osiander, and Starke are worthy of attention.

104. Jordan, *Judges*, 177.

105. Jordan, *Judges*, 177. Cf. Gunn, *Judges*, 38: "The Protestant Reformation saw interest in Judges surge. The book spoke to burning issues of civil authority and the relationship between religion (Church) and State, issues that tore Europe apart during the sixteenth and seventeenth centuries. It was a book about war, the overthrow of enemies, and the divine calling of leaders."

106. See Gunn, *Judges*, 60.

Judges and had an impact on the Puritans.[107] Vermigli's approach was clearly christological, utilizing typological and, occasionally, allegorical interpretation.[108] According to Vermigli:

> Since Christ is called the goal and perfection of all holy Scripture, there remains for us to assert how these acts of the judges also may and ought to refer to him, and how they prophesy about him to us . . . [and] so these private deliverances of the Jews that happened under the judges, since they are contained within the principles of redemption, which is given unto mankind by Christ, these necessarily relate the same redemption to us, as they were certain assured parts and figurative shadows, and because they had the very same author, namely Christ.[109]

While being christological in its orientation, his work is applied time and again to the political situation of his day.

Richard Rogers's thousand-page commentary (1615), which builds self-consciously on the foundation of Vermigli's work, is an early example of modern commentaries on the whole book, though it suffers from reading the book through the lens of Heb 11 and thereby seeing the judges as examples of faith.[110] In a discussion on the rightful use of princes to exercise force, Martin Luther (1523) does see in Samson (not a political ruler, according to Luther) an exception to the rule because he was endowed with divine favor: "'First become like Samson,' [Luther] suggests, 'and then you can also do as Samson did.'"[111]

For John Milton, writing in 1651, both Samson and Ehud provide justification for violence against tyrannical rule and even regicide.[112] While Milton appealed to Ehud in his justification of the execution of King Charles I, his view was resisted by his opponents (Royalists and Presbyterians).[113] The English Calvinist Joseph Hall (1574–1656) warns his contemporary "butchers of princes" not to presume that they have been sent by God, lest they experience

107. Jordan, *Judges*, 178.

108. For a helpful discussion of the relationship between Vermigli's hermeneutical approach and that of the church fathers/early medieval interpreters on the one hand and the medieval scholastics on the other see Jenkins, "Commentary on Judges," 231–48.

109. Translated by and cited in Jenkins, "Commentary on Judges," 233.

110. For Vermigli's work as a foundation, see Jordan, *Judges*, 178. For the judges as examples of faith, see Groves, "Judges," 411.

111. Cited in Gunn, "Judges," 91.

112. Gunn, "Judges," 91.

113. *Tenure of Kings and Magistrates* (1649); referenced in Gunn, *Judges*, 38.

the revenge of God.[114] Although Protestant interpreters of these tumultuous times were convinced that Judges spoke into their political and ecclesiastical contexts, they clearly did not agree *how* Judges spoke and *what* it was saying to them.

In general, the Puritans, for good or ill, drew heavily on Judges to illuminate political, moral, and ecclesiastical matters (e.g., Jonathan Edwards's lengthy reflections on Jephthah's vows to address issues of vow/covenant making in his day).[115] Matthew Rowley's recent dissertation examines in detail the use of Scripture and the view of divine providence that afforded American Puritans justification for violence against Royalist Episcopalians, Irish Catholics, Scottish Presbyterians, and Native Americans; although the work focuses on the exodus and conquest narratives, Judges (particularly the Gideon narrative and the civil war against the tribe of Benjamin) was an important biblical text.[116] James Byrd states that "the Song of Deborah (Judges 5) was the most cited passage in over a century of colonial war sermons (1675–1800)."[117] Deborah's song was popular not only among colonial preachers but also among English Civil War preachers, particularly as a motivation for soldiers to kill for their country.[118] Closely related to the Puritans, the Scottish Covenanters returned again and again to Judges for instructions for their times. The Battle of Dunbar provides a good example of this. Drawing from the example of Gideon, the Covenanters dismissed from their ranks soldiers who were not sincere in their commitment to the Covenant. To their surprise, Cromwell's army annihilated the reduced army.[119] Thus, Judges not only provided political teaching but also provided leverage for military action.

The political dimension of Judges was an obvious focus during the Protestant Reformation and its antecedents. Of course, it was also used for inspiring spiritual and religious revival. For example, Edwards sees in Ehud's call for support inspiration for support of the New England revival in 1742.[120] Similarly, Edwards interprets Deborah's curse against Meroz (5:23) as a curse from

114. *Contemplations* (1615), ix.3; cited in Gunn, *Judges*, 39.

115. Groves, "Judges," 411. For a helpful summary of premodern Christian interpretation (from the ante-Nicene to post-Reformation) see Martin, "Unheard Voice of God," 39–53. I'm indebted to Matthew Rowley who in a private correspondence indicated that the vast amount of Puritan reflection on Judges may warrant a volume all on its own.

116. Rowley, "Godly Violence."

117. Byrd, *Sacred Scripture, Sacred War*, 73.

118. Byrd, *Sacred Scripture, Sacred War*, 74.

119. Benedict, "Religion and Politics," 166.

120. Gunn, *Judges*, 44.

Christ against those who oppose the revival.[121] Judges continued to be used as providing examples of faith for contemporary Christians to follow; however, increasingly, voices emerged that found the behavior in Judges (including that of the leaders in the book) troubling.[122]

Judges in Art, Music, and Theater

Judges has also been the source for much artistic inspiration. Wilbur Sypherd's 1948 monograph unearths an astounding number of artistic works on the story of Jephthah alone.[123] According to Sypherd, of the many popular themes and figures that artists, poets, and musicians have depicted, "none of these themes has had, I venture to say, so wide and so varied an appeal [as has the story of Jephthah and his daughter]."[124] Sypherd supposes to have discovered more than 300 plays and poetic depictions of the story of Jephthah and his daughter, more than 170 musical productions, and approximately 100 other artistic representations, almost all of which derive from the modern period.[125]

Karin Schöpflin reflects on the depiction of Samson in European poetry, particularly in the works of Geoffrey Chaucer (1340–1400), Hans Sachs (1494–1576), John Milton (1608–1674), and Alfred de Vigny (1797–1863). In summary she notes:

> In Chaucer Samson appears a little like Superman defeated because of domestic affairs—a hero outside, and a fool at home. In Sachs he is at last interpreted as a type of Christ—a loser in the eyes of the world, but God's champion. In Milton he is a man who realizes and recognizes his own fault and folly and responsibility which adds moral energy and motivation to his returned physical strength—a hero who knows he has been a fool. And de Vigny's Samson is a hero who consciously acts as a fool because man always makes a fool of himself in his relation with woman.[126]

Jean-Jacques Rousseau's *Le Lévite d'Ephraïm* (1762) although a "prose poem based on the last narrative in the biblical book of Judges . . . raises a pressing issue: to what extent is violence, whose ultimate expression is expunging other

121. Gunn, *Judges*, 62.
122. See the introduction in Gunn, *Judges*, 9–13.
123. Sypherd, *Jephthah and His Daughter*.
124. Sypherd, *Jephthah and His Daughter*, vii.
125. See Thompson, *Reading the Bible with the Dead*, 45.
126. Schöpflin, "Samson in European Literature," 195.

people, mandated and thus justified by the establishment of community?"[127] Klaas Spronk has examined the depiction of Samson in the fine arts, commenting on the appearance of Samson in images from the early sixteenth century to the early twentieth century, and what that says about the artist and the figure.[128]

Judges in the Late Modern Period and Beyond

The modern period brought reflections on Judges from women interpreters of Judges in an unprecedented way. Marion Ann Taylor and Christiana de Groot have compiled a helpful collection of excerpts from some thirty-five nineteenth-century female interpreters of Judges from a variety of socio-economic and religious backgrounds.[129] Many of the female interpreters in this volume were convinced that the texts of Judges speak into their situations, but wrestled with the historical and cultural distance between the world of Judges and that of their own day; they utilized a variety of means to bridge that distance.[130] The *Woman's Bible Commentary* also provides valuable essays on the depiction of women in Judges as well as the history of the reception of these narratives by both male and female interpreters.[131] Women interpreters of the past demonstrate an ambivalence with regard to their reception of Judges, showing a desire to learn from its teaching but also resisting the oppression of women in the book and some of the assumptions (e.g., the unequal standard for men and women in the book).[132]

The idealizing tendency in the interpretation of Judges could not be sustained indefinitely. As early as the eighteenth century, Voltaire harshly critiqued the treachery of Ehud's assassination of Eglon in the entry on "Fanaticism" in his *Philosophical Dictionary* (1764).[133] This critical evaluation of Judges would trickle down to the laity as it did a century and a half later in the Sunday School class of the English minister R. Rhondda Williams who said quite boldly to his pupils:

127. Morgenstern, "Strangeness, Violence, and the Establishment of Nationhood in Rousseau," 360. See also the essay on early Christian humanist interpretation of Jephthah's sacrifice in Nyquist, "Plight of Buchanan's Jephtha," 331–54.

128. Spronk, "Looks of a Hero," 197–209.

129. Taylor and de Groot, *Women of War, Women of Woe*. Seven of the eight chapters in this volume are focused on female interpretations of Judges (the other is focused on the interpretation of Rahab in Joshua).

130. See the introductory essay, Taylor and de Groot, *Women of War, Women of Woe*, 1–18.

131. Newsom, Ringe, and Lapsley, *Women's Bible Commentary, Revised and Updated*, 113–41.

132. Taylor and de Groot, *Women of War, Women of Woe*, 15.

133. Gunn, "Judges," 91.

> You may imagine, then, that this Book of Judges is not pleasant to read—much of it is quite ghastly. You must not go to it for any ideals of life, or learn anything about your own duty at the present time, except as you can see that it is your duty not to imitate the ways of most of the people of whom you read in it.[134]

While in the history of the reception of Judges, such a view would be unthinkable, a shift took place such that stories of Judges had become viewed by some as simply too repugnant to hold any enduring moral or spiritual value.

Judges and Modern Biblical Criticism

Many factors no doubt contributed to the radical reinterpretation of Judges in the modern period. Whether a symptom of this shift or a contributing factor, modern scholarship on the book of Judges gradually broke with the traditional view of Judges as Holy Scripture and spawned interpretations that were in keeping with the nature of the perceived object of study, namely, an ancient human text. A critical reassessment of the Hebrew text, new archaeological evidence, and discovery of ancient Near Eastern texts and cultures propelled a reevaluation of Judges. Interpreters felt increasingly liberated from the constraints of religious dogma and ecclesiastical tradition and strove for "objective," "scientific" research in keeping with "academic freedom." Scholarly interest in Judges tended toward its value as a witness to what exists "behind" the text—the sources of its composition, the "real" history of the settlement period, and such.

A detailed account of the results of modern biblical criticism on Judges is not necessary for our purposes.[135] We are more interested in the character and approach to interpretation that this kind of scholarship exhibited. Sasson has helpfully identified a number of foci (accents as he calls them) that distinguish modern scholarship on Judges.[136] First, modern interpreters focused on sources, trying to discern with a profound attention to detail the textual sources that lay behind the book of Judges as we have it today. Initially, scholars discovered in Judges the four sources (J, E, D, and P) that were key to the Documentary Hypothesis with regard to the Pentateuch, and they proposed a compositional history similar to that of

134. Cited in Gunn, *Judges*, 9.

135. Interested readers can consult any number of good summaries of modern Judges scholarship. See esp., Butler, *Judges*, xxxvi–lxxiv.

136. Sasson, *Judges 1–12*, 20–26.

the Pentateuch.[137] Second, modern scholarship focused on redaction history, and, accordingly, they gave attention not only to the sources but also to how those sources were taken up, shaped, and edited over time. Martin Noth's monumental Deuteronomic History (DH) theory is significant in this regard and spawned countless scholarly revisions. Third, modern scholarship on Judges focused on cultural and social contexts. This focus was certainly aided by the discovery of texts and material evidence from a wide array of ancient Near Eastern cultures, and interpreters were driven to bring their import to bear on the interpretation of Judges. Fourth, modern scholarship focused on archeological evidence, trying to discern to what extent the narratives of Judges align with the material evidence from the Late Bronze Age to the Early Iron Age found in the Fertile Crescent. Fifth, modern scholars focused on the epic style, discerning how much the heroic narratives of Judges conform to the epic mode of historiography.

Modern biblical criticism has much to offer toward the goal of theological interpretation of Judges, provided it is reframed properly. The rigor and attention to minute textual details is undeniable and commendable. This commitment to meticulousness often yielded "observable discrepancies" in the text (doublets, shifts in the use of divine names, etc.), and although the explanations are not always satisfactory in my mind (resorting to theories of multiple authorship) these observable tensions in the text are almost always worthy of reflection (for rhetorical purposes). The command of the Hebrew language and other Semitic and cognate languages evident in modern scholarship is impressive. Moreover, setting Judges properly within its ancient Near Eastern context is essential, and comparative studies help us to see rightly the cultural and social similarities and differences between Judges and its counterparts.

While many in the scholarly guild still held to some notion of inspiration, that was increasingly ruled out as a guiding principle in the academic interpretation of Judges. Moreover, one cannot deny that modern biblical scholarship had a profound impact on one's sense of the uniqueness, trustworthiness, and inner coherence of the book. In some cases, Judges was seen not just as a product of its time and place, it was a subpar one at that.

Judges and the Literary Turn

Although source and redaction criticism continued throughout the twentieth century and are still practiced to this day, the tides began to change in

137. I wrote a brief overview of modern biblical criticism and Judges, complete with references in Beldman, *Completion of Judges*, 10–15. I summarize that here.

reaction to their atomizing tendency in the 1960s and 1970s. A watershed moment in this regard was James Muilenburg's presidential address at the Annual Meeting of the Society of Biblical Literature in 1968.[138] In that address Muilenburg sounded a clarion call, advocating a focus on rhetorical criticism with a chief interest

> in understanding the nature of Hebrew literary composition, in exhibiting the structural patterns that are employed for the fashioning of a literary unit, whether in poetry or in prose, and in discerning the many and various devices by which the predications are formulated and ordered into a unified whole. Such an enterprise I should describe as rhetoric and the methodology as rhetorical criticism.[139]

Many scholars, including those interested in Judges, took up the call, and in the subsequent decades, articles, book chapters, monographs, and commentaries emerged, taking Judges seriously as a literary production in its own right.[140] This scholarly literature is vast and diverse, but a number of common themes surfaced. With few exceptions scholars agreed that

> (1) Judges consists of three parts, namely, the introduction, main section, and end section. . . ; (2) the introduction is an appropriate exposition for the book as a whole, providing a schematized account of battles between Israel and the Canaanite nations, and an initial hermeneutical schema which plays out in the judges accounts in the main section; (3) the book evidences a pattern of progressive deterioration or degeneration of the Israelites (and their judges) over the course of the book; (4) chs. 17–21 represent the completion of the downward spiral, the events of these chapters epitomizing the moral, spiritual, and social disintegration of Israel in the time between the death of Joshua and the rise of the monarchy. Thus, on the whole, scholars regard chs. 17–21 as a fitting conclusion to the book, a coda or dénouement which brings completion to the plot and themes which are developed previously in the book.[141]

Thus, the historical turn in Judges scholarship in the late nineteenth century lost ground to the literary turn in the late twentieth century. This shift in focus

138. Published as Muilenburg, "Form Criticism and Beyond," 1–18.

139. Muilenburg, "Form Criticism and Beyond," 8.

140. I have surveyed this literature in some detail in Beldman, *Completion of Judges*, 15–50.

141. Beldman, *Completion of Judges*, 51.

was by and large not motivated by theological concerns, and the historical value of Judges was in some cases downplayed or ignored altogether for literary purposes. Nevertheless, the attention to the patterns of meaning and the literary features of Judges as a whole vouchsafed obvious fruit for theological reflection on Judges.

Judges and the Postmodern Turn

As the literary turn was well under way in Judges scholarship, another turn of sorts was taking place, namely, the postmodern turn. Lagging slightly behind the broader cultural and literary revolution that took place in the 1980s and 1990s, biblical scholarship (including that of Judges) witnessed the application of a spate of new methods to biblical interpretation. In his helpful survey of the most recent trends in Judges scholarship, Alan Hauser notes the cornucopia of new interpretative approaches to Judges, among which he identifies social scientific criticism, deconstructive criticism, postcolonial criticism, feminist criticism, structuralist criticism, ideological criticism, gender criticism, cultural criticism, and reception history.[142] At their very best, these approaches show the potential of opening up aspects of Judges that scholars and other interpreters of the past have ignored or distorted. For example, in Old Testament literature, Judges is unparalleled in its treatment of a diversity of female characters. By virtue of this fact, it is rich ground for feminist interpretation, which has provided keen insights into both the nobility of female characters and their exploitation in the book.

The methods that have emerged in the wake of the postmodern turn are diverse and evidence a variety of interests; for these reasons we should avoid painting them all with the same brush. The methods tend to share a motivation to take seriously the reader's perspective in the task of interpretation. Whereas historically oriented interpretation of Judges was focused on what exists *behind the text*, and literary-oriented interpretation focuses on the patterns of meaning *in the text*, postmodern approaches attempt to take seriously what is *in front of the text*. The danger is that texts become no more than an echo chamber for a reader's own interests and perspective, but that need not be the case. As with historical and literary approaches, properly framed postmodern methods of interpretation can illumine the text of Judges and aid in our hearing of the book.

142. Hauser, "Judging Judges Scholarship," 437–42.

Conclusion

Judges invites us into a world of adventure, tragedy, uncertainty, and intrigue. As we enter into this world, we encounter in a fallen and broken world the very real human struggle to exist in the world as God intended humanity to be. The stories are told with sophistication, pathos, and creativity. We also enter this world alongside centuries of fellow travelers, struggling as they have done to make sense of this mysterious world. The task for us is to articulate for our times and embody the eternal truths that emerge from these powerful and explosive narratives.

Theological Commentary

The Exposition

The prologue or exposition of Judges provides the necessary background information for the core and end sections of the book. It consists of two parts. The first chapter describes the transition of Israel from the conquest to the settlement periods and recounts the Israelite "mop-up campaign" against the remaining Canaanite residents of the land. The second section (2:6–3:6) provides the interpretive framework for understanding the whole period of the settlement. In between these two parts is a linking section that interprets the problem of the settlement period as Israel's failure to rid the land of the Canaanites (2:1–5).

1:1–2:5: Israel's Increasingly Unsuccessful "Mop-Up Campaign"

Context and Title (1:1a)

Judges starts with the words, "After the death of Joshua" (1:1). These opening words function in a number of important ways. Most obviously, the phrase "After the death of Joshua" serves as a temporal marker, indicating that the narratives that follow occurred after the exploits of Israel's great military leader. The book of Judges should be regarded, therefore, as the continuation and next chapter in the story of God and his dealing with his people.

This phrase also indicates that an understanding of the biblical book of Joshua and the history leading up to it is crucial for setting the context for Judges. As mentioned above, God's people are at a pivotal juncture in Judges. At the end of Joshua, we read that Yahweh has followed through on all the promises to the patriarchs and Israel has pledged their unswerving allegiance to Yahweh and his covenant. We expect great blessing to spill out in the book of Judges at such a time as this! This expectation makes what readers do encounter in the book of Judges all the more shocking and tragic.

The opening phrase also functions like the book's title, evoking the opening words of the book of Joshua. There we read that "After the death of Moses" Yahweh commissions Joshua as the leader of Israel and assures him of success as long as he follows the Torah of Moses (Josh 1:1–9). Already before his death, Moses announced to the people that Yahweh would lead them in the conquest of Canaan and that Joshua would be Yahweh's appointed human leader in that conquest (Num 27:15–23; Deut 31:3; cf. Josh 1:1–9).[1] What unfolds in the rest of the book of Joshua after the note about Moses's death is the portrayal of the relative success of Israel as they conquer the land under the leadership of Joshua.

That the beginning of Judges evokes the beginning of Joshua in this way builds up certain expectations.[2] We may expect that just as Joshua succeeded Moses as the leader of Israel, so too will another leader emerge to succeed Joshua. However, in Judges, the leadership vacuum that the death of Joshua created is not obviously filled, and the leadership *structure* following Joshua's death is apparently left undefined. Who will follow Joshua as the leader of the twelve tribes in this new phase of their existence? Should we expect a change in the kind of political structure that would govern Israel and if so what political system will be put in place?

One would expect that the obvious moment for Joshua to appoint a successor would have been after the covenant renewal ceremony in Shechem and before he dismissed the people to their inheritances. The precedent for such an expectation is Moses's appointment of Joshua as leader following the covenant ceremony on the plains of Moab (Deut 29–30 and 31:1–8). Amit is probably right to suppose that

> when Joshua made the covenant in Shechem without appointing a successor, but sent each man to his inheritance, he acted according to the expectation that the people would serve God alone and would fulfill its part

1. Note the similarities between Yahweh's commissioning of Joshua in Josh 1:7–8, i.e., to observe the Torah of Moses and not turn aside from it, "to the right hand or to the left," and the instructions for kings in Deut 17:18–20.

2. The opening of Judges necessitates that one read Judges in relation to Joshua according to Boling, *Judges*, 15. Similarly, Webb writes, "To the extent that the present narrative *assumes* the reader's familiarity with another narrative (in this case the story of Joshua's career and death) it makes itself dependent on that other narrative for its own intelligibility"; Webb, *An Integrated Reading*, 81 (emphasis original). See also Wong, *Compositional Strategy*, 27–77.

> in the covenant. The appearance of the judges, God's messengers, was the result of the violations of the covenant and the accompanying punishment.[3]

The second part of the exposition confirms this role of Israel's judges/deliverers.

The death notice at the beginning of Judges is peculiar in terms of the book's chronology. After the note about Joshua's death it appears that the following section (1:1b–2:5), arranged geographically, recounts further battles between the tribes and the Canaanites. The battles reported in 1:1b–2:5 collectively represent a "mop-up campaign" to drive out the remaining Canaanites from the promised land.[4] Given the note about Joshua dismissing the people and his death notice in 2:6–10, we cannot be certain if this mop-up campaign happened before or after Joshua's death.

In any case, this first section of the exposition provides essential information for making sense of the unfolding narrative of the book. It explains the continued presence of the foreign nations in Canaan following the conquest as a result of the Israelites' failure to drive out the Canaanites. As Michael Fishbane notes, the existence of these nations indicates "the deliberate violation of older injunctions which commanded the removal of the nations of Canaan."[5] The culture and especially the religious practice of the foreign nations set the context for the Israelites splitting their allegiance between Yahweh and the foreign gods or else rejecting their allegiance to Yahweh altogether (2:1–2). Moreover, although this section is arranged geographically, it also shows the progressive failure of Israel to completely subjugate the land, from Judah's relative (though not complete) success to Dan's failure to drive out the Amorites. Israel's progressive failure on the battlefield is bound up with their failure to obey Yahweh, and coheres with the author's general aim to portray the period of the Judges (at least on the surface) as one of progressive decline for the nation of Israel.

Divine Inquiry and Answer (1:1b–2)

In the leadership vacuum Israel appears at first to be on the right track. The author of Judges portrays a united Israel gathering to seek divine guidance as they devise their battle plans.[6] Younger maintains that this inquiry of Yahweh (וישאלו . . . ביהוה/*wayyišʾălû . . . bayhwh*) is substantially equivalent to the

3. Amit, *Book of Judges*, 99.

4. See Butler, *Judges*, 9–18.

5. Fishbane, *Biblical Interpretation*, 203.

6. Butler notes that the answer one would expect, given the death of Joshua, is that an individual would be named to lead Israel; however, the unexpected answer is a tribe; Butler, *Judges*, 19.

obtainment of Yahweh's will by means of the Urim of the high priest (. . .ושאל האורים/*wəšāʾal* . . . *hāʾûrîm*; e.g., Num 27:21).[7] The reader's optimism grows as Yahweh elects Judah and assures victory with the words "I have given the land into his hand," the same language found repeatedly in Joshua (e.g., 6:2; 10:8; 11:8).[8]

Judah's Victories and Failure (1:3–20)

What we might expect to read after Yahweh's explicit election of Judah to lead in the battle is that Judah goes into battle and that Yahweh grants them complete victory. What the author does in fact report is that immediately Judah makes a pact with Simeon (1:3), and although Judahites are quite successful in battle, the land *is not* given completely into their hand.[9] By and large, 1:3–20 simply indicate the lands, cities, and peoples that Judah (and to a lesser extent Simeon) conquered, without much detail. However, interspersed in these reports are fuller accounts of particular battles/events.

Judah is successful in their first skirmishes with the Canaanites. Yahweh gives the enemy armies "into their hands" in the first instance (v. 4). The narrative of 1:5–7 tells of the Canaanite king Adoni-bezek's capture, mutilation, and death. By severing the king's big toes and thumbs, the Israelites would not only have humiliated him but also rendered him useless in battle (unstable on his feet, and unable to wield a sword, spear, or bow), a common yet cruel and unusual punishment for prisoners of war in the ancient Near East.[10] Although Adoni-bezek regards his treatment as divine retribution, the narrator is silent in this regard and it falls to readers to assess his treatment. Block regards the treatment of Adoni-bezek negatively, an early example of the canaanization of Israel (i.e., employing a Canaanite ethic in the treatment of captives rather than "looking to Yahweh for ethical guidance").[11] Webb on the other hand thinks the perspective of Adoni-bezek is a window into the narrator's authoritative perspective—the king has received what he deserves.[12] The narrator reports that the king died as a prisoner of war in Jerusalem (v. 7).

7. Younger, "Judges 1," 215.

8. Younger, *Judges and Ruth*, 64.

9. 1:19b notes that the tribe of Judah was not able to drive out the inhabitants of the plain on account of their enemy's chariots.

10. Walton, Matthews, and Chavalas, *IVP Bible Background Commentary*, 242. Block, *Judges*, 90.

11. Block, *Judges*, 91.

12. See Webb, *Book of Judges*, 100.

Next the text notes Judah's complete destruction of Jerusalem (v. 8). We are not told whether this happened before or after they brought Adoni-bezek captive there, so we are left to speculate. Moreover, Judah's destruction of Jerusalem in this verse is difficult to square with 1:21, which speaks of Benjamin's failure to drive out the Jebusites in Jerusalem, and Josh 18, which situates Jebus/ Jerusalem in Benjamin territory. Judah's destruction does not necessarily indicate their political hold on the territory so it is possible Jebusites moved into the area after the vacancy brought about by Judah.[13]

Verse 9 summarizes the southern expansion of Judah, which is recounted in more detail in 1:10–18.[14] After reporting Judah's success against the Canaanites in Hebron, the narrator provides the second "narrative digression" in Judah's campaign report (the first being that of Adoni-bezek).[15] Here the chime of wedding bells joins the sound of the battle trumpets. Israel's hero from the past graces the pages of Judges as Caleb offers his daughter Achsah's hand in marriage to the brave warrior that would capture Debir. While this may seem offensive to our modern sensibilities, within the cultural norms of his day, Caleb was trying to secure the best possible husband for his daughter.[16] Othniel passes the test, and he and Achsah are married (v. 13). The narrator includes a curious note about Achsah procuring valuable springs in addition to her assumed dowry, and Caleb's consent (vv. 14–15). This curious anecdote "provides a delightful picture of normal and positive social relationships as they functioned in this early phase of the conquest. This is one of the few accounts in the book where all the characters are cast in a favorable light."[17] Moreover, it provides both a link to Israel's past (via Caleb) and a link to what is to come (i.e., Othniel will be the first deliverer in the cycle of deliverers).

Further successes of Judah are recounted in 1:16–18, including territories occupied by the Philistines in the coastal areas. A summary evaluation of Judah's campaign appears in v. 19 in what seems like an incongruous statement. The first part of the verse alludes to 1:2 ("Yahweh was with Judah") but the second part states that all was not well, because they could not gain control of the plains because of the presence of iron chariots. By leaving this statement to the end it may surprise the reader because by all accounts so far things seem to be going according to plan. According to Webb, "Like an admission reluctantly made, it is held over until all the possibilities for a

13. Butler, *Judges*, 8.
14. Webb, *Book of Judges*, 102.
15. Quotation from Block, *Judges*, 93.
16. Block, *Judges*, 94.
17. Block, *Judges*, 94.

positive comment have been exhausted."[18] This is a pivot point in chapter 1, as the subsequent tribes become less and less successful. Finally, the narrator includes a note about the success of Caleb and his possession of Hebron (v. 20), in spite of great odds (the sons of Anak were of large stature and greatly feared: Deut 2:10; 9:2; Num 13:28, 33) and in fulfillment of the prophecy of Moses in Deut. 1:36 (cf. Josh 14:6–9). The account of Judah's battles, then, ends on a note of Judah's failure and Yahweh's faithfulness.

Many scholars perceive a pro-Judah bias throughout Judges, but if that is indeed the case, then it would require careful nuance. Marc Brettler's opinion that Judah is acquitted of any fault because the chariots made it "impossible" for Judah to drive out the valley-dwellers seems unlikely.[19] The implication is that Yahweh's power over the foreign nations is limited by chariots, a notion that would not only seem quite unusual in Judges, but is also undercut later in the book when Deborah and Barak gain a victory over Sisera and his nine hundred chariots (4:12–16).[20]

The note about Judah forming an alliance with Simeon after being divinely elected to lead is curious—in Trent Butler's words "a surprise."[21] Block and others may be correct that this is a natural alliance, given their kinship (both were sons of Jacob and Leah), the proximity of their tribal allotments, and, perhaps, the size of the tribe of Simeon (Simeon was by far the smallest tribe).[22] Be that as it may, Judah's alliance with Simeon after being divinely elected to lead has struck some commentators as problematic. Lillian Klein, for example, perceives here the introduction of irony, a literary device that she argues pervades the book:

> Yahweh tells Israel (here Judah) specifically what to do, but Israel only partially heeds Yahweh's command: Judah immediately establishes a battle pact with his brother Simeon. Thus, from the outset, Israel exerts self-determination, evidencing automatic trust in *human* perception. These verses may be

18. Webb, *Book of Judges*, 108.

19. Brettler, *Judges*, 100.

20. I am not convinced by the theory that Judges is pro-Judah (see also Block, *Judges*, 57), but some scholars, while holding this view, also admit that Judges does at times reveal the faults of Judah. E.g., Butler notes, "[Judah] apparently chose not to face the settlers in the valley, being content to remain in the hill country. Thus, typical of Israelite history writing, no one gets a clean slate. Even the heroes are painted with their faults clearly showing, David being example number one"; Butler, *Judges*, 26. See also O'Connell, who states, "Thus, while the concluding summary of 1:19 is generally positive (in contrast to the other tribes), it is tempered by the realization that not even Judah was entirely without fault"; O'Connell, *Rhetoric*, 64.

21. Butler, *Judges*, 20.

22. Block, "Period of the Judges," 88–89. See also Webb, *Integrated Reading*, 83.

> regarded as introducing the ironic configuration of the book—the implicit difference in perception between Yahweh and Israel and Israel's insistence on following human perception.[23]

Judah's alliance with Simeon after the explicit divine command for Judah to lead may, in isolation, be regarded as benign, but given the wider context it is entirely plausible that the author intended to introduce, already in the opening sentences of the book, a subtle clue that all is not as it should be. This seems to be confirmed in the ensuing narrative. The note in 1:19 about Judah not being able to capture the plains opens up a gap in the reading, causing the reader to question *why* they were unsuccessful when Yahweh ensured their success, a question that seems all the more pertinent as we continue to read about the progressive failure of the subsequent tribes.

The Increasing Failure of the Other Tribes (1:21–30)

The tribe of Benjamin is the first after Judah to gain the disapproval of the narrator. That they failed to "drive out" the Jebusites from Jerusalem (v. 21) creates the circumstances that will be important for the narrative of the Levite and his concubine in chapter 19—they did not lodge in Jerusalem because the foreign Jebusites were living there (19:11–12) so they went on to Gibeah where the atrocity took place.

The narrator shifts focus from the southern tribes (Judah, Simeon, and Benjamin) to the northern tribes starting with the "house of Joseph" in 1:22. Here we encounter the third anecdotal narrative in chapter 1. The note that "Yahweh was with them" should not raise the expectation that they will be successful or that what follows is divinely sanctioned, given the similar language in 1:19. The Josephites scout the city of Bethel, engage the help of one of its inhabitants, and successfully capture the city and devote it to utter destruction (vv. 23–25a). Following through on their promise to the man to show him "covenant faithfulness" (חסד/*ḥesed*; v. 24b), they spare the unnamed man and his family (v. 25b). The result of all of this is that Bethel is established as an Israelite city, but the Canaanite city of Luz is also established (albeit in a different location) and is vouchsafed longevity (i.e., "to this day"; v. 26). Although echoes of the story of Rahab and the defeat of Jericho are discernible in this story, unlike Rahab the unnamed Luzite makes no profession of faith in Yahweh and rather

23. Klein, *Triumph*, 23. See also Younger, *Judges and Ruth*, 65. Niditch regards this as reading into this chapter "theological messages that do not appear until ch. 2"; Niditch, *Judges*, 38.

than being enfolded into the covenant community of Israel, as Rahab was, the man departs and reestablishes the Canaanite city.[24] Moreover, the making of a covenant treaty with Canaanites is clearly prohibited in Deut 7:2 (cf. Josh 9) and is the source of divine displeasure and judgment in Judg 2:1–5. We should, therefore, follow the narrator's hints of disapproval with regard to the actions of the Josephites.

The increasing failure of the tribes is highlighted in the remaining verses of chapter 1 (vv. 27–36). An inability to "drive out" the Canaanite people, cohabitation, and Canaanite forced labor become the norm. Manasseh failed to drive out the inhabitants of a number of cities, and the Canaanites lived among them, being put to forced labor (1:27–28). Ephraim failed to drive out the Canaanites in Gezer, and the Canaanites lived among them (1:29). Zebulun failed to drive out the Canaanites in Kitron and Nahalol, and the Canaanites lived among them, being put to forced labor (1:30).

A subtle shift in language takes place in the reports of the failure of Asher and Naphtali. The now customary language of not driving out the inhabitants appears, but then rather than noting that the Canaanites dwelt among the Israelites, the situation is reversed. The Asherites and the Naphtalites "lived among the Canaanites," the latter featuring now as "the inhabitants of the land" (v. 32, 33). Whereas before the Canaanites dwelt among the Israelites (suggesting Israel had the upper hand), the situation is such that the Israelites are dwelling among the Canaanites (implying Canaanite domination). In the case of the Danites, the shift in situation is even more pronounced—the Amorites clearly have the upper hand. The Amorites drove the Danites into the hill country and maintained control of their inhabited land (1:34–36). For the first time, the Canaanite inhabitants are the subject and the Israelite tribe is the object, and the account ends indicating the borders of the *Amorite* territory. Thus, while the narrative sows seeds of doubt already with the campaign of Judah (at least as early as 1:19, but perhaps in retrospect already in the coalition of Judah and Simeon in 1:3), by the time the reader reaches the end of this battle section little doubt remains that something is terribly wrong.

In summary, the narrator emphasizes the progressive degeneration by the results of the battles (the relative success of Judah, to the failure of Benjamin, Manasseh, Ephraim, Zebulun, Asher, and Naphtali to drive out the Canaanites, and finally to the Canaanites driving the Danites into the hills) but also by the deliberate mode of narration. In the case of the first four tribes after Judah (with the exception of Joseph) the Canaanites are said to have lived among the tribes (1:21, 27, 29, 30), whereas the Asherites and Naphtalites are

24. Block, *Judges*, 103–4.

said to have lived among the Canaanites (1:32, 33).[25] Moreover, the construction of verbal subjects in these verses highlights the progressive degeneration of Israel over the course of the battle campaign: up until the account of the Danites the tribes are the subject of the verbs (e.g., the house of Joseph [v. 22], Manasseh [v. 27], Ephraim [v. 29], and so on). In the account of Dan, the Amorites are the acting subjects and the account ends, ironically, indicating the geographical borders of the Amorites (as opposed to the tribal allotment that should have belonged to Dan).

The effect of all of this is that the initial optimism that emerges with the united tribes inquiring of Yahweh and receiving assurance of success deteriorates as the narrator recounts the battle results. The reader is left to ponder why Israel did not succeed in conquering the land. The answer comes, at least in part, in the address of the "heavenly envoy" that follows (2:1–5).[26]

The Messenger of Yahweh Confronts Israel's Disobedience (2:1–5)

The episode in 2:1–5 marks a shift in the exposition of Judges. Whereas in chapter 1 the narrator tells the events of Israel's mop-up campaign with little overt evaluation, in this passage and what follows the evaluation is obvious. Thus, we encounter report (ch. 1) and interpretation (ch. 2), and the prognosis is not good.[27]

The narrator introduces us to the "messenger of Yahweh" in 2:1, a divine representative who will appear periodically in the book. Often translated as "angel," Yahweh's מלאך/*mal'āk* is a spokesperson for God, often speaking in his voice. "Angel" may bring connotations to modern readers that are not appropriate (cute, chubby, winged beings)—in biblical usage, the "angel" of God is often indistinguishable from humans and can be confused with human beings.[28]

The messenger clarifies Israel's lack of success in covenant terms. He starts by reminding the people of Yahweh's works on their behalf (v. 1b). Yet, in spite of Yahweh's redemption of Israel from Egypt and his binding himself to the Israelites in an unbreakable covenant, the Israelites have not obeyed Yahweh (v. 2). They have covenanted themselves instead with the inhabitants of Canaan and have not eradicated the pagan forms of worship in Canaan. The result is

25. Younger, "Judges 1," 219.

26. Boling, *Judges*, 64.

27. Block, *Judges*, 109.

28. There is a long tradition going back to the early church fathers—and that still exists today—that the angel of Yahweh in the Old Testament is a preincarnate representation of Jesus; see Elwell and Beitzel. "Angel of the Lord," 90. This interpretation seems difficult to substantiate.

that Yahweh would no longer drive out the inhabitants of Canaan (v. 3). This makes sense of the failure of the military campaign that precedes 2:1–5 but also sets the context for the period of the Judges, one that is characterized by Israel's threat of assimilation into the Canaanite cultural and religious identity.

Confronted in this way, "all the people of Israel" are moved to tears. Anyone who has children of their own or has been around children long enough will know that crying does not necessarily correspond to contrition. We should not miss the notable lack of repentance and contrition in the emotional reaction of Israel. They are upset but not repentant. Again, this does not bode well here at the very beginning of the book.

2:6–3:6: Israel's Rebellion and the Announcement of the Cycle

The Death of Joshua and the End of an Era (2:6–10)

In the second part of the exposition (2:6–3:6), the narrative pulls back and offers a wide-angle view of the whole period of the settlement. The narrative recapitulates Joshua's dismissal of the people to their inheritances (2:6; cf. Josh 24:28). We read that "the people served Yahweh all the days of Joshua, and all the days of the elders who outlived Joshua, who had seen all the great works that Yahweh had done for Israel" (2:7). "Serving Yahweh" is the narrator's way of referring to undivided allegiance to Yahweh as king. The messenger of Yahweh spoke of breaking covenant (2:1b–2), but this is another way of saying that the people had abandoned their allegiance to Yahweh.

Judges 2:8–10a reports the death and burial of Joshua and the passing of that whole generation. In 2:10 we arrive at the narrative present: "And another generation arose after them that did not know Yahweh or the work that he had done for Israel" (2:10b). "To know" (ידע/*yādaʿ*) goes beyond mere cognition; it denotes intimacy with the object of "knowing," as is evident so often in the Bible when a husband "knows" his wife and a baby is conceived! When God is the object of human knowing it involves, among other things, appropriate worship and obedience. The term has significance within the context of the covenant, and its appearance here defining the generation that "*did not know* Yahweh nor the work he had done" does not, according to Boling, merely mark the passage of time but also a fundamental change in the situation of the Israelites and their relationship with Yahweh.[29]

The generation that did not know Yahweh was also ignorant of the things

29. Boling, *Judges*, 72.

he had done on behalf of Israel. Primarily in view here is Yahweh's great act of delivering the people from the clutches of Pharaoh and subsequently binding them to himself in covenant relationship at Sinai. It also refers to his care for Israel in the wilderness years and his doing battle for them during the conquest. The Israelites' faith and identity were founded on Yahweh's historic relationship and care for the people. That is why they were instructed on the plains of Moab to continually tell the stories of Yahweh's great deeds to their children and their children's children, to actualize them in the memorial festivals (Unleavened Bread, Passover, Booths, etc.), and to celebrate them in songs of praise.[30] In these ways they would know Yahweh, and in turn know their own true identity as his people. By "remembering" (another thick term that goes far beyond mere cognition), Israel would be properly oriented to God and properly oriented to the world. The sad reality is that in just one generation they had forgotten.

The Cycle Announced (2:11–23)

As opposed to the previous generation that knew Yahweh and served him (v. 7), this generation did not know him and "did evil in the sight of Yahweh and served the Baals" (2:11). The narration in 2:11–13, in fact in this whole chapter, seems rather repetitive, but the repetition serves to emphasize the point so that there is no mistaking the problem of Israel in the settlement period. The political struggle that would characterize the settlement period is a symptom of God's displeasure over Israel's idolatry. A change in governance model will not begin to solve their problems. Only undivided allegiance to King Yahweh will turn the tide—or break the cycle, as the case may be.

As mentioned above, Amit holds that Joshua did not appoint a leader in his place on the expectation that Israel would uphold the covenant and serve Yahweh alone; the appearance of the judges/deliverers, according to Amit, "was the result of the violations of the covenant and the accompanying punishment."[31] The "violations of the covenant" and the "accompanying punishment" to which Amit refers are two elements in the so-called judges cycle, introduced in this second part of the exposition (2:6–3:6) and then demonstrated in the core section of the book (3:7–16:31):

30. I'm grateful to my friend A. J. Culp who in conversation introduced me to this triad of (1) story, (2) song, and (3) ritual and how these three are key dimensions of Israel's identity formation. This triad will emerge elsewhere in this commentary.

31. Amit, *Book of Judges*, 59.

1. The Israelites do evil in the eyes of Yahweh.[32]
2. Yahweh's anger is aroused, and he sends foreign nations to punish the Israelites.
3. The Israelites cry out to Yahweh for deliverance.
4. Yahweh sends judges/deliverers to save the Israelites.
5. The land experiences a period of rest.
6. The deliverers die, and Israel becomes more corrupt in their persistent idolatry.

To be sure, a common denominator in all of the cycles in the book of Judges is the appearance of a judge/deliverer.[33] Judges 2:6–23, constituting in effect the announcement of the plot of Judges, seems to confirm the central role of leadership in the period of the judges.[34] This key section of Judges very deliberately associates the perpetuation of the cycle and the lack of divinely appointed leaders in Israel. However, the role of Israel's judges/deliverers was not merely to deliver the people from the immediate threat of foreign oppression, but also presumably to return the people to covenant fidelity and to eradicate the influence of the gods of the Canaanites.[35] A careful reading of this section makes it clear that leadership, or the lack thereof, was not the chief of Israel's problems during this period. Indeed, Yahweh is moved to pity by Israel's crying out, and indeed he sends a series of deliverers to rescue them. In the core section of Judges, Israel's deliverers are by and large successful in saving Israel from the foreign oppression, but the foreign oppression is a result of the more deep-seated issue, which is Israel's infidelity. Gideon is the only judge who is reported to have made any strides to eradicate the idolatry in Israel (6:25–27). However, even this initiative seems to be annulled by Gideon's eventual fashioning of the ephod, which Israel "whored after" (8:27; cf. 2:17).

The limited success of Israel's deliverers in turning the people back toward covenant obedience and faithfulness is already clearly evident in the exposition of Judges in 2:16–23. In fact, the exposition prepares the reader for the progressive deepening of Israel's corruption, in spite of Yahweh's being "with the judge":

> They did not listen to their judges, for they whored after other gods and bowed down to them. They soon turned aside from the way in which their

32. This expression clearly connotes covenant violation; see Judg 2:11–13.

33. It is apparent that there are variations in the cycle of the judges even though as a general rule the pattern of sin—Yahweh's anger—foreign oppression—Israel's crying out—Yahweh's sending of a deliverer—Israel's deliverance guides the central section of Judges.

34. For a study on the phenomenon of plot announcements particularly in Genesis, see Turner, *Announcements*.

35. Amit, *Book of Judges*, 75.

> fathers had walked, who had obeyed the commandments of the LORD, and they did not do so. . . . But whenever the judge died, *they turned back and were more corrupt than their fathers*, going after other gods, serving them and bowing down to them. They did not drop any of their practices or their stubborn ways (2:17, 19; emphasis added).

The author of Judges thus presents Israel's history between the conquest and the rise of monarchy as a perpetual cycle. In terms of leadership, the cycle is perpetuated by means of the judges/deliverers in two important ways. On the one hand, the judges/deliverers prevent, by means of military success, the certainty of either annihilation by or assimilation with the foreign nations. By sending the judges, Yahweh is portrayed as preserving the nation of Israel from extinction. On the other hand, the inability of the judges/deliverers to induce religious reform, to return the Israelites to covenant faithfulness and to obedience to the commandments appears to guarantee the perpetuation of the cycle. As Amit notes, "The reader becomes convinced of the judges' ability to deliver the people, together with their inability to guarantee loyalty to God after their deaths."[36]

Verses 20–23 reiterate Yahweh's purpose in allowing the foreign nations to remain in the land. Yahweh's messenger indicated that Israel's rebellion resulted in Yahweh leaving the nations to act as a painful thorn in their flesh and their gods as a snare to them (2:3). Here Yahweh indicates that their covenant disobedience means that Yahweh will not drive the nations out as a test of their allegiance. This repetition may make what follows in the opening verses of chapter 3 a bit perplexing.

The Nations That Yahweh Left to Test Israel (3:1–6)

Judges 3:3, 5 lists the various nations that remained in the land and that we encounter in the cycle of judges. Verse 4 repeats again the test of allegiance that these remaining nations would cause. However, 3:1–2 provide what seems like another purpose for the remaining nations, namely, to teach the ways of warfare to the generations who had not experienced it. This may seem incongruous with the previous stated reasons for leaving the nations in the land. However, the generation of Israelites in chapter 1 disobeyed God by not conducting holy warfare (as difficult as that is for modern readers), so the subsequent generations would have to learn it, not because they were inexperienced warriors and

36. Amit, *Book of Judges*, 75.

needed to learn how to fight as such, but so that they might learn to obey God in ways their ancestors failed to do.[37] There does seem to be some irony here. Had the previous generation obeyed the divine directive to conduct holy war against the Canaanites, there would be no need for the subsequent generation to learn warfare.

The exposition ends on a sour note. Verse 6 reports the daughters of Israel being given in marriage to Canaanite husbands and vice versa, and it reemphasizes Israel's allegiance to the Canaanite gods. The previous verse speaks of Israel settling down with the various Canaanite nations, and we get the sense in the end that they are at home among the enemies or worse: at one with the enemy. Butler notes, "Rather than enemies in holy war, we now find one big happy clan, all giving and receiving one another's children in marriage to cement the clan ties."[38] They are literally and symbolically sleeping with the enemy. Thus ends the exposition, preparing the way for the cycle of rebellion, oppression, and deliverance.

The Cycle of Judges

3:7–11: The Othniel Cycle

The first in the cycle of judges recounted in the main body of the book is that of Othniel. On the heels of the exposition, the account of Othniel fits perfectly the paradigm set in the exposition (particularly 2:11–23):

Exposition	Othniel account
Israel does evil in the sight of Yahweh by abandoning Yahweh and serving the Baals (2:11–13).	Israel does evil in the sight of Yahweh by forgetting Yahweh and serving the Baals (3:7).
Yahweh's anger is aroused, and he sells them into the hand of the surrounding nations (2:14–15).	The anger of Yahweh is aroused against Israel, and he sends the king of Mesopotamia against them (3:8).
The Israelites were in terrible distress (2:15b) and they groaned because of their oppression (2:18c).	The Israelites cry out to Yahweh (3:9a).

37. See the section on violence in Judges below (pp. 279–85).

38. Butler, *Judges*, 60.

Exposition	Othniel account
Yahweh raised up judges who saved Israel (2:16a).	Yahweh sends Othniel to save them (3:9b).
The judges saved the Israelites (2:16b, 18a).	Othniel prevails against Cushan-rishathaim (3:10).
Yahweh saves Israel all the days of the judge (2:18a–b).	The land has rest 40 years (3:11a).
The judged died and the Israelites become more corrupt (2:19).	Othniel dies (3:11b).

In comparison to the narratives that follow, the details of the account of Othniel and his deliverance of Israel are few and brief, but as the first account in the cycle of judges, the Othniel narrative corresponds well to the expectations that the exposition anticipates. The exposition provides the paradigmatic framework that characterizes the period as a whole whereas the Othniel account exemplifies the paradigm in a concrete example.[39]

The Othniel cycle begins just like all the other cycles after it with Israel doing evil in the eyes of Yahweh. Verse 7 clarifies the substance of this evil they perpetrated when it says "They *forgot* Yahweh their God and *served* the Baals and Asheroth" (emphasis added). First, God's people forgot. The Hebrew word for "forget" (שׁכח/šākaḥ) appears in the book of Judges only here in 3:7, but that should not diminish its significance. The word appears more than a dozen times in Deuteronomy, as Moses carefully instructs Israel not to forget (1) what they have seen Yahweh do for them (Deut 4:9), (2) the covenant Yahweh made with them (Deut 4:23), (3) their own rebellion against Yahweh (Deut 9:7), and most importantly (4) Yahweh himself who rescued them from Egypt (Deut 6:12; 8:11, 14, 19; 32:18). In Scripture, remembering and forgetting of this kind is not merely cognitive, but is identity-forming. Remembering Yahweh and what he had done on their behalf would orient their individual and collective lives toward Yahweh and allegiance to him. Thus, a certain logic follows from the fact that Israel first *forgot* Yahweh but then second, they *served* the Canaanite gods. By forgetting their identity, which was forged in relationship to Yahweh, God's people oriented their lives in accordance with their allegiance to the Canaanite gods.

Some ambiguity surrounds the identity and geographical origins of the foreign king whom Yahweh sets against the Israelites.[40] Even his name, which

39. This has led some commentators to question the historical veracity of the account of Othniel.

40. See Block, *Judges*, 152–53; Butler, *Judges*, 64–65.

could be rendered "Twice-Wicked Cushan," may be more of a symbolic title than a proper name. However, here as in the rest of this first cycle, the details are not as important as showing how the cycle ideally plays out. After an eight-year period of servitude, the people cry out to Yahweh and Yahweh uses Othniel (through the power of Yahweh's Spirit) to save his people, after which follows a forty-year period of peace.

J. Clinton McCann makes the intriguing point that the language used here (and in other places in the judges cycle) identifies each cycle in the book as a miniexodus: "each episode of the cyclical pattern throughout the book of Judges should be understood as a sort of new exodus, God's gracious deliverance of the people from an oppressive, death-dealing situation."[41] Each cycle of oppression and redemption, therefore, provides an opportunity for Israel to remember Yahweh and what he had done for them and to reorient their lives in allegiance to him. Sadly, it seems, these are missed opportunities for God's people.

Although the narrative does not provide any information about the leadership of Othniel following his act of saving Israel, the ordering of the phrase in 3:11—"The land had rest for forty years, and then Othniel son of Kenaz died"—draws a link between the time of peace and the span of Othniel's life after his deliverance.[42] This may infer a leadership role for Othniel that maintained the well-being of Israel for as long as he lived.

Readers are already familiar with Othniel from the short narrative in the exposition (1:11–15), where Othniel is established as a leader, one who is courageous and successful on the battlefield. He, therefore, provides a bridge between the period of conquest and the period of settlement and exemplifies the kind of leadership one would expect from the expositional material.[43] It seems reasonable to suppose, therefore, that the account of Othniel appears where it does (following the expositional material) to demonstrate what an ideal leader may look like.[44]

Although scholars have frequently regarded the Othniel account as an editorial afterthought, more recently scholars have suggested that it serves as an important standard against which the other judges/deliverers ought to be

41. McCann, *Judges*, 42.

42. Amit, *Book of Judges*, 78–79.

43. Amit, *Book of Judges*, 166.

44. Klein thinks it significant that Othniel is the "younger" brother, indicating that perhaps he is not the most likely choice of a leader: "In a society strongly influenced by primogeniture, the likelihood that the offspring of a younger (literally 'smaller' with implications of 'unimportant') brother will become the leader of the elder's descendants warrants attention. . . . In Judges, the 'younger brother' motif works in two directions: it 'exposes' the pattern of younger brothers taking over in the sequence of Judges narratives and it reaffirms the providential"; Klein, *Triumph*, 34.

measured. According to the design of the book, the Othniel account fits the pattern set in the exposition—"a concretization of the exposition"—and provides the reader with a measure of optimism (at least for the time being) regarding the potential of the judge-model for leadership in Israel.[45]

3:12–30: The Ehud Cycle

Ehud is next in the cycle of judges/deliverers. A left-handed "Benjamite" (literally, "son of the right hand"), Ehud is an oxymoron.[46] Ehud seems like an unlikely character to deliver Israel, but in Judges the reader will come to expect Yahweh to provide unexpected means of deliverance. Ehud is just the first in a string of unlikely deliverers. The account of Ehud may be difficult for modern readers, as it raises questions about the role of deception and gruesome violence in God's redemptive plans.

With regard to the cyclical pattern, as mentioned in the introduction, it is essential not only to recognize it, but also to give attention to the creative ways that the author utilizes the pattern, reinforces it, and also at times deviates from it. The author rarely slavishly follows the pattern, and where we discover nuances and variations we ought to pay attention because there is sure to be some significance to it. All five elements of the cycle are present in the Ehud account, providing a skeleton for Judg 3:12–30. Although the Ehud account is not very long, the narrator fleshes out the details of that skeletal frame in a way that goes beyond the previous turn of the cycle (i.e., Othniel). Here we encounter much more description, narrative texture, plot twists, humor, and so on.

Introduction to the Ehud Cycle (3:12–15)

Verses 12–15 provide the introduction to the story. The expected cyclical elements appear in these verses but notice the progression and intensification in the way they are presented. Verse 12 mentions twice Israel's persistence in doing "evil." In this turn of the cycle, the narrator notes that Yahweh "strengthened" the hand of the Moabite king Eglon against Israel. Forming a coalition with the Ammonites and the Amalekites, Eglon "struck" Israel, leading to an eighteen-year period of Israelite servitude under the Moabites (more than double

45. Quotation from Amit, *Book of Judges*, 166.

46. Concerning this and other wordplays in the Ehud narrative see Ogden, "Special Features of a Story," 408–14.

the length of time that they served the Mesopotamian king in the Othniel cycle).[47] Moreover, dimensions of the Moabite oppression included the occupation of an Israelite city (v. 13)—the "city of palms" likely refers to Jericho and would serve as a strategic operational headquarters for the Moabite king—and the regular paying of tribute to Moab (vv. 15 and 17).[48]

Verse 15 includes the third and fourth elements of the cyclical pattern: (3) the people of God cry out to God to deliver them from their oppressive situation and (4) Yahweh raises up a deliverer. The narrator not only identifies Yahweh's deliverer as Ehud, but also provides his tribal lineage and his left-handedness. Moreover, even before Yahweh elects him to be a deliverer, Ehud has been engaged by the people as a courier, bringing their tribute to the Moabite king.

The introduction of Ehud subtly highlights irony in the situation. Ehud's name means "Where is the glory/majesty?" Butler notes that already here the tension of the narrative emerges: "Israel sends their deliverer, [whose name is] 'Where is majesty?' to pay tribute to his majesty Eglon. How can tribute be a form of deliverance?"[49] Moreover, the word used for "tribute" in this verse, a form of payment that a victorious king demanded from a subjugated people, is the same word commonly used in the Old Testament for a sacrificial offering made to God, particularly the grain offering that was brought to the tabernacle.[50] Thus, Ehud's name does raise a particularly pertinent question: Where is the glory in a context where God's people are bringing their tribute/offering not to the feet of their true King at the place where his glory dwells (at that time, the tabernacle) but to the feet of a foreign king!

The narrator introduces Ehud, including his father's name, his tribe, and the curious note about his left-handedness. Both the patriarch Benjamin and his tribe have a somewhat ambiguous past. Although his father Jacob favored Benjamin along with his brother Joseph (Jacob's only sons by his wife Rachel), at his death Jacob (prophetically) declares that his descendants will be a tribe of ravenous wolves, devouring prey by day and dividing the spoils by night (Gen 49:27). The very earliest audience of the book of Judges would have immediately associated the tribe of Benjamin with King Saul's disastrous reign and would likely have regarded a Benjamite deliverer like Ehud with suspicion (especially if the audience was from the south). To top that off, Ehud was left-handed. The

47. The Moabites and Ammonites find their ancestral roots in the incestuous relationship between Lot and his two daughters (Gen 19:30–38).

48. Block, *Judges*, 158; Butler, *Judges*, 69.

49. Butler, *Judges*, 69–70.

50. Webb, *Book of Judges*, 171. Cf. Gen 4:3, 4, 5; Exod 29:41; 30:9; 40:29; 1 Sam 2:29; 3:14; Isa 66:20, etc. This word is used throughout Leviticus and Numbers to specifically refer to the "grain offering" (see, e.g., Lev 7).

term "left-handed" means something like impeded or restricted in the right hand. This could mean that Ehud had some kind of injury or impediment that had disabled the use of his right hand that necessitated left-handedness in this case.[51] However, Judg 20:16 refers to seven hundred choice Benjamite warriors who were left-handed and yet exceptionally skilled at warfare (they were, e.g., experts at stone-slinging). In this light, it may be that Benjamite warriors would train in such a way that they strengthened the use of their left hand (they bound/impeded their right hand in training exercises), making them ambidextrous and giving them an edge in battle over their right-handed opponents. We cannot know for sure whether Ehud had some kind of impediment in his right hand or whether he was skilled in using his left hand (as well as his right) in battle. However, seemingly random information in Old Testament narrative often becomes vital for the unfolding narrative, and this is the case with Ehud's left-handedness.

Ehud's Assassination of Eglon (3:16–25)

In 3:16 the story gets interesting. Before leading one of the convoys to bring the expected tribute to Eglon, Ehud crafts a sword and conceals it by strapping it under his garments to his right thigh. It is quite possible that king Eglon's guards did check that Ehud and his men were not armed. Given that Ehud strapped the weapon to his right leg because he was left-handed, the weapon went undetected.

The narrator draws attention in 3:17 to Eglon's girth. Old Testament narrative rarely includes physical traits when describing characters, so when it does we do well to pay attention (e.g., Esau's hairiness in Gen 25:25; Goliath's great height and impressive physical presence in 1 Sam 17:4–7; Bathsheba's beauty in 2 Sam 11:2). The note that Eglon was "an exceedingly fat man" is not necessarily a criticism, but it highlights that the king was accustomed to quality, healthy food, and his opulent diet was provided in part by the Israelite tribute. Moreover, the adjective is most often used to describe healthy animals that are without blemish and ready for sacrifice. Thus, "Eglon is pictured as very pleasingly plump on the one hand and as a perfect creature for sacrifice on the other. His physique also sets him up for Ehud's plan."[52]

51. See, e.g., Cundall, "Judges," 76, who maintains that Israelites would have regarded this as a physical defect.

52. Butler, *Judges*, 70. Cf. Webb, *Book of Judges*, 172; Chisholm, *Commentary on Judges and Ruth*, 183.

Ehud's assassination plan unfolds in stages. It starts, as we have already seen, when he fashioned and concealed his chosen weapon (v. 16). Then, after he and the other tribute-bearers had delivered payment to Eglon and were on their way home, Ehud dismisses those with him and returns back to the Moabite outpost. The text indicates that the place where Ehud turned back was at "the idols near Gilgal"—more on that shortly. Upon his return and with a desire to get Eglon alone, Ehud says to the king that he has a secret "message" (דבר/*dābār*) for him (v. 19a). The Hebrew word דבר/*dābār* can and often does mean "word/message" but can also signify "thing/object" or even "experience," a feature of the word that in its context here Block considers "delightfully ambiguous."[53] Ehud achieves his intended outcome—the promise of a secret message intrigues the gullible Moabite king enough that he dismisses his guards (v. 19b)—and once he has Eglon alone, he indicates again that he has a דבר/*dābār* for the king, this time specifying the divine origins of his דבר/*dābār*. Eglon stands to receive this divine "thing" (v.20).

In 3:21–22 we reach the structural center of the Ehud cycle—everything so far has been building up to the stealthy assassination of Eglon (e.g., Ehud's left-handedness, Eglon's obesity, the guard's dismissal) and the rest of the narrative unfolds as a result of it. In three swift actions, Ehud's plan is complete: he "reached," "took," and "thrust." In gruesome detail, probably intended to mock Eglon and the enemies of Israel, the narrator describes the whole sword, including the hilt, being swallowed up in Eglon's girth and excrement issuing out.[54]

With the execution complete, Ehud makes his escape. Ehud acts decisively, and we get the sense that he has given thought to his escape plan. The guards' absence grants him a stealthy withdrawal, and the forethought to lock the door bought the needed time to escape (vv. 23–25). Although it is true that his plans were well-hatched and unfolded smoothly, events unfold in ways that Ehud could not have expected and that contributed to his success. Ehud could not have anticipated the messy results of his attack on Eglon, but while he was making his escape the smell from the chamber combined with the locked doors caused the guards to assume the king was relieving himself and prevented them from disturbing the king. One can imagine the nervous glances between the guards as they waited and waited, each passing moment becoming excruciatingly longer and more awkward than the last. When they cannot bear it any longer, they fetch the key and discover their master lying on the floor, dead.

53. Block, *Judges*, 165.

54. The phrase "and dung/filth came out" is not straightforward but likely means that the violent execution also resulted in the loosing of Eglon's bowels. Thus, Block, *Judges*, 168, notes, "When Eglon fell to the ground and expired, his bowels relaxed and discharged their contents."

Ehud Rallies the Troops and Victory Is Gained (3:26–30)

In 3:26, the focus of the narrative turns to what transpires with Ehud during the time of Eglon's guards' indecision. The author includes another, seemingly incidental reference to the "idols" (פסילים/*pěsîlîm*) that we encountered in 3:19. Ehud's battle cry and the ensuing victory seem almost secondary after the detailed account of the assassination of Eglon, so much so that some commentators regard it as anticlimactic.[55] And yet, the cycle will not be complete until the Israelites are liberated from the Moabite oppression; thus, 3:26–30 recount the events that unfold toward that end and as a result of Ehud's decisive action.

The "hill country of Ephraim" to which Ehud travels to muster an army (v. 27) is a range of mountainous territory that includes territory not only from the tribe of Ephraim but also from the tribes of Benjamin and Manasseh. However, the narrator refers to those who answer Ehud's summon to arms as the "people" (literally "sons") "of Israel" (v. 27), giving the sense of national support. Ehud assures his army that Yahweh will grant the victory, and indeed, they capture the fords of the Jordan River, cutting off the Moabite army from possible military reinforcement and also preventing retreat. Verse 29 represents a complete reversal of 3:13. Whereas Eglon and his coalition army "struck" Israel, 3:29 says that the Israelite army "struck" about ten thousand strong and seasoned Moabite warriors, leaving no survivors. This is the deliverance and liberty that the Israelites cried out for in 3:15, and it ushers in an eighty-year period of peace (v. 30), the longest period of rest recorded in the book of Judges.

The second cycle is complete. Although the five elements of the cycle are all there, the Ehud cycle contains texture, surprise, and detail that go much beyond the Othniel cycle. Significant in the Ehud cycle is the intricate interplay between human and divine action. Amit has pointed out that the story of Ehud's liberation from Moabite subjugation is moved forward by a careful combination of human planning and tactics and what appears on first glance to be coincidence or chance. Ehud's successful assassination attempt on Eglon, king of Moab, was indeed a result of Ehud's careful planning (e.g., his fashioning and concealing of his weapon, his request for a private audience, his stealthy retreat); however, his success depended on a number of important coincidental factors (e.g., the guards not finding the concealed weapon, the private context for the actual murder, the guards, embarrassment about entering the upper chamber and consequently their delay in entering). As Amit notes, "This rhetorical technique, in which chance events and planned tactics appear alongside one

55. See Butler, *Judges*, 72.

another, convinces the reader that Ehud's ability to act as a tactician depends upon God's wish to deliver his people."[56]

In concert with the divine agent, the human agent, Ehud, successfully leads Israel out from the oppression of the foreign enemies. Over the course of the short narrative Ehud morphs from a lone assassin to the rallying leader of Israel. Careful attention indicates that the language emphasizes Ehud as the unmistakable leader of Israel: "he was in the lead"; "Follow after me"; "they went down after him." Modern readers may have difficulty reconciling Ehud's crafty and brutally violent tactics with the divine will. The consequence of Ehud's leadership is the subjugation of Moab by the "hand [יד/*yād*] of Israel" and the ensuing eighty years of rest. Whatever we might say about Ehud's tactics, Yahweh orchestrated events through them. Take, for example, the motif or *Leitwort* of the Hebrew word for "hand" (יד/*yād*) in the narrative.[57]

Ehud is a "left-handed" man (3:15)
Israel's tribute to Moab was sent "by his hand" (3:15)
Ehud carries out the assassination of Eglon "with his left hand" (3:21)
Ehud indicates that Yahweh has given the Moabites "into your [Israel's] hands" (3:28)
Moab is subdued "under the hand of Israel" (3:30)

This repeated word suggests the progression from the successful assassination by the hand of Yahweh's chosen deliverer, to the promise that Yahweh will deliver the Moabites into Israel's hand, and finally to the subjugation of Israel's enemies not by the hand of the deliverer as the reader might expect but by the hand of the Israelites themselves. The last occurrence of the *Leitwort* also indicates the unity of the Israelites as they battle against the enemies under the leadership of Ehud.

It appears, therefore, that in this second turn of the cycle of the judges Yahweh provides Israel with an able, albeit unlikely, deliverer who unites the tribes against the Moabites and brings about a period of peace. Very significant by virtue of its absence is any kind of *religious reform*. The appearance of פסילים/*pěsîlîm* ("the images/idols") twice in the narrative (3:19, 26) is conspicuous. On first glance these "idols" feature as geographical markers—a place near Gilgal

56. Amit, *Book of Judges*, 173.

57. Alter describes a *Leitwort* as such: "Through abundant repetition, the semantic range of the root-word is explored, different forms of the root are deployed, branching off at times into phonetic relatives (that is, word-play), synonymity, and antonymity; by virtue of its verbal status, the *Leitwort* refers immediately to meaning and thus to theme as well"; Alter, *Art of Biblical Narrative*, 95.

where Ehud "turned back" (v. 19) or "passed over" (v. 26). Although Ehud passes over these images without giving them any attention, perhaps the reader is not intended to pass over them without pause. Of course, there is some debate over what precisely these פסילים/*pĕsîlîm* are referring to. According to tradition, Gilgal had historical and cultic significance. Upon crossing the Jordan into the promised land, Joshua had twelve memorial stones set up at Gilgal (Josh 4:20), and Gilgal was the location of Israel's first Passover meal in the land (Josh 5:10). The פסילים/*pĕsîlîm* may be referring to the memorial stones, but Block rightly notes that it would be unlikely to refer to these stones, marking as they do such a significant moment in Israel's history with such a "pejorative" term that in the Old Testament "always denotes sculpted pagan cult images."[58] According to Block these פסילים/*pĕsîlîm* are probably to be regarded as a subtle indication of the paganism that had crept into an established cultic site in Israel.[59] If this is the correct interpretation of the פסילים/*pĕsîlîm* in 3:19 and 3:26 then perhaps the author intended to cast a shadow of doubt over the leadership of Ehud. At the very least the reference reminds readers what the exposition made explicit: that the foreign oppression of Israel is only a symptom of Israel's real problem, namely, their rejection of Yahweh in favor of Canaanite gods.

Ehud is one of many complex characters in the book of Judges. On the one hand he is characterized as successful in ridding Israel of the foreign military and political oppression; on the other hand he failed at a more fundamental level in ridding Israel of the foreign religious influences.[60] Ehud's leadership

58. See Block, *Judges*, 163–64.

59. Block, *Judges*, 165.

60. Some scholars are less charitable in their assessment of Ehud. See Christianson, "Fistful of Shekels," 58–78, who sees moral ambiguity at work in the Ehud narrative. Frolov goes further and regards Ehud not as an exemplary leader but one who engages in "terrorist" activity; see Frolov, *Judges*, 111–13. Klein regards Ehud as deceptive and dishonorable, and that his deceptive means are not in accord with the divine will; whereas Amit understands the divine agent working through human ingenuity, Klein sees Yahweh as absent from the action; see Klein, *Triumph*, 37–39. O'Connell suggests that Ehud's inability to rid the land of the idols as well as a subtle characterization of Ehud as a self-promoting, self-glorifying savior, subtly undermine his integrity. He admits, however, that the narrative serves the purpose of ridiculing Israel's enemies and glorifying Yahweh, who is portrayed as controlling circumstances surrounding the deliverance by the hand of Ehud; see O'Connell, *Rhetoric*, 84–100. O'Connell's theory that Judges is pro-David and anti-Saul propaganda should be kept in mind in assessing his interpretation of Ehud. According to his theory, the tribes of Benjamin and Judah symbolically represent Saul and David respectively and thus it would not serve his theory well to have a Benjamite cast in a favorable light. I cannot help but think that O'Connell's theory has caused him to read Ehud more critically than the narrative warrants. As indicated above, his lack of religious reform is problematic, but I find it difficult to see criticism, even subtle, in the narrative of his political and military endeavors.

brings liberation and a significant period of peace, but his failure to bring about comprehensive religious reform guarantees the perpetuation of the cycle. At the end of the second cycle, the reader is still anticipating the leader who will vouchsafe a solution to Israel's problem, highlighted in the book's exposition (2:6–3:6), of covenant infidelity.

3:31: Shamgar

The third judge/deliver is Shamgar, and his account amounts to a single brief verse: "After him was Shamgar the son of Anath who killed six hundred of the Philistines with an ox goad, and he also saved Israel" (3:31). The narrator's account of Shamgar, like that of the other so-called "minor judges," falls outside the cyclical framework. Amit classes him as a delivering judge by virtue of his incredible victory against the Philistines with an unusual weapon, namely, an ox goad, and the specific phrase "he also saved Israel."[61] Given his name, which appears to be Hurrian, and his connection with Anath, a goddess according to Canaanite mythology, Shamgar is most likely not an Israelite.[62] If this is indeed the case, then Shamgar continues an emerging theme of Yahweh bringing about the deliverance of Israel by unusual and unexpected leaders. Although the account is brief, it is absolutely clear that Shamgar is a successful deliverer, in the line of Othniel and Ehud. The foreign pedigree of Israel's leadership at this point may, as Block suggests, indicate the author's depiction of the degenerating situation in Israel: "The dearth of native leadership in Israel represents one more symptom of the Canaanization of Israel."[63]

4:1–24: The Deborah/Barak/Jael Narrative[64]

The emerging theme of Yahweh using unexpected individuals with unusual tactics to deliver Israel becomes even more pronounced in the third narrative cycle

61. Amit, *Book of Judges*, 79.

62. Younger maintains that "the only scholarly agreement is that Shamgar son of Anath was not an Israelite"; Younger, *Judges and Ruth*, 129. However, Butler questions this consensus; Butler, *Judges*, 74. For summaries of the identity of Shamgar see Butler, *Judges*, 73–74; Younger, *Judges and Ruth*, 128–31; Block, *Judges*, 172–75.

63. Block, *Judges*, 175.

64. As will become clearer below, the narrative is not entirely clear who in the narrative is ultimately the deliverer, whether Deborah, Barak, or Jael. Therefore, to avoid jumping to conclusions I will not refer to the third cycle as the Deborah cycle or the Barak cycle.

in Judges, a narrative thick with irony.[65] Whereas the Ehud cycle was longer and more detailed than the Othniel cycle before it, the narrative section alone of the Deborah/Barak/Jael cycle is more in-depth than the Ehud cycle. Moreover, embedded in the narrative cycle is the Song of Deborah (Judg 5), which more than doubles the amount of attention the narrator gives to this third cycle.

The third in the cycle of judges breaks down as follows:
Introduction to the Deborah/Barak/Jael Cycle (4:1–3)
Introduction of Deborah and the Call of Barak (4:4–9a)
Armies Assembled and Battle Lines Drawn (4:9b–13)
Israel's Victory over Sisera's Army (4:14–16)
Sisera's Demise (4:17–22)
The End of Canaanite Oppression (4:23–24)

I will provide a structural outline of the Song of Deborah (ch. 5) after the commentary on the narrative section here, but it is important to note that the narrative cycle is not complete until after the Song in 5:31 where the narrator includes the expected fifth element of the cycle (the number of years the land experienced rest).

Introduction to the Deborah/Barak/Jael Narrative (4:1–3)

The opening verses of the Deborah/Barak/Jael narrative follow the pattern set in the exposition and demonstrated (with some variations) in the cycle of judges:

1. Israel does evil in the sight of Yahweh (4:1).
2. Yahweh responds by sending foreign oppression, in this case in the form of Jabin king of Canaan and Sisera his military commander (4:2).
3. The number of years of oppression (4:3).
4. Israel cries out for deliverance (4:3).

It is worth repeating that literary patterns are helpful not only in building expectations in the reader but also, by means of variations in the patterns, in requiring readers to adjust their expectations and drawing significance from those variations. This third cycle begins almost exactly as the second cycle begins, with Israel again doing "evil in the eyes of Yahweh"; however, the narrator

65. For a comprehensive survey of recent scholarship on Judg 4 and 5 see Mayfield, "Accounts of Deborah," 306–35.

includes a reference to Ehud's death. In the introduction, I indicated that the events recorded in the book of Judges do not always follow a linear chronology; in other words, the sequence in which we find the events in the book of Judges may not have been the precise sequence in which they occurred in history. Verse 1 sets the context of chapter 4 in the wake of Ehud's death. This suggests that the events in chapter 4 did indeed happen after the events of Ehud's deliverance and the ensuing period of peace.[66]

In 4:2 the language of Yahweh "selling" Israel into the hands of foreign enemies shows up again (cf. 2:14; 3:8). The reference to "Jabin king of Canaan, who reigned in Hazor" presents a number of challenges. In Josh 11:1–15, the armies of Israel defeat a Canaanite army (reinforced with countless chariots) that was led by none other than a "Jabin king of Hazor" (Josh 11:1). Moreover, the text in Joshua indicates that the city of Hazor and its inhabitants were devoted to utter destruction (*ḥerem*) and was completely burned with fire (11:10–15). Because of the obvious parallels, it might be easy, as some commentators do, to consider the account in Judges to be a distorted adaptation of the event recorded in Josh 11, but this is not the only explanation for the similarities. The name "Jabin" is likely a royal title or a dynastic name, in which case we would expect to find more than one "king Jabin."[67] That the Jabin of Judg 4 reigns from Hazor is difficult, given that it was completely destroyed, and archaeology seems to suggest it was not built up again until the time of Solomon. It could be, as Webb and Block suppose, that a remnant of the Jabin dynasty escaped the destruction of Joshua's conquest and reestablished the dynasty to some extent in Hazor, but the historical issues surrounding this are difficult to resolve.[68] King Jabin does represent a powerful and uniting Canaanite force, and though at the very end, the narrative will return to Jabin and Hazor, after their introduction they fade into the background and the narrative focuses on the commander of Jabin's army, Sisera, also introduced in 4:2.

Verse 3 emphasizes that Sisera carried out a cruel reign. Butler translates 4:3b as "he *vehemently tormented* the sons of Israel for twenty years."[69] The period of foreign oppression is two years longer than the previous period of domination under Eglon and twelve years longer than Cushan-rishathaim's

66. The narrator makes no reference to Shamgar here, but Shamgar does make an appearance in the Song of Deborah (5:6). It seems likely that Shamgar was a contemporary of Deborah and that the events of his deliverance happened simultaneous to the events of Deborah and company.

67. Webb, *Book of Judges*, 180; Block, *Judges*, 188.

68. Webb, *Book of Judges*, 180; Block, *Judges*, 188–89.

69. Butler, *Judges*, 79 (emphasis added).

dominance before that. Sisera's fleet of nine hundred iron chariots made him an unstoppable military force. The narrator seems to be highlighting a progressive intensity in the length and cruelty of the foreign oppression from one turn of the cycle to the next.

Introduction of Deborah and the Call of Barak (4:4–9a)

In the place where the reader has come to expect Yahweh to "raise up" (cf. 2:16, 18; 3:9, 15) a deliverer, the narrative introduces Deborah without the formulaic language of Yahweh raising her up. The introduction of Deborah (4:4–5) highlights her role as prophetess, as wife, and as judge. Deborah's base of operation is in the hill country of Ephraim (v. 5). Whereas in the previous cycle, Ehud mustered the troops in this region and marched them south, in this cycle the action will move from this location northward.[70]

By virtue of her prophetic and judicial activity, the narrative portrays Deborah as already holding a leadership position, and perhaps as the would-be deliverer.[71] The appearance of a female leader in Israel may strike the reader as unusual. As Butler puts it,

> This emphasis on the character's gender and multiple offices turns the reader's world upside down. The hope for Israel lies not in a man Yahweh calls specifically for the situation but in a female judge and prophet. This turn of events might not seem so radical to today's audience, but it would have seemed unthinkable to the Israelites of the time. What has happened to leadership in Israel?[72]

Butler may be right that the notion that Israel would depend on a female deliverer would be surprising, but in the unfolding narrative of Judges, readers already at this point may be starting to expect the unexpected.

Deborah was clearly a judge—she "was judging Israel at that time" (v. 4)

70. Webb, *Book of Judges*, 133.

71. Herzberg, "Deborah and Moses," 15–33, argues that the narrator casts Deborah as a type of Moses.

72. Butler, *Judges*, 84. Yee, on the other hand, argues that the social structure of premonarchic Israel, with its strong kinship and residential connections, blurred the lines between the domestic and public realms and thus provided a context in which a female like Deborah could take up a significant military leadership role. She admits, however, that even in this context women in military leadership positions was not the norm (she refers to such instances as "the confusion of gender roles" in "anomalous situations in war"); see Yee, "By the Hand of a Woman," 110–12.

and the Israelites went to her "for judgment" (v. 5).[73] Given that the exposition indicates that it was the judges that delivered Israel, readers might be inclined to assume that Deborah is the appointed deliverer. In fact, some commentators espouse this view.[74] However, the omission of the expected phrase that Yahweh raised up Deborah should prompt some questions, chief among which might be: Is Deborah the deliverer or should we expect someone else to emerge?[75] Moreover, the noticeable omission of the formulaic language of "raising up" is not the only reason that readers might be suspicious of Deborah as Israel's designated deliverer. Block maintains that upon a close reading, "the presentation of Deborah as a savior of her people is more apparent than real," and he lists no less than twelve questions rising from the narrative itself that would raise doubt about the presentation of Deborah as the expected deliverer.[76] Indeed, although the pattern of the cycle might cause us to expect that Deborah will deliver Israel from the threat of the Canaanite forces, we soon learn that another, perhaps more likely individual seems to be designated for the role of deliverer.

In her function as prophetess, Deborah appoints Barak as the divinely designated deliverer in 4:6.[77] The Hebrew word for "hand" (*yād*) appears again as a *Leitwort* in this narrative.[78] Although Yahweh had sold Israel "into the hand" of Jabin (v. 2), he assures Barak through his prophetess Deborah that he will deliver Jabin and his whole army "into your hand" (v. 7).

The theme of leadership in Judges takes a distinct turn with Barak, as he is the first deliverer who exhibits reluctance (if not downright refusal) to lead. We will see this reluctance-to-lead motif again in the next cycle (6:15–18, 36–40), but with the unmistakable assurance of divine help, Barak's hesitation is surprising. This turn of events adds to the irony of the narrative: the election of a male leader seems to restore the reader's expectations, but expectations are

73. Many scholars regard these phrases as implying Deborah's legal or judicial role (e.g., holding court or settling disputes). Block, on the other hand, suggests that according to the vocalization of the MT v. 5b should be rendered "And all the sons of Israel went up to her for *the* judgment" (emphasis added). Thus, according to Block, "when 'the sons of Israel' come to Deborah for 'the judgment,' they are not asking her to solve their legal disputes but to give them the divine answer to their cries, which is described in the following verse"; Block, *Judges*, 197.

74. See, e.g., Moore, *Judges*, 113. See also Cundall, "Judges," 82, who refers to Deborah as "the savior of her people."

75. This deviation from the expected pattern is a good example of what Smith calls "retrospective patterning." On the perception of poetic structure and specifically the technique of retrospective patterning see Smith, *Poetic Closure*, 8–14.

76. See Block, *Judges*, 193–194. See also Amit, "Judges 4," 91–92.

77. Amit, *Book of Judges*, 80.

78. See also the appearance of יד/*yād* in the Deborah/Barak narrative in 4:9, 14, 21, 24, and also in the Song of Deborah (5:26).

thrown back into confusion as the chosen leader refuses to lead![79] An unwilling leader, Barak's response to Deborah's call to lead amounts to an ultimatum: "If you will go with me, I will go, but if you will not go with me, I will not go" (4:8). It would not be unprecedented for a leader in Israel to refuse to lead without the presence of Yahweh (e.g., Moses in Exod 33:15–16). However, Barak was already assured of Yahweh's presence in his call to lead. Although Deborah assures him that Yahweh will go before him into battle, Barak seems to prefer the presence of Deborah rather than the presence of Yahweh.[80]

Deborah agrees to go with Barak but her response makes it clear that Barak will not be credited with the deliverance of Israel. The consequence of Barak's hesitation is that "Yahweh will sell Sisera into the hand [*yād*] of a woman" (4:9) as opposed to the hand of Barak (4:7). The reader might deduce at this point, at least according to a linear reading of the Deborah/Barak narrative, that the implication is that Deborah will deliver Israel, that she is the woman that will defeat Sisera. However, this is a story with "many twists and complications," and not until the end of the narrative does the reader comprehend that another twist awaits: the woman into whose hand Yahweh will deliver Sisera is not Deborah.[81] This narrative, as Butler notes, "is a story of reversal in which the final hero emerges only after the reader has formed entirely different expectations. It is a story of seduction and murder, but that lets the ending determine the nature of the entire narrative."[82]

Armies Assembled and Battle Lines Drawn (4:9b–13)

Judges 4:9b–10 and 4:12–13 are like mirror images: first, Deborah and Barak go to Kedesh and Barak summons an army of ten thousand soldiers from the tribes of Zebulun and Naphtali; second, Sisera, upon hearing of the gathered Israelite army, musters his own forces and moves them into place for battle.

Right in the middle of the descriptions of the respective armies making ready, the narrator includes a note that seems on first glance to be random and out of place. In the context of the narrative, 4:11 interrupts the flow of the story, standing awkwardly as it does between the assembly of the Israelite army and Sisera's mustering of his chariots to meet the Israelite forces. We are introduced

79. Butler, *Judges*, 84.

80. Or perhaps Barak regarded Deborah's presence as assurance of the divine presence; see Butler, *Judges*, 84.

81. Quotation from Butler, *Judges*, 85. Cf. Hackett, "Violence and Women's Lives," 357.

82. Butler, *Judges*, 85.

to a certain Kenite named Heber.[83] The Kenites had ancestral links to Moses's in-laws and as Judg 1:16 notes, they had some kind of association with the tribe of Judah and settled with Judah. Those associations (with Moses and Judah) would normally be positive, but the note here in Judg 4:11 indicates that Heber had "divided" or "separated" from these associations and moved a good distance to the north. Apart from Heber's proximity to the mounting battle between the Israelite forces and Sisera's army, we have no indication what role Heber will play in the unfolding story. Here is a fine example of the genius of biblical storytelling—the narrator drops a seemingly irrelevant piece of information that will play a significant role in the outcome of the story. Chisholm notes,

> The original audience would know enough about Israelite storytelling style to realize this tidbit of information would prove to be important in the unfolding plot. This Heber would somehow play a role in the approaching battle. But how so? Does his identity as a Kenite mean he was on Israel's side (cf. 1:16), or does his departure from Kenite territory to northern Israel suggest the possibility that he had defected to the Canaanites? We must wait and see.[84]

All will be revealed but not until after the Israelite and Canaanite armies do battle.

Israel's Victory over Sisera's Army (4:14–16)

Similar to the previous cycle, the battle report in this third cycle is brief and to the point; although a necessary aspect of the cycle, it almost seems secondary and subordinate to other, apparently more important details of these events. The battle scene begins in 4:14 with Deborah summoning Barak to action and it ends only a few verses later in 4:17 with a comical picture of Israelite foot soldiers chasing down the fleeing chariots and completely annihilating Sisera's army.

Determining precisely who is leading the Israelite forces is a challenge. Barak had mustered and led the ten thousand troops from Zebulun and Naphtali (as divinely instructed), but the hint in 4:10 is that this sizable army was not sufficient as it adds "and Deborah went with him." When Sisera summons nine hundred chariots to meet Barak in battle, Deborah urges Barak to engage Sisera

83. His name seems to connote association or company and is related to the verb "to unite" or "to be joined to."

84. Chisholm, *Commentary on Judges and Ruth*, 229.

with a promise that Yahweh would precede him and deliver Sisera "into your hand" (v. 14): "Arise, for this is the day that Yahweh has given Sisera into your hand. Has not Yahweh gone out before you?" From all appearances, Deborah takes a decisive role in the battle; however, from this point, Deborah disappears from the narrative altogether until she appears again in chapter 5 to sing the song of victory with Barak.

While Barak successfully annihilates the army of Sisera, the narrative makes two things clear: (1) the success of the battle is a result of Yahweh's intervention (v. 15: "Yahweh threw into confusion Sisera and all his chariots and all his army at the edge of the sword before Barak"); (2) Sisera makes his escape in the midst of the confusion of battle (v. 17). The battle is indeed over but the story is still awaiting an ending.[85]

Sisera's Demise (4:17–22)

The account of Jael's crafty assassination of Sisera is a fascinating narrative in its own right, but in the context of the Deborah/Barak narrative it stands as a "surprise ending."[86] The seemingly irrelevant note in 4:11 about Heber the Kenite's (Jael's husband) estrangement from the Kenites begins to make sense when the reader reaches 4:17. Heber had cut ties with Israel and had aligned with King Jabin. In other words, Heber and his household were traitors to Israel and were now Canaanite collaborators. These circumstances, however, are ambiguous and do not prepare the reader for the assassination plot that unfolds later in the narrative. In fact, the expectation is quite likely the opposite: based on the Canaanite treaty one would expect that Jael invited the commander of Jabin's army in order to provide him with protection. Although the narrative does not indicate Jael's motivation for slaying Sisera, as the narrative unfolds we realize that the treaty is a pretext for Jael's offer of protection but in the end marks a fatal mistake on the part of Jabin's commander.[87] Moreover, Deborah's prophecy that Yahweh would deliver Sisera "into the hand of a woman" is fulfilled, albeit by unusual and unexpected means.[88]

Fleeing desperately for his life, the once-great Sisera encounters Jael, the wife of an ally—this must have seemed like such good luck to Sisera. The words

85. Cf. Butler, *Judges*, 103.

86. Butler, *Judges*, 86.

87. See the discussion and various opinions on Jael's motivation in Butler, *Judges*, 100–101.

88. "The description of the murder in verse 21 is sudden and unexpected, and is not explained by or connected with any motivations alluded to in the text"; Amit, *Book of Judges*, 212.

of Jael's invitation are song-like, according to Barry Webb, "Jael is like a siren, singing her victim aside to his destruction."[89] Jael offers protection, hospitality and care, and Sisera naively accepts them—a mistake that will cost him his life. The events that unfold inside Jael's tent—the private intimacy, the betrayal of trust, the swift and violent brutality of the deed—are reminiscent of Ehud's assassination of Eglon. Like a mother with her trusting child, Jael settles Sisera down, draws a blanket over him and even provides him with some milk and adjusts the blanket into place. Ordering Jael to keep watch at the tent door (v. 20), Sisera, convinced he has escaped all danger, drifts off into a deep sleep.

Nothing quite prepares us for what happens next. The conditions are set for Jael, the wife of an Israelite traitor, to break ties with Canaan and cast her lot with the people of Yahweh. The sequence of events in 4:21 seem to proceed in slow motion: Jael takes hold of the tent peg, she puts a hammer in her other hand, she stealthily tiptoes over to Sisera and drives home the tent peg through his temple, the tent peg being driven so hard it went into the ground. Sisera was dead by the hand of a heroic female. This decisive blow marks the end of Jabin's oppressive regime.

The scene ends in 4:22 with the hero Jael emerging from the tent to meet Barak. It seems a bit comic that Barak is pursuing the man whom Jael, by her cunning, had already dispatched. Barak appears to be trying to circumvent Deborah's prophecy—this pursuit of Sisera represents his journey on the "way/road" which will, he no doubt hopes, lead to his glory (see 4:9a). However, the glory has already been gained by the woman of Deborah's prophecy (4:9b). Jael invites Barak into her tent, and he discovers the corpse of Sisera, the tent peg still in place. The stranglehold of Canaanite oppression has been broken.

The End of Canaanite Oppression (4:23–24)

In case the reader has become sidetracked by the subplot of Sisera's demise, the final unfolding of the narrative in 4:23–24 represents a sort of circular ending as the story returns to the ultimate undoing of Israel's true enemy. These verses make clear that although Jabin is subdued by "the hand [*yād*] of the people of Israel," they are successful in defeating Jabin ultimately by means of God's leadership (v. 23).[90] As mentioned, the cycle of Deborah/Barak/Jael is not complete until the notice at the end of chapter 5 (v. 31b), but what can we say in summary

89. Webb, *Book of Judges*, 193; cf. Block, *Judges*, 206.
90. Amit, *Book of Judges*, 213.

so far regarding the state of leadership and the situation in which the people of God find themselves?

The Deborah/Barak narrative continues the motif of the unexpected deliverer. Othniel is probably the most likely of Israel's deliverers, Ehud is a crafty left-handed "son of the right hand" (i.e., Benjamite), and Shamgar wielding an ox-goad is a foreign deliverer. In fact, as the Deborah/Barak story unfolds it is not entirely clear at all which individual is the deliverer. Amit explores in some detail the question of who in the Deborah/Barak narrative is the deliverer, examining each of the main characters of the story in turn.[91] Deborah plays a key role as mediator between Yahweh and Barak, and once the reader is aware that she is not the woman into whose hand Yahweh would deliver Sisera, Deborah disappears from the narrative. Barak is the deliverer elect but his reluctance to take on the role results in Yahweh electing another, even though Barak does have some success in battle.[92] Jael no doubt has a pivotal role as she solves the riddle of Deborah's prophecy and slays the great commander of Jabin's army (4:9), but by the time she enters the action Israel has already achieved success on the battlefield.[93] In the final analysis, Amit determines that

> The various indicators prove that our story has one main hero: the Lord. . . . There is a balance in the portion of the other characters in the story, and the various indicators do not suggest an advantage of any particular human figure above the others. Is this phenomenon to be seen as pure accident? It seems to me that the author preferred to exploit this balanced technique in order to stress the greatness of God's action.[94]

Indeed, leadership reaches a crisis point in the Deborah/Barak narrative. As mentioned, at this point in the book we have come to expect the unexpected with regard to leadership, but in this narrative the unexpected would be comic if it were not so tragic as the reader is led to expect first, the unexpected deliverer (the woman Deborah), second, the expected but unwilling deliverer (Barak) and ultimately, third, the unthinkable deliverer

91. Amit, *Book of Judges*, 214–18.

92. Amit maintains that even in these successes Barak is overshadowed by either a woman or Yahweh; Amit, "Endings," 216.

93. The Deborah/Barak narrative does not include what has become an expected element of the judge's cycle, namely, the death notice of the judge/deliverer. Judges 5:31 does include the expected formula regarding the period of "rest" for the land ("And the land had rest for forty years") but it is not accompanied by the death notice of the judge/deliverer (see 3:11; 3:30/4:1), which contributes to the ambiguity regarding who is the human deliverer in the narrative.

94. Amit, *Book of Judges*, 216.

(Jael the wife of a traitor). As Tammi Schneider states, "The story focuses on Israel's plight and her need to rely on foreigners and women as a result of the decline in Israel's leadership. The decline is not because of Deborah's actions, which are praised, but because she had to carry them out at all, since the men would not."[95] It seems clear that in the Deborah/Barak narrative leadership has reached an all-time low in the context of the book of Judges to this point. Even so, equally clear is that the narrative depicts these events according to the pattern set in the exposition and played out in the narratives of Othniel and Ehud. Yahweh sends the foreign nations to punish Israel's disobedience and as a result of Israel's crying out, he provides deliverance (see the formulaic statement regarding the period of rest in 5:31c), even if that is executed through unexpected means and through various twists and turns in the narrative. As the reader continues into the Gideon/Abimelech narrative the theme of the crisis of leadership intensifies even further, but the Gideon/Abimelech narrative is far more open-ended, resisting the kind of closure that is apparent in the previous narratives.

Finally, the narrative in this third cycle focuses entirely on political and military matters. The beginning of the Othniel account explicitly attributes the foreign oppression to Israel's abandoning Yahweh and serving Baal and Asheroth (3:7). In the Ehud cycle, Israelite idolatry is hinted at twice in key places in the narrative—a kind of subtle reminder that the problem in Israel is their disloyalty to Yahweh. The Deborah/Barak/Jael narrative in Judg 4 contains no explicit allusions to Israel's idolatry and covenant unfaithfulness. Of course, the formula that starts the cycle ("the Israelites again did evil in the eyes of Yahweh"; 4:1) is a clear indictment against the Israelites for covenant unfaithfulness, but still it is curious that the narrative does not draw that out further. Perhaps the narrator is subtly drawing readers into the reality of Israel's own dulling of sensitivity to their own idolatrous society. The deliverers so far have brought military victory and liberty, but we do not get the impression they are dealing with the "religious" root of the problem. Perhaps the sense we should be getting at this point is: nobody is dealing with idolatry and trying to bring about a renewal of covenant faithfulness, so why even mention it. So the focus of the narrative becomes military and political, but the shift in focus does not mean the narrator approves—the absence of religious language or themes is a rhetorical technique that lulls us into the reality of the situation. The Gideon cycle which follows will jolt readers as it focuses at points squarely on idolatry and covenant fidelity. But before moving there we need to consider the Song of Deborah.

95. Schneider, *Judges*, 82.

5:1–31: The Song of Deborah

If the Song of Deborah was composed soon after the events that inspired it, then Judg 5 "is beyond question one of the oldest elements in our present book of Judges."[96] This ancient text, therefore, was taken up by the author of Judges much later and embedded in the author's account of the history of the settlement period. Although not unprecedented, the Song of Deborah provides a rare opportunity to compare the relationship between a narrative account of events and a poetic depiction of/reflection on the same events. Some readers may feel uneasy about the different ways that the narrative and the song depict the events. Of course, it is easy to spot the similarities but what are we to make of the differences? Suffice it to say that narrative and poetry communicate in different ways for different purposes, and in the case of Judg 4 and 5, there is no need to see these as contradictory accounts.[97]

The Song of Deborah and the Song of Moses (Exod 15:1–18) are the best biblical examples of the relationship between prose and poetry. In fact, the parallels between these two songs and their circumstances (both being poetic victory songs that were sung after the events they are celebrating) are too obvious to ignore—they deliberately invite comparison (and contrast).[98] The Song of Deborah is often regarded as a kind of hymn of praise to Yahweh, ultimately crediting him with victory and akin to the Song of Moses in this regard.[99] However, I wonder whether a comparison between these two songs (and other similar songs in the Bible) might nudge us to different conclusions—the comparison seems to reveal that something distinct is going in on the Song of Deborah. We will return to that after the analysis of the song itself.

The Hebrew text of the Song of Deborah is fraught with challenges. In the following commentary I attempt as much as possible to avoid very technical discussions and debates. Those interested in that kind of discussion can find it in the more technical commentaries.[100]

96. Cundall, "Judges," 90.

97. For a good discussion of the relationship between the narrative account in Judg 4 and its poetic counterpart in Judg 5, I recommend consulting the thorough discussion of these matters in Butler, *Judges*, 158–78.

98. For a summary of many of the similarities, see Chisholm, *Commentary on Judges and Ruth*, 217; Wong, "Song of Deborah as Polemic," 22.

99. E.g., Webb, *Book of Judges*, 206 "So the Deborah-Barak episode . . . concludes with a victory hymn in praise of Yahweh and his loyal supporters, but especially Yahweh himself." Chisholm, *Commentary on Judges and Ruth*, 235: "This song of victory was appropriate because all kings needed to know of the royal splendor and power of victorious Yahweh, the God of Israel."

100. E.g., Butler, *Judges*, 113–58; Boling, *Judges*, 101–16.

Narrative Context of the Song (5:1)

The narrator introduces the Song of Deborah here in 5:1 as a song sung by both Deborah and Barak. This may indicate that it might be more appropriate to call this the "Song of Deborah and Barak"; however, the first-person ("I") throughout the song and the self-reference in 5:7 ("I, Deborah") more closely associates the song to Deborah than to Barak. Moreover, the verb at the beginning of 5:1 is in the third-person feminine singular ("then she, Deborah, sang"), which also gives pride of place to Deborah in the singing of the song.[101] That said, other voices do appear in the Song. For example, the summons to Deborah ("Awake") and to Barak ("Arise") may be a chorus of singers joining in on the song that is led by the two lead singers.[102]

The Hebrew construction of this verse clearly connects the singing of the song with the events of the previous chapter, indicating temporal sequence, and the phrase "on that day" is a reference to the day of deliverance. Webb draws attention to the fact that this verse is reminiscent of Moses's song of deliverance after the exodus and Yahweh's defeat of Pharaoh and his army of charioteers.[103]

The Summons to and Cause for Praise (5:2–8)

The song begins in 5:2–3 with an invocation and a summons. Deborah invokes the assembly to "bless Yahweh" on the basis of those who voluntarily took up the battle call. For someone of lower status to "bless" someone greater (in this case Yahweh) is to praise or exalt the latter.[104] The summons to the "kings" and "princes" in 5:3 refers presumably to the foreign kings. Deborah witnesses not only to the people of God but also to the nations about what has just transpired. Her song is, nevertheless, to Yahweh, who has a particular relationship with Israel (i.e., "the God of Israel").

Verses 4–5 depict in powerful and cosmic language the terrifying appearing of Yahweh (i.e., theophany). This picture of the coming of Yahweh is carefully structured:

101. Butler, *Judges*, 136.
102. Butler, *Judges*, 136.
103. Webb, *Book of Judges*, 206.
104. Block, *Judges*, 221.

A. Yahweh goes forth from Seir and Edom
  B. the earth trembles
    C. the heavens drop (water)
    C′ the clouds drop water
  B′ mountains quake
A′ Before Yahweh the God of Israel

These verses depict Yahweh as the mighty divine warrior. The poet carefully chooses locations that would recall the major events of Israel's past. Sinai is the place that Yahweh, on the basis of his victory over Egypt, forges an unbreakable bond (a covenant) with Israel, and from there his mighty presence led them through Seir and Edom. The present context (the victory over Jabin, Sisera, and their armies) is part of a continuous revelation that is like the marching of Yahweh through time. The storm imagery associated with the "march" of Yahweh is the kind of language that is often associated with the Canaanite god Baal. In these verses, the Canaanite kings and princes whom Deborah had summoned are confronted with the stark reality that Yahweh and not Baal is the true God and storm-bringer who grants victory to his people.[105]

A notable shift takes place in 5:6. The poem will now focus (1) on the immediate context of Canaanite oppression at the hand of Jabin, and (2) on the details of the battle itself. Even more significant is the focus on the human actors. To be sure there are references to Yahweh in the rest of the poem, but they seem on the whole to be secondary (or else simply incidental) to the actions of the human participants in these events.

The rise of Yahweh in 5:4–5 is here paralleled with the rise of Deborah in what the poem describes as perilous times. The Canaanite oppression caused traders and other travelers to avoid the major travel routes for fear of attack and/or theft.[106] The heavy hand of the Canaanites also had terrible consequences for Israelite villages (v. 6).[107] Deborah's rise to a place of authority and leadership (i.e., "as mother") was a decisive turning point. This sense of self-importance is curious. The Deborah/Barak/Jael cycle so far has been nothing but positive toward Deborah, and although the purpose of this note may not be negative it does seem to stand out. In the next cycle of judges (that of Gideon), a similar pattern appears: Gideon expresses that the source of the victory is Yahweh (7:15)

105. Block, *Judges*, 223.

106. Butler, *Judges*, 138; Block, *Judges*, 225.

107. It is not certain if v. 6 means that villages languished and actually ceased to exist, or if the inhabitants of the villages cut themselves off from travel and cloistered themselves inside their own villages; see Butler, *Judges*, 138.

but when the time comes he urges the troops to shout as their war cry "For Yahweh and for Gideon" (7:18, 20).

Verse 8 is difficult to translate, and commentators disagree about its interpretation. I tend to agree with Butler: Israel had pledged allegiance to foreign gods and perhaps even made treaties with the foreign powers, but this still led to military oppression ("war was at the gates").[108] Being preoccupied with survival, the Israelite troops were not properly prepared for warfare and lacked the basic military tools ("shield" and "spear").

Willing Volunteers (5:9–13)

The references to the military leaders, to those who were "willing" to join the battle, and the invocation to "bless Yahweh" in 5:9 connect back to 5:2. Here Deborah expresses her (maternal?) admiration. Deborah next invokes both the rich (those who ride "white donkeys" and sit on "carpets") and the ordinary "pedestrians," presumably all segments of Israelite society, to hear and ponder the triumphs of Yahweh.[109] Verse 11 shifts to the village centers: the water wells where all villagers would regularly visit. The poet invokes the people to tell the victory of Yahweh in these places too. In light of the introduction in the book of Judges, which sets the book among the generations of Israelites who had forgotten ("they did not know") Yahweh and the mighty acts he had done on behalf of Israel (2:10), Deborah's summons here is surprising. Butler seems justified to wonder whether 5:11 might be "a bit of hyperbole."[110] Verse 11 ends with the "people of Yahweh" setting off to the place of battle (the gates; see v. 8).

At this point in the song, with the people of Yahweh ready to engage the Canaanite armies, listeners anticipate action. Here in 5:12 we encounter an abrupt change of speaker, as Deborah and Barak are called to action, spurred on perhaps by the congregation listening to the song. The voice(s) urges Deborah to rise up in song again and Barak to bring about a reversal of the situation—to bring captive the Israelites who are captive to the Canaanites. The voice changes again in 5:13 (note the first-person singular "me") and continues the action of v. 11. Deborah or per-

108. Butler, *Judges*, 140.

109. Alter translates v. 10a as "Riders on pure-white she-asses, sitting on regal cloths"; Alter, *Ancient Israel*, 133. For those "who walk by the way" as ordinary citizens of Israel see Butler, *Judges*, 141; and Webb, *Book of Judges*, 210. Block sees the rich in v. 10 as referring to Canaanite merchants and as a critique of their sense of security; see Block, *Judges*, 228. This would make sense of vv. 6–7, which indicate that the Canaanite oppression drove the population from Israel off the main roadways and confined the citizens of Israel to their villages.

110. Butler, *Judges*, 141.

haps (more likely) Barak recounts how the meager army of Yahweh, the "remnant" or "survivors" of the Canaanite oppression, marched down "against the mighty."[111]

Tribal Participants and Tribal Abstainers (5:14–18)

The section in 5:14–18 functions as a roll call, highlighting three groups among the people of Israel: those who willingly participated in the battle (vv. 14–15a), those who resisted the call to arms (vv. 15b–17), and those whose heroism on the battlefield made them worthy of special honor (v. 18).[112] The list of participants has at least two functions, as Webb has helpfully pointed out: the list of tribes "builds up expectancy that there is to be a truly great battle, such as the theophany of verses 4–5 foreshadowed. At the same time, it reveals a lack of unity among the tribes—an issue that will assume growing importance in the remainder of the book."[113] Missing altogether from this roll call are the tribes of Judah and Simeon, the two southern-most tribes. These two tribes had led the tribes in the "mop-up" campaign in Judg 1, so their absence from the roll call in Deborah's song is noticeable. Did the rift between the northern and southern tribes, evident much later in Israel's history, exist already this early in the nation's formation? Whatever the case, the song does not appear to be critical of Judah and Simeon for their absence (as it is, e.g., of the tribes listed in vv. 15b–17). The Canaanite threat in this cycle was a northern threat so perhaps it was acceptable that the coalition forces would comprise the northern tribes.[114]

In the first part of the roll call—those who willingly supported the military effort—the poet organizes the list in order of the kind and intensity of support that each tribe offered:

1. A contingency of Ephraimites ("some from Ephraim")
2. The tribe of Benjamin with their *troops/military companies*
3. *Commanders* from Machir[115]
4. The Zebulun participants who "*wield the commander's scepter*"
5. The "*chieftains/captains*" of Issachar, showing *solidarity with and loyalty to* Deborah and Barak and displaying *no hesitation in battle*

111. Butler, *Judges*, 142.

112. Block, *Judges*, 231–32.

113. Webb, *Book of Judges*, 203.

114. On the tribal organization evident in these verses see the thorough discussion in Butler, *Judges*, 142–47.

115. Machir is a prominent clan in the tribe of Manasseh, whose ancestor (Machir) was the son of Manasseh (see Gen 50:23); Webb, *Book of Judges*, 211.

Having recounted the increasing support of these tribal representatives, Deborah shifts focus in 5:15b–17 to those who, for one reason or another, could not be bothered to engage in warfare. The poet publicly shames two tribes to the southeast (Reuben and Gad) and two tribes to the northwest (Dan and Asher) for their indifference and lack of resolve to heed the battle summons.[116] Here we encounter a spirit of tribal self-interest and a lack of national cohesion among the tribes. Although this tribalism manifests itself as disinterest in this cycle, in the following cycles it breeds resentment and gives birth to intertribal warfare.

Finally, in 5:18 the poet praises the heroic attitudes and actions of the tribes of Zebulun (already mentioned in v. 14) and Naphtali. The people of Zebulun relativized their own lives (they "scorned their life to death") for the sake of the liberty of all Israel from the tyranny of the Canaanites, as did Naphtali "taking the most strategic points in the battle zone."[117]

The Battle (5:19–23)

In the broadest of brushstrokes, the song depicts the battle itself. The kings of Canaan fought (v. 19a) and failed (they received no victor's plunder; v. 19b). Even with all their might and the force of their countless charioteers, they are, of course, no match for the cosmic forces of the stars (v. 20) and torrential rivers (v. 21). These cosmic images are reminiscent of the theophany of 5:4–5. It seems that Yahweh's instrument for throwing the Canaanite army and chariots into disarray in 4:15 was the flooding of the Kishon (notice the effect of the torrential waters of the Kishon on the horses in v. 22).[118] Again here we have evocations of the exodus from Egypt, and Yahweh's defeat of Pharaoh and his charioteers by means of the Red Sea.

The curse of Meroz in 5:23 comes as a bit of a surprise. The identity of Meroz is a mystery and has been the subject of much speculation. We might have expected this statement in the roll call in 5:14–18, although the roll call there focuses on tribal involvement. Its placement here contrasts sharply the utterly damning curse on Meroz for having no role whatsoever in the battle with the overwhelming expressions of blessing on Jael for her decisive role in the battle in the following verse. Thus, according to Block, "Meroz represents

116. The reference to Gilead (a region and not a tribe) is likely meant to evoke the tribe of Gad and perhaps part of the tribe of Manasseh (not including the clan of Machir) in the regions east of the Jordan River; see Webb, *Book of Judges*, 213.

117. Webb, *Book of Judges*, 213.

118. Webb, *Book of Judges*, 214.

those Israelites who have taken their stand on the side of the Canaanites; Jael represents those non-Israelites who have taken their stand on the side of Israel."[119]

Jael's Heroism and the Mother of Sisera's Desolation (5:24–30)

If the curse of Meroz is deliberately juxtaposed with the blessing of Jael, then in 5:24–30, the exultation of Jael is contrasted with the misery of Sisera's mother. The two halves of this section of the poem (vv. 24–27 and vv. 28–30) each center around a woman connected to Sisera (Jael, the one who took his life, and his mother, the one who gave him life). Whereas the first half takes place in the privacy of Jael's tent, the second half takes place in Sisera's home or his mother's home as she waits in vain for his return.

Similar to the narrative account of these events in chapter 4, the poem spends less time on the details of the battle and more time on the intricate details of the assassination of Sisera. The poem slows right down when it comes to the moments leading up to and including the violent end of Jabin's commander. The poem is a celebration of the defeat of Israel's enemies, and Block is surely correct when he notes that "The killing of Sisera is described with savage pleasure."[120] As the poem crawls to its climax, "the shortening of the lines in Strophe 17 (v. 27) describes the action with a tantalizingly slow sequence of verbs that present [Sisera's] 'fall'":[121]

> Between her feet he bowed down,
>   he fell,
>   he lay.
> Between her feet he bowed,
>   he fell,
>   where he bowed,
>   there he fell,
>   destroyed.

With the final word "destroyed" ringing in our ears, the poem shifts to focus on Sisera's mother. The Song of Deborah is the expression of praise from a "mother in Israel" because of victory (5:7c), but for the mothers in Canaan there can only be wailing as a result of defeat. Although it is not apparent that

119. Block, *Judges*, 239.
120. Block, *Judges*, 240.
121. Younger, *Judges and Ruth*, 155.

the poet includes 5:28–30 to present Sisera's mother as an object of sympathy, the pathos of her situation is moving.[122] In the briefest of pen strokes the poet vividly describes her miserable circumstances. She peers longingly out the window, hoping against all hope that she will see Sisera's chariot returning on the horizon, and she expresses aloud the anxiety of her spirit—why hasn't my son returned yet (v. 28)? Her attendants try to assure her with logical explanations for the delay—explanations she tells herself to ease her vexed mind (v. 29).

Surely Sisera is preoccupied by the spoils of war, and that accounts for his delay, or so Sisera's mother and her attendants try to convince themselves. The items described here are the choicest booty and at the top of the list is "a woman or two"—actually these Canaanite speakers consider the female spoils of war as nothing more than female organs ("a womb or two") to be exploited by the likes of Sisera and his men. The callousness with which Sisera's mother and her female attendants speak of rape in 5:30 is jolting and indicates what would have been the fate of the Israelite women had Sisera and his armies been victorious. It is also ironic, because Sisera is lying dead at the feet of one of these potential "wombs."[123] In all of this, the poet subtly mocks the calamity that has befallen their would-be oppressors.

Divine Invocation against All Israel's Enemies (5:31a)

With the miserable picture of Sisera's mother and her vain hope etched in the minds of readers, the poem draws to a conclusion. The final word, addressed once again to Yahweh, is one of curse on Yahweh's enemies and blessing on "those who love" Yahweh. There are a number of assumptions and implications in this short prayer. In context, the Canaanite armies and especially Sisera's brutal end exemplify the kind of fate that the poet desires for all of Yahweh's enemies. In the context of Judges, however, we may feel that Deborah (or whoever's voice is speaking in 5:31a) should be careful what she prays for, because it is by no means the case in Judges that Israel is always on the side of Yahweh.[124]

This caution becomes all the more necessary in the contrast of the

122. Cf. Webb, *Book of Judges*, 217: "there is strong pathos in the episode, since the aftermath of the battle is now seen from the woman's perspective, and who could not feel for a mother who has lost her son?"

123. Schneider, *Judges*, 96.

124. Butler, *Judges*, 157; Polzin, *Moses*, 167; Block, *Judges*, 244; Webb, *Book of Judges*, 217.

"enemies" of Yahweh with "those who love" him. The root verb of this participle is אהב/'āhēb—"love"—and it evokes the sense of commitment, loyalty, and faithfulness. Understood in light of the covenant made at Sinai and confirmed on the plains of Moab, this is referring to those who have an unswerving "covenant commitment."[125] Butler notes: "Such a call to love Yahweh has roots in the formulation of the Decalogue (Exod 20:6; Deut 5:10; compare Josh 22:5; 23:11). Love of God is shown by obedience (Deut 7:9; 11:1; 30:20; 1 Kgs 3:3; Isa 56:6) and faithfulness (Ps 31:23)."[126] Again, as we find this kind of "love" for Yahweh so rarely in Judges, this seems a very dangerous prayer, and there may be a deliberate sense of irony here.[127] In any case, the final chord that the poem strikes is one of the persistence and permanence of the lovers of Yahweh.[128]

Narrative Cycle Conclusion (5:31b)

The notice about the land having rest for forty years signals that the third cycle is complete. The great victory over Jabin and his armies yielded only about a generation of peace before another cycle will begin again. This should be somewhat worrying compared with the eighty-year period of rest of the previous cycle (3:30).

I have already provided some general remarks about the narrative account of Deborah, Barak and Jael (see above), but before we move on to the Gideon cycle, it is worthwhile reflecting on the song as well. The song is clearly a victory song that celebrates the defeat of Jabin, Sisera, and the Canaanite armies. Song, as well as story and ritual, were significant identity-forming activities that God's people were to utilize to remind them of their history and relationship with Yahweh. What kind of identity, we might ask, might the Song of Deborah, with its themes and emphases, reinforce? Viewing the song in isolation, we can discern that Yahweh plays a primary and crucial role in the victory, and that much emphasis (positive and negative) is also put on the human actors in the events.

However, if we compare the Song of Deborah with other biblical victory songs, particularly the Song of Moses in Exod 15 the picture that emerges is

125. Block, *Judges*, 244.

126. Butler, *Judges*, 157.

127. The deliberate irony is not by the poet but by the author who incorporated the song into the book of Judges.

128. The reference to the sun in this verse may be part of a polemic against the worship of the sun; see Block, *Judges*, 244; Webb, *Book of Judges*, 218–19.

more ambiguous.[129] Hardly a verse goes by in Exod 15 without reference to the name, the activity, or some kind of attribute of Yahweh. In the Song of Moses, Yahweh is not just the primary actor, he is the only actor, apart from the futile efforts of his enemies. In the Song of Deborah, if we limited the references to Yahweh only to those where he acts, we would essentially be left with the theophany (5:4–5), and we might add to that the "triumphs of Yahweh" that the people at the wells should sing about (v. 11) and the lack of help Yahweh received when he was acting against the mighty (v. 23). The only other references (v. 2, 3, 9, 11, 23, 31) are either invocations to bless or praise Yahweh, or else are incidental to the action of the events (e.g., the reference to the "people of Yahweh" in v. 11b). The exploits of the human actors, on the other hand, get sustained coverage in the poem. Whereas Moses's song ends with the eternal reign of Yahweh, Deborah's song ends with the strength and permanence of God's people.

I cannot help but agree with Gregory Wong that the role of Yahweh, although present, is indeed eclipsed by the role of the human agents. Is this the kind of identity-forming song that would arouse unswerving commitment to Yahweh and his covenant, or would it simply reinforce the ambivalence of God's people to be the people he was calling them to be? If the rest of the book is any indication, we might be inclined to conclude that this song was of the latter kind. There may be enduring instruction here for contemporary people of faith about the kinds of worship songs we sing—are they theocentric songs that inspire commitment to God and a more faithful witness to him or are they anthropocentric songs that celebrate human achievement and leave us comfortable with the status quo?

6:1–8:35: The Gideon Cycle

At the center of the book of Judges is the cycle of narratives concerning Gideon and his son Abimelech.[130] The author has drawn events from the lives of Gideon

129. In this regard see Echols, *"Tell Me, O Muse,"* (see ch. 4); in this detailed study, Echols reads the Song of Deborah alongside the Song of Moses (Exod 15), as well as the deliverance song of David in 2 Sam 22 (with Ps 18) and Hab 3. The conclusion he reaches is that each of these songs unambiguously attributes the victory to Yahweh, whereas the Song of Deborah ascribes victory to the human actors in the events. Echols regards the Song of Deborah as a secular heroic poem (the heroes being the human figures). It should be noted that Echols regards the references to Yahweh in the Song of Deborah to be later additions and therefore excises them from his comparison, which does influence his conclusions. However, even without removing these references, the Song does seem to relativize the role of Yahweh when compared to these other texts. See also Echols, "Eclipse of God," 149–52.

130. Gooding was the first to make a substantial argument for what he refers to as sym-

and Abimelech and carefully crafted them into a complex literary unit that includes a number of subplots but that resonates with the themes and developments of the book as a whole. The accounts of Gideon and Abimelech continue threads in the development of the theme of leadership, but this theme develops in new ways with Gideon/Abimelech. Whereas the previous narratives (of Othniel, Ehud, and Deborah/Barak) bring about a degree of balance at the end, readers are left with a sense of irresolution at the end of the Gideon/Abimelech narratives, a sense that persists in the following cycles (i.e., Jephthah and Samson).

One can discern two main parts to the Gideon/Abimelech narrative. The first section follows the pattern of the cycle, beginning with Israel doing evil in the sight of Yahweh in 6:1 and ending with subjugation of the foreign enemy and the notice of the land having rest in 8:28. However, the narrative continues beyond the boundaries of the cycle. It follows the legacy of Gideon through his son Abimelech in the second section (8:29–9:57). Judges 8:29–35 functions as a transition, providing Gideon's obituary, which also functions as an introduction to Abimelech.

The Gideon cycle itself, which ends with the formulaic note about the land experiencing rest (6:1–8:28) is by far the longest cycle in the book to this point and also the most complex. The behavior of the chosen deliverer and the people of God is the most troubling behavior we have encountered in the book so far as well. The role of Yahweh in the Gideon cycle is also unprecedented in the book so far. Yahweh interacts at length (sometimes through a messenger) with Gideon in his call and in the confirmation and assurances of victory, and the narrator recounts extensive quotations of the words of Yahweh.[131] It is not insignificant that although Yahweh speaks multiple times in this cycle, he goes silent just before the battle itself and does not speak again in this cycle. As Younger notes, "Yahweh and Gideon will be in almost constant dialogue with

---

metry in the structural design of the book of Judges, with the stories in the first half of the book demonstrating symmetry with the stories in the second half of the book. The pattern he perceives is of the type of A-B-C-D-C′-B′-A′; see Gooding, "Composition," 70*–79*. Some but by no means all scholars follow Gooding's structuring of the book, but by virtue of the length of the Gideon/Abimelech narrative and its placement after the stories of Othniel, Ehud, and Deborah/Barak and before the Jephthah and Samson narratives, it is difficult to deny the central place given to the narratives of Gideon and Abimelech.

131. Although the narrative identifies Gideon's divine interlocutor at times as "the messenger/angel of Yahweh" (6:11, 12, 20, 21, 22), as is often the case in the Old Testament "the messenger/angel of Yahweh" and Yahweh himself are indistinguishable. Even in this call narrative Gideon's interlocutor is identified as Yahweh; see 6:14, 16, 25.

one another in the sequence of events leading up to the battle (6:25, 36, 39; 7:2, 4, 7, 9). This will prove ironic in light of the final outcome of the Gideon cycle."[132]

As with the events of the previous cycle, the events in the Gideon cycle are set once again in the northern regions of Israel.[133]

Introduction to the Gideon Cycle (6:1–10)

The complex of stories surrounding Gideon is framed according to the expected cyclical pattern.

1. Israel does evil in the sight of Yahweh (6:1a)
2. Yahweh responds by delivering them into the hand of the Midianites (6:1b)
3. Israel cries out to Yahweh (6:7)

This is now the fourth time that readers of Judges have encountered the cyclical pattern and by this time we should be adept at not only recognizing the pattern but also identifying nuances in the way the cyclical pattern is used.[134] In terms of the first and third elements of the pattern, the narrator this time around stays fairly consistent.[135] We should not forget that the note about Israel doing evil in the eyes of Yahweh in 6:1a follows the previous verse which ends the Song of Deborah and calls for Yahweh's enemies to perish!

Whereas the period of oppression from the first cycle up until this point has been increasing—from eight (Othniel), to eighteen (Ehud), to twenty (Deborah et al.)—in the Gideon cycle the period of oppression is only seven years. It seems the quality of Israel's oppression under the Midianites, however, makes up for the lesser quantity of years, as the narrator explains in excruciating details the nature of the conditions the Israelites endured in the seven years (vv. 2–6a). According to Webb, "The pitiful decline in their lifestyle is conveyed by piling detail upon detail: they live in dens and caves

132. Younger, *Judges and Ruth*, 176.

133. Webb, *Book of Judges*, 219, holds that this similarity makes the Gideon cycle a "natural sequel" to the previous cycle.

134. In fact, this is the fifth time, if we include the introduction of the cyclical framework in 2:11–23.

135. The Ehud and Deborah/Barak/Jael cycles both begin with the same form of the Hebrew verb יסף/*yāsap* ("to add to/increase") together with an infinitive of the verb עשׂה/ʿāśâ, often translated as "Israel *again* did." The Gideon cycle does not include the verb יסף/*yāsap* and just jumps in using a finite form of the verb עשׂה/ʿāśâ.

like animals; their produce is destroyed, and their livestock is carried off by the enemy."[136]

The primary oppressor is Midian, but once again (cf. the coalition of Moabites, Ammonites, and Amalekites in 3:13) foreign forces collaborate to make life extremely bleak for the Israelites. This time the Midianites along with the Amalekites and the "people of the East" constituted God's scourge against Israel (6:3). The ancestors of the Midianites and Amalekites were ancient enemies of God's people, and they trace their roots to the offspring of Abraham with his concubine Keturah (Midian—see Gen 25:1–6) and the grandson of Esau (Amalek—see Gen 36:12, 16) respectively.

The situation of Israel under the oppression of these people groups is dire. The narrator paints a vivid picture of the horrors perpetrated against Yahweh's people. Driven from their homes, the Israelites are forced into hiding. Whenever they tried to produce crops for food, the foreigners and their livestock, pictured as a devastating swarm of locusts, would pillage the land, leaving a wake of destruction and bareness. Starving, destitute, and on the run, the seven years of oppression took their toll. In short, "Israel was brought very low because of Midian" (v. 6a). The intensity of foreign oppression had reached critical mass, far more intense than anything described yet in the book of Judges. With nowhere to turn, the Israelites cry out to Yahweh (v. 6b).

At this point in the cycle the narrative breaks from the pattern. Attentive readers expect that according to the cyclical pattern Yahweh would respond to Israel's distress by raising up a judge/deliverer. In the previous cycle, the language of Yahweh raising up a deliverer is not present but in its place the narrator introduced Deborah. In this cycle, something unexpected and unprecedented takes place, namely, Yahweh sends a prophet and confronts the Israelites with the reality of their covenant disloyalty.

The prophet appears in response to the people's distress cry (v. 7). His message is more important than his identity, as the narrator only says that he was sent by Yahweh. The message comes in covenant language and is a word of judgment. It recounts Yahweh's action on behalf of Israel (cf. 2:10) not only in the great redemptive acts of the exodus (vv. 8b–9a) but also in the conquest (v. 9b). On this basis, God declared himself as Yahweh, the God of Israel, and demanded loyalty (they must not fear the foreign gods; v. 10a). The divine word spoken through the prophet ends with the indictment: God's people have failed (v. 10b).

The last time Israel was challenged by a word from Yahweh was in the exposition (2:1–3). The similarities (and indeed the differences) between the

136. Webb, *Book of Judges*, 222–23.

communication of Yahweh's messenger in 2:1–3 and his prophet in 6:7–10 are striking. Each is prefaced on the basis of Yahweh's deliverance of Israel from slavery in Egypt and his giving of the promised land; each confronts the Israelites with their infidelity (the former in the language of making a covenant with the inhabitants of the land and failing to break down their altars; the latter in terms of fearing the gods of the inhabitants of the land); and each directly challenges Israel's disobedience with precisely the same phrase (2:2; 6:10): "But you have not obeyed my voice."

Is it significant that the prophetic message recounted here at the center of the book resonates so apparently with the words of the divine messenger in the prologue? Having arrived at this point in the narrative after the accounts of Othniel, Ehud, and Deborah/Barak, readers may have gotten sidetracked by the political and military matters of the book. The placing of the Gideon account, which starts off with the divine word of the unnamed prophet, at this point in the book serves to reorient readers back to the central problem of the book. That central problem is not Israel's political or military shortcomings, but rather concerns Israel's infidelity to Yahweh and his covenant with them. Placed at the beginning of the book's central narrative, the prophetic word is a reminder that Israel's disobedience and unfaithfulness have been perpetuating the cycle as recounted thus far. In this way, Judg 6:7–10 provides a retrospective understanding of the previous narratives. However, it also points forward. The prophetic word implies that the key to Israel finally breaking the cycle of the judges is a religious reorientation on the part of Israel—a renewed commitment to Yahweh and his covenant.

Moving forward, readers may be optimistic that Gideon will be instrumental in this change, and indeed his first acts as leader are to destroy the altar of Baal and the Asherah and to build an altar to Yahweh in their place. The unfolding account of Gideon indicates, however, that not only did Gideon fail to turn the hearts of the Israelites toward Yahweh, he actually instigates false worship (8:24–27) with the result that after his death the people are further entrenched in their infidelity (8:33–35).

One final observation is worth noting regarding the word of Yahweh emerging at the beginning of this central narrative of the book, especially in comparison to the similar message in the prologue. Conspicuous by virtue of its absence in chapter 6 is the kind of response that Israel had to the divine word in 2:1–5. There Israel responds with lamentation: "[All the people of Israel] lifted up their voices and wept . . . and they sacrificed to Yahweh there."[137] The reader

137. Even here it is not certain whether Israel's reaction is one of conviction and repentance or whether they are lamenting the announced judgment.

might expect Israel in the face of their infidelity once again to weep or engage in penitential rituals, but instead there is no response at all! The silence is deafening. The prophet's message apparently has no effect on the Israelites, let alone the grief they expressed in 2:4–5. Rather, following the prophetic indictment, the scene changes and the stage is set for the call narrative of the next judge/ deliverer in Israel's cycle of judges.

Gideon's Call (6:11–24)

In the Gideon cycle the theme of leadership takes an unexpected turn. Gideon's reluctance to accept the call to lead may be reminiscent of Barak, but Gideon's call narrative itself contains the formal elements of other call narratives in the Old Testament and resonates particularly with that of Israel's preeminent leader Moses (Exod 3–4).[138] Is the deliberate connection between the call of Moses and the call of Gideon for the purpose of portraying Gideon as "the quintessential biblical hero," as Susan Niditch puts it?[139] Butler, in my mind, seems closer to the mark when he argues that the call-narrative genre is used here for a different purpose than in other call narratives.[140] Of course, expected literary types can function in any number of different ways, and Butler suggests that the call-narrative genre in this context is intended as a parody to portray Gideon not as a second Moses but as an "antitype to Moses."[141]

The call narrative of Gideon begins in 6:11 with the "angel" or "messenger" of Yahweh appearing on the property belonging to Gideon's father. The exact nature of this individual is difficult to pin down. Nothing in his physical appearance causes Gideon to think he is anything but a human being, and yet the messenger does have supernatural abilities (v. 21) and the unfolding events cause Block to conclude that he is no mortal prophet but "a heavenly visitor."[142] In any case, the importance of the messenger is that he is the spokesperson for Yahweh himself—when he speaks, he speaks the words of Yahweh such that the narrator will indicate that Yahweh himself replies to Gideon, even though

138. See the chart in Younger, *Judges and Ruth*, 174–75; Block, *Judges*, 257. Cf. also the call narratives of Saul (1 Sam 9–10), and Jeremiah (Jer 1); Butler, *Judges*, 199.

139. Niditch, *Judges*, 89.

140. Butler, *Judges*, 200.

141. For differences in genre use, see, e.g., the Song of Deborah and the Song of Moses, which are both victory songs but they function, in my opinion, very differently, the former emphasizing the role of the human actors and the latter emphasizing the role of Yahweh. Butler, *Judges*, 200.

142. Block, *Judges*, 259.

it is clear that this is mediated through the messenger (e.g., vv. 14, 16). We also meet Gideon (which means "hacker"[143]) for the first time in 6:11, while he is covertly beating out grain in a winepress, an unlikely spot for this process but one that would conceal him from the Midianite raiders.

The way Gideon's interaction with the divine messenger unfolds is awkward, unexpected, and filled with irony. The messenger begins with a greeting that emphasizes Yahweh's presence and addresses Gideon as a "mighty man of valor" (v. 12).[144] Gideon's response is prickly and expresses his frustration and doubt. In essence, Gideon's first response raises a number of questions that challenge Yahweh's fidelity in his dealing with Israel (6:13):

> Please[145] my lord, if Yahweh is with us then why has all this happened to us? Where are all his wonders that our fathers recounted for us, saying, "Did not Yahweh bring us up from Egypt?" But now Yahweh has forsaken us and given us into the palm of Midian.

In isolation, Gideon's questions seem innocent enough, but on the heels of the prophetic word in 6:7–10 his questions seem unwarranted to say the least. The prophet made it clear that it was Israel and not Yahweh who had broken covenant and not obeyed the voice of Yahweh.[146]

In light of Judg 2:10, which sets the context of Judges in the generations of Israelites who did not know Yahweh and his works on behalf of Israel, it is curious that Gideon does show an awareness of these mighty acts of Yahweh. This raises a theological question: What does it mean to "know" God and his redemptive works? Clearly Gideon's ancestors passed down the stories (at least some of them) but this did not result in a genuine "knowledge" of Yahweh. Gideon's first words seem more like the bitter words of a sulking, self-pitying child who is bearing the consequence of his own actions. It was not Yahweh who had forsaken Israel (v. 13) but Israel who had forsaken Yahweh.

In 6:14 the narrator notes that Yahweh himself turns to answer Gideon. Gideon's skewed interpretation of the situation has not dissuaded Yahweh from using Gideon to save the people. His command for Gideon to go "in this your strength" is ambiguous, and probably means the strength of Yahweh's call upon him to be a warrior of valor, rather than the "strength" of his belligerent re-

143. Block, *Judges*, 258, thinks Gideon ("Hacker") is likely a nickname and that Jerubbaal was his real name.

144. It is not at all clear that the messenger is using this phrase to describe who Gideon is. It's more likely that a mighty man of valor is what Yahweh is calling Gideon to be.

145. בִּי/*bî* is a particle of entreaty; see BDB, 106.

146. Younger, *Judges and Ruth*, 175.

sponse to the divine call.[147] Yahweh's penetrating question "Have I not sent you?" forces Gideon's hand—does he trust and will he obey the divine summons or will fear and unbelief continue to cripple him?

Remarkably, Gideon does find a way to try to evade the responsibility of leadership, in spite of a divine commission and the assurance of Yahweh's presence. In his reply to this commission Gideon verbalizes his misgivings and offers excuses why he is not eligible for the leadership role he is being called to fill (6:15):

> "Please, my lord, how can I save Israel? Look, my clan is the poorest[148] in Manasseh, and I am the least/youngest[149] in my father's house."

These are more like weak excuses of a fearful individual rather than legitimate exemptions for leadership, particularly for those familiar with Israel's stories, which often center around unqualified characters that take up leadership roles in spite of overwhelming odds.

The notion that Gideon's objections come from a place of humility does not hold up to critical scrutiny as other indications in the text suggest that Gideon is not being altogether truthful. Gideon seems to be suggesting that he is of a low social and familial status.[150] This is patently false. Butler notes, "He calls his family the poorest one in the tribe, yet his father owns property and supports a worship place for Baal as we will soon learn. Far from being the poorest or weakest in the tribe, Gideon's father is a clan leader and one of the strongest economically and politically in the tribe."[151] In addition to the fact that Gideon is the son of a clan leader and belongs to a wealthy household that included a cultic shrine, we learn in 6:25 that his father possessed at least one, but probably a number of bulls.[152] Add to this the fact that Gideon himself

147. Webb, *Book of Judges*, 230; Block, *Judges*, 260.

148. Lit. "low, weak, poor, thin"; BDB, 195.

149. Lit. "least, insignificant, young"; BDB, 859. Butler translates ואנכי הצעיר בבית אבי/*wĕʾānōkî haṣṣāʿîr bĕbêt ʾābî* as "and I am the baby in my father's house"; Butler, *Judges*, 181. Amit also understands this phrase as referring to Gideon as the youngest of his father's offspring; see Amit, *Book of Judges*, 254.

150. Amit holds that Gideon's reference to his clan indicates a family military unit, and that as the youngest he may not even be eligible to go to war; see Amit, *Book of Judges*, 254. See also Boling, *Judges*, 132, on בית אב/*bêt ʾāḇ* as a military unit.

151. Butler, *Judges*, 203.

152. There is debate over the translation of this verse and particularly the meaning of פר השני/*par haššēnî*; however, each of the interpretations of פר השני/*par haššēnî* ("prime bull," "exalted bull," "second bull") implies that Gideon's father possessed more than one bull; see the discussions in Butler, *Judges*, 186–87; and Block, *Judges*, 266–67.

has a number of personal servants (at least ten but again most likely more; see 6:27), Gideon's objections based on his social and/or economic standing ring false. Gideon is projecting a false sense of humility and inadequacy to avoid his call to deliver Israel.

Yahweh sees through this facade. In 6:16 he repeats that his presence is with Gideon, a reality that overcomes any shortcomings that Gideon may possess or objections that he might raise. With Yahweh's presence, victory will be a simple task.

This is not enough and still Gideon resists. Only a test will give Gideon the confidence that (1) the source of the call is in fact divine and (2) he does in fact have divine favor.[153] Gideon requests that Yahweh's messenger remain there until Gideon has time to prepare and bring his "gift" or "offering," and the messenger acquiesces: "I will remain until your return" (v. 18).

Gideon carefully prepares and cooks a huge meal, much more than a single person could eat in a sitting, and he presents it to the messenger (v. 19). After giving careful instructions about how the food should be arranged, the messenger sets it aflame with his staff and then mysteriously vanishes.

Up until this point, we might wonder whether or not Gideon was fully aware of the identity of his visitor. Younger maintains that Gideon failed to recognize that it was Yahweh and holds that this is most clearly evident in Gideon's "preoccupation with tangible manifestations of the divine" (see also 6:36–37, 39; 7:10–15; and esp. 8:24–27).[154] Here is perhaps the biggest difference between the call of Moses and the call of Gideon: although Moses did raise objections, he never questions who it is who is calling him, whereas Gideon requires a sign to determine which deity is calling him.[155]

There are other indications that Gideon failed to recognize Yahweh. Until the moment that Yahweh performs the sign (i.e., consuming Gideon's meal with fire) Gideon (1) refers to Yahweh in the third person (see esp. 6:13) and (2) refers to Yahweh/the messenger of Yahweh as אדון/*'ādôn* ("lord" or "master"). Only after the miraculous sign does it finally dawn on Gideon that the divine visitor is Yahweh, and he appropriately declares "Alas, lord Yahweh! I have seen the messenger of Yahweh face to face" (v. 22). Gideon up until this point seems hesitant and perhaps even fearful, but the revelation that his visitor is Yahweh literally puts the fear of death in Gideon. This becomes apparent by Yahweh's reassuring response: "Peace to you. Do not fear. You will not die" (v. 23). Gideon responds appropriately by building an altar to Yahweh there, pro-

153. Block, *Judges*, 262.

154. Younger, *Judges and Ruth*, 175, 180, 182.

155. Bluedorn, *Yahweh Versus Baalism*, 77.

viding perhaps a glimmer of hope for Gideon, who thus far in the narrative is not inspiring much hope for positive leadership in Israel. On the other hand, the sacrifice may be an act of superstition in which the terrified Gideon meant to appease the deity. Gideon was, after all, raised in a home with a shrine to Baal and would be accustomed to the appropriate way to manipulate ancient Near Eastern gods. The scene closes as it opens, with a reference to Ophrah and the Abiezrite clan. How ironic that the place where Gideon was called, where he saw the messenger of Yahweh "face to face," and where he constructs an altar of worship to Yahweh, is the place where Gideon will later set up an idolatrous shrine that will become a snare to all Israel (8:27). But again, according to the logic of ancient Near Eastern religion the most appropriate place for Gideon to set up a shrine would be the place where he experienced the divine.

Yahweh (through Gideon) Battles the Canaanite Deities (6:25–32)

Given that Gideon is specifically called to deliver Israel from the oppression of Midian (6:14, 16), what transpires next in the narrative (6:25–32) comes as a surprise. Typically, one would expect first the call (in Gideon's case the summons to "strike the Midianites as one man" in 6:16) and then the fulfillment of the call (i.e., Gideon doing battle with the Midianites). Thus, Block states, "Under normal circumstances the narrative should have proceeded directly from v. 24 to vv. 33–35, and then on to 7:1."[156] Interrupting Gideon's commission (6:11–24), his call to arms (6:33–35) and Gideon's military campaign against the Midianites (7:1–8:28) are two testing narratives. In the first, Yahweh tests Gideon and in the second Gideon tests Yahweh.

In the evening of the day that Gideon was initially called by Yahweh, he is party to another divine visitation. This time we are not told how Yahweh's message comes to Gideon, but simply that "Yahweh said to him" (v. 25). Yahweh's instructions are detailed, methodical, and about as specific as they could be. The indecisive, fear-ridden Gideon does not need to think and plan but simply carry out the instructions as they are given.

The instructions of Yahweh in 6:25–26 provide, by implication, some key information for understanding the wider circumstances of the events. Preeminent is the fact that in Gideon's own household exist an altar to Baal and a shrine to Asherah. Many commentators note the blatant blending of the worship of Yahweh with that of the Canaanite gods; for example, Butler notes in this regard, "The family has taught Gideon the traditions of the peo-

156. Block, *Judges*, 265.

ple of Yahweh (v. 13), but they practice the rituals of Baal."[157] Secondarily, the wealth of Gideon's family is clearly on display here. Although the Hebrew text is difficult in 6:25, Yahweh seems to be calling Gideon to take two bulls from his herd—one that is used to heavy labor to pull down the stone altar and another premier bull ("seven years old") as a sacrificial animal.[158] Having two bulls and probably more besides, Gideon's family was anything but poor. Add to this the fact that in 6:27 Gideon chooses ten men from among his servants (implying a larger pool of servants he was drawing from), Gideon and his family are exceptionally affluent, which contradicts Gideon's assessment of his social standing in 6:15.

Yahweh commands Gideon to destroy his father's pagan shrine: to dismantle the altar to Baal and to cut down the Asherah pole.[159] On the very site of this pagan cultic site Gideon is called to build an altar to Yahweh and to make a burnt offering on it, an act, according to Block, in which Yahweh is reclaiming the paganized land for himself.[160] Yahweh's mission for Gideon exposes the syncretism that certainly existed in Gideon's household but presumably affected the Israelites more broadly. As Israel's leader and thus their representative, Gideon was meant to be an example of covenant fidelity to Yahweh. As long as the pagan cult remains in his own household, the integrity of Gideon's leadership would be in question. Perhaps even more importantly, this symbolic act removes any doubt as to the source of the coming victory over the Midianites. Had the pagan cult remained in Gideon's father's house, the Israelites might suppose that his success was a result of the power of the pagan gods he worshiped. In an evocative symbolic act, Yahweh calls upon Gideon effectively to sacrifice the pagan gods on the altar to Yahweh.[161]

It would seem that Gideon passes Yahweh's test of his fidelity by immediately carrying out Yahweh's orders: "And Gideon took ten men from his servants and did what Yahweh had told him" (6:27a). However, there is a twist. Rather than letting the reader draw their own conclusions, the narrator explicitly states in 6:27 the less than admirable motivation for Gideon's

157. Butler, *Judges*, 205.

158. For a good summary of the textual difficulty see Webb, *Book of Judges*, 233–35 (especially n. 40).

159. Chisholm sees this action as part of a more broad-ranging polemic in Judges in which Yahweh is shown to be superior to the Canaanite gods; see Chisholm, "Yahweh Versus the Canaanite Gods," 170–71. Cf. Endris, "Yahweh versus Baal," 176.

160. Block, *Judges*, 267.

161. Note 6:26b: "Take the second/prize bull and offer it as a burnt offering on the wood of the Asherah that you cut down." On the sacrifice of the Asherah to Yahweh see Butler, *Judges*, 205, following Bluedorn, *Yahweh Versus Baalism*, 96.

immediate action: "But because he was [too] afraid of his father's household and of the men of the city to do it by day, he did it by night."[162] Gideon is truly a complex individual and his character will develop over the course of the ensuing narrative, but he is still showing himself fearful even in obeying the very specific divine command.[163] His actions in this case, according to the narrator, derive not primarily out of a proper fear of Yahweh but out of fear of his family and friends.[164]

Regardless of his motivation, Gideon obeys the divine order that night. Moreover, here at the center of the book the problem of idol worship, which according to the prologue is the chief issue of the book/period of the Judges, is explicitly combated for the first time in the book of Judges. The first-time reader of Judges may at this point wonder: Is this a turning point in the narrative? Does this powerful symbolic act anticipate an advance on the part of Israel toward covenant faithfulness?

In the ensuing narrative, the men of the town discover the altar to Yahweh in the place of the dismantled pagan shrine (v. 28). Gideon's earlier fear of retaliation proves to be justified. After an investigation into the matter, the townsfolk determine that Gideon is the perpetrator of, what is in their mind, an act of sacrilege, and they sentence Gideon to death (vv. 29–30). That the people of the town come to the defense of Baal is illuminating. Israel's primary problem in the period of the judges as it is articulated at the beginning of the book, namely idolatry and infidelity with regard to Yahweh and his covenant, has remained until this point in the narrative of Judges unspecified, but here at the center of the book it emerges with force. Not only is Ophrah engaged in idol worship, but they fail to understand the symbolic significance of Gideon's act; whereas they ought to have perceived the folly of their idolatry and turned their allegiance toward Yahweh, they instead remain entrenched in their commitment to Baal and advocate on Baal's behalf. As Butler notes, "the Israelites of Ophrah have proven themselves to be perfect Canaanites, protecting Baal in the face of Yahweh's self-evident victory."[165] The significance of this event, however, is not lost on the patron of the now defunct pagan shrine. In a surprising turn of events, Gideon's father Joash turns the legal case against Gideon into a case against Baal and Baal's

162. Block, *Judges*, 267, notes that it is rare for Hebrew narrative to provide a character's internal motivation. Thus, it is all the more significant that the narrative here in 6:27 states in no uncertain terms that it was fear of his kin and townsfolk that moved Gideon to carry out Yahweh's orders at night.

163. Cf. Gideon's fear of death implied in 6:23.

164. See Butler, *Judges*, 206.

165. Butler, *Judges*, 206.

contenders.[166] The townspeople relent, and it appears Gideon has passed Yahweh's test. This part of the narrative closes with Gideon getting a new name: Jerubbaal, with this explanation: "Let Baal contend against him because he broke down his altar" (6:32b).

Although Yahweh's test of Gideon interrupts the call of Gideon to deliver Israel and his military action to that end, there is something fitting about this turn of events. Amit notes, "[the reader] expects the stage of the deliverer's appointment to be followed by liberation, and by Gideon's struggle with the Midianites. However, at God's command Gideon first declares war against the Baal and sets out against the people of his town."[167] As mentioned earlier, the prophetic message of Judg 6:7–10 makes absolutely clear that the problem facing Israel is not in the realm of politics or military strategy, but has to do with allegiance: To whom will Israel commit themselves? Sinai casts Yahweh as the divine king and provides the blueprint for life in Yahweh's realm. The references to the redemption from Egypt and the terms of the covenant at the start of the Gideon narrative (6:7–10) deliberately evoke the Israelites' failed commitment to Yahweh, their true king. Here in 6:25–32, the narrative casts Yahweh as the divine king who demonstrates his rule over against gods that would usurp his reign. The narrative is now poised to exhibit Yahweh's deliverance through his chosen leader Gideon.

Gideon (with Yahweh) Battles the Midianites (6:33–7:23)

The story of deliverance seems back on track in 6:33, with the coalition of Canaanite armies moving into Israelite territory and encamping in the Jezreel Valley. The formidable character of this vast army is emphasized: "*all* the Midianites, the Amalekites, and the people of the East" (emphasis added). Whereas in the previous cycle, Sisera mobilizes his army in response to Barak's marshaling of his troops (4:12–13), here the Canaanite armies jolt Gideon into action.[168]

With this threat on the northern doorstep, Gideon blows the battle horn, summoning first his own clan (the Abiezrites), and then sending messengers throughout his own tribe Manasseh and to the surrounding tribes of Asher, Zebulun, and Naphtali (6:34–35). Remarkably, Gideon's clan (those who were

166. See Butler, *Judges*, 206. One interpretation is that Joash, in coming to the defense of Gideon, has broken his allegiance to Baal. Another interpretation is that Joash has not abandoned his commitment to Baal, but as a good Baalist he allows Baal to fight his own battles. See, e.g., Block, *Judges*, 270.

167. Amit, *Book of Judges*, 226.

168. Butler, *Judges*, 207.

ready to execute him in the previous narrative), his tribe, and the neighboring tribes all respond to Gideon's summons and go up to meet him. Block writes, "This raises an extremely important question: Why are Gideon's clansmen, tribesmen, and countrymen so ready to respond to him? Are they impressed with his leadership ability or his courage? Do they recognize him as the 'Valiant warrior,' whom the messenger of Yahweh had addressed in v. 12?"[169] Clearly, up until this point Gideon is a reluctant leader, seized by fear and doubt. Readers might conclude that Gideon has overcome his trepidation, but the subsequent narrative (Gideon's testing of Yahweh with the fleece) rules that option out. The success of Gideon's battle summons, rather, is a result of the presence of Yahweh with Gideon, empowering him for his divine commission.[170] Previous to Gideon the only other leader in Judges empowered with Yahweh's Spirit is Othniel, the first in the cycle of the judges (3:10).[171] As Yahweh had declared (v. 12) and promised (v. 16), so he delivers as Yahweh's Spirit "clothes" Gideon (v. 34).

The narrative of Israel's deliverance from the Midianite threat is interrupted yet again (vv. 36–40). In spite of his inhibitions Gideon finds himself at the head of a sizable army (see 7:3). With the army poised and ready for his command, Gideon once again demonstrates his doubt and his need for certainty from Yahweh by asking for a sign. Perhaps at this point we should not be surprised, but the brashness of Gideon's unbelief is astounding! Essentially he is acknowledging what Yahweh has said but is not quite sure he can trust it: "If, *as you have spoken*, you will save Israel by my hand . . . [perform this sign of the fleece] . . . then I will know that you will save Israel by my hand, *as you have spoken*" (vv. 36–37; emphasis added). And yet, Yahweh condescends to provide Gideon with the assurances he so desperately desires.

In this familiar story, Gideon tests God twice by means of a fleece. In the first test, Gideon declares that he will trust God to deliver Israel by his hand if the fleece that he lays out in the evening is wet and the ground around it dry in the morning. In the second test, the instructions are reversed: the fleece is to be dry while the ground remains wet. In both cases God humors Gideon in an attempt to allay his doubt. The details of this narrative are worthy of note as we consider the character of Gideon and his role as leader, especially given that "laying out the fleece" has become something of a metaphor for discerning the will of God for contemporary believing readers.

First, the use of the divine name changes in 6:36–40 from the more

169. Block, *Judges*, 271.

170. See Block, *Judges*, 272; and the discussion of Yahweh's Spirit in Butler, *Judges*, 208.

171. However, the remaining major judges subsequent to Gideon, Jephthah and Samson, are both explicitly empowered by Yahweh's spirit (see 11:29; and 13:25; 14:6, 19; 15:14).

personal name of Yahweh as he is revealed at Horeb and Sinai to the more generic name of Elohim. The older diachronic approaches see here a clear indication of the E source, but others suggest that the shift in divine name serves a rhetorical purpose.[172] For example, Butler maintains, "By replacing *Yahweh* with *Elohim*, the narrator places some distance between Gideon and God, distance that had not been there when Gideon was making his commitments and following God's leadership."[173] Some scholars see in the shift an indication of Gideon's difficulty to distinguish Yahweh from the pagan gods (in this case Baal) or perhaps even a deliberate appeal to Baal apart from Yahweh.[174] The latter views would be supported by Younger's conclusion that the "fleecing process" is a clear example of pagan ancient Near Eastern divination practices.[175] According to John Beck, both Baal and Yahweh claimed control over the production of dew and so the test served to demonstrate which deity was sovereign.[176]

Second, it is difficult to comprehend how this narrative of Gideon testing "Elohim" could be regarded as characterizing Gideon in a positive light, that is, as an individual of faith. In spite of repeated promises, five times by Younger's counting, that Yahweh will deliver Israel by the hand of Gideon, Gideon remains resolute in his doubt and demand for further signs.[177] Moreover, one sign using the fleece is not enough for Gideon and he requires a second.[178] J. Cheryl Exum notes, "No character in the book receives more divine assurances than Gideon and no one displays more doubt. Gideon is, significantly, the only judge to whom God speaks directly, though this privilege does not allay his faintheartedness."[179] Block puts it bluntly: "The request for signs is not a sign of faith but of unbelief."[180]

172. For Elohim as indicating the E source, see, e.g., Moore, *Judges*, 198.

173. Butler, *Judges*, 209.

174. For Gideon's problem distinguishing Yahweh from other gods, see Block, *Judges*, 273. For the view that he is appealing to Baal, see Polzin, *Moses*, 170–71: "since Gideon like his fellow citizens, has been a Baal worshiper who was recently put to the test by Yahweh, it may be that Gideon is now intent upon putting his own god to the test—whoever he may be, probably Baal—in a time of crisis. With Yahweh *and* 'God' on his side, how can he lose?" (171; emphasis original).

175. Younger, *Judges and Ruth*, 188.

176. Beck, "Gideon," 37.

177. Younger, *Judges and Ruth*, 185; the five times are 6:36; 7:2, 7, 9, 14–15.

178. Perhaps the fleece in the first test absorbed the moisture from the evening dew and retained the moisture even after the dew dried up the following morning. In such case, Gideon may have realized his blunder (i.e., that there was a natural explanation for the wet fleece and the dry ground) and thus requests another round of testing. Butler, *Judges*, 209, suggests as much. See also Younger, *Judges and Ruth*, 188.

179. Exum, "Centre Cannot Hold," 416.

180. Butler, *Judges*, 272–73.

Third, the narrator depicts God as eerily silent in this fleece testing narrative. Gideon initiates the fleece testing ("And Gideon said to Elohim"), and though God does indeed deliver on both of Gideon's requests for a sign, he does not respond verbally. Silence, of course, is difficult to interpret. Is the old dictum "actions speak louder than words" at work here? Is God simply and graciously responding to Gideon's request? Or is there something more to the silence? Is this a silence of disapproval? It is difficult to be sure but clearly the promised word of Yahweh is not sufficient to give Gideon the confidence he needs to lead the Israelite army.

Fourth, the need for two signs of the fleece may point to Gideon's ineptitude. According to the natural order of things, the wool fleece would have absorbed the moisture from the dew so that when the morning came the sun would have dried the ground, but the fleece would have naturally remained damp. No doubt realizing his blunder, Gideon requests a second sign that would require a miracle. Things are not boding well for Israel's new leader. All of these subtleties of the text and the broader context should probably give contemporary readers pause before drawing in the fleecing test as a paradigm for discovering God's will today.

The narrative picks up in 7:1 where it left off in 6:35 with Gideon and his army encamped opposite of the Midianite camp. The scene is set for the now long-expected battle, but yet again the battle is delayed. This time Yahweh initiates another test of sorts, requiring Gideon to put his complete trust in Yahweh. Comparing Gideon's motivation for requesting the sign of the fleece and Yahweh's motivation for culling the Israelite army reveals an intriguing irony. Gideon desires certainty that his "hand" (יד/*yād*) will be the means of Israel's salvation: "If you will save Israel by my hand" (6:36). Yahweh, on the other hand, wants to dispel any confidence that the Israelites may have in their own power or ability; he pares the Israelite army to a mere three hundred men, "lest they glorify themselves over against me, saying, 'my [own] hand [יד/*yād*] has delivered me'" (7:2).[181] Moreover, whereas in 6:36–40 Gideon confronts God and manipulates God to give him a sign while God remains silent, here in 7:1–8 Yahweh first engages Gideon and gives Gideon his orders while Gideon remains quiet. That fearful Gideon is struck dumb as his army is deliberately dwindled down to a mere three hundred soldiers is understandable.

Gideon's army is culled in two stages. First, Yahweh instructs Gideon to give a pass to "whoever is fearful and trembling" (v. 3) The fact that more than two-thirds of the troops (twenty-two thousand of the thirty-two thousand

181. The "hand" motif is strong in the Gideon narrative. The word יד/*yād* appears no less than sixteen times over the course of chs. 6–8. See 6:14, 36, 37; 7:2, 5, 7, 8, 9, 11, 14, 15, 20; 8:3, 6, 7, 15.

men) take their leave is indicative of the lack of resolve of Gideon's army and the intimidation they felt at the prospect of facing the Canaanite forces. Given Gideon's track record, it is remarkable that he maintained his resolve having lost so many men.[182] However, Yahweh is not finished yet.

Commentators have puzzled over the drinking test that Yahweh devises to further reduce the number of troops (vv. 4–7). The attempt is made to draw some significance between the drinking test and military fitness. On the one hand are those who argue that those who lapped the water like dogs were more attentive and alert (a good quality for a solder) than those who knelt; on the other hand are others who hold the exact opposite: the kneelers were more alert and better suited for military action.[183] Younger maintains that the process has no significance and is "based on purely arbitrary criteria."[184] If there is a greater significance to the test, it is apparently lost to us. However, the test fulfills the primary purpose that Yahweh had intended. In 7:7, he addresses Gideon again, promising Gideon that the three hundred are enough for the victory Yahweh has planned, and he instructs Gideon to dismiss the others (i.e., the kneelers). Still remaining silent, Gideon seems compliant, sending everyone but the three hundred "to his tent."[185] This scene ends with Gideon looking out over the Midianite camp, stretched out in the valley below. Surely, the battle scene will come next.

One last time the battle report is delayed as Yahweh yet again provides fearful Gideon with assurance of victory. That very night Yahweh commands Gideon to take his three hundred troops, and, with Yahweh's assurance of victory ("I have given [the Midianite camp] into your hand"), invade the Midianite camp (7:9). However, Yahweh accounts for Gideon's fear and adds this proviso: "If you are afraid to go down, then go down to the camp with Purah, your young servant. And you will hear what they are saying, and afterward your hands will be strengthened, and you will go down into the camp" (7:10–11). Without hesitation, Gideon eagerly takes Yahweh up on his offer, clearly implying that he is still full of fear in spite of miraculous signs and divine assurances. Verse 12 describes the overwhelming vastness of the Midianite army and their camels—a truly formidable scene!

182. Webb, *Book of Judges*, 242.

183. For a helpful roundup of interpretations see Butler, *Judges*, 212–13.

184. Younger, *Judges and Ruth*, 189.

185. It is not entirely clear if sending the majority to their "tents" (Hebrew root אהל/*'ōhel*) in 7:8 is what Yahweh had in mind when he indicated in 7:7 that they should go to their "place" (מקם/*māqōm*). The Hebrew word מקם/*māqōm* has quite a range of meaning including city, place of human abode, locality. However, it can also mean a "station" where soldiers are placed or a military "post." Some hold that the majority were not in fact sent home but to the military camp; see Block, *Judges*, 277; Butler, *Judges*, 213.

At this point we may be wondering: What will be sufficient enough to allay Gideon's fear and motivate him to embrace his leadership role? The answer presents itself in 7:13–14 and consists of a Midianite soldier's dream and his companion's interpretation of it. The man dreamed that a loaf of bread rolled into the camp, hit the tent and overturned the tent; his comrade is sure of the meaning: "This is none other than the sword of Gideon the son of Joash, a man of Israel. God has given into his hand Midian and all the camp" (7:14). This revelation causes a dramatic change in Gideon: he immediately worships and then actively takes up his leadership role. There does seem to be some irony in the fact that in the end what prompts Gideon to action is not Yahweh's repeated verbal and symbolic assurances, but the dream of a foreign soldier and his companion's interpretation of it.[186] Verse 15 is the last time Gideon worships.[187]

Gideon rallies his three hundred men with the assurance that Yahweh has delivered the Midian armies into their hand (v. 15b). He divides the men into three groups, instructs them to station themselves at strategic locations outside the camp, and charges them to do as he does: at the sound of his horn, they are to blow their own horns and cry out "For Yahweh and for Gideon" (vv. 16–18).

The events recounted in 7:15–18 are pivotal—they represent a significant turning point in the portrayal of Gideon, in the fourth cycle, and in the book as a whole. The decisive action of Gideon, according to Block, "reflects an amazing personal transformation."[188] Gone for good is Gideon's spirit of fear and hesitation. Though we may expect (or at least hope) a spirit of humility and obedience would take its place, instead fear and hesitation give way to *self*-confidence and *self*-importance. At this point, Gideon is willing to share the glory ("and for Gideon") but as events unfold he becomes more and more the power-crazed tyrant, eliminating anyone who stands against his quest for absolute power.

At long last, 7:19–23 reports the events of the main battle. As with the previous cycles, the battle report is brief. Essentially, the narrator reports that the events of the battle unfolded as Gideon had instructed. We now learn how the clay jars and the torches mentioned in 7:16 are used to create a sense of intimidation and chaos. Amidst the pandemonium, Yahweh turns the Canaanite soldiers against each other (v. 22a). Those who managed to escape the swords of their fellow Canaanites flee south and east, back into the desert.[189]

186. Younger, *Judges and Ruth*, 190.

187. Younger, *Judges and Ruth*, 191. See the discussion in Culp, *Puzzling Portraits*, 78–81, regarding the lack of an object for the verb "worship." Culp and others contend that this deliberately creates ambiguity regarding the object of Gideon's worship. Is Gideon really worshiping Yahweh, or perhaps himself or even Baal? The reader must wrestle with this troubling question!

188. Block, *Judges*, 281.

189. Block, *Judges*, 283.

Similar to the battle in the previous cycle, the battle against the Midianites is over in just a few verses; moreover, after the initial victory against the Midianites a chase ensues followed by the defeat and death of those who fled—similar to the escape and murder of Sisera in chapter 4.[190] Verse 23 provides a curious and puzzling bit of information; with the Midianites on the run, we are told that troops from the tribes of Naphtali, Asher, and Manassah are rallied and take up the pursuit. We can be quite certain that Gideon recalls here the army that had originally taken up his summons—the 22,000 fearful men (v. 3) and the 9700 kneelers (v. 6) whom Gideon had dismissed.[191] Was it Gideon's plan from the beginning to draw on these men as a reserve army in spite of Yahweh's design to use the army of 300? Retrospectively, it seems that is precisely what Gideon had planned (at least with regard to the kneelers). Yahweh had commanded that the men who had been culled should be sent "each to his place/abode" (מקם/*māqōm*) but when it comes time to dismiss them Gideon sends "each to his tent" (אהל/*'ōhel*). By recalling these troops, Gideon has undermined the whole purpose behind reducing the army—that the people would recognize that Yahweh grants the victory.[192] Gideon has taken matters into his own hands.

Gideon and Ephraim (7:24–8:3)

Apparently, the reserve armies are insufficient in Gideon's estimation. While in hot pursuit of the fleeing Canaanites, he sends messengers to summon the tribe of Ephraim to take and hold strategic locations. "All the men of Ephraim" take up the call, are successful in battle, and they capture and behead two Midianite princes (vv. 24–25). Surely the victory is now complete, and rest will ensue.

However, the story is not over, and as it drags on things seem to spiral out of control. What happens next is like the scene from a movie (8:1–3). We can imagine the bloodied and tired warriors of Ephraim coming before Gideon and callously tossing the severed heads of the Midianite princes at his feet. The tension is palpable, as the Ephraimites bring their complaint: why hadn't

190. Block, *Judges*, 283, notes the progression from the previous cycle to this cycle: "The sight of the enemy in flight amplifies the picture of Barak's pursuit of Sisera in 4:17. In place of one individual pursuing another, however, we now witness the remnant of an entire camp fleeing from a force of three hundred Israelites."

191. Block, *Judges*, 283; Butler, *Judges*, 215; Webb, *Book of Judges*, 249.

192. See esp. Block, *Judges*, 283–84; and the roundup of commentators who see this as undermining Yahweh in Butler, *Judges*, 215–16. However, Webb, *Book of Judges*, 249, regards Gideon's recalling of the army as quite a natural decision and does not identify any negative connotations in the text.

Gideon summoned them when he first went to battle? The text indicates that "they contended vehemently with him" (v. 1b).[193] We are not told why Ephraim feels slighted but should be curious how Gideon will respond.[194] At this point, Gideon calculates that a careful diplomatic response would be prudent. He appeals eloquently to their vanity. Anything that Gideon had achieved pales in comparison to the mighty feat of the Ephraimites (vv. 2–3): "Elohim" gave the Midianite princes "into your hands [יד/*yād*]." With these words, Gideon defuses a potentially explosive situation.

Gideon Settles the Score (8:4–21)

Although the transformation of Gideon is not fully complete until the end of the chapter, the events surrounding his pursuit of the Midianite kings, including his dealings with the Israelite cities of Succoth and Penuel, represent a significant phase in his metamorphosis.

The deaths of the Midianite princes did not end the war, and in 8:4 the action follows Gideon and his three hundred men—"exhausted and in pursuit." Gideon, it seems, has bigger fish to fry! At this point in the narrative we are in the dark, but for some reason Gideon is absolutely resolute in his pursuit of the Midianite kings. Judges 8:4–21 unfold as follows:

A Gideon requests help from Succoth, is denied help, and promises revenge.
  B Gideon requests help from Penuel, is denied help, and promises revenge.
    C Gideon captures the Midianite kings Zebah and Zalmunna.
A′ Gideon exacts revenge on Succoth.
  B′ Gideon exacts revenge on Penuel.
    C′ Gideon exacts revenge on Zebah and Zalmunna.

As Gideon and his three hundred men are pursuing the two kings of Midian, Gideon asks first Succoth (8:4–7) and then Penuel (8:8–9) for aid—sustenance for the exhausted men. Both towns refuse, mocking Gideon for his lack of success. In both cases, Gideon promises that he will in fact be victorious and when he is he will certainly return to deal with their disrespectful snub.

193. Alter *Ancient Israel*, 150. Block, *Judges*, 285, notes that the Hebrew verb used here (ריב/*rîḇ*) is a "legal term, which appeared earlier in 6:2, [and] means 'to contend, to challenge, to conduct a legal case.'"

194. Niditch, *Judges*, 103, argues that because they were not called out to war they would not be entitled to the spoils of war nor the glory of victory. This, according to Niditch, accounts for the tension between Ephraim and Gideon.

Gideon does indeed catch up with the Midianites forces (vv. 10–11). Only in 8:10 do we get a clear sense of the size of the Canaanite army and their devastation at the hands of Yahweh and the Israelite army. The army of 120,000 sword-wielders had been reduced to a mere 15,000 men. Even so, that is still a sizable foe for Gideon and his 300 men. This time Gideon does not hesitate for a moment. Gideon and his force rout the remaining Midianite army, pursue the fleeing Midianite kings, and take the two kings captive (8:11–12).

On his return trip, Gideon makes good on his promise of revenge on the towns of Succoth and Penuel. Gideon flogs the seventy-seven leaders of Succoth as he had vowed (8:13–16). Upon his return to Penuel he not only tears down the tower of Penuel as he had promised but his thirst for vengeance is quenched only when the men of the city are dead (8:17). The Song of Deborah already indicated a lack of unity among the Israelite tribes. The incident between Gideon and Ephraim demonstrated outright hostility among the Israelite people, though in that instance, bloodshed was averted. Here is the first time in the book where Israelites shed the blood of fellow Israelites . . . and it won't be the last.

The scene shifts in 8:18 to Gideon's dealing with the Midianite kings Zebah and Zalmunna. We might be wondering why on earth is Gideon so hell-bent on pursuing these kings, and 8:18–21 provide the answer. Having relentlessly pursued these two kings and finally captured them, Gideon initiates the conversation with this question: "Where are the men whom you killed at Tabor?" Nothing in the narrative thus far prepares the reader for the revelation that these kings are responsible for the deaths of Gideon's brothers, as their answer indicates: "As you are so are they: each resembled the sons of the king."

This revelation, a "surprise element" in the narrative, helps to explain the recklessness with which Gideon pursued the Midianite kings (they killed his brothers), but even more significantly it subtly but unmistakably foregrounds the connection between Gideon and kingship.[195] This event, according to Butler, "allows the narrator to introduce an important theme into the book of Judges, that of kingship. . . . For the first time, the thought is slipped into the reader's mind that Gideon may have come from royal stock, or that he may be on the road to royal rule."[196] Similarly, Webb notes, "this verse provides the first link between Gideon himself and kingship. In the eyes of the two kings of Mid-

195. Quotation from Butler, *Judges*, 220.

196. Butler, *Judges*, 220. This may also shed light on the social standing of Gideon's clan and household, a standing that he downplays in his call narrative but which, by all accounts, is significant indeed. Perhaps a link exists between cult-centralization in Gideon's household and his family's political and royal aspirations.

ian, Gideon's murdered brothers *each had the bearing of a royal son*. Literally, they were like the 'sons of the king (*hammelek*).' It indirectly raises the issue of how king-like Gideon himself has become in his own eyes, and in the eyes of his followers," not to mention in the eyes of his enemies![197]

Furthermore, two peculiar actions of Gideon with regard to these two kings are also revealing. He urges his young firstborn son to carry out the execution of Zebah and Zalmunna. Not unlike the "early" Gideon, his son is too afraid to do this deed. Why would Gideon demand such a thing of his young son? A number of things may be going on here, but at the very least it seems that Gideon is attempting to confer some leadership experience, perhaps symbolically, on his firstborn son, who is after all the most obvious successor according to a model of hereditary rule.[198] This episode ends with Gideon killing the Midianite kings himself and seizing the special ornaments of the royal camels (v. 21). Of course, a successful warrior laying claim to the spoils of his victory is not unprecedented, but is there a deeper significance to Gideon appropriating for himself symbols of royalty?[199] The subtle (and not so subtle) clues suggest that Gideon is behaving like royalty.

King Gideon—A King like the Kings of the Nations (8:22–27)

One might expect that the climax of the Gideon story would be his victory over the Midianites; however, the structure of the narrative suggests that Gideon being offered dynastic rule and his fashioning of the ephod (8:22–28) constitute the climax, followed by an epilogue that reports Gideon's death and legacy (8:29–35).[200] Apparently impressed with Gideon's military feats, the men of Israel demand the establishment of dynastic rule beginning with Gideon and his offspring. The request initially strikes one as surprising—in Butler's words, "a totally unexpected narrative twist."[201] With the foreign enemies subdued,

197. Webb, *Book of Judges*, 258 (emphasis original).

198. See Webb, *Book of Judges*, 259 who notes, "the fact that Jether is Gideon's *firstborn* raises the issue of succession in some sense, and the way Gideon commands Jether to *Arise and kill* Zebah and Zalmunna instead of doing it himself entails a delegation of power to him that is highly suggestive" (emphasis original). See also Butler, *Judges*, 220.

199. See Block, *Judges*, 299

200. Butler, *Judges*, 221 says at this point in the narrative, "Finally, we approach the narrator's climactic moment." See also Webb *An Integrated Reading*, 146: "With this [the offer of dynastic rule], Gideon has reached the peak of his power and influence, and this, rather than his victory over the kings becomes the true climax of the second movement and, retrospectively, of the story as a whole."

201. Butler, *Judges*, 221.

the pattern of the cycle raises the expectation that the Gideon cycle has run its course, but in fact the narrative continues. The choice of words in 8:22 gives the impression that all of Israel (a collective singular which is literally "the man of Israel"[202]) is united and speak with one voice in their demand for a king.[203] This is the first time since the exposition at the beginning of the book that Israel is portrayed as acting cohesively.

Gideon's response to the offer of hereditary kingship sounds pious and orthodox: "I will not rule over you, nor will my son rule over you; Yahweh will rule over you" (v. 23). What are we to make of this exchange between the Israelites and Gideon? First, the request indicates that the Israelites acknowledge a problem in the stability of their nation, but also that they think that the solution to the instability is political; in other words, according to the Israelites the institution of defined and continuous (hereditary) leadership will bring the political stability they desperately desire. Moreover, their choice of Gideon to inaugurate this institution of leadership exposes their working assumption that good leadership is defined by political and military prowess. However, this line of thinking should immediately arouse the suspicion of the careful reader of Judges at this point.

As we have seen, the problem of the Israelites in this period in their history and as framed by the book of Judges is not primarily a political or military one, but has to do foremost with Israel's religious orientation. By demanding dynastic monarchy Israel is (rightly) acknowledging their need to break out of the cycle, an important insight here at the center of the book. However, their desire also demonstrates that they have fundamentally failed to understand the impetus that is driving the cycle, namely, their infidelity with regard to Yahweh and his covenant.

Second, while the narrative suggests that the Israelites have misinterpreted the cycle that has been driving their immediate history, it also suggests that they have not rightly interpreted the deliverance they have just experi-

202. In Hebrew: איש־ישׂראל/*'îš-yiśrā'ēl*. Block, *Judges*, 296–297, notes, "while we can only speculate about how many men were in the delegation that approached Gideon, the narrator sees them as representing the entire nation . . . the author deliberately characterizes them as (lit.) 'the men of Israel' . . . making this look like a pan-Israelite assembly offering rule over the entire nation."

203. The word "king" (מלך/*melek*) does not appear here but it seems certain that this is what the Israelites have in mind. Block supposes that the narrator may have deliberately avoided the term מלך/*melek* because the actions of the מלך/*melek* that the Israelites look to Gideon to perform belong exclusively to Yahweh; see Block, *Judges*, 297. See also Butler, *Judges*. Many commentators simply assume that kingship is the mode of rule that the Israelites had in mind: Moore, *Judges*, 229–30; Boling, *Judges*, 159–61; Younger, *Judges and Ruth*, 203–10; Ryan, *Judges*, 62; Niditch, *Judges*, 105–6.

enced by means of Gideon's leadership, though perhaps for good reason.[204] In choosing Gideon to deliver Israel from the Midianite oppression, Yahweh went to great lengths to remove any doubt that he was the ultimate source of Israel's deliverance. His reason for whittling down the initially large Israelite army was so that they would know that their deliverance is not by means of human strength but by the "hand of Yahweh" (7:2). However, as the narrative unfolds Gideon progressively undermines—perhaps even usurps—Yahweh's role in this regard, first by sharing with Yahweh in the glory of the battle (7:18; 20) and by then conducting the war against Midian as if it were his own personal vendetta.[205]

Gideon himself undermines Yahweh's reduction of the army when he calls out Israelite reinforcements from the surrounding regions (7:23, 24) after the initial success of the band of three hundred in 7:19–22.[206] Whereas the intent of Yahweh intervening in the political and military affairs of Israel in the book of Judges thus far, and particularly in the Gideon narrative, is always to encourage the Israelites to put their trust in Yahweh, the actions of Gideon have been to effect the opposite. Webb states, "The slayer of kings has *ipso facto* achieved kingly status in the eyes of his followers, who now attribute their escape from the Midianite yoke directly to him, and make this the basis of their offer that he and his family should rule Israel in perpetuity."[207] As the narrative continues the reader realizes that their confidence in Gideon leads them not only to trust in a human deliverer but also leads them (back) into pagan worship (8:24–27).

The exchange between the Israelites and Gideon in 8:22–23 is significant, third, for the response of Gideon Clearly Gideon's character has developed over the course of the narrative, from the fearful and sign-seeking individual in chapter 6, to the increasingly confident military general in chapter 7, and finally to the relentless punisher and cold executioner in chapter 8. Given his swelling confidence in his leadership role, one would expect that Gideon would immediately seize the offer of dynastic kingship rather than politely refusing it. However, as pious sounding as his response seems, it is, arguably, a calculated manipulation of religious orthodoxy to advance his own personal and political agenda.[208] The literary context, as Webb points out, makes a

204. Block, *Judges*, 297–98, also makes this argument.

205. See Boling, *Judges*, 152: Gideon "took the federal militia into the field, beyond the river, in pursuit of merely personal vengeance."

206. See Klein, *Triumph*, 57–58; Block, *Judges*, 283; Bluedorn, *Yahweh Versus Baalism*, 146–48; Butler, *Judges*, 215.

207. Webb, *Book of Judges*, 262.

208. Some scholars maintain that Gideon was genuine in his refusal of kingship. E.g., Niditch, *Judges*, 105, writes, "In no uncertain terms, the hero rejects dynastic monarchy, for Yhwh is king." Similarly, Ryan, *Judges*, 62, maintains, "[Gideon] refuses the offer to be Israel's dynastic

positive evaluation of Gideon's motivations difficult to maintain: "From the outset of the second movement of the narrative [8:4–28] he has acted more and more like a king, especially in his dispensing of summary justice on those who have resisted his authority. In crossing the Jordan he had already exceeded his commission and begun to move toward the kind of rule that is now offered him."[209] However, is there any further evidence that suggests that Gideon was less than sincere in his refusal of hereditary kingship? In short, yes, the evidence is overwhelming!

We have already seen the first cluster of clues that Gideon had royal aspirations in his dealings with the Midianite kings (his resemblance to a son of a king, his command to his firstborn son to execute Zebah and Zalmunna, his seizing of the royal crescents). As the narrative continues the evidence mounts. A second cluster of clues to Gideon's kingly motives center around his request of gold and the fashioning of the ephod. No sooner had Gideon "refused" the offer of kingship than he requests that the assembly yield to him some of their spoils of war (v. 24). The request of a share of the spoils of war is, according to Block, doubly significant. It represents a symbolic gesture of the Israelites' submission as vassals to Gideon, a status they yield without hesitation. Also, the large quantity of gold that Gideon's request garners "takes on the character of a royal treasure. Seventeen hundred shekels of gold amounts to 43 pounds [20 kg]. This is indeed a treasure fit for a king!"[210] Additionally, among the Israelites' offering, the text specifically identifies items that symbolize royalty: "crescent amulets, pendants, and purple garments worn by the kings of Midian" and "the collars that were around the necks of their [the kings'] camels" (v. 26).[211] The collection of war spoils supports the notion that Gideon was taking on a kingly role.

Verse 27 notes that Gideon made an ephod. Following the collection of the spoils of war, the narrative says: "And Gideon made it into an ephod and set it up in his city, in Ophrah. And all Israel whored after it there, and it became a snare to Gideon and to his household" (8:27). The ephod of itself is benign enough and on its own may not arouse suspicion. It is sufficiently plain from elsewhere in the Old Testament that an ephod was an elaborately designed high-priestly garment (see Exod 28, 35, 39; Lev 8) that the high priest donned when seeking the divine will for specific circumstances (e.g., 1 Sam 23:9–12; 30:7–8). Lesser ephods also appear in biblical narrative (e.g., a linen ephod) that are also

---

king and reminds the 'men of Israel' that they live in a theocracy, Yahweh rules over them and they are to remain in covenant loyalty."

209. Webb, *Book of Judges*, 263.

210. Block, *Judges*, 299–300.

211. Block, *Judges*, 300.

associated with priestly or tabernacle-related offices (1 Sam 2:18; 22:18), and in one case David wears a linen ephod (2 Sam 6:14). However, based upon the kinds of materials that the Israelites offer for the ephod, we can safely assume that Gideon's ephod is in the likeness of the high-priestly ephod.[212]

Conspicuous because of its absence is any mention of a high priest who could legitimately wear Gideon's ephod. Block suggests a link between the ephod here and an Akkadian cognate *epattu*, "which, in several Old Assyrian texts apparently refers to the costly garments worn by high officials and/or draped over images of the gods."[213] According to Block "ephod" in the context of Judg 8:26–27 is a synecdoche, referring to the garment but also an image over which the garment was placed.[214] Younger agrees, noting that the amount of gold and use of the term "set up" suggest a cultic image or idol in addition to the ephod.[215] Another telling piece of evidence in identifying Gideon's ephod comes from the end section of the book of Judges itself. In chapters 17–18, Micah fashions an ephod that is associated with carved images and later becomes part of the cultic center in Dan.

The most positive interpretation of Gideon's actions in this matter is that the making of the ephod is consistent with his sincere rejection of kingship. In other words, the ephod would provide the means of determining the will of the only true king, Yahweh.[216] According to this understanding, Gideon had pious intentions and could not have anticipated that this symbol of Yahwism would become a means of apostasy. In my opinion, this seems unlikely given the character of Gideon leading up to and subsequent to this event. That aside, Gideon's culpability, it would seem, is bound up with what precisely he "made" and "set up." This sight became an idolatrous place of worship, implying more than simply a linen garment.

Thus, either Gideon was ignorant or willfully indifferent regarding the proper worship of Yahweh. The result of his action, however, is devastatingly clear: national apostasy. Gideon and his household become ensnared by this "ephod" (which calls into question whether this is purely a symbol of Yahwism),

212. So Webb, *Book of Judges*, 264.

213. Block, *Judges*, 300.

214. A synecdoche is a figure of speech in which the whole of a thing is represented by a part of the thing.

215. Younger, *Judges and Ruth*, 205–6. See also Butler, *Judges*, 222.

216. See, e.g., Ryan, *Judges*, 65. Webb supposes that "the ephod which Gideon made was probably intended as a symbol of divine government according to the Mosaic ideal," but he admits that the episode is "unnervingly" similar to the golden calf incident in Exod 32; Webb, *Book of Judges*, 264. Even Niditch, who generally regards Gideon as a hero, sees the ephod incident as evidence of a character flaw in Gideon (though she does not specify if this is a case of Gideon's good intentions gone awry or if he willfully led Israel into apostasy); Niditch, *Judges*, 105–6.

but more significantly the whole nation, "all Israel," falls into the trap of Gideon's "ephod."

Does Gideon's fashioning of the ephod betray any latent royal aspirations? Block maintains that the fashioning and setting up of the ephod is typical of a monarch's function as sponsor of the cult. Of course, this would not be the only time in Israel's recorded history that a royal figure dedicated the spoils of war for cultic purposes. For example, in 1 Chr 26:26–27, David and his armies dedicate war booty for the maintenance of the temple. Furthermore, this would not be the only time that the setting up of a cultic center in a strategic location would serve political purposes. Jeroboam set up the golden calves at Bethel and Dan for the expressed purpose of keeping the citizens of the Northern Kingdom loyal to him (1 Kgs 12:28–29). We should also note the role of ancient Near Eastern kings in the maintenance of cultic shrines and images. It seems no mistake that Gideon sets up the shrine in his home city. Thus, Gideon's request of the spoils of war, the specific items that the Israelites yield, and Gideon's fashioning of the ephod, and his strategic placement of it all have potential royal overtones and seem to run contrary to Gideon's verbal refusal of hereditary kingship.

As pious as his rejection of hereditary kingship sounds, Gideon misunderstands the divine economy in Yahweh's kingdom. Hereditary monarchy is no less legitimate a form of government than rule by elders or charismatic leaders. Nevertheless, any and all kinds of political government that blatantly disregard Yahweh's intention for Israel, forged in the Sinai covenant and enshrined in the Torah, are illegitimate.[217] Deuteronomy 17:14–20 is clear about the qualities of a king and of the three prohibitions (he should not acquire many horses, many wives, or much silver/gold). Gideon falls prey to the latter two, and of the prescriptions mentioned Gideon is not clearly chosen by Yahweh to be king and he does not write down and observe the Torah. Thus, the irony of the situations thickens: Gideon verbally rejected kingship to honor Yahweh as the divine king (which demonstrates his lack of understanding regarding the kingdom of Yahweh, which made provisions for kingship), but actually conducts himself like a king in all sorts of ways that dishonor the divine monarch and display his disregard for Yahweh's sovereign rule. Leadership in Israel has most certainly reached a new low with Gideon.

The epilogue of the Gideon cycle (8:29–35) provides further evidence of Gideon's royal ambitions. But first the final element of the cycle appears in 8:28.

217. Niditch may go too far in seeing in Judges (as in Deut 17:14–20) a kind of grudging acceptance of kingship as a political reality. However, I think it is correct to see a measure of ambivalence with regard to the type of political governance, as long as the rule facilitates covenant fidelity. See Niditch, "Judges, Kingship, and Political Ethics," 63.

The Land Experiences Rest (8:28)

As we have come to expect, the cycle is completed with a note about Israel's foreign enemies being "subdued" (see 3:30; 4:23) and the land experiencing rest. A kind of symmetry exists between the beginning of the cycle (6:6a) in which "Israel was brought low" because of the foreign oppression and the end of the cycle (8:28b), which states that as a result of their subjugation the Midianites "no longer raised their heads." The period of rest during the days of Gideon is forty years in length, the same number of restful years that followed Deborah/Barak/Jael (5:31b).

Gideon's Legacy . . . and Progeny (8:29–35)

With the final element of the cyclical pattern, we expect the Gideon cycle to be complete. This final section seems to serve both as an epilogue to Gideon's story and an introduction to his son Abimelech's story. On first glance, 8:29–35 seems an appropriate ending to Gideon's narrative, summarizing his "retirement" years, his progeny, and rounding off with a note about his longevity, death, and burial in good patriarchal fashion (cf. Gen 25:8; 35:29; Job 42:17). What did Gideon get up to in his "retirement" years? What was the character of his life after his military success? And why is this information included here?

Verse 29 refers to Gideon as "Jerubbaal, son of Joash." This seems a subtle reminder that although he once tore down the altar to Baal, he is very much his father's son—one who looks like a king's son (8:18) and who establishes an idolatrous household shrine. What follows provides clear evidence that Gideon fancied himself a king and conducted himself accordingly.

Gideon accumulated a harem of "many wives" (including at least one concubine) and he sired seventy plus one sons (not to mention daughters).[218] Private citizens do not generally establish a harem and have dozens and dozens of children. If at this point there was any doubt about Gideon's royal ambitions, the name Gideon himself gives to his son should eliminate it altogether. Gideon names his son Abimelech, which translates *My-Father-Is-King*!

Webb is right to suggest that "Gideon's household as it is described in these verses looks far more like that of a ruler than of a private citizen. Indeed,

218. Hauser holds that Gideon had made a treaty with Shechem, "the treaty sealed by Gideon's marriage to a Shechemite concubine," and he cites examples in 2 Sam 3:3; 1 Kgs 3:1; 7:8; 11:1–3 where marriage serves to seal treaties. Each of these cases involves Israelite kings, either David or Solomon; Hauser, "Unity and Diversity," 299; also referenced in Butler, *Judges*, 222.

it seems that his retirement was more symbolic than real."[219] Block supposes that the establishment of Gideon's hometown as the cultic center meant that Ophrah effectively became Gideon's capital, and the note in 8:29 that Gideon "dwelt/sat" connotes enthronement (cf. Pss 9:7; 29:10; 61:7; 102:12; Isa 10:13; Lam 5:19).[220] Indeed, "Jerubbaal, the uncrowned king, goes back home to live out his remaining years, or perhaps to live enthroned his remaining years."[221]

Verses 33–35 indicate the situation after Gideon's death. The amazing feats that Yahweh performed in and through Gideon seem to have no effect. The Israelites "whore" after the Baals and make "Baal-Berith" ("Baal/master of the Covenant") their god. The narrative now turns to focus on Gideon's son "My-Father-Is-King," further demonstrating the legacy of Gideon.

Leading up to Gideon we have observed movement in the types of Israelite leaders. Othniel stands as the paragon: a proven warrior, a Judahite, and one who by all accounts acted decisively and unhesitatingly to deliver Israel. Ehud is the first in a series of unlikely or unexpected leaders. He was left-handed and from the tribe of Benjamin, but like Othniel he successfully led the Israelites into battle against the foreign oppression. As a foreigner Shamgar seems an unlikely deliverer, but he too saved Israel. In the Deborah/Barak narrative Deborah's gender qualifies her to be an unexpected deliverer but that role seems reserved for Barak. In the end Barak's fear and hesitation disqualify him and the honor of victory would go to a woman—not Deborah but Jael, the wife of an Israelite traitor. In the first half of his narrative, Gideon resembles his predecessor Barak: hesitant, fearful, and unwilling to lead unconditionally. However, in the second half of the narrative, Gideon's cowardice turns to confidence, his doubt to determination, and his (false) self-deprecation to self-aggrandizement. In the transformed Gideon, readers encounter an unprecedented kind of leadership, namely, one driven by personal revenge and the thirst for power.

The Gideon narrative contains a number of firsts. Gideon is the first in the cycle of Israelite leaders to confront idolatry by tearing down the altar to Baal and Ashtoreth, but by the end he becomes the first deliverer to effect pan-Israelite idolatry and apostasy. Gideon is clearly not the first leader to defeat Israel's enemies on the battlefield, but he is the first judge confronted with internal strife. In the case of Ephraim he acts with diplomacy but then in the cases of Succoth and Penuel he exercises harsh punitive action against, and execution of, fellow Israelites. The Gideon narrative raises the possibility of

219. Webb, *Book of Judges*, 267.
220. Block, *Judges*, 300–301.
221. Butler, *Judges*, 222.

human kingship for the first time and portrays, arguably, the dealings of Israel's first de facto king. Kingship as an institution is not the problem in the Gideon account, but rather the fact that Gideon is conducting himself as a king like the Canaanite kings.

Butler sums up the Gideon account well: Gideon begins, appropriately with humility,

> but a humility that almost stifles any leadership potential, a humility that brings him to test God, not trust God. Gradually, Gideon becomes the leader who contests with God for honor in victory. Ultimately, Gideon becomes the vengeful leader who neglects the needs of his troops, angrily punishes enemy kings, unreasonably carries out personal vendetta, and finally hides behind humble theological statements as he enjoys a royal lifestyle.[222]

Gideon delivered Israel and brought rest to the land. He even combated idolatry early in his career, but his legacy is the nationalization of Baal worship and an experiment with hereditary monarchy of the Canaanite kind that ends in disaster.[223]

9:1–57: The Reign of Abimelech

The exploits of Gideon's son Abimelech stand outside the cyclical framework. The land may have experienced rest (from warfare) as a result of Gideon's deliverance, but it is soon to be thrown into turmoil under Abimelech. The theme of kingship that the Gideon cycle introduced and developed gets explored in more detail in the Abimelech account. It's as though the narrator wants to pursue further the consequences of kingship of the Canaanite sort. Several pieces of information from the epilogue of the Gideon cycle (8:29–35) are key for the unfolding story of Abimelech.[224]

222. Butler, *Judges*, 251.

223. Block, "Will the Real Gideon Please Stand Up?" 362–63, 365, notes that in the final chapter of the Gideon account (ch. 9) the narrator consistently refers to Gideon by his alternative name, Jerubbaal, which befits his character as a Baalist.

224. In addition to the basic fact that Abimelech is introduced in 8:31, we also learn he was the son of Gideon's concubine (not one of his "many wives"); Abimelech's mother is from Shechem, Abimelech has seventy brothers, and Israel had accepted Baal-Berith as their god.

Abimelech Becomes King (9:1–6)

Abimelech's story begins with his conspiracy to seize absolute rule. Abimelech sows the seeds of this plot in the town of his birth and with his mother's family and clan—from here his rule would expand. The seventy sons of Gideon are clearly regarded as a threat to Abimelech, and he appeals to his mother's family, clan, and the whole of Shechem on the basis of kinship ("I am your bone and your flesh"; v. 2). The appeal works and the "lords of Shechem" (בעלי שכם/*ba'ălê šĕkem*) support Abimelech because "he is our brother" (v. 3). This is the first time in Judges where a major leadership role is determined by popular choice rather than divine election. Loyalty to Yahweh should have been the cohesive force, uniting the people of God; it should come as no surprise that when Yahweh is rejected tribalism and self-interest (which are latent in the choice of Abimelech as king) become the guiding principles.[225]

The funds the Shechemite leaders give to Abimelech derive from the temple of Baal-Berith. Although we learned in 8:33 that the Israelites had made Baal-Berith their god, the information that a temple to Baal-Berith existed in Shechem is a new piece of information.[226] As Webb notes, Shechem "was a place of huge symbolic importance" by virtue of the fact Abraham built his first altar to Yahweh there (Gen 12:6–7) and that it was the place of covenant renewal after the conquest (Josh 24:1–28).[227] The place so significant for Yahweh and his covenant with Israel is now a place devoted to *Covenant-Baal* (Baal-Berith), and the launching place geographically and symbolically for Abimelech's royal conspiracy.

Like his father before him, Abimelech is motivated by principles and practices of Canaanite kingship. In line with these motivations, he surrounds himself with a band of goons whom he hires with the temple funds (v. 4), and they journey to Ophrah to eliminate the most obvious threats to his royal claim. The narrator expresses in one brief, chilling statement Abimelech's systematic murder of all but one of his seventy brothers "on one stone" (v. 5). Having seemingly eliminated potential usurpers, he returns to Shechem where the citizens conduct his coronation event (v. 6).

225. Webb, *Book of Judges*, 270.

226. Could this indicate a preexisting rivalry between Ophrah and Shechem, both being places of sacred shrines?

227. Webb, *Book of Judges*, 269–70.

Jotham's Parable (9:7–21)

The scene shifts in 9:7 to the only son of Gideon to escape Abimlelech's murderous plot, Jotham, as he receives the news of his half-brother's coronation. From the vantage point of Mt. Gerizim, which looks out over Shechem, Jotham tells a parable to the Shechemites. According to the parable, trees are seeking a king to rule over them. They ask in turn the olive tree (vv. 8–9), the fig tree (vv. 10–11), and the grape vine to reign over them (vv. 12–13), and each in their turn declines the offer of kingship.[228] Finally, the trees approach the bramble with the same offer (v. 14). Unlike the previous three, brambles do not provide fruit and are good for nothing—they cannot provide shade (as promised in v. 15) and their thorns are harmful to anyone who gets close to them.[229] In any case, the bramble accepts on the condition that the offer of the trees is indeed genuine—if not, the bramble vows that fire will come to consume the trees (v. 15).

Having told his parable, Jotham makes his case against the Shechemites (vv. 16–20). In the form of an if/then clause, Jotham urges the Shechemites to consider their motivation for making Abimelech their king.[230] Were their motives pure and upright and were they appropriate in light of all that Gideon had done in delivering them from Midian oppression? If so, Jotham wishes them all the best (though this is of course tongue in cheek because clearly Jotham does not think they acted in good faith). The conditional clause ends with a curse: If they have not acted with integrity, let the Shechemites and Abimelech destroy each other (v. 20).[231]

Much has been made of this parable, and many scholars maintain that it represents a clear antimonarchy perspective. However, as Jotham explains, this is not an indictment against kingship as a leadership model in Israel but

228. Schöpflin, "Jotham's Speech," 16, draws a link between the noble trees' rejection of kingship and Gideon's rejection of kingship. Contra Ogden who thinks it pointless to question whom the trees represent; Ogden, "Jotham's Fable," 303.

229. Block, *Judges*, 318.

230. Butler, *Judges*, 242. I can't help but wonder about Jotham's own motivation for coming forward. Of course, his seventy brothers were slaughtered by Abimelech and he only narrowly escaped, so his hatred of Abimelech is understandable. However, his challenge seems like a perfect blend of revenge and political maneuvering. Is this a case of "like father . . . like son"? E.g., notice how he associates himself with "his father's house" and represents Abimelech as the son of a "maidservant" and a relative of the Shechemites (v. 18). He uses Gideon's name and reputation to his advantage, and there is no reference to the hand of Yahweh in defeating the Midianites. In the end, his words do function prophetically and Abimelech and the Shechemites destroy each other as he had hoped.

231. Butler, *Judges*, 242.

against the kind of king the Shechemites elected and their reasons for doing so. Thus, Webb rightly notes:

> The issue is not kingship as such, but whether it was right for them to make this particular man king and, in doing so, to support and participate in his slaughter of Gideon's seventy sons . . . [Jotham's] basic charge is that the rulers of Shechem have debased goodness into expediency, and covenant faithfulness into tribalism. Their behavior has been inexcusable, and (as the *fire* of the fable has warned) they will pay a high price for it.[232]

With his murderous and tyrannical brother in power, Jotham is not safe. This section ends with Jotham making a stealthy retreat to live out his days in hiding, at least as long as Abimelech is around (v. 21).

Abimelech's Demise (9:22–57)

Verse 22 indicates that Abimelech ruled for three years before everything began to unravel. Intriguing is the fact that 9:22 says that he ruled "over Israel," which gives the impression of *all* of Israel and not just the Shechemites. In any case, this kind of hereditary monarchy did not provide political stability and Abimelech held onto power for a mere three years.[233]

Judges 9:23–57 recounts the downfall and eventual death of Abimelech. The narrator states clearly at the very beginning (vv. 23–25) and then again at the end (vv. 56–57) that God was at work in the events of Abimelech's downfall. God sowed discord between Abimelech and the Shechemites as a consequence of the evil that Abimelech and the Shechemites had done in murdering Gideon's seventy sons. The theological purpose frames the narrative of Abimelech's demise. In accordance with Jotham's parable, the fire of Abimelech, the bramble king, consumes the people of Shechem (v. 49), and in the process Abimelech himself is consumed (vv. 53–54).

The first indication that Abimelech's hold on Shechem is slipping appears in 9:25. The "lords of Shechem" (בעלי שׁכם/*baʿălê šĕkem*), presumably the same "lords of Shechem" who had crowned Abimelech as king (see vv. 3–6), set a trap for Abimelech and also robbed all the passersby (v. 25). This strikes me as reminiscent of the time of Jabin's oppression of Israel when, as the Song of Deborah indicates, it was not safe to travel the regular travel routes (5:6), and

232. Webb, *Book of Judges*, 277.
233. Webb, *Book of Judges*, 280.

it is suggested that the situation in Israel with Abimelech as king was no better than being under foreign oppression. As Abimelech is receiving word of this activity (v. 25b) an outright rebellion is brewing.

Verses 26–29 introduce Gaal and describe his rebellion against Abimelech. Gaal comes from the root *gaʿal* ("to loathe") and Gaal is indeed a hater, especially when it comes to Abimelech.[234] The lords of Shechem enthusiastically embrace Gaal and arrange a festival in "the house of their god(s)," which becomes the context for reviling Abimelech. Notice that in his bid for being king in Shechem, Gaal uses the same argument as Abimelech; whereas Abimelech does have ties to Shechem (his father's concubine was a Shechemite), why serve him when you could serve Gaal who is a descendant of the original founder Hamor (Gen 33:18–19).[235] Gaal undermines the legitimacy of Abimelech's rule and openly taunts and challenges him to battle.

Apparently, Abimelech still has some support in Shechem, and Zebul warns him of Gaal's treason and instructs him to prepare for battle (vv. 30–33). Abimelech does so (v. 34). Moreover, Zebul buys Abimelech's forces time by deceiving Gaal concerning the approaching armies (vv. 35–36). Up until this point, Zebul must have gained the confidence of Gaal by feigning support, but in 9:38 he drops the pretense and openly mocks Gaal. Abimelech gains the victory over Gaal and his armies, driving Gaal and his relatives from Shechem (vv. 39–41).

The next day, Abimelech moves against the city of Shechem itself. When the Shechemites go out of the city and into the fields (perhaps to see what damage the previous day's battle had caused), Abimelech uses their vulnerability to his advantage. While part of his army is slaughtering unarmed civilians in the fields (v. 43), Abimelech uses the other part to capture the city, kill its citizens and utterly destroy the city (vv. 44–45).

Apparently, the temple of El-Berith remained intact, perhaps because it was outside the city or in part of the city not yet destroyed by Abimelech's forces.[236] It seems El-Berith was powerless to save the remaining lords of Shechem against the bramble king. Abimelech seizes the opportunity of the trapped lords. The narrator describes rather vividly the image of Abimelech himself taking up an axe, cutting firewood, bearing it upon his shoulder, and then laying it at the foot of the stronghold (v. 48). In a statement curiously similar to Gideon's statement on the eve of his battle with the Midianites (7:17), Abimelech instructs his men to do just as they have observed him doing. The

234. See Block, *Judges*, 325, who thinks the name "looks suspiciously like a nickname."

235. Webb, *Book of Judges*, 282–83; Block, *Judges*, 326.

236. For the former view see Webb, *Book of Judges*, 290; and for the latter view see Block, *Judges*, 331.

stronghold is set ablaze, and Jotham's parable comes true—the bramble king has literally consumed his subjects with fire. The city is completely annihilated. But what about the part of Jotham's parable that predicts also the consumption of Abimelech with fire? The final verses (vv. 50–54) recount Abimelech's final ruin.

The text does not indicate why Abimelech turns his attention to Thebez, perhaps to reestablish his power in the region.[237] Like Shechem, Thebez has a tower to which the inhabitants flee when Abimelech attacks. No doubt counting on a similar outcome of his use of fire on the stronghold of Shechem, he plans to use fire on the Thebez tower. Upon his approach, Abimelech is struck by a millstone, dropped from the top of the tower by a woman. The crushing of Abimelech's skull by a woman using an unconventional weapon is reminiscent of Jael's assassination of Sisera.[238] There also seems to be some irony in the fact that Abimelech who killed his seventy brothers "on one stone" (v. 5) meets his death as a result of a stone (a millstone). Not wanting the shame of being known as one who was killed by a woman, Abimelech commands his armor-bearer to finish him off, which his armor-bearer seems quite willing to do (v. 54).

Rhetorically, the death of Abimelech is like dowsing a fire with water. The narrator notes, "When the men of Israel saw that Abimelech was dead, each one went back to his place/home" (v. 55). As Block notes, "with the death of their leader not only had this military adventure ended, but the Israelite experiment with Canaanite kingship also had fittingly aborted."[239] The story of Abimelech's demise ends here as it started in 9:22–24, indicating that what happened was retribution for Abimelech's treachery.

What can we say about the purpose and message of the narratives about Abimelech? They stand outside the cyclical pattern and so surely, they are significant. We should note first of all that with Abimelech the leadership model in Israel has changed. Abimelech manipulates matters in such a way as to establish himself as king over all Israel (see 8:22). The judges emerged as leaders for particular times of crisis in order to bring deliverance and peace. In the case of Abimelech, for the first time in Judges, an individual propels himself into a leadership role *during a time of peace*. Moreover, in this narrative kinship ties influence the election of leadership in a way that is unprecedented in the book, a motif that will appear in subsequent narratives (e.g., the Jephthah narrative and the civil war in chs. 20–21). Tracing the theme of leadership in Judges, we might ask, what is one to make of the leadership of Abimelech?

237. Block, *Judges*, 333.
238. Webb, *Book of Judges*, 293.
239. Block, *Judges*, 334.

There is no question that clues from the text cast Abimelech in a very bad light. For example, Abimelech surrounds himself with unprincipled mercenaries ("worthless and reckless men"; 9:4) to act as his royal guard, and the parable of Jotham functions as a prophetic denouncement of Abimelech's rule (9:7–21). Moreover, the narrator states in 9:23 that "God sent an evil spirit" between Abimelech and the lords of Shechem, and the last note in the Abimelech narrative says that Abimelech's demise was divine recompense for his murderous means of gaining power (9:56). However, attention to the function of the cycle in Judges is revealing.

With the end of one cycle readers expect the cycle to begin again. While the formulaic phrase "And Israel did evil in the eyes of Yahweh" does not appear in the Abimelech narrative, such is apparently implied in the transition from Gideon to Abimelech:

> As soon as Gideon died, the people of Israel turned back and prostituted themselves with the Baals. They set up Baal Berith as their god. The Israelites did not remember Yahweh, their God, who saved them from the hand of all their enemies who surrounded them. They did not show steadfast love to the house of Jerubbaal (that is, Gideon) in return for all the good that he had done to Israel (8:33–35).

However, Yahweh does not raise a foreign nation to oppress Israel for their evil ways, and, therefore, the cry for deliverance and Yahweh raising up a deliverer are also absent. Whereas Yahweh raises up the previous leaders to deal with military threat, Abimelech emerges in a time of (military) peace, fueled by his thirst for power and following the lead of his father who instituted in deed (if not in word) a royal dynasty. Thus, the attentive reader recognizes in the Abimelech narrative a break in the cycle, but not the kind that will lead to the flourishing of Israel and the path of covenant faithfulness. Rather, as Butler perceptively notes, "The result of such a dynastic approach to leadership is disaster, destruction, and death for all."[240] Indeed, the narrative of Judges as a whole seems to pivot on the account of Abimelech. Elements of the cycle will emerge once again in subsequent narratives but the leadership in the following stories (Jephthah and Samson) will be characterized by the kind of self-serving rule we observe in Abimelech.

In the final analysis, we saw that Gideon's leadership is a failure, but a comparison with his son's reign indicates that leadership has reached new depths under Abimelech. Abimelech is much more overt and calculating in

240. Butler, *Judges*, 251.

his seizure of leadership in Israel than his father was before him. Whereas leadership was foisted upon Gideon and he only gradually develops into his leadership role, Abimelech desires power from the start and will stop at nothing to seize power. To satisfy his passion for revenge Gideon, somewhat understandably, executes in cold blood the two Canaanite kings who had killed his two princely brothers; in contrast, Abimelech murders his seventy princely brothers to eliminate any potential usurpers to his royal rule. Whereas his father lives out his life and dies at a good old age (8:32) having brought peace to Israel (at least in terms of the foreign oppression), Abimelech dies a shameful death in the context of warfare against his fellow Israelites (9:53–54). If we feel as though the situation in Israel is spinning out of control, then we are in tune with the purpose of the narrative. What will pull Israel out of this terrible vortex of their own doing?

10:1–5: Tola and Jair

Five short verses indicate the exploits of Tola and Jair. Aside from his lineage ("the son of Puah, the son of Dodo, a man of Issachar") and dwelling (in Shamir), Tola is said to have arisen after Abimelech and to have saved Israel (10:1). The narrator indicates that "he judged Israel twenty-three years" before reporting his death and burial in Shamir (v. 2). The judgeship of Jair, a Gileadite, lasted twenty-two years, and he died and was buried in Kamon (vv. 3 and 5). Additionally, the narrator includes the note that Jair's thirty sons each rode a donkey, and these thirty sons had thirty towns (v. 4).

It is difficult to determine with certainty how these notices fit into the design of the book as a whole, given that the cyclical framework is absent. Webb may be correct in inferring that the introduction of Tola ("After Abimelech there arose to save Israel Tola") implies that in the wake of Abimelech Israel needed saving.[241] However, Block's argument from silence may be overinterpreting these "minor judges" (or "secondary governors," as he refers to them) when he suggests that they, like Jephthah, emerge as leaders in Israel "without the apparent involvement of God."[242] Amit regards Tola and Jair, along with Ibzan, Elon, and Abdon following the Jephthah narrative, as "consecutive judges" on the basis of the phrases "after him . . . there arose" and "after him . . . judged" and the absence of the cyclical formulas. The placement of these judges in the book may, therefore, have more to do with historical factors than

241. Webb, *Book of Judges*, 298.
242. Block, *Judges*, 337.

the author's theological or rhetorical purpose, and the brevity of the accounts may be attributed to the assumed annalistic sources available to the author.[243]

On the basis of his analyzing the key words "rose" (קום/*qûm*), "judged" (שׁפט/*šāpaṭ*) and "delivered" (ישׁע/*yāšaʿ*) in the so-called minor judges and in the book as a whole, Butler perceives these terms as providing a structural framework that binds chapters 10–16 and ties these chapters "back to the framework of ch. 3 and its role-model judges."[244] The effect, according to Butler, is that "These structural markers almost make the reader think the narrator has started over on a second path."[245] This observation on Butler's part is all the more intriguing in light of the fact that the Abimelech narrative represents a break in the cyclical pattern of the judges and a pivotal moment in the book. Again, the narratives of Jephthah and Samson pick up elements of the cycle, but as will become evident, the cycle from this point is deeply broken, just as the preceding leaders of Israel are deeply broken. Moreover, after the Gideon cycle there is no more "rest" in the land.

Is the narrator indeed striking a new course subsequent to Abimelech? As we trace the theme of leadership, should we now expect a new kind of leader to emerge, and if so what kind? The answers to these questions will emerge in the remaining narratives of the final two major judges.

10:6–12:7: The Jephthah Cycle

So far, the author has been fairly consistent in the use of the elements of the cyclical framework.[246] The only significant deviation is that in the case of Deborah and Gideon in the place where we expect the language of "Yahweh raising up [the deliverer]" something else appears (i.e., the introduction of Deborah and her call of Barak, and Gideon's call narrative). All the other five elements of the cycle appear in the first four cycles of judges, even if the details of the stories change. After the narrative of Abimelech and the short notes about Tola and Jair, we are clearly plunged right back into the cycle, but it won't be long before we realize that even the cycle is starting to break down, reflecting in a way the deterioration of the people of God and their leaders.

The Jephthah narrative is structured around five dialogues, which Block refers to as "dialogical episodes, each of which involves a confrontation and a

243. Block, *Judges*, 336; Butler, *Judges*, 257.

244. Butler, *Judges*, 256.

245. Butler, *Judges*, 256.

246. Of course, the minor judges and the Abimelech narrative are outside and therefore do no conform to the cyclical framework.

resolution."[247] These confrontations provide the basic structure for the whole of the narrative of Jephthah (10:6–12:7).[248]

Episode 1 Yahweh versus Israel (10:6–16).
Episode 2 Jephthah versus Gilead (10:17–11:11).
Episode 3 Jephthah versus Ammon (11:12–28).
Episode 4 Jephthah versus his daughter (11:29–40).
Episode 5 Jephthah versus Ephraim (12:1–6).

The Jephthah cycle is a tragic story. It follows the deteriorating trajectory that we have observed unfolding in Judges.

Yahweh versus Israel (Episode 1) (10:6–16)

The extended exposition in 10:6–16 leading up to the emerging leadership of Jephthah indicates that the state of Israel is dire indeed. The formulaic "Again the children of Israel did evil in the eyes of Yahweh" begins the narrative (v. 10a) but is followed in the rest of 10:6 by a scathing description of their infidelity. The narrator provides a litany of gods that the Israelites served (the Baals and Ashtoreths, the gods of Syria, Sidon, Moab, Ammon, and Philistia). In addition to the overwhelming number of gods they worshiped, Webb points out the perversity of the fact that in the list are the deities of the people that had oppressed Israel earlier in the book.[249] Verse 6 closes with a summary statement of the problem with language that brings us back to the problem as it is identified at the beginning of the book (2:13): they "forsook" Yahweh, the one divinity that they ought to have been "serving."

This provokes the anger of Yahweh (v. 7; the second element in the cycle). The new depth of Israel's depravity is matched by the new depth of oppression that they experience at the hands of the Philistines and the Ammonites (vv. 8–9):

> [The Philistines and Ammonites] shattered and crushed the children of Israel in that year. For eighteen years [they oppressed[250]] the children of

247. Block, *Judges*, 342.

248. Block, *Judges*, 342. For the structuring of the Jephthah account according to these dialogues see also Polzin, *Moses*, 176–81; and Webb, *Integrated Reading*, 41–78. Chisholm, *Commentary on Judges and Ruth*, 338–39, discerns essentially the same structural boundaries as presented here.

249. Webb, *Book of Judges*, 301.

250. The syntax at this point is difficult and requires smoothing out. See the proposals by Butler, *Judges*, 253; Webb, *Book of Judges*, 300.

> Israel who were beyond the Jordan in the land of the Amorites, which is in Gilead. The Ammonites crossed over the Jordan to fight, even against Judah, against Benjamin, and against the house of Ephraim. Israel was exceedingly distressed.[251]

The narrator appears to go to great lengths to emphasize Israel's dreadful state of subjugation. This is worse than the seven terrible years of oppression during Gideon's life and it lasts for much longer too (eighteen years).

As the reader has come to expect, the next element in the cycle (the Israelites crying out to Yahweh) appears in 10:10, but we should also notice a difference. For the very first time in the book of Judges the "crying-out" formula is accompanied by words of confession: "We have sinned against you, for we have abandoned our God and served the Baals" (v. 10b). The Israelites clearly articulate the problem of idol worship and for the first time they repent of it! This confession is hugely significant for at least two reasons.

First, it prompts a reevaluation of the nature of this element of the cycle. In other words, it raises the question: does the "crying out" elsewhere in the book imply a confession of sin or is the added confession in this context something additional to the "crying out"? In the vast majority of cases in the OT, the use of זעק/*zāʿaq* constitutes a plea for help from distress and not a confession of sin. A notable example of זעק/*zāʿaq* appears in the exodus narrative where the Israelites "cry out" to God for relief from their oppressive slavery in Egypt (Exod 2:23).[252] From the wider context, the reader knows that Israel is not in Egypt as a punishment for some wrongdoing and, therefore, a confession of sin is unnecessary. In only two cases in the Old Testament does זעק/*zāʿaq* occur in the context of a confession of sin, and in each of these cases, like here in Judg 10:10, the confessional dimension of the crying out is explicitly stated.[253] It seems reasonable to conclude, therefore, that where the verb זעק/*zāʿaq* is not accompanied by an explicit confession of sin, the reader should regard it as merely a plea for help in a time of distress and not a cry of confession.[254] Thus,

251. It is interesting that the southern tribes emerge for the first time in any meaningful way since ch. 1.

252. Compare this usage of זעק/*zāʿaq* in 1 Sam 4:13; 5:10; 7:8, 9; 8:18; 12:8; 15:11; 28:12; 2 Sam 13:19; 19:4; 1 Kgs 22:32; Isa 14:31; 15:4, 5; 26:17; 57:13; Jer 11:11, 12; 20:8; 25:34; 30:15; 47:2; 48:20, 31; Ezek 9:8; 11:13; 21:12; 27:30; Hos 7:14; 8:2; Jonah 1:5; Mic 3:4; Hab 1:2; 2:11; Pss 22:5; 107:13, 19; 142:1, 5; Job 31:38; 35:9; Lam 3:8; Esth 4:1; Neh 9:28; 1 Chr 5:20; 2 Chr 18:31; 20:9; 32:20.

253. There appear to be two other uses of זעק/*zāʿaq* in the Old Testament, namely, the calling of an assembly (Josh 8:16; 1 Sam 14:20; 2 Sam 20:4, 5; Joel 1:14) and the issuing of a proclamation (Jonah 3:7; Zech 6:8).

254. Hoyt considers the issues related to Israel's repentance in Judges. She concludes on

up until this point in the cycle of judges Israel's turning to Yahweh is purely pragmatic—they turn to Yahweh when they need him and abandon him in times of peace when they have no need for him.

This observation leads to a second reason why this confession is so significant. With the continuation of the cyclical pattern after a brief hiatus under the leadership of Abimelech, the unprecedented confession of sin may represent a sign of hope that the cycle is about to be broken once and for all. A return to covenant faithfulness on the part of Israel is what the keen reader has been hoping for, which makes Yahweh's response to the confession all the more surprising.

In 10:11–14 Yahweh rejects their confession in what Block classifies as a "modified judgment speech."[255] First, he rehearses his previous actions on their behalf, reminding them of the long list of enemy nations, starting with Egypt, from whom he had delivered them (vv. 11b–12). When the Israelites had cried for help, Yahweh had rescued them. He then accuses them of rejecting him and committing themselves to other gods (v. 13a). Finally, he passes his sentence: he will no longer deliver the Israelites from their enemies (v. 13b). His final instructions are dripping with sarcasm: "Go and cry out to the gods that you have chosen. Let them deliver you in your time of distress" (10:14).[256]

The Israelites plead one last time for Yahweh to deliver them, and they "turned away from the foreign gods in their midst and served Yahweh" (10:16a). Is this true remorse and a return to covenant fidelity on the part of Israel, or is it a calculated effort to manipulate Yahweh into action? The answer lies in part on how one translates the phrase that follows.

Most modern English translations render this verse something along the lines of "He could bear Israel's misery no longer" (NIV).[257] The phrase "he could bear" here is a rendering of the idiomatic phrase ותקצר נפשו/*wattiqṣar napšô*, which could be translated more literally "And his soul/person was short." This idiom appears four times elsewhere in the Old Testament (Num 21:4; Judg

---

the basis of lexical usage, narrative features, and references outside of Judges that Israel does not display genuine repentance in the book of Judges. Hoyt, "Reassessing Repentance," 143–58 (for her discussion of the special case of repentance in 10:10–16 see pp. 151–53). Contra Frolov, who consistently throughout his commentary refers to the "crying out" formula as "repentance"; see, e.g., Frolov, *Judges*, 17, 18.

255. Block, *Judges*, 346.

256. Endris proposes that Yahweh's harsh rejection of Israel's plea is understandable only in light of the Gideon/Abimelech narratives, which evidence Israel's obstinate apostasy in spite of Yahweh symbolically defeating Baal; see Endris, "Yahweh versus Baal," 189.

257. Block, *Judges*, 348, notes the following translations follow a similar interpretation: NLT, NASB, NRSV, REB, NAB, NJB.

16:16; Job 21:4; Zech 11:8), and in those contexts it suggests a kind of extreme form of impatience. Webb surmises, "[W]hen used of a personal response to a situation קצר [*qṣr*] normally expresses frustration, impatience, exasperation, anger—inability to tolerate the situation any longer."[258] What exactly is frustrating Yahweh beyond toleration? Is Yahweh's frustration on account of Israel's misery (i.e., their extreme oppression at the hands of the Philistines and the Ammonites), as the modern translations imply? Block's analysis indicates that עמל/*ʿāmāl* could be interpreted either as "pain/trouble" or as "hard work/effort."[259] The sense of hardship is certainly attested in the Old Testament usage of עמל/*ʿāmāl* (e.g., Gen 41:51; Num 23:21; Deut 26:7; Isa. 10:1; Jer 20:18). However, the notions of mischief (Pss 7:14; 10:7, 14; 140:9; Job 15:35; Prov 24:2) and toil (Pss 73:16; 90:10; עמל/*ʿāmāl* in the sense of toil is a *Leitwort* in Ecclesiastes) are also attested. Moreover, Block notes that if the sense of misery were intended here the Hebrew word צרה/*ṣārâ* ("distress"), which is found in 10:14, would be expected.[260] Thus, a number of commentators regard Yahweh's frustrations as being directed not to the misery of Israel's oppressive circumstances but to Israel's desperate ploy to garner Yahweh's help. For example, Robert Polzin renders the statement as "[Yahweh] grew annoyed with the troubled efforts of Israel," and for Block, "The Israelites' present efforts are intolerable, and the attempts to wrest deliverance from him are an affront."[261]

Admittedly, the terminology in 10:16b is ambiguous, but another piece of this puzzle suggests that Polzin, Block, and others are justified in interpreting עמל/*ʿāmāl* in the way that they do. We have observed that this extended exposition in the Jephthah narrative includes the first three elements in the judges cycle, namely, (1) Israel does evil in the eyes of Yahweh, (2) Yahweh deliverers them into the hands of foreign oppressors, and (3) Israel cries out to Yahweh for deliverance. If Yahweh is moved by Israel's confession and changes his mind regarding his commitment not to save them, then readers would rightly expect that immediately following Yahweh's change of heart the next element in the cycle would appear, i.e., Yahweh raising up a deliverer. However, the narrator is eerily silent with regard to the fourth element in the cycle. What comes next in the narrative (10:17–18) highlights the leadership vacuum, with the Ammonites setting up camp in Israelite territory and the Israelite assembly at a loss as to

258. Webb, *Integrated Reading*, 47.

259. Block, *Judges*, 349.

260. Block, *Judges*, 349.

261. Polzin, *Moses*, 177; Block, *Judges*, 349. Even Webb, who supposes עמל/*ʿāmāl* refers to Israel's distressing situation, admits that it is "a completely apt term to describe Israel's desperate attempts to get Yahweh to help them"; Webb, *Book of Judges*, 306–7.

who should lead! In fact, not only does Yahweh not provide a deliverer, for the rest of the narrative he is silent and aloof.[262]

If the narrator's statement in 10:16b is ambiguous, Yahweh's action—or rather inaction—should dispel any confusion about his regard for Israel's confession and reform. In the history of his dealing with his people, Yahweh has not failed to change his mind or a course of action on the basis of true repentance, so it seems reasonable to conclude that Israel's confession lacked a genuine sense of repentance and thus failed to move Yahweh to raise up a deliverer. Block states it well:

> The repentance is external only; theirs is a conversion of convenience. The covenant God who has been slighted despite his repeated gracious interventions on the nation's behalf and abandoned in favor of the more exciting and physical deities of Canaan has grown tired of their calls for help. He sees through their empty cry. These people are interested only in relief from their oppressions. Because their confession lacks sincerity, Yahweh will withdraw.[263]

At the end of this first episode that pits Yahweh and Israel in opposition, the tension is not broken. The Israelites have for the moment cast aside their idolatrous ways, but it is one thing to rid the camp of the Canaanite gods and quite another to wipe them from the hearts and desires of the people. The subsequent actions of the people will show just how deep-seated the Canaanite way of being has become. However, the question remains: will Yahweh intervene on their behalf? By the time we get to 10:16 we really cannot be sure that he will.

Jephthah versus Gilead (Episode 2) (10:17–11:11)

Conditions are unbearable for the Israelites, but a storm is brewing it seems. Verse 17 indicates that the Ammonites had mobilized for battle, and without any kind of leadership the "children of Israel" also congregate (v. 17). Their lack of leadership is apparent, and the leaders of Gilead offer a permanent leadership position in Gilead to the man who would lead the battle (v. 18).

262. Indeed, at a number of points in the narrative individuals evoke Yahweh's name, but this does not indicate his endorsement of the people or events. The one exception to Yahweh's remoteness in the Jephthah narrative is in 11:29 which states that "The Spirit of Yahweh came upon Jephthah."

263. Block, *Judges*, 349.

The introduction of Jephthah does not occur until 11:1, but the material leading up to his introduction (10:6–10:18) serves as an integral backdrop for Jephthah's story.[264] Being the son of a harlot and as such at odds with his brothers (compare Abimelech), Jephthah continues in the line of the unexpected leader. However, in the introduction to Jephthah, the narrator characterizes him as a "mighty warrior" (11:1), which was likely what drew the leaders of Gilead to him, but he had gathered around himself a posse of "worthless men" (again, cf. Abimelech). Whereas in the exposition of the Jephthah narrative the Israelites appeal to Yahweh and are rebuffed, they now seek a human leader to provide them with the help they so desperately need. A comparison between the circumstances and dialogue in Episode 1 and those of Episode 2 reveals the change in situation.[265]

Episode 1	Episode 2
Israel rejected Yahweh	The Gileadites rejected Jephthah
The Israelites are oppressed by the Ammonites	The Gileadites are oppressed by the Ammonites
The Israelites appeal to Yahweh whom they had rejected	The Gileadites appeal to Jephthah whom they had rejected
Yahweh sarcastically rebuffs the Israelites	Jephthah rebuffs the Gileadites
The Israelites "repent" and repeat the appeal	The Gileadites "repent" and repeat the appeal
Yahweh will not be manipulated to help the Israelites	Jephthah will help the Gileadites to his own advantage

The way the narrator frames these two episodes seems to suggest that the people's hope is that Jephthah has taken on the role of Yahweh, that in the absence of divine help the people put their hope in Jephthah.

Jephthah proves himself to be shrewd in manipulating situations and people to get his way. A misfit among his own kin and tribe (vv. 2–3), Jephthah desires vindication, but more than that he craves a leadership role in Israel, so much so that the account of Israel's deliverance in the Jephthah narrative takes a back seat to his hunger for acceptance, power, and self-

264. Webb's literary analysis of 10:6–12:7 is a superb handling of this narrative; see Webb, *Book of Judges*, 299–343.

265. The following chart is an amalgamation of the comparisons in Block, *Judges*, 354, and Webb, *Book of Judges*, 313–14.

aggrandizement. This is clearly evident in Jephthah's negotiations with the Gileadites.

Two leadership types emerge in the dialogue between Jephthah and the elders of Gilead (vv. 6–10), namely, קצין/*qāṣîn* and ראש/*rō'š*. Amit suggests that the former "refers to military leadership (Josh 10:24)" while the latter "refers to tribal-judicial authority (Exod 18:25; Deut 1:15; 1 Kgs 8:1)."[266] Admittedly, קצין/*qāṣîn* appears three times in the Old Testament with the sense of ruler more generally (i.e., not necessarily limited to military leadership; see Isa 1:10; Mic 3:1, 9), but the two terms are used as distinct roles in the context of the Jephthah narrative. Moreover, the elders of Gilead specify how they understand these distinct roles. Having found themselves without a general to lead them into battle, the elders of Gilead offer Jephthah a role as military commander (קצין/*qāṣîn*): "Come and be our *commander* so that we can fight against the sons of Ammon" (v. 6).

Jephthah's initial rebuff indicates his shrewd awareness that the current situation holds out a golden opportunity for him not just to be a military commander (קצין/*qāṣîn*) but to emerge as a tribal leader (ראש/*rō'š*). Sensing that Jephthah has the upper hand in these negotiations, the elders promise that if he leads them in battle, Jephthah will "be head [ראש/*rō'š*] over all the inhabitants of Gilead" (v. 8c). Jephthah agrees to the terms, and in doing so invokes Yahweh's name: "If you bring me home again to fight the Ammonites, and Yahweh gives them over to me, I will be your head [ראש/*rō'š*]" (v. 9). Apparently inspired by Jephthah's "piety," the elders call Yahweh to witness that they "will do according to your [Jephthah's] words" (v. 10).[267] In a surprising turn of events, this episode concludes (v. 11) with Jephthah returning to Gilead with the elders, and upon his return he is sworn in "at Mizpah" as both military commander (קצין/*qāṣîn*) *and* political leader (ראש/*rō'š*). This is unexpected not only because Jephthah receives the honor of political ruler before he wins the battle, but also because the text says that Jephthah "spoke all his words before Yahweh at Mizpah." There is no evidence to suggest that Mizpah was a sacred center, so the note that Jephthah was sworn in there seems unusual.[268]

266. Amit, *Book of Judges*, 86. On the other hand, Frolov, *Judges*, 217, holds that "Although the exact nature of [קצין/*qāṣîn*] cannot be ascertained with any degree of confidence . . . it can hardly be higher than that of the group's 'head.'"

267. Jephthah's invocation of Yahweh appears pragmatic. So Block, *Judges*, 355, who maintains, "His appeal to Yahweh sounds pious—a tacit recognition of Yahweh as the national deity—but like Abimelech he was driven only by self-interest."

268. Block, *Judges*, 356, supposes that Jephthah's real intent is to witness before the army camped at Mizpah (mentioned earlier in the narrative: 10:17) rather than before Yahweh.

A subtle yet notable shift has taken place here with regard to the role of leadership in Israel. Up until this point in the book of Judges leadership positions emerge for the purpose of providing deliverance from foreign oppression (the exception being Abimelech). Jephthah reverses this. He manipulates the circumstances in such a way that the foreign oppression and his promise of deliverance become a pretext for his rise to power. To state it in other words: whereas previously leadership is the means for deliverance, in the case of Jephthah deliverance has become a means for establishing his own leadership position. This is the first evidence that Israel's deliverance from oppression has become secondary to other goals and motivations. Perhaps none of this should come as a surprise, since Yahweh's active role in the narrative, at least at this point, is absent. It is important to recall that the fourth element in the cycle does not occur in the Jephthah cycle—Jephthah is not Yahweh's choice but the choice of the people.

Jephthah versus Ammon (Episode 3) (11:12–28)

Jephthah demonstrates finesse as a statesman and further negotiation skills in his diplomatic parley with the king of Ammon, going to great lengths to negotiate terms of peace before resorting to battle.[269] He conducts himself with regal authority, approaching the Ammonite king as an equal. Block states, "[H]e acts remarkably kinglike, dispatching envoys (*mal'ākîm*), negotiating directly with the king of Ammon, dealing with the conflicting issues as if they were personal between him and the Ammonite king, and claiming the land as his own."[270] Also remarkable about this exchange between Jephthah and the Ammonites is his keen knowledge of Israel's history. He recalls with detail the events of the years following the exodus. Like Gideon he knew the history, but it is not at all clear his knowledge of Israel's story has the kind of identity-forming function that it was intended to have.

O'Connell has identified in Jephthah's message to the Ammonite king

269. Contra O'Connell, *Rhetoric*, 196, who believes that Jephthah evidences no concern for a peaceful resolution and that in Jephthah's mind military combat is a foregone conclusion. Moreover, O'Connell holds that the Ammonite king is the one suing for a peaceful settlement. This seems unlikely for at least two reasons. First, Jephthah initiated the negotiations. If warfare is inevitable what would be the advantage of sending the diplomatic envoy, except perhaps as a show of bravado? Second, Jephthah's tragic vow in the next episode betrays his lack of confidence regarding the forthcoming battle. This same sense of foreboding is likely driving his concerted attempt to come to peaceful terms with the king of Ammon and avoid battle.

270. Block, *Judges*, 358.

various features of the ancient Near Eastern lawsuit (ריב/*rîb*) genre.[271] In order to support Israel's claim on the land, Jephthah presents historical argumentation in 11:15–22 (the circumstances surrounding Israel's taking of the land after they had come out of Egypt) and theological argumentation in 11:23–24 (just as Israel is satisfied with the land that Yahweh has given them, so too should Ammon be satisfied with the land that their god Chemosh has given them).[272] Jephthah rounds out his case by suggesting that since this dispute dates back three hundred years, the statute of limitations, as it were, must certainly nullify the Ammonite king's claim on the land (vv. 25–26). Finally, Jephthah declares his innocence and invokes Yahweh to decide the case: "May Yahweh, the Judge, judge today between the sons of Israel and the sons of Ammon" (vv. 27–28).

What is one to make of Jephthah's correspondence with the king of Ammon? If the significance of this event is measured by the amount of narrative time the narrator devotes to this event (according to Block's calculation more than one-third of the whole of the Jephthah narrative) then we ought to conclude that this exchange is very significant.[273] Block asserts that "The image this episode creates of Jephthah is filled with ambiguity," though in the final analysis he feels that Jephthah's speech betrays syncretism, a pragmatic sort of Yahwism, and the suspicion that he "has no reservations about manipulating God for his own use."[274] Webb interprets this episode with more charity, regarding Jephthah as a monotheist who operates in the interest of Israel.[275] According to Webb,

> He takes his leadership responsibilities seriously, and discharges them with maturity and impressive skill. Most of all, he knows that it is Yahweh who rules the world, including his own part of it, and not Jephthah himself. He realizes that he is utterly dependent on God for the victory he hopes for, and stakes all on God giving it to him. That is faith, and it may well be this moment in Jephthah's life that the writer to the Hebrews had in mind [Heb. 11:32].[276]

Butler too perceives the faith of Jephthah at work in this episode: "Jephthah places everything in the hands of Yahweh, the Judge, to decide. Gideon had called Yahweh the only king (8:23). Now Jephthah names him the 'judge' or

271. See O'Connell, *Rhetoric*, 358.

272. Block, *Judges*, 362, finds an ad hominem argument here (is the king of Ammon better than Balak king of Moab who made no claim on the land).

273. Block, *Judges*, 357.

274. Block, *Judges*, 364.

275. Webb, *Book of Judges*, 322, 325.

276. Webb, *Book of Judges*, 325.

שֹׁפֵט (*šōpēṭ*). . . . This appears to set Yahweh up as the absolute ruler of Israel no matter what title one wants to use."[277]

Perhaps the answer lies somewhere in the middle. I am not convinced by Block's interpretation of Jephthah's theological argument, namely, that the Ammonites should be satisfied with the land that Chemosh gives them just as the Israelites are satisfied with what Yahweh gives to them. In this argument, according to Block, Jephthah "displayed contempt for his own theological traditions. Orthodox Yahwism acknowledges only one God, who is also Israel's covenant Lord. Yahweh alone determines the boundaries of the nations."[278] However, on this argument alone, Jephthah is no less orthodox than the psalmist, who for rhetorical purposes refers to other gods (e.g., Pss 58 and 82). Jephthah's argument could just as likely be a case of him conceding the point as of evidence of syncretism.[279] On the other hand, Webb perhaps overstates Jephthah's complete reliance on Yahweh to deal with the Ammonite threat. Even Jephthah's profession that Yahweh is the "judge" and final arbiter could be subject to suspicion. Butler perceptively connects this profession to Gideon's profession of Yahweh as king in 8:23. In the context of the Gideon narrative, a disconnect exists between Gideon's profession and his actions (i.e., he declines the offer of kingship on the basis of Yahweh's kingship but acts for all intents and purposes as Israel's king). The comparison between Gideon's less-than-genuine acknowledgement of Yahweh's kingship and Jephthah's assertion of Yahweh's ultimate judgeship perhaps should give readers pause concerning Jephthah's motivations behind the statement. In any case, at this point in the narrative Jephthah musters all of his rhetorical and logical skills in the hopes that he can avoid a military confrontation with the Ammonites. To be sure, evidence of Jephthah's allegiance to other gods is lacking, but he does seem to place a good deal of trust in his own leadership and diplomatic ability.

This returns us to the theme of leadership, and why the narrator reserves such an inordinate amount of space to Jephthah's exchange with the king of Ammon. The previous episode demonstrated Jephthah's deep-seated desire to rule. Jephthah was not content with a military leadership role but manipulated the situation so as to assure himself an enduring political rule. Moreover, it was not enough for the Gileadites to offer political leadership; Jephthah required assurances that they will keep their word, which he re-

277. Butler, *Judges*, 286.

278. Block, *Judges*, 362. Of course scholars debate when in Israel's history "orthodox Yahwism" in fact emerged.

279. So Webb, *Book of Judges*, 322, who notes, "It is possible that it is merely something to concede for the sake of argument, as his best chance of getting his adversary to accept the legitimacy of Israel's claim to the territory in question."

ceives when they call Yahweh as their witness. Now the only obstacle to his rise as tribal leader is the Ammonite threat. The reader may not help but wonder if at this point Jephthah is having doubts about his ability to gain victory over the Ammonites on the battlefield. Could this account for his concerted effort to resolve the situation diplomatically? If that is the case, this episode demonstrates Jephthah pursuing his own self-interest on his pathway to political control. To be sure, the best interests of Israel align in this instance with his own, but in my estimation the removal of the Ammonite threat is important to Jephthah only insofar as it is the necessary condition of his political advancement.

Despite Jephthah's best diplomatic efforts he is unable to avert a military confrontation with the Ammonites (v. 28). The Ammonite king is unwilling to negotiate. Military engagement is inevitable.

Jephthah versus His Daughter (Episode 4) (11:29–40)

The two events that occur next, at the start of the fourth episode, are each in their own way quite unexpected. That they occur almost simultaneously is most shocking. First, 11:29 states "The Spirit of Yahweh came upon Jephthah." The endowment of Yahweh's Spirit on Israel's deliverer is by no means unprecedented. The Spirit of Yahweh came upon Othniel (3:10) and Gideon (6:34; cf. Samson: 13:25; 14:6, 19; 15:14). However, the movement of Yahweh in endowing Jephthah with his Spirit is unexpected given Yahweh's earlier determination not to intervene to deal with the Ammonite threat (10:13). The most reasonable interpretation of this endowment of Yahweh's Spirit is that Yahweh will in the end work through Jephthah to alleviate Israel's experience of oppression, and that, as in the case of Othniel and Gideon, "Jephthah's activity that immediately follows is a consequence of the Spirit coming upon him."[280] This would associate the endowment of the Spirit (v. 29a) with Jephthah's travel through Gilead, Manasseh, Mizpah, and to the place where the Ammonites are camped (v. 29b), presumably to garner troops for the looming battle.

The next event is Jephthah's tragic vow (vv. 30–31), made all the more tragic because, unbeknownst to Jephthah, Yahweh has already determined to use him to deliver Israel. Immediately after the narrator describes the Spirit coming upon Jephthah and Jephthah's journey to the battlefield, we read,

280. Webb, *Book of Judges*, 327.

> And Jephthah vowed a vow to Yahweh, "If you will indeed give the sons of Ammon into my hand, what/whoever comes out from the doors of my house to meet me when I return in peace from the sons of Ammon will be Yahweh's, and I will offer it up as a burnt sacrifice.

The reader learns later that the vow leads to the sacrifice of Jephthah's daughter, but what did Jephthah have in mind when he made this vow? Did he anticipate human sacrifice? The language is ambiguous and could refer to an animal or a human. Boling has discovered the practice of accommodating livestock in Iron Age dwelling places, but Amit and Webb maintain that the phrase "to meet me" makes it more likely that Jephthah had human sacrifice in mind when he made the vow.[281] Whether Jephthah intended human sacrifice or not, his vow provides deep insight into his character and motivations. His impressive diplomacy has failed to remove the final obstacle in his securing the position of tribal head. His vow betrays his increasing doubt concerning his ability to deliver Israel from the Ammonite threat. It is a last ditch effort to manipulate Yahweh to come to his aid.[282] According to Webb, "Jephthah has everything to lose if the battle goes against him, including his life (see 12:3), but also his position in his clan and tribe, and that clearly means a great deal to him."[283] Jephthah's quest for power (perhaps symbolic of his vindication among his tribe and kin) is so important to him that he is literally willing to sacrifice anything (short of his own life) to secure it.

If we suspected that the actual deliverance of Israel from the Ammonite oppression is of secondary importance to other interests in the Jephthah narrative, the narrator's account of the battle should confirm this suspicion (vv. 32–33). The narrator includes no grisly details of the assassinations of key foreign enemies as in the case of Ehud killing Eglon, Jael murdering Sisera, or Gideon executing Zebah and Zalmunna. Nor does the narrator include detailed battle reports as in the accounts of Ehud, Deborah/Barak, and Gideon (or for that matter Abimelech). Rather, in a mere two verses the narrator summarizes the campaign against the Ammonites:

281. Boling, *Judges*, 208; Amit, *Book of Judges*, 88; Webb, *Book of Judges*, 329. Butler asserts that this is representative of the views of many scholars; Butler, *Judges*, 288. Moore, *Judges*, 299, does not perceive any ambiguity: "that a human victim is intended is, in fact, as plain as words can make it; the language is inapplicable to an animal, and a vow to offer the first sheep or goat that he comes across—not to mention the possibility of an unclean animal—is trivial to absurdity."

282. Webb maintains that the vow reveals a deep psychological angst, associated with Jephthah's feeling of rejection; see Webb, *Book of Judges*, 328.

283. Webb, *Book of Judges*, 328.

> Jephthah crossed over to the Ammonites to fight against them, and Yahweh gave them into his hand. And he struck them from Aroer to the vicinity of Minnith, twenty towns, and as far as Abel-keramim. It was an exceedingly great slaughter. So the sons of Ammon were subdued before the sons of Israel (vv. 32–33).

The narrator apparently knows the audience is holding its breath after Jephthah's vow, and he does not waste any more time than necessary to confirm that indeed the conditions of the vow have been met. Jephthah's vow has created a complication in the plot that minimizes the importance of the deliverance account. With Israel free of foreign oppression, the cycle should end in peace, but because of Jephthah's dysfunction the narrative seems to be spiraling out of control. As the audience keenly anticipates what will transpire next, the narrator jumps forward in time to Jephthah's triumphal return to his dwelling (v. 34a).

Echoing the vocabulary of the tragic vow, Jephthah returns to his house and the horrifying reality hits Jephthah (as it does the reader)—"Look [הִנֵּה/*hinnê*]!—his daughter, coming out to meet him with tambourines and dancing" (v. 34b). Indeed, "victory turns to horror."[284] As expected, Jephthah is undone, signified by the tearing of his clothes (v. 35a). However, Jephthah's grief, as indicated by his dialogue with his daughter, is focused on himself. Rather than taking responsibility he accuses his daughter as the cause for his calamity: "Alas, my daughter, you have brought me very low. You yourself[285] have become my calamity. I have opened my mouth to Yahweh and I cannot turn back" (11:35). With all the grace and dignity lacking in her father, Jephthah's daughter accepts her fate, and after a time of bereavement she is sacrificed on the altar of Jephthah's ambition and pride (vv. 36–39).

Jephthah believes that his daughter is to blame for this tragic turn of events and that the vow cannot be undone, but he is patently incorrect on both counts. Clearly, the vow was his doing and his daughter was an innocent party.[286]

284. Butler, *Judges*, 290.

285. The appearance of the second-person pronoun is understood as emphatic.

286. Few commentators would argue that Jephthah's daughter is blameworthy in this narrative. Ryan and Reis, however, are two notable exceptions. Ryan maintains that Jephthah's daughter volunteers herself for sacrifice: "she willingly offers herself as her father's vow-victim. . . . She is more than submissive to her father; she is submissive to the idea of sacrifice." For his complete argument see Ryan, *Judges*, 88–92. Reis, "Spoiled Child," 279–98, is more biting in her criticism of Jephthah's daughter. From the few sentences that Jephthah's daughter speaks Reis surmises that she is disrespectful (286) and rude (288, 293). According to Reis, she is a spoiled child, the "archetypal 'daddy's girl'" (291). Reis even perceives evidence that Jephthah's daughter is a worshiper of heathen idols (286). For Reis, Jephthah's only fault with regard to his daughter is his overindulgence: "He speaks to her with the all-embracing parental love of even an errant child, but she does not return his affection in equal measure" (288).

Moreover, assuming for argument's sake that the vow is indeed irrevocable, Block maintains that two options are open to Jephthah to avert the sacrifice of his daughter.[287] First, Jephthah could simply have broken his vow in a self-sacrificial act, taking the consequent curse of the vow upon himself and sparing his daughter. Second, Lev 27:1–8 concerns instructions for an individual who makes a vow of a person to Yahweh. Hartley says concerning these laws:

> Anyone may make a vow of a person to Yahweh. In the neighboring cults such a vow was the means of devoting a person to the sanctuary for service, for participation in the cultic ritual, or for sacrifice, especially if the vow concerned a child (cf. 18:21; 20:2–5). The making and the fulfillment of such a vow in Israel, however, had to take a different course, because human sacrifice was banished, and the servants at the sanctuary, for the most part, were Levites . . . an Israelite who makes a vow of oneself or of a family member to God is to fulfill that vow by contributing to the sanctuary a predetermined payment.[288]

First Samuel provides at least one other example of a rash vow, eerily similar in some of the details to the Jephthah account, that is apparently dealt with in this manner. In 1 Sam 14:24 Saul vows that anyone who eats food before the Philistines are defeated will be cursed (i.e., put to death). As the story continues, Saul's own son, who was unaware of the vow, eats some honey. Saul is determined to put him to death, but the people protest and ransom Jonathan. So a means of substitution is available in the cases of such vows. In any case, whether or not Jephthah had an intimate enough knowledge of the Torah to be aware of this option is another question. Pamela Reis maintains that given Jephthah's familiarity with Israelite history he would also have been acquainted with the legal tradition associated with such a vow.[289] Butler, on the other hand, thinks this gives too much credit to Jephthah and lacks support in the text.[290]

Thus, at least two options are available to Jephthah to save his daughter, but Jephthah is either unwilling to accept the consequences or (in the case of the second option) ignorant of the law. After a brief stay of execution, the narrator reports that Jephthah "did with her according to his vow that he had vowed" (v.

287. According to Miller, Jephthah's belief that Yahweh would want him to keep the "foolish oath" is itself evidence of Jephthah's skewed moral compass; Miller, "Moral Formation," 106–7.

288. Hartley, *Leviticus*, 480–81.

289. Reis, "Spoiled Child," 292.

290. Butler, *Judges*, 292.

39). Some commentators have attempted to argue that Jephthah did not in fact offer his daughter as a burnt offering but rather fulfilled his vow by dedicating her to perpetual virginity or to fulltime service at Yahweh's sanctuary.[291]

The reticence of the narrator to describe in detail (or even to name the action) by no means indicates that Jephthah did something other than offer his daughter as a burnt offering.[292] As Butler notes, "though the narrator's language here may involve circumlocution, it does not involve ambiguity . . . Jephthah does what he told God he would do."[293] Even Roger Ryan, who regards Jephthah's vow as an act of piety and devotion to Yahweh, maintains that Jephthah did indeed follow through with the literal sacrifice of his daughter:

> When it comes to making the sacrifice, Jephthah does not use an alternative form of "offering" such as consigning his daughter to a solitary life in a sanctuary where she is denied the prospect of marriage or children. He does not use the get-out-of-a-vow-for-a-fee option (Lev 27:1–8). He does not refuse to fulfill his vow which may save his daughter but bring retribution upon himself.[294]

Jephthah's sacrifice demonstrates that nothing will stand in the way of his political ambitions.

The episode involving Jephthah and his daughter ends with a reference to "Jephthah the Gileadite," bringing a level of closure to the whole of the Jephthah account thus far. Having soundly defeated the Ammonites and fulfilled his vow, the once-estranged son of Gilead is finally vindicated. However, the narrative does not end here but continues on. The final episode in the Jephthah narrative indicates that Jephthah's daughter is only the first victim of Jephthah's ruthless ambition and ego.

Jephthah versus Ephraim (Episode 5) (12:1–6)

In circumstances similar to the gathering of the Ammonite forces, the Ephraimites prepare their armies to move against the Gileadites (12:1a). As they had

291. Keil and Delitzsch, *Commentary on the Old Testament*, 2:280, trace this view back to a handful of rabbis in the Middle Ages. More recently see Landers, "Did Jephthah Kill His Daughter?" 28–31.

292. This seems to me a good example of what Sternberg refers to as foolproof composition; see Sternberg, *Poetics of Biblical Narrative*, 50–57.

293. Butler, *Judges*, 292.

294. Ryan, *Judges*, 90.

done in the Gideon cycle, the Ephraimites claim Jephthah failed to include them in the campaign against the Ammonites, and they threaten to burn down Jephthah's house over his head (v. 1b). Jephthah once again engages dialogue, defending himself (vv. 2–3), but he seems much more determined to do battle with the Ephraimites than he did with the Ammonites. Before the narrator explains the real reason for Jephthah's thirst for Ephraimite blood (i.e., they had slighted Jephthah and the Gileadites, calling them "fugitives from Ephraim and Manasseh"), Jephthah ceases his negotiations with Ephraim and engages them in battle (v. 4a).

The narrator provides more detail in the telling of Jephthah's vengeful campaign against his fellow Israelites (vv. 4–6) than in the account of the battle against the Ammonites. Jephthah and his Gileadite army soundly defeat the army of Ephraim. Capturing the ford of the Jordan, Jephthah's army identifies the fleeing Ephraimite soldiers with a test of pronunciation. Apparently, the Ephraimites had an idiosyncratic way of pronouncing *šibbōlet* (שׁבלת). If they used the Ephraimite pronunciation (i.e., *sibbōlet*) they were summarily slaughtered. The casualties are staggering as Jephthah's army slays forty-two thousand Ephraimites (v. 6c).[295]

The narrator ends with the simple note, "Jephthah judged Israel six years. Then Jephthah the Gileadite died and was buried in his cities in Gilead" (12:7).[296] The Jephthah narrative has provided a number of surprises but that the final element in the typical judge cycle ("the land had rest x number of years") is absent from the Jephthah cycle should come as no shock after everything is told. Jephthah left death in his wake, but he seems to get his wish, which the narrator (ironically) highlights: he died a Gileadite and was buried in Gilead.

The narrator does not paint Jephthah as evil incarnate, but Jephthah does represent a new low in the string of deliverers. Comparison with the actions of the previous two leaders (Gideon and Abimelech) bears this out. All three demonstrate a thirst for power; Gideon initially did not want to lead but gradually desired ultimate power, while Abimelech and Jephthah both strove for political power from the start. Each of the three engages in military action against their fellow Israelites because of a personal affront. For their unwillingness to support him in battle, Gideon punished the men of Succoth, and he broke

295. Smith connects Jephthah's slaughter of the large number of Ephraimites with his sacrifice of his single daughter, as familial/domestic problems become compounded exponentially on the national level; see Smith, "Failure of the Family, Part 1," 208. Cf. Janzen, "Why the Deuteronomist Told about the Sacrifice," 339–57.

296. The plural form of עיר / *ʿîr* in this context has prompted debate. Butler, *Judges*, 297, notes that some believe that Jephthah was dismembered and buried in various locations (so Reis, "Spoiled Child," 291). For others the plural is the result of a textual error.

down the tower of Penuel and killed the city's men. Abimelech utterly destroyed Shechem, killing all the inhabitants, and razed the city of Thebez because these cities rebelled against him. Neither of these compares with Jephthah, who massacred forty-two thousand Ephraimites because they insulted the honor of Jephthah and the Gileadites. Moreover, Gideon is able to diffuse a similar situation with the Ephraimites without resort to bloodshed.

A comparison of the treatment of kin is also revealing. Gideon relentlessly pursues his enemies to avenge his murdered brothers, an action which is perhaps justifiable and at least understandable. Abimelech kills his seventy brothers in a calculated effort to eliminate any potential usurpers. Although certainly not excusable, one can make sense of the logic of Abimelech's action. Jephthah's sacrifice of his daughter in the name of Yahweh, on the other hand, is unthinkable. Jephthah and Gideon are akin, however, with regard to their relationship to Yahweh: Gideon professes the kingship of Yahweh and Jephthah says with his mouth that Yahweh is the ultimate judge but for both these expressions appear to be nothing more than lip service.

The Jephthah cycle raises a number of questions, as Butler has shown, revealing the deep crisis of leadership in the wake of Jephthah's rule: "Is this the type of leadership Israel needs? Can Israel not find a leader who will bring the nation together rather than destroy its parts? Must Israel's leaders come from the unqualified and outcasts, the unwilling and untrusting? Are women the only heroes and martyrs in Israel? Has God finally given up on this people?"[297] The crisis of leadership has reached a new level in the person of Jephthah. Yahweh was indeed instrumental in saving the Israelites from the Ammonite threat but what kind of leadership is adequate to save the Israelites from destroying themselves? Moreover, it seems Israel has reached new depths in the process of their canaanization: self-serving, vengeful leadership, child sacrifice, Israelites warring against Israelites with devastating causalities. The cycles are moving from bad to worse.

12:8–15: Ibzan, Elon, and Abdon

Before the narrative of Samson gets underway, the narrator provides another string of so-called "minor" or "consecutive" judges. Like the notices concerning Shamgar (3:31), Tola, and Jair (10:1–5), these accounts provide little more information than the judge's name, place of birth, number of years he judged, death notice, and place of burial. The narrator does include infor-

297. Butler, *Judges*, 296–97.

mation regarding the progeny of Ibzan and Abdon. Moreover, the text does not say that these judges saved/delivered the Israelites, another aspect that these judges share with Tola and Jair (though not with the first minor judge, Shamgar). This may mean that the years during which they judged were times of peace in Israel, but readers must infer that—the text is silent. The periods of Ibzan, Elon, and Abdon's judgeships are notably shorter (seven, ten, and eight years respectively) than Tola and Jair before them (i.e., twenty-three and twenty-two years respectively). Like the short account of Shamgar and those of Tola and Jair, the scant information makes it difficult to determine what these accounts contribute to the themes and purposes of the book. On the other hand, perhaps Webb is correct that the cataloguing of minor judges in this way contributes to the sense that the narrative, reflecting the state of Israel, has lost the plot.[298]

Amit argues that the consecutive judges (Tola, Jair, Ibzan, Elon, and Abdon) do fit with the overall editorial design of the book. The grouping of these accounts, according to Amit, gives the impression of continuous rule: "After him, x judged Israel. . . . After him. . . ," and so on. Amit believes that the editorial design is such that the absence of a period of sin and punishment in the accounts of the consecutive judges is associated with continuous rule. In other words, these periods when Israel's leadership is uninterrupted prevent a new cycle from starting and thus stem the tide of sin and punishment. For Amit, the book as a whole is an apology for monarchy, which holds out the hope for stable, continuous leadership in Israel. Thus, "The editor needed the consecutive judges in order to present the advantages of consecutive rule."[299] The sparseness of these minor judges accounts makes Amit's interpretation tentative. Moreover, her understanding of the minor judges is influenced by her view that Judges is preparing the reader for the inevitability of monarchy as the solution to Israel's problem in the judges period, a view that I find difficult to square with the evidence in the book. However, Amit may be on to something in questioning their significant placement after the Gideon/Abimelech narratives and in probing into their contribution to the theme of leadership and particularly the notion of monarchy.

One thread that runs through the minor judges demands attention and may shed some light on the anomalous minor judges. The narrator's reference in this final string of minor judges to Ibzan's thirty sons and thirty daughters (v. 9) and Abdon's forty sons and thirty grandsons (v. 14) is intriguing. The two references combined immediately call to mind the previous minor judge Jair,

298. Webb, *Book of Judges*, 346.

299. Amit, *Book of Judges*, 85.

who had thirty donkey-riding sons.[300] These notes also deliberately call forth comparison with Gideon's seventy sons. Moreover, the sizeable number of offspring of Jair, Ibzan, and Abdon contrasts sharply with Jephthah whose line ended when he sacrificed his only offspring, and also with the barren couple (Samson's parents) whom the narrator introduces in the next chapter (ch. 13).[301] Why the interest in progeny, and why does this apparent motif only occur in the second half of the book (starting with Gideon)?

Younger points out that the minor judges fit a one-two-three pattern, that is, the first appearance of a minor judge reports only on Shamgar (3:31), the second includes both Tola and Jair (10:1–5), and the third consist of Ibzan, Elon, and Abdon (12:8–15). This pattern, Younger supposes, functions "to reinforce the overall message of the cycles section . . . they strengthen the message of moral declivity that is communicated in the cycles section."[302] Can the scant accounts of the minor judges really support such a view, and if so how?

Younger argues that Shamgar is the ideal minor judge, significantly placed in the first half of cycles of the judges. Albeit an unexpected deliverer (something he shares with his fellow deliverers) he does "save Israel." The narrator is more reserved with the next minor judge, Tola. Whereas Shamgar "saved Israel," Tola "arose to save Israel." This is admittedly a subtle point, but the text is ambiguous as to whether or not Tola was successful in bringing deliverance. Younger also wonders why a member of the tribe of Issachar is living in the hill country of Ephraim, a fact that may be cause for some reservation.

Younger believes the narrator's criticism is less subtle with regard to Jair. According to Younger the reference to Jair's thirty sons (implying a harem), their thirty donkeys, and their thirty cities in a region named after Jair exposes Jair's preoccupation with material wealth and power. "In this respect he is pictured in the mold of Gideon."[303] Webb maintains, "In the light of the Gideon episode and its sequel there is a suggestion, in the mention of the numerous sons of certain judges, that from Gideon onwards judgeship was always on the verge of turning into kingship, in which sons would succeed their fathers to office."[304]

300. That Abdon's seventy sons/grandsons rode on donkeys also ties this compilation of minor judges with the previous.

301. Smith, "Failure of the Family, Part 1," 289, detects here a chiastic structure: 70: The number of Gideon's children (8:30). 30/30/30: the sons/donkeys/cities under Jair (10:4). 1: The lone offspring of Jephthah (11:34). 30/30/30: The sons/daughters/daughters-in-law of Ibzan (12:9). 70: The total number of Abdon's sons and grandsons (12:4).

302. Younger, *Judges and Ruth*, 278.

303. Younger, *Judges and Ruth*, 279.

304. Webb, *An Integrated Reading*, 161. See also Gooding, "Composition," 79.

After Jair, Ibzan has a sizable harem as well and produces not only thirty sons but thirty daughters as well. Younger notes, "to have thirty sons and thirty daughters (sixty children!), one must have a substantial harem (between thirteen and twenty-four wives) and the resources to support such a harem (i.e., monarchic-type resources)."[305] Moreover, motivated by his desire for a wider network of political alliances and a more extensive power base, Ibzan makes marriage agreements for his sons and daughters from "the outside/abroad." Most assume this to mean that Ibzan went outside *his clan* to secure husbands and wives for his offspring but the text is not specific on this point.

Younger finds nothing definitive in the account of Elon, but regards Abdon as the climax in the trend of swelling monarchic airs among the minor judges. Compared to the other minor judges, Abdon has the largest number of sons. His sons and grandsons ride on donkeys, symbolic of their "royal-type power over their region."[306] The mention of Abdon's thirty grandsons riding donkeys suggests to Younger that Abdon's rule is extended to the third generation.

The clincher for Younger's argument that the progression of the minor judges follows the progression in the cycles (i.e., a progressive degeneration) is the final note in the minor judges accounts. Younger maintains,

> There is tremendous irony at this point. The final phrase of verse 15 states that this last of the noncyclical/minor judges is buried not in Israel but "in the hill country of the Amalekites." Whose land is this? Have the Israelites dropped to such a level of living that they are being absorbed into the peoples of the land? This is not the note we would have hoped the noncyclical/minor judges' presentations to end on.[307]

Amit and Younger both come to the conclusion that the minor judges ought to be read particularly in the shadow of the Gideon narrative, and that they in some way represent symbols of or precursors to dynastic monarchy. However, the ways Amit and Younger interpret these figures are fundamentally at odds. Amit perceives that the minor judges portray stable rule that keeps the Israelites faithful. These examples of consecutive rule provide a sweet taste of what dynastic monarchy has to offer. Younger, on the other hand, believes the minor judges represent just the opposite. They progressively demonstrate the negative trappings of monarchic rule, namely, wealth, influence, and power. Younger's argumentation does at times seem to stretch

305. Younger, *Judges and Ruth*, 277.
306. Younger, *Judges and Ruth*, 278.
307. Younger, *Judges and Ruth*, 278.

the textual evidence, but Amit fails to deal adequately with the extra details that the narrator does supply, especially the abundance of offspring. Thus far, the book of Judges has implicitly undermined qualities typically associated with good leadership: wealth, power, political alliances, military strength, and so on. If these qualities are not explicitly undermined, they are certainly subordinated to obedience to Yahweh. Therefore, for the narrator to suggest that power, wealth, or continuous rule is the answer to the unrest in Israel would seem unlikely at this point in the book. Rather, the hints in these accounts suggest that the minor judges in the latter half of the book have the qualities that the pagan nations value, further evidence that Israel is becoming increasingly canaanized.

13:1–16:31: The Samson Cycle

After the brief interlude chronicling the final minor judges, readers are thrust back into the cycle in 13:1. The Samson cycle is long and is certainly entertaining, but it is filled with ambiguity—according to Webb, "It contains riddles, and in a sense that is what the whole story is—a riddle, an enigma, like Samson himself."[308]

Samson is clearly unlike any of the previous deliverers. As I have highlighted along the way, Israel's deliverers up until this point (with the exception of Othniel) all have traits or characteristics that make them unexpected leaders:

- Ehud is the left-handed Benjamite ("son-of-the-right-hand").
- Shamgar is likely a foreigner.
- Deborah is a woman, Barak is unwilling to lead without the support of Deborah, and Jael is the wife of an Israelite traitor.
- Gideon is fearful and unwilling to lead.
- Abimelech is the son of a concubine and a usurper.
- Jephthah is an illegitimate son of a prostitute, an outcast, and a brigand.

Regardless of their faults, these unlikely deliverers led the Israelite armies into battle against their foreign enemies and delivered the Israelites from oppression.[309]

Of all the deliverers, Samson appears on the surface to be the most likely deliverer. He is born under miraculous circumstances and ordained to lead even before his birth. He is set apart for special service by virtue of his (prenatal)

308. Webb, *Book of Judges*, 346.

309. Though Jephthah does not bring rest to the land.

Nazirite status. Samson is brash, bold, and fearless, and displays none of the hesitancy that some of the other deliverers manifest. Moreover, Samson has exemplary physical strength. Above all, from an early age Samson is said to experience a good measure of divine favor (13:24b–25). As Block notes, "Unlike the earlier deliverers, most of whom began with serious disadvantages, this deliverer will start with the advantage of a godly heritage and the early hand of God upon him."[310] In a book in which expectations are upset at every turn, it is difficult to determine if such traits should inspire hope or if they are sure signs that Samson is destined to disappoint.

Even though he personally does significant damage to Israel's enemies, he is ultimately a failure, and in some ways provides a kind of mirror image of the Israelites collectively, as we will see. The Samson narrative breaks down into three basic sections, each of which ends with a summarizing statement:

(1) Samson's birth narrative (13:1–25)
(2) Samson's marriage (14:1–15:20)
(3) Samson's demise and death (16:1–31)[311]

Samson's Birth Narrative (13:1–25)

Verse 1 kicks off the sixth and final cycle with the formulaic "Again the sons of Israel did evil in the eyes of Yahweh, and Yahweh gave them into the hands of the Philistines for forty years." Again, Israel's rebellious ways put them in the crosshairs of the Philistine nation (cf. 10:7). We learn in 15:20 and then again in 16:31 that Samson judged Israel twenty years, so for the first time in the book, the period of oppression extends beyond the life of Israel's deliverer.[312]

Although the Samson narrative commences with the expected cyclical formulas, once again the cycle is not complete, indicating that circumstances in Israel have reached an all-time low. Most significantly, the Israelites do not cry out to Yahweh for deliverance (element #3 in the cycle). This creates a gap in the reading. Are they so thoroughly canaanized that they are content to be oppressed by the Philistines? After their (pseudo) confession in the Jephthah narrative have they lost confidence in Yahweh? Is there another explanation for their failure to cry out? Whatever the case, the missing cyclical element of Israel crying out to Yahweh should be cause for great concern. Whereas in the previous cycle, the people cry out and Yahweh does not raise up a judge, here

310. Block, *Judges*, 418.

311. Amit, *Book of Judges*, 267–68; Younger, *Judges and Ruth*, 281; Webb, *Book of Judges*, 347.

312. Webb, *Book of Judges*, 350.

in the Samson narrative the circumstances are reversed: the people fail to cry out, but Yahweh determines to raise up a deliverer anyway.[313]

In the place of the formulaic "And Yahweh raised up for them a deliverer, x son of y," the narrator includes an extensive birth narrative, including angelic birth annunciations, a barren couple's miraculous conception, signs, promises of the coming child's uniqueness, and so on. This seems to create a sense of hope and expectation.

Samson's family is from the tribe of Dan and dwell in Zorah. We recall from Judg 1:34–36 that the Danites failed to drive the Amorites from their tribal allotment. Zorah is in the south of Israel, west of Jerusalem.[314] Reconstructing the chronology from Judg 17–18, which recounts the migration of the Danites north only two generations removed from Moses (18:30), we can conclude that the events in the Samson cycle are some of the earliest in the book.[315] In this context we are introduced to Samson's parents, childless and barren (v. 3b)

Once again, the messenger of Yahweh appears to bring a word of hope—hope not only for the barren couple, but for Israel. Appearing to Manoah's wife, the messenger indicates that her years of waiting are over. She will conceive and have a son (v. 5), and Yahweh has plans for her son. Samson is the only person in the Bible whose Nazirite status is life-long (vv. 4–5); in normal circumstances the Nazirite vow extended for a finite period of time (Num 6:1–20). However, the narrator makes clear that in spite of the special circumstances, the one who will be born to Manoah and his wife will only "begin to save Israel from the hand of the Philistines" (v. 5c).

In 13:6–7 Manoah's wife reports to her husband all that she has experienced. The narrator has informed readers that the visitor was the messenger of Yahweh, but Manoah's wife is clearly unsure of the identity of the visitor. She is by no means certain that she has encountered the messenger of Yahweh.[316] She relays the message that they will have a child and that he will be a Nazirite, curiously leaving out the part that he will begin to deliver the Israelites from the Philistines.

What follows is perplexing. We might expect a note about the conceiving of a child and his birth, as the messenger reported.[317] Instead, the narrative continues to limp along as Manoah seeks his own encounter with the divine

313. Chisholm regards the omission of Israel's crying out as an example of stylistic variation in Judges; see Chisholm, "What's Wrong with This Picture?" 177–78.

314. Webb, *Book of Judges*, 350.

315. Based on the fact that the Danites are still in the south at this point.

316. There are many similarities between the encounter between Samson's parents and the divine messenger and the encounter between Gideon's encounter with the same.

317. Block, *Judges*, 406. Block refers to 1 Sam 1:20 as an example.

messenger and takes control of the situation. Not content with his wife's second-hand account, Manoah prays that Yahweh would send the "man of God" back to them so that he might know what to do regarding the child (v. 8). If we put ourselves in Manoah's shoes, perhaps his disbelief is understandable—he has just been told that after a visit from a strange individual in the field, his once-barren wife is pregnant! We can sympathize with Manoah's desire to meet this stranger.

God answers Manoah's prayer, but again sends the messenger to Manoah's wife so that when he does appear, Manoah's wife has to fetch him (vv. 9–10). Block notes that Manoah uses two tactics to take control of the situation and in both cases the divine messenger denies him the satisfaction.[318] First, he requests that the messenger tell him all that he has told Manoah's wife, ensuring that he receive the same respect as his wife (vv. 11–12). The messenger essentially says (I am paraphrasing here), "It's like I said to your wife: no alcohol and no unclean food—make sure she avoids those things" (vv. 13–14). The answer is curt, to the point, and does not add anything to what Manoah's wife already heard. Second, he tries to exercise his authority over the messenger by (1) offering him hospitality by means of a meal (v. 15) and (2) by insisting that the messenger tell Manoah his name (v. 17). In both cases, the messenger does not yield to Manoah's demands. He refuses the meal and instructs Manoah instead to offer it to Yahweh as a sacrifice (v. 16a); moreover, he indicates that his name would be incomprehensible to Manoah and therefore will not be yielded (v. 18).

The narrator makes explicit in 13:16b that Manoah was unaware that he was dialoguing with Yahweh's messenger. His true identity is revealed when Manoah makes the burnt offering and the messenger mysteriously ascends in the midst of the flames (v. 20a). Finally recognizing his visitor, Manoah fears death (vv. 21–22)—the way Manoah has been trying to manipulate and bully the visitor perhaps his response is justified! With the appearance of fire, the fear of death, and the recognition of the identity of the divine messenger after an involved dialogue we are reminded of Gideon and his call narrative. This time it is not the messenger himself that assures the fearful human, but Manoah's wife who emerges as the voice of reason (v. 23), assuring him that none of this would have taken place had Yahweh intended to kill them in the end.

Finally, 13:24 announces Samson's birth. The narrator does not find it necessary to tell the details of Samson's childhood. The few details that the narrative does provide should fill us with anticipation as we read that Yahweh blessed the boy and that Yahweh's Spirit began to stir in Samson (v. 25). It seems the situation in Israel is poised for change.

318. Block, *Judges*, 406.

Samson's Marriage (14:1–15:20)

In this second section of the Samson cycle, we see Samson in action, his character, motivations, and temperament. He is not at all what we might expect from the previous section. Younger has identified a number of intriguing parallels between chapter 14 and chapter 15, such that the latter is almost a mirror image of the former.[319]

One of Samson's very first actions in the narrative is his seeing and desiring "one of the daughters of the Philistines" (vv. 1–2), and all of the events of chapters 14–15 are consequences of Samson's "fateful" encounter with the Philistine woman. This is not the behavior we might expect from one in whom Yahweh's Spirit is stirring. When he demands that his parents arrange his marriage to her, his mother and father appropriately respond that he ought not marry a foreigner (v. 3a). On the heels of the previous narratives (Jephthah and Gideon), observing parents with an interest in their child's spiritual and moral welfare is refreshing.[320]

Samson's response, however, is troubling: "Take her for me, for she is right in my eyes" (v. 3b; cf. v. 7). A variation of the idiom "right in my eyes" appears in the refrain of Judg 17–21 (17:6; 18:1; 19:1; 21:25) to capture the anarchy evident in those chapters, and the idiom is a kind of flip side to the formulaic "The Israelites did evil in the eyes of Yahweh" in the cycle of judges (3:7, 12; 4:1; 6:1; 10:6; 13:1). This phrase suggests that the standard for right and wrong is determined by the individual without regard for divine moral standards.[321] Samson's motivation for taking this daughter of the Philistines (i.e., "she is right in my eyes") is symptomatic of almost all of Samson's actions as they are recorded in Judg 13–16. Doing right in his own eyes is Samson's modus operandi. Block exaggerates only slightly when he asserts that "Never in the entire Samson narrative does he operate in anyone's interest but his own."[322] The narrative of Samson provides plenty of examples of Samson's modus operandi at work, as we will see.

The narrator interjects in 14:4a to provide a vital piece of information, namely, that Yahweh was at work in these circumstances to move against the Philistines. Theologically, this is difficult to navigate. Samson desired something that God had expressly forbidden (Judg 3:6; Exod 34:11–16; Deut 7:3) and yet God is at work behind this. Does this make God the author of evil? Did he incite

319. Younger, *Judges and Ruth*, 300.

320. Though Younger, *Judges and Ruth*, 301, maintains that Samson's parents are more concerned about the social implications of their son marrying an outsider.

321. Block, *Judges*, 426.

322. Block, *Judges*, 470.

this sinful desire in Samson? Or did God allow the sinful desire of Samson so that he could use it in his larger plan? At the very least, we can identify that in this moment the problematic motivations and desires of Samson and Yahweh's interest align.

The second half of 14:4 is also significant. This is the only place in the book where a foreign nation is said to have "ruled/had dominion" (משל/*māšal*) over Israel. Outside of the Samson narrative this verb appears in only two other contexts. In Judg 9:2, Abimelech persuades the Shechemites that it would be better for him to rule them rather than having his seventy brothers "rule" (משל/*māšal*) over them. The other usage occurs in 8:22–23, the incident when the Israelites offer Gideon hereditary monarchy. They ask Gideon to "rule" over them and he responds by saying that he will not "rule" over them and neither will his sons "rule" over them because Yahweh will "rule" them—in each case the Hebrew verb is משל/*māšal*. Regardless of Gideon's motivation for saying so, confessing that Yahweh was the only proper one to "rule" was clearly the orthodox thing to say.

However, the narrator indicates in 14:4b that the Philistines carried out a role that rightfully belongs to Yahweh. On the heels of the statement immediately prior to 14:4b, perhaps there is a double meaning here. On the one hand, the circumstance in which Yahweh must use the twisted motivations of a character like Samson is one in which Yahweh's rightful place as king ("to rule") is being usurped by the Philistines. On the other hand, Yahweh is orchestrating events in such a way as to overthrow the illegitimate rule of the Philistines and reemerge as Israel's rightful ruler and king again.

Verses 5–7 recount the journey that Samson and his parents make to Timnah, beginning with them setting off to Timnah and concluding with them arriving and the confirmation that the Timnite woman was indeed "right in Samson's eyes." Along the way we encounter the first of Samson's miraculous feats. Apparently separated from his parents, Samson encounters an agitated lion in the vineyards of Timnah. Empowered by Yahweh's Spirit, Samson kills the lion, tearing it in two with his bare hands (v. 6). The narrator notes that he kept the ordeal with the lion from his parents, which is intriguing given that secret-keeping is not something that Samson is very good at doing later in the cycle. After Samson speaks to the Timnite woman and he confirms his initial assessment (v. 7; cf. v. 3b), he and his parents apparently return home.

Time passes, and Samson is ready to return to Timnah for his wedding day (v. 8). For reasons the narrator does not share, Samson revisits the place where he killed the lion. Just as he was surprised by the appearance of the lion in 14:5, so he is surprised to discover that honeybees now occupied the lion carcass—both discoveries are signaled by the Hebrew הנה/*hinnê* (traditionally translated as "lo/behold"). Samson is a man who satisfies his desires no matter the consequences to him or those around him and so he scoops out the honey, goes on his way eating, and shares some with his parents. Again, we are told that he kept the source of the honey from his parents (v. 9). This is the first time that Samson willingly breaks his Nazirite vow by eating food tainted by the corpse of the lion.[323] Not only that, he shares the unclean food with his parents, defiling them in the process. All of this is done with such nonchalance. First pursuing a Philistine woman who is "right in his eyes" and now callously ignoring his Nazirite status, Samson is proving to be a disappointing leader in this sixth turn of the cycle of judges.

Block maintains that the swarm of honeybees in the carcass of the lion has further significance. First, this phenomenon bears the imprint of God's activity, since bees do not naturally inhabit dead bodies.[324] Second, the imagery and choice of vocabulary suggest to Block that the colony ("community") of bees is meant to be a picture of the Israelite people. In the midst of death and decay, the people of God were to be a community that produces sweetness and blessing for all to enjoy.[325] If this is true, this is a timely reminder in the final cycle of the book. Israel was called to be a holy nation and kingdom of priests for the sake of the blessing of the gentile nations. They have failed and rather than spreading the sweet and nourishing honey of blessing they are propagating death and decay all around.

Samson seems quite willing to violate the customs of torah, as evidenced in the disregard for his Nazirite status, but 14:10b indicates that he was quite attentive to the Philistine customs, such that Webb notes, "Samson is behaving like a Philistine."[326] The thirty companions that the Philistines conscripted "to be with him" (v. 11) may demonstrate more the Philistines' need for keeping an eye on this outsider than their desire for making him feel welcomed and at ease.[327] Samson regards them as competitors and engages them with a riddle. That he sets the stakes so high indicates Samson's confidence in besting the thirty Philistine companions. This development will be the catalyst for bitter conflict between Samson and the Philistines.

With the stakes agreed upon (thirty garments), the deadline set (the seven days of the wedding feast), his competitors engaged (vv. 12–13), Samson presents his riddle in two poetic lines of a mere three words each:

323. Younger, *Judges and Ruth*, 302, maintains that already at the time of the killing of the lion, Samson had defiled himself, requiring a sacrifice at the tabernacle to "reboot" his Nazirite vow according to Num 6:9–12.

324. Block, *Judges*, 429.

325. Block, *Judges*, 429.

326. Webb, *Book of Judges*, 370; cf. Block, *Judges*, 431.

327. Webb, *Book of Judges*, 370–71; Block, *Judges*, 431–32.

From-the eater	comes-forth	food
And-from-the-strong	comes-forth	a-sweet-thing.

There is a level of poetic and rhetorical sophistication to Samson's riddle, which may surprise us, coming as it does from a brute like Samson. At the heart of the riddle is the paradox of the consumer of food producing food and the strong thing/person producing sweetness.[328] However, given that the honey in the lion carcass emerges from Samson's own personal experience and appears to be unique and anomalous, the riddle seems entirely unfair.[329] Was Samson just playing with his Philistine hosts, provoking them with an unsolvable riddle? Whatever his motivation, the situation devolves over the course of the feast.

Of course, the thirty Philistines cannot solve the riddle (v. 14b), so they turn on Samson's bride, threatening her and her father's whole household with death if she cannot find out the answer (v. 15). The threat of death by burning is the second time that the motif of fire appears in the Samson cycle (cf. 13:20), and it is certainly not the last. The unnamed bride has a choice: Will she show loyalty to Samson (who does indeed have the capacity to save her and her household, though she does not have evidence of this yet) or will she cast her lot with the Philistines? Admittedly, she faces an impossible choice and in the end her allegiance to her nation does not save herself or her family.

The Timnite bride uses every resource she has to persuade Samson to reveal the secret; it is intriguing that in response to her appeal to his loyalty to and trust of her, Samson tells her that he has not even told his parents; why then should she expect to be told (v. 16b)? The irony here is multilayered. In betraying her loyalty to Samson, his bride appeals to his loyalty and in response Samson relativizes his loyalty to his bride, indicating that his commitment to his parents is stronger than that to his bride; and yet, he shows a deep level of disrespect to his parents by callously giving them defiled food to eat (another secret he has kept from them). Samson's loyalties are clear—he is committed to himself and will use people if it does him good or satisfies some kind of desire (i.e., is "good in his eyes"). However, another one of Samson's character traits emerges in this episode, namely, that he is susceptible to the relentless harassing of Philistine women. Thus, on the final day of the feast and the deadline for solving the riddle, Samson reveals his secret to his bride (v. 17).

328. Block, *Judges*, 433.

329. Webb, *Book of Judges*, 371, notes that this riddle would be solvable only if it were customary for honeybees to make hives in the carcasses of dead animals, but the indications in the text suggest the opposite (that the beehive in the lion carcass was anomalous).

At the final moments of the seventh day, the Philistines reveal the answer (v. 18). They formulate their answer poetically, in two three-word lines:[330]

What	is-sweeter	than-honey?
And-what	is-stronger	than-a-lion?

They give the right answer, which Samson concedes; however, their answer may be a riddle itself, aimed at mocking their "guest." Block suggests that the Philistines' answer exposes the strong man's weakness. Obviously, Samson is stronger than a lion because he killed one with his bare hands, and yet there is a single thing that is both sweeter than honey and stronger than Samson himself: the sweet words of Samson's bride had overpowered the powerful Samson, in spite of his own resolve. Thus, according to Block, "From the narrator's perspective, despite Samson's great physical strength and the force of his Nazirite vow, he is completely helpless when confronted with the love of women."[331]

Furious, frustrated, and bitter, Samson immediately responds, again poetically in two three-word lines (v. 18b):

If-not	you-plowed	with-my-heifer,
Not	would-you-have-solved	my-riddle.

Block notes that Samson's comparing his bride to a young cow "is as disparaging in Hebrew as it is in English."[332] Moreover, the notion of "plowing" has not only an agricultural sense (his bride was used in service to the Philistines) but also has crude sexual connotations.[333]

In 14:19, the narrator indicates that for a second time Yahweh's Spirit animates Samson. He procures the thirty garments that he waged on the riddle by killing thirty inhabitants of the prominent Philistine coastal city Ashkelon, approximately thirty kilometers (twenty miles) west. Having delivered the garments, he returns to "his father's house." What is the mental state of Samson at the end of all of this? Does he return humbled and chastised? Having been burned, has he learned his lesson not to play with fire and is he determined

330. Block, *Judges*, 435.
331. Block, *Judges*, 435.
332. Block, *Judges*, 436.
333. Webb, *Book of Judges*, 374.

now to avoid personal contact with the Philistines? The narrator makes explicit that none of his hot anger has dissipated and he returns home "burning with anger" (v. 19b).[334] This episode which started with Samson seeing the Timnite woman and desiring to marry her (vv. 1–2), ends with the Timnite being given to his "best man" (v. 20). Samson's unabated fury and his wife being married off to one of Samson's competitors (unbeknownst to him) foreshadow the next clash between Samson and the Philistines.

Chapter 15 opens up a new episode, but one clearly connected to chapter 14. The reference in 15:1a to the harvest indicates the passing of time, but the dry fields of unharvested wheat crop will be an important feature in the unfolding story (see v. 5). The narrator indicates that from Samson's perspective he is going to visit "his wife," and Samson's own words in 15:1b indicate that he regards her as "his wife." We know better. When Samson's expectations meet reality it's like a match meeting gasoline! The anger that by this time had dissipated (in v. 1 Samson is returning with a gift and the expectation of intimacy with his wife) is ignited as he learns from the Timnite woman's father that she had been married off to another. Samson is by no means appeased by the father's explanation or his offer of his younger daughter in marriage (v. 2). His words are chilling: "This time I will be guiltless from the Philistines when I execute evil/injury against them" (v. 3).[335]

Samson may have been out of his head with fury, but he does have the clearness of mind to conceive of an astoundingly creative if not perverse and devastating way to exact his revenge. The motifs of (1) Samson's strength and agility, (2) fire, and (3) the bizarre use of animals converge in Samson's second major clash with the Philistines. The three hundred foxes tied in pairs tail to tail with a blazing torch between them and set loose among the fields of the Philistines (v. 4) effect a major economic blow to the Philistines. The wildfire consumes not only the harvested ("shocks") and unharvested ("standing") grain but also the Philistine vineyards and olive groves (v. 5). This devastating blow means not only the immediate loss of yield (wheat, grapes, and olives), but also represents the loss of a season of work in the case of the wheat field and several years of work in the case of the vineyards and olive groves.[336]

334. This is the common Hebrew idiom, which more literally could be translated as "his face/nose burned."

335. For the nuances of the translation of this verse see Block, *Judges*, 440; Webb, *Book of Judges*, 375–77; Butler, *Judges*, 314, 340.

336. From the time vines and olive trees are planted to the time that they would yield a full crop would be years, so not only is that time lost, it would take several more years as the Philistines would have to replant the vineyards and olive groves.

Tit for tat—when the Philistines discover who is behind the scorched-earth tactic they retaliate in kind, burning Samson's former bride and her father (v. 6), ironically a destiny she was trying to avert when she made a deal with the Philistines in the first place. The cycle of retaliation continues to spin. In reaction to the fiery murder of his bride and her father, Samson vows (v. 7) and then exacts his own retaliation (v. 8a). The precise meaning of the idiomatic phrase "hip upon thigh" is lost to us but may indicate some kind of hand-to-hand combat at which Samson dominates, apparently inflicting many casualties.[337] Samson seems satisfied with this victory and he withdraws to a cave at Etam Rock perhaps hoping to be left alone.[338] This is not to be.

In retaliation, the Philistines garner an army and deploy to the territory of Judah (v. 9). Judges 15:9–17 is the only section in the Samson narrative in which Israelites apart from Samson and his family appear. When the Philistines encamped at Judah, almost immediately the men of Judah engage the Philistines in diplomatic parley (v. 10). The Judahites are appropriately alarmed at the imminent threat that the Philistines pose, and they inquire why they have come out to battle.[339] The Philistines express their desire to bind Samson (the commencement of another notable motif in the remainder of the Samson cycle) and exact their revenge for the havoc he has been wreaking among them (v. 10b).

Block is indeed correct when he maintains that what comes next is crucial for understanding the troubling state of affairs in Israel at the time.[340] The Judahites muster three thousand men and confront Samson. In essence, they accuse Samson of upsetting the status quo: "Do you not know that the Philistines rule over us? What is this you have done to us?" (v. 11). That the Judahites express their conviction that the Philistines—not Samson or another Israelite and certainly not Yahweh—are their proper rulers and the extent to which they will go to perpetuate that rule is indicative of the state of affairs in Israel.[341]

They then express their determination to bind Samson and turn him over to the Philistines. Surprisingly, Samson agrees (v. 12). His only request is that

337. See Block, *Judges*, 442.

338. The location of Etam is unknown; Webb, *Book of Judges*, 380; Block, *Judges*, 380. However, based on 15:9–11 Etam must have been in the vicinity of Lehi in Judah.

339. I cannot help but wonder if the Judahites' question may suggest that the Israelites (or at least Judah) had some kind of diplomatic understanding with the Philistines. If not, their questions appear out of place.

340. Block, *Judges*, 444.

341. Contra Butler, *Judges*, 342. I am not convinced by Butler's argument that Judah is being portrayed benignly (or even positively) in this episode. O'Connell, *Rhetoric*, 277, admits that this episode may be portraying Judah negatively, even though he understands the book to be pro-Judah rhetoric to support the Davidic dynasty over against Saulide rule.

they must vow that his own countrymen do not attack him (v. 12). We cannot be sure of Samson's inner motivation here. Is he resigned to his fate but cannot bear the shame of his own fellow Israelites murdering him? Does he have a plan to further his campaign against the Philistines and see this as an opportunity? Whatever the case, he allows the men of Judah to bind him and hand him over to the enemy.

The irony here is astounding: Israel's would-be deliverer is bound by the people he is meant to deliver, and they deliver him over to the oppressors from whom he is meant to deliver them. The hand motif emerges in 15:13, and it reinforces the sense of irony. Elsewhere in the book either Yahweh gives the Israelites into the hand of foreign enemies or gives foreign enemies into the hand of Israelite armies or often the judge/deliverer. Here the men of Judah express twice that they intend to bind Samson and give him "into the hands of the Philistines" (vv. 12a and 13a). Here in the final cycle is the first and only time in the book that Israelites deliver a fellow Israelite (let alone their chosen deliverer) into the hands of their enemies. Moreover, the Judahites' assertion that the Philistines are ruling Israel should not come as a shock at this point, as the narrator expressed this in 14:4 using almost the exact phrasing as in 15:11. However, that Judah is so willing to accept this reality and will go so far as to deliver Samson to the Philistines to maintain Philistine rule is unthinkable and marks an all-time low in the book of Judges.

In 15:14 the Judahites fade into the background and the attention focuses back on the Samson/Philistine rivalry. Webb identifies the parallels between Samson's encounter with the lion in 14:5–6 and the Philistines here in 15:14–15: just as the lion comes "roaring to meet Samson" so the Philistines come "shouting to meet him"; at this point in both episodes "Yahweh's Spirit rushed upon Samson." In the earlier case the Spirit empowers Samson to "tear" the lion in two whereas in this case the Spirit enables him to "strike down" one thousand Philistines.[342]

The fire motif appears in 15:14, but in this case it is Yahweh's Spirit that like fire melts away the ropes that bind Samson, freeing him to engage the Philistines. The donkey jawbone is a weapon of convenience, and Samson puts it to good use for his purposes (v. 15). The narrator notes that the jawbone was "fresh," perhaps suggesting that some remaining flesh and blood still clung to the makeshift weapon.[343] Being fresh it would have stood up better for the purpose that Samson wields it than if it had been dried out and brittle from age. More significantly, the narrator is subtly emphasizing that once again Samson has willingly violated his Nazirite vow by taking hold of the remnants of a dead

342. Webb, *Book of Judges*, 385.
343. Webb, *Book of Judges*, 387.

animal.[344] The killing of one thousand men at one time is staggering and is Samson's most significant victory up to this point. This, as Webb notes, "is the crashing climax of the whole train of events that was set in motion by his trip to Timnah and demand to have a Philistine wife at the beginning of chapter 14."[345]

Samson is already a proven poet (14:14, 18b), and having struck a great blow against the Philistines, he breaks forth in a poetic victory song (v. 16). In two short two-cola lines and commanding sophisticated use of poetry (a word play between the Hebrew words for "donkey" and "heap," parallelism, and meter), Samson sings of his victory over his enemies. This is not the kind of victory song of Israel's tradition (e.g., Exod 15 and Deut 32:1–43), and it moves beyond the Song of Deborah/Barak (Judg 5), which highlights the achievement of humans at the expense of Yahweh. Block notes, "With typical narcissistic flair Samson immortalizes his fabulous victory over the enemy."[346] With no mention of the source of his victory (namely, Yahweh's Spirit), Samson puts the focus where Samson always puts the focus—on himself. In Israel's tradition, victory songs are meant to remind the generations of the great deeds of Yahweh on behalf of his people, and here Samson, a man gifted with language, misses a perfect opportunity for doing just that . . . a sign of the times.

The narrator includes the seemingly unnecessary detail about Samson throwing away the jawbone after he finished his poem (v. 17a). There is something so vivid about this image—the tragic and complex hero casting aside his weapon of convenience. Immediately after (v. 17b) he discards the jawbone, he "reclaims it from oblivion by incorporating it into a name for the place where all this happened: *Ramath-lehi* (Jawbone Hill)."[347] In case Samson's song is lost in oblivion, the renaming of the battle location ensures that no one will ever forget his epic accomplishment.[348]

Just when we think this episode is complete, the narrator includes an epilogue (vv. 17–20). Samson's great thirst provokes him to call on Yahweh for the first time in the cycle. Commentators disagree about what to make of Samson's prayer. On the one hand, Samson declares himself a "servant" of Yahweh, credit's Yahweh for performing "this great salvation," and seems to demonstrate dependence on Yahweh by virtue of crying out to him in the first place. Moreover, Block notes that the prayer indicates that Samson fancies himself a second Moses in the wilderness.[349] According to this interpretation, Samson's prayer

344. Block, *Judges*, 445.

345. Webb, *Book of Judges*, 385.

346. Block, *Judges*, 445.

347. Webb, *Book of Judges*, 388.

348. Block, *Judges*, 446.

349. Block, *Judges*, 446. This is not to say that Block interprets Samson's prayer positively (as

is an expression of his faith and trust in Yahweh, and the narrator is presenting him positively.[350]

On the other hand, perhaps Samson's expressions of humility and faith are simply a matter of Samson using the right words to get what he wants from Yahweh. There may be a hint of accusation in the prayer—it's as though Samson is saying, "Having achieved this victory, Yahweh, are you going to let me die?" Furthermore, Samson's disdain for the Philistines in his use of the pejorative "uncircumcised" (the same term his parents use in trying to persuade him not to pursue the Timnite in 14:3) rings false. Samson has demonstrated a keen fondness for Philistine culture and (especially) Philistine women so that it's difficult not to regard this distancing himself from the "uncircumcised" as expedient when he makes the request of Yahweh. Finally, the parallels between Samson and the Israelites in their wilderness wandering are difficult to overlook, and if they are deliberate, they are not likely to be flattering to Samson.[351]

How then should we evaluate Samson's prayer? My own sense is that it is in line with his character so far and does amount to Samson manipulating the situation to look out for Samson. And yet, Samson is a complex character—perhaps one of the most complex human characters in the whole of Judges.[352] There is something admirable and also tragically self-destructive about Samson. In this prayer he does display knowledge of Yahweh as the source of deliverance, but it's almost as though something deep within Samson cannot allow himself to be dependent upon anyone but himself. If he uses prayer to manipulate Yahweh then he is still the ultimate source of his own salvation, rather than asking for and receiving salvation as Yahweh's gift. We will encounter a similar pattern in his prayer to Yahweh in the final moments of his life (16:28–30).

Regardless of Samson's motivations, Yahweh provides the gift—a fountain of water miraculously gushes, and Samson is rejuvenated (v. 19ab). The place is renamed En Hakkore—"The Spring of the Caller"—once again memorializing Samson himself (v. 19c). This middle section of the Samson cycle (ch. 14–15) ends with the puzzling note about Samson judging Israel for twenty years in the "days of the Philistines" (v. 20). This is intriguing for a number of reasons. First, we expect a note like this at the conclusion of the account, and yet the

---

demonstrating Samson's faith in Yahweh); Block holds that the prayer is simply another indication of Samson's self-centeredness and self-interest (447).

350. Although cautious, Webb (*Book of Judges*, 389–90) regards this as "one of Samson's finest moments." For other positive interpretations of Samson's prayer see the references in Butler, *Judges*, 343–44.

351. See Younger, *Judges and Ruth*, 309 contra Webb, *Book of Judges*, 390.

352. Though rivaled by Gideon in this regard.

Samson cycle continues.[353] Second, as Block highlights, it is hard to imagine Samson in a leadership role as judge, let alone for two whole decades.[354] Third, the narrator's designation of this period as the "days of the Philistines" indicates that during Samson's judgeship the land had no rest and in spite of Samson's victories, Israel was still an occupied and enslaved nation.

Samson's Demise and Death (16:1–31)

The author masterfully portrays the gradual downfall and death of Samson in this final chapter—both literally and metaphorically—of Samson's life. This final section of the Samson cycle includes a brief account of Samson's visit to a prostitute in Gaza (vv. 1–3), the story of his relationship with Delilah, centering around her betrayal of Samson and ending with his capture (vv. 4–22), and the details of his humiliation and death at a Philistine feast, as well as his burial and legacy (vv. 23–31).

The amount of time between the events in chapter 16 and the slaughter at Lehi in the previous chapter is uncertain.[355] Regardless, what happened in Gaza (vv. 1–3) serves as an appropriate transition from Samson's early activity and his final days. We are not told what business Samson had in Gaza, the most southwestern of the five major Philistine cities. What we are told connects back to his initial encounter with his Timnite bride: he sees a foreign woman, he desires her, and, in this case, he sleeps with the prostitute (v. 1). This forbidden liaison creates the perfect context for the Philistines to trap their arch nemesis. Learning from earlier mistakes, the Philistines set a trap, patiently waiting for the morning to dawn when they intended to snare their enemy and finish him once and for all (v. 2).[356] Not one to be outfoxed, Samson slips out under the cover of dark, and escapes the city by an incredible feat of strength: heaving the city gates from the ground (v. 3). Not content just to tear down the gates, in vintage Samson style, he carries them to the Judahite city of Hebron (some forty miles up hill).[357]

Block identifies the myriad questions that this brief story does not answer.[358] So what is its purpose? The story draws us back to see that after many

353. See, e.g., the very last verse in the Jephthah cycle (12:7).

354. Block, *Judges*, 448.

355. The relationship with Delilah leads to Samson's captivity and eventual death (vv. 23–31) so those events happened after his twenty-year judgeship. Although we cannot be certain, it is probably safe to assume that the events at Gaza also took place after that.

356. Webb, *Book of Judges*, 394.

357. Block, *Judges*, 451.

358. Block, *Judges*, 449–51.

years, Samson hasn't really changed much, certainly not for the better. He still likes what he "sees" in foreign women and goes after them no matter the cost. He relies on his own strength and ingenuity when in a tight spot. Something about Philistia draws him back, again and again. We are also alerted to the fact that the Philistines' hatred of Samson has not cooled. They remained determined to put an end to their mortal enemy and revert to their tactic of using Samson's taste for Philistine women as a trap for snaring Samson. These three verses, thus, also ominously foreshadow Samson's imminent ruin, as the Philistines will continue to use the Philistine women in Samson's life to further their ambitions. At this point, we may feel the noose tightening around Samson's neck, even though in this instance he narrowly escapes it.

Verse 4 introduces the elaborate story of Samson and Delilah, which ends with his capture, humiliation and, ultimately, his death. Although Samson was in the northern territory of Judah (Hebron) in the previous verse, the following events take place in the Valley of Sorek, within Philistine territory. The narrator notes this time that Samson "loved" a woman of this place. We can discern a progression here. In his previous two encounters with Philistine women, Samson "sees" them, and the object of his perception becomes the object of his desire. We are not told (nor do we get the sense) that Samson loves the Timnite or the prostitute in Gaza.[359] Here in 16:4 the situation is different—he loves in this case, and this level of affection and commitment clouds his vision with tragic consequences.[360] Also different from the other two liaisons with foreign women is the fact that the female antagonist is named. We cannot be certain of the meaning of Delilah or whether it has rhetorical significance, though suggestions regarding its connotations include "flirtatious," "praise/glorify," "languishing/delicate," and "night/darkness."[361]

Having briefly set the scene, the narrative jumps immediately into the conspiracy plot. The conspiracy occurs at the highest level—the lords of the Philistines (most likely referring to the heads of the five Philistine states or their representatives) make a proposition to Samson's lover (v. 5). Whereas previously the Timnite woman was threatened into cooperation, Delilah is offered an astronomical sum of money to betray Samson.[362] Their experience with Samson, most recently in Gaza, indicates that Samson's strength is extraordinary. Delilah's

359. Of course, Samson's Timnite bride accuses him of not loving her (14:16) and far from setting her straight, he tells her that his trust in her is subordinate to his trust in his parents (from whom he kept secrets).

360. Cf. Webb, *Book of Judges*, 399.

361. See the discussion in Webb, *Book of Judges*, 398 ("night/darkness" is based on a pun).

362. For a discussion of the relative size of this payment see Block, *Judges*, 455; Webb, *Book of Judges*, 400.

mission is to determine the mystery of his great strength and the means by which the Philistine lords might circumvent his strength. They make their malicious intentions clear to Delilah: once this mystery is revealed they will "bind" and "torture"[363] him. They want their revenge on their enemy once and for all.

How will Delilah respond to the prospect of her lover being captured and tortured? Verse 4 indicates that Samson loved Delilah, but the narrator does not explicitly state whether or not Delilah reciprocated that love. Delilah is a woman of action, and her actions speak volumes. Notice that she does not respond verbally to the proposition of the Philistine lords; rather the proposition is presented and immediately following that she begins to carry out her role in the agreement (i.e., she pleads with Samson to reveal the secret of his strength). In fact, the sequence of events from 16:5 to 16:6 (they offer her the sum of silver and immediately "she said to Samson") suggests that all the interested parties—the Philistine conspirators, Delilah and Samson—are under one roof; otherwise we would expect the narrator to signal a change of scene (e.g., "and Delilah departed from there," or "And Samson came there," or "And the Philistine lords departed from there"). If Delilah has any kind of affection for Samson, that is subordinated to her desire for wealth. She wastes no time in carrying out the plan and achieving her desire.

Delilah's question is forthright—she does not conceal the overarching intention. She asks him to reveal the secret of his strength and "how you could be bound to be tortured" (v. 6). These terms "bind" and "torture" are the very same words the Philistine lords state as their goal in this scheme in the previous verse (v. 5). At this point we might expect Samson to be able to sniff out the plot and recognize the danger that this circumstance presents. Although in Gaza Samson slipped the noose, here we see the noose drawing in around Samson's neck. Samson cannot be oblivious to the danger he is in, but he is confident in his own strength to deliver himself should things go wrong—his love for Delilah overrules the risk of the situation.

Delilah's scheming and Samson's deception progress in a repetitive pattern (vv. 6–9, 10–12, and 13–14); on the fourth and climactic repetition Samson reveals his secret and the plot unfolds (vv. 15–21).[364] Block sums up the sequence well:

> The first and third episodes are held together by the number seven: seven fresh undried tendons (I) and seven locks of hair (III). But the tension

363. This Hebrew verb has the sense of torture, humiliate, or afflict, and is the verb used by the Levite in 20:5 to describe what the men of Gibeah did to his concubine (i.e., they gang-raped her all night, leaving her for dead; cf. 19:24).

364. Webb, *Book of Judges*, 400.

> increases from episode to episode as Samson teases Delilah, toys with her countrymen, and moves ever closer to the brink of disaster. The result is an artful building of suspense, which heightens the reader's impatience with this man who is both extraordinarily powerful and extraordinarily stupid.[365]

It is important to notice the progression of these episodes as variations take place within the set pattern. Samson's deceitful answers to Delilah's request move from the absurd (binding with seven fresh/undried animal tendons), to the plausible (binding with new ropes), to the dangerously-close-to-the-truth (weaving his seven locks of hair into a loom and fixing the loom).[366] In each of the first three episodes, Samson effortlessly breaks free of his binding upon being alerted to Philistine threat. Through the progression of episodes, three parties of conspirators seem to be moving in concert. First, Delilah of course is consistent through the episodes, manipulating the situation to its goal. Second, the Philistine lords are there in the first episode, providing the animal tendons but they disappear till the climactic fourth episode. Third, Delilah commissions a number of attendants to lie in wait so they might ambush Samson when he is finally bound—these are mentioned in the first two episodes but not in the third and fourth episodes. Although Delilah's request is consistent through the episodes, the rhetoric gets more intense as the episodes unfold—whereas in the first episode she simply states her request, in the second and third she accuses him of mocking her and lying to her.

In the fourth episode (vv. 15–22), all indications suggest that the dance that Samson and Delilah (and the Philistines) have been engaged in has reached a climax. The narrative slows down and provides more detail than the previous ones.[367] Delilah intensifies the pressure on Samson, again accusing him of mocking her and especially appealing to his love and affection for her (v. 15). In 16:16 the narrator vividly describes Delilah's relentlessness, day after day hounding Samson in pursuit of his secret, so that he is exasperated to the point of death. Breaking under the pressure, Samson bares his soul to Delilah (v. 17a).[368]

Samson explains to Delilah that because he is a Nazarite, his hair has never been cut—this is the secret of his strength. If she were to cut his hair, his strength would depart (v. 17b–c). This is the very first time in the whole Samson cycle that we know for certain that Samson was aware of his Nazirite

365. Block, *Judges*, 457.

366. Block, *Judges*, 457, notes that not only did Samson probably mean the first one to be ridiculous, he also shows further disregard for his Nazarite status as contact with undried animal tendons would have made Samson ceremonially unclean (i.e., a violation of his status).

367. Block, *Judges*, 458–59; Webb, *Book of Judges*, 403–4.

368. Block, *Judges*, 459.

status: "When Samson opens his heart, we find something there which we had always expected but had never been sure of. Samson's actions have been so at variance with what was said to his mother in chapter 13, and the law . . . concerning Nazirites in Numbers 6, that there has always been a question mark about whether he really knew who he was. But now that doubt is removed."[369] Samson seems to regard his hair as a kind of good luck charm, the secret to his strength. In reality, his uncut hair is meant to be symbolic of how he ought to be set aside, devoted for service to Yahweh. Of course, violations of his vow would have consequences but not in a magical way.

Samson's confession in 16:17 leaves us at this particular point in the narrative with no doubt as to his awareness of his special status as a Nazirite. This does pose a serious question at this point in the reading: What should we make of his repeated violation, and now his confession to Delilah regarding his status and strength, in light of the revelation that he has always been fully aware of his special status? In this regard, Block notes that "Samson's problem with his vow is not so much that he violates it; he simply does not take it seriously. Like his strength, and the people around him, it is a toy to be played with, not a calling to be fulfilled."[370] Block is right that Samson does display a wanton disregard for his actions in relation to his status, but there may be more to it than this.

Webb makes the intriguing case that Samson is not so much indifferent to his Nazirite status as he is resentful of it.[371] To say that Samson has a propensity for anything Philistine would not be too much of an exaggeration. He has an unexplained draw to be in Philistine territory and mix with the Philistine people, he attempts to learn Philistine culture and customs, and he has an irresistible attraction to Philistine women. Webb notes that his "separateness" always put him at odds with the Philistines—not only did Yahweh's Spirit drive him against them, even when he wanted to stop the conflict (15:7), it seems circumstances were against him.[372] Samson's phrasing when he finally reveals his secret to Delilah is slightly different than the other instances. In 16:17 he says that if his hair is cut he will become weak "like every other man." The Hebrew word used here (כֹּל/*kōl*) has the sense of whole/all and connotes in context commonality with all men, whereas in the other instances (vv. 7 and 11) Samson says I will become weak like "one" (אחד/'eḥāḏ) man.[373] Is it possible

369. Webb, *Book of Judges*, 405; cf. Block, Judges, 459.

370. Block, *Judges*, 459.

371. Webb, *Book of Judges*, 405–6.

372. Webb, *Book of Judges*, 405.

373. The Hebrew text in the third instance (v. 13) is corrupted, so we can't be sure what

that as Samson reveals his secret he inadvertently stumbles upon the deepest desire of his heart? Grossman thinks so: "[Samson] reveals to her how he can become like every man, tasting these words for the first time. But maybe it is not a weakness, an illness, to be like everyone else. Maybe this is what Samson, in his heart of hearts, has wanted his whole life."[374] Samson is divinely set apart and called for a special purpose—to bring liberation and salvation—and all he wants is to be free of his specialness and have that deep sense of belonging, which in his mind means to be like every other Philistine. As Webb puts it:

> He had to fight them, but it was never what he wanted. All he had wanted was what *every* man wanted if he dare admit it: sex, love, and freedom from the too narrow confines of his upbringing. But Samson's Naziriteship had dogged him at every turn, and become an unbearable burden. That is what he told Delilah when he opened his heart to her. I don't want to be special any more. Bring the nightmare to an end. Shave my head and make me normal.[375]

We will return to this key insight into the inner psyche of Samson and what it might mean for the narrative cycle more broadly, but at this point it is vital to recognize that although Samson gets his wish—his hair is cut and he becomes like every other man—his new reality by no means sets him free, but rather makes him vulnerable to the terrible bondage he will experience at the hands of those Philistines among whom he so desires to find acceptance.

From 16:18–20a Delilah emerges as the primary actor.[376] She "sees," she "sends and summons" the Philistine lords, she "puts him to sleep," she "summons" the barber, and finally she "begins to torment him." In 16:17 the narrator indicates that Samson "told her all his heart," and although we are not told why, Delilah is perceptive enough to discern that this is the case (as revealed in v. 18)—she "perceives" that he had revealed his heart. This is the start of Delilah's actions in 16:18–20a. With this sure conviction, Delilah summons the Philistine lords who had apparently by this time given up hope of her discovering Samson's secret, and they return with cash in hand (v. 19).

Delilah puts Samson to sleep (v. 19), though we are not told how. Commentators have repeatedly noted the maternal/foetal image that Samson sleep-

---

phrase Samson uses there, but it's reasonable to suspect that it is the same in the first and second instances, changing only in the fourth instance.

374. Grossman, *Lion's Honey*, 133–34.

375. Webb, *Book of Judges*, 406 (emphasis original).

376. Block, *Judges*, 460.

ing soundly on the lap of Delilah evokes.[377] There is something most pitiable about Samson's situation here. As far as we know from the narrative, Delilah is the first/only woman that Samson loves. We may surmise that Samson loves his mother (though the narrative is silent on that point), but even in that relationship we get hints of tension (e.g., the keeping of secrets). At the moment he bares his soul to the woman he loves, of whom he should be most suspicious, Samson falls asleep on her lap, an action that would in other situations demonstrate his sense of vulnerability, trust, and security. Is it possible that in sharing his deepest secret and making himself vulnerable he is revealing his deepest desire to find the kind of unconditional maternal love and acceptance that he found in no other place?[378] If so, he is about to experience the worst betrayal imaginable.

Delilah exploits Samson's trust and vulnerability. Remarkably, it does not occur to Samson that she would cut his hair because when she wakes him to tell him that the Philistines had come for him, he is sure things will play out as they had done previously—he would shake loose from whatever strictures were on him and be free (v. 20). Little did he know that "his strength had left him" (v. 19c) and that "Yahweh had left him" (v. 20c)—for the narrator these two are one and the same thing. The Philistines waste no time and Samson's humiliation is swift and immediate (v. 21). Block captures the irony of Samson's demise well:

> Overnight this man is transformed from one whose life is governed by sight and whose actions are determined by what is right in his own eyes into a blind man with eyes gouged out. Overnight a life of coming and going as he pleases turns into a life of bondage and imprisonment. Overnight, the person who had spent his life insulting and humiliating others becomes the object of their humiliation. Overnight a man with the highest conceivable calling, the divinely commissioned agent of deliverance for Israel, is cast down to the lowest position imaginable: grinding flour for others in prison. Samson's sun has set.

Just as the narrator paints a bleak and hopeless new reality for Samson, in a sentence pregnant with significance the narrator provides a glimmer of hope.[379] Simply put, Samson's shaved hair begins to grow again (v. 22).

Verses 23–30 fast-forward to the final day of Samson's life—a day his

377. E.g., Webb, *Book of Judges*, 406; see the roundup of commentators who take this view in Butler, *Judges*, 351.

378. See Grossman, *Lion's Honey*, 130–34.

379. Block, *Judges*, 463; Webb, *Book of Judges*, 407.

mother already alluded to before his birth (13:7). The context is a sacrificial feast in honor of the Philistine god Dagon.[380] The pretext for the celebration is Dagon's giving of their great enemy Samson "into their hand" (v. 23), and when Samson is paraded before the partying Philistines their purpose is confirmed: they praise Dagon for delivering Samson "into their hands" (v. 24). The narrative highlights an ironic twist to the יד/*yād* ("hand") motif that has appeared time and again in Judges. Throughout we have observed Yahweh either giving Israel into the "hand" of foreign oppressors or delivering those foreign oppressors into the "hand" of the Israelites and/or their leaders. Here although they celebrate Dagon's delivering Samson into their "hand" little do they know that Samson's humiliation and captivity will provide the context for the end of Samson's beginning to save Israel from the "hand" of the Philistines, foretold by Yahweh's messenger at Samson's birth announcement (13:5). It is literally while in the "hand" of the Philistine servant boy (v. 26) that Samson deals the final blow against his enemies.

At the height of the festivities, Samson is brought out to "entertain" the Philistines (v. 25)—a summons that was meant to further degrade Samson. With the help of the servant boy, blind Samson positions himself strategically between the structural supports of the edifice. The narrator notes that it was a packed house: not only were all the Philistine lords in attendance, so were three thousand female and male onlookers (v. 27). Despised, abandoned, humiliated, and alone among a crowd that holds nothing but the deepest contempt for him, Samson gropes in darkness for purpose. Foxes have holes and the birds of the air have nests, but the son of Manoah has no place to rest his head. Restless among his own kin, and despite his every effort, he finds no acceptance among the Philistines. However, now, in this foreign "house" (בית/*bayit*: vv. 26, 27, 29, 30), Samson will find his rest.[381]

For only the second time in this narrative cycle, Samson appeals to Yahweh. We long for Samson at this point to embrace his divinely given purpose and to abandon himself and his pride, giving himself totally to Yahweh here at the end. That longing would be in vain. Although he "cries out" to Yahweh and in so doing he acknowledges his own vulnerability and dependence, in predictable Samson fashion, Samson's ego features largely in his prayer. As Block notes, "Samson has no corporate sense. His preoccupation is expressed in 'remember me,' 'strengthen me,' 'let me get my revenge,' 'for my two eyes,' and 'let me die!' (v. 30)."[382] And in predictable Yahweh fashion, Yahweh works in, through, and

380. For a discussion of the deity Dagon see Webb, *Book of Judges*, 411–12.

381. Grossman, *Lion's Honey*, 141–42.

382. Block, *Judges*, 468.

despite flawed human motivations to achieve his purpose. Although Yahweh doesn't respond verbally and the narrator does not explicitly say that Yahweh answered Samson's prayer, we should assume that Yahweh is behind Samson's final superhuman feat: "He pulls the pillars with all his strength and only then, as they begin to crack and move, does he learn that his God has not abandoned him after all."[383] The temple comes down, the Philistine lords perish, the three thousand Philistine women and men perish . . . and Samson too perishes. Only in his death and in answer to his prayer does Samson find solidarity with the Philistines. At the end of this scene the narrator notes that Samson's death toll in the circumstances of his own death was higher than his victims while he lived—quite a legacy (v. 30c).

Verse 31 constitutes an epilogue to the whole of the cycle. In an unexpected turn of events, his brothers (the narrator makes no mention of siblings) and father's household came to Gaza to retrieve his body and give it a proper burial in his father's tomb. Samson is not left abandoned, forgotten and "at rest" among the slain Philistines. Here at the end is a beautiful and profound sense of solidarity and kinship that seems lacking throughout the narrative. As Webb notes, "His being laid in *the tomb of his father Manoah* completes the theme of reconciliation and brings the whole frenzied movement of his life to its eventual point of rest."[384]

Rest.

Yes, Samson in the end finds a place of rest. At the end of the Samson cycle and what's more at the end of the cycles as a whole, we ought to be left wondering about the status of the land. Glaring because of its absence is the final element of the cycle, namely, the land experiencing rest. As if to emphasize Samson's limited success in delivering Israel, the narrator gives no indication at the end of the Samson narrative of the customary period of rest that the land experienced as a result of Samson's leadership. In fact, the last time in the book of Judges that the narrator indicated that the land had rest was after Gideon defeated the Midianites (8:28). What will break this cycle that seems to be spinning out of control? Samson's amazing feats of strength are in retrospect inadequate to bring about the deep sense of rest that Israel so desperately needs. The final note of the Samson cycle—"He judged Israel for twenty years"—is, in context, disappointing.

Having considered the whole of the Samson cycle, what are we to make of it? Samson seems to be motivated by what seems good to and for Samson. This kind of human autonomy runs counter to the biblical notion of wisdom, which

383. Grossman, *Lion's Honey*, 142.

384. Webb, *Book of Judges*, 415 (emphasis original).

begins and is motivated by the fear of Yahweh (cf. Proverbs). The cycle provides plenty of examples of Samson's modus operandi at work. The first regards his Nazirite status. Scholars have debated to what extent the characteristics of Samson's Nazirite status correspond to the instructions for Nazirite vows in Num 6:1–21. Regardless of that relationship, Judg 13:4–5 (cf. vv. 7 and 14) provides the particular stipulations of Samson's Nazirite status, namely, prohibiting his consumption of "wine and strong drink" and unclean food, and refraining from cutting his hair. The narrator explicitly indicates that Samson violates two of these terms of Samson's Nazirite status—namely, he eats defiled food (14:8–9) and allows his head to be shaved (16:19)—and the narrator may imply that Samson also broke the third condition at the "feast" that he had prepared (14:10).[385]

Second, Samson has a weakness for foreign women. His liaisons with three Philistine women (the Timnite woman in ch. 14, the Gaza prostitute in 16:1–3, and Delilah) become pretexts for Samson's conflicts with the Philistines, but in light of the narrator's remarks about Israel's intermarriage with the Canaanites (3:6), Samson's proclivity for foreign women is troubling.

Third, Samson's acts of deliverance (if that is even an appropriate way to refer to them) amount to no more than personal clashes with the Philistines. Greenstein notes, "Unlike the other judges—and most other Israelite heroes—Samson does not lead his people in combat, nor does he on any occasion fight for the sake of their welfare. Each of his battles takes the form of personal vendetta."[386] Samson fights when it seems right in his eyes. Moreover, although the number of Philistines he kills in battle is remarkable for a single warrior, Samson's death toll pales in comparison to the acts of deliverance that the other judges perform. Ehud's army slays ten thousand Moabites (3:29), Deborah and Barak go up against Jabin's army which consisted of "nine hundred chariots of iron, and all the men who were with him [Sisera], from Harosheth-hagoyim to

385. BDB, 1059, defines משׁתה/*mišteh* as "1. feast, banquet (occasion for drinking, drinking-bout) . . . 2. drink (late)." Greenstein, "Riddle of Samson," 240, supposes that Samson broke all three. Johnson regards the placement of the specific references to Samson's Nazirite status (in the context of his birth announcement and leading up to his death) as a thematic frame, highlighting that "Samson's career is an utter failure"; Johnson, "What Type of Son Is Samson?" 278. Chisholm holds that the violation of Samson's Naziritehood is somewhat ambiguous, with the only clear violation being the cutting of Samson's hair; see Chisholm, "Identity Crisis," 155–62. Emmrich has a different take on Samson's Nazirite status. He holds that Samson does indeed violate his Nazirite status but that Yahweh is unconcerned with the ritual purity of Samson's status and uses events like Samson's killing of the lion and eating the honey from the carcass as a symbol of Israel's entering Canaan (an unclean nation) and eventual flourishing in the land (symbolized by the honey production); see Emmrich, "Symbolism of the Lion," 67–74.

386. Greenstein, "Riddle of Samson," 239–40.

the river Kishon (4:12; cf. 4:3),[387] and Gideon and his three hundred soldiers defeated an army which was "like locusts in abundance; their camels were innumerable, as the sand on the seashore in abundance" (7:12).

According to the narrator, the three thousand Philistines Samson killed at his death totaled more than those he had killed in his life (16:30), so in total he slew no more than six thousand of Israel's enemies. Again, for a single warrior this number is impressive, but in terms of the Philistine threat, six thousand casualties is a paltry number. Yes, Samson *begins* to deliver Israel from the Philistine oppression but only when it aligns with his own purposes.

Samson's amazing feats of physical strength at the expense of the Philistines do not justify his overall disappointing behavior. What are readers to make of the narrative of Samson and its function in the book? Samson represents the depths of bad leadership in Israel. In fact, by all accounts Samson demonstrates not only a complete lack of regard for his leadership role and the calling to which he was called before his birth, but quite possibly a resentment about his special calling. If there is complacency bordering on resentment on the part of Samson in terms of his calling, this is reflected in the complacency of the Israelites as a whole in the Samson narrative. As mentioned, unlike in the previous cycles, in the Samson cycle the Israelites do not cry out to Yahweh for help. It may be reading too much into this to say that their lack of crying out to Yahweh constitutes their contentment with the status quo (i.e., the Philistine domination). However, the episode with the men of Judah at about the center of the Samson narrative confirms such suspicions (15:9–13).

The narrative also portrays a deliverer with the most promising potential, but who demonstrates a lack of regard for doing anything except what serves his own purposes. Breaking his vows, having devious illicit relationships with foreign women, and generally doing what is right in his own eyes, Samson is portrayed as a microcosm of Israel as a whole.

Edward Greenstein's elaborate argument is that the whole of the Samson narrative represents a riddle that reveals that Samson is an allegory of Israel, epitomizing the depths of their degradation.[388] For example, his in-

387. An example of chariot to cavalry to infantry ratio is attested in a sixth century BC inscription (the inscription of Sargon II). Fuchs deduces from this inscription that "The ideal composition of a substantial Assyrian force at the end of the 8th century . . . regarding chariots, cavalry, and infantry seems to have been 1:10:200"; Fuchs, "Assyria at War," 399. According to this ratio nine hundred chariots would be supported by nine thousand mounted soldiers and one hundred eighty thousand foot soldiers. Granted this is an Assyrian army from several centuries after the period portrayed in the book of Judges, but it at least provides a helpful reference point.

388. Greenstein, "Riddle of Samson," 254.

terest in foreign women is a picture of Israel's prostituting themselves with the foreign gods. His status as a Nazirite corresponds to Israel's special covenant status before Yahweh and his breaking of the Nazirite vows is a figure of Israel's covenant apostasy. Samson's crying out to Yahweh echoes Israel's practice of crying out to Yahweh, and the list goes on. Greenstein may press the analogy too far, but it seems certain that the narrator portrays Samson in such a way so as to evoke the similarities. Samson is an image of Israel as a whole.[389]

If this rogue leader is a picture of Israel, can we draw anything from the analogy apart from the dire state of the Israelites? Samson's story, in the end, is rather tragic. Samson meets his death in the direst of circumstances: humiliated by his enemies, blinded, forced into base servitude, in captivity, and abandoned by Yahweh—or perhaps not completely abandoned by Yahweh. Up until his final moment Samson is experiencing horrendous suffering, which is perhaps made all the worse because it is all of his own making.[390] When Samson cries out to Yahweh, the narrator does not state explicitly that Yahweh had returned, but Samson's prayer is indeed answered. There may be a hint of hope for Israel in the story of Samson but this is clearly not redemption without cost.[391] Samson had to lose everything to find redemption.

Is this the lesson that Israel will have to learn? Will it take blindness, humiliation, and foreign captivity before Israel genuinely recognizes and returns to Yahweh? Whatever the case, the Samson narrative is the grand finale in the cycle of the judges, depicting Israel's leadership in a deep crisis. The book of Judges started by portraying the problems in Israel associated with the leadership vacuum after the death of Joshua. At the end of the cycle of the judges, the reader may be puzzling over what would have been better, no leadership or the kind of leadership that Samson exemplifies?

389. This seems to be a popular view more recently, but it is not new. Webb, *Book of Judges*, 416, identifies this view implicitly in John Milton's *Samson Agonistes* (1671), in which the Danites, when they regard Samson's captive condition, cry: "O mirror of our fickle state."

390. For a fascinating interpretation of Samson as a "case of horrendous evil in which it is the sufferer's own doing that his life was wrecked as it is" see Stump, "Samson," 199–217.

391. Exum perceives an analogy between Samson and Israel. She notes, "Samson provides a model for Israel. Just as Samson moves from his humbled (female) position to reclaim his 'rightful' superior status, so too Israel will eventually, under David, make the transition from the weak and oppressed nation to the powerful oppressor of its enemies, beginning with the Philistines"; see Exum, *Fragmented Women*, 91.

The End Section

The transition from the Samson cycle (chs. 13–16) into Judg 17 marks a new and final section of the book of Judges, consisting of chapters 17–21. The "end section" consists of two main parts: the story of Micah and the Danites (chs. 17–18) and the account of the Levite and his concubine, which leads to civil war between the tribe of Benjamin and the other tribes (chs. 19–21).

The end section is conspicuous because it breaks from what the reader has come to expect of the cycle of judges (3:7–16:31).[392] The foreign enemies of Israel, who functioned as the scourge of Yahweh and were a constant threat to the peace and prosperity of the Israelites, are no longer problematic in the end section.[393] In fact, in the end section Israel's sole threat to unity and peace is no longer external but internal—the Israelites have become their own worst enemy, a reality that is anticipated earlier in the cycles (Gideon, Abimelech, Jephthah, etc.). In addition, the five-fold structure of the judges cycle that we have come to expect no longer appears in the end section. Furthermore, there is less of a focus on individual people in the end section than in the judges cycle (only two people are specifically named in the end section, Micayehu/Micah and Jonathan, the latter of whom remains nameless until the very end of the account). The interest seems to focus on social relationships (mother/son, father/son, priest/parishioner, employer/employee, husband/wife, father-in-law/son-in-law, tribal community/tribal community).

Even though the end section is a distinct section of the book, it stands out, as we will see, as the logical ending of the book. For example, while in the end section the author has abandoned the five-fold structure of the cycle, that structure (which always leads back into Israel's idolatry) is actually reflected on the macro level with the worst kind of idolatry (ch. 17–18) and violent anarchy (19–21) represented in the end section. Moreover, the final cycle of judges (ch. 13–16) is already preparing the reader for an imminent change of tactics. First, at the beginning of the Samson account the narrator indicates that once again the Israelites did evil in the eyes of Yahweh, and that he subsequently delivered them into the hands of the Philistines (13:1). Immediately, the narrative begins the story of the life of Samson without any

392. Webb, *Book of Judges*, 419.

393. In fact, the two references to foreigners are significant in this regard. The reference to the people Laish in ch. 18 emphasizes their peace and security, and the illegitimacy of the Danite campaign conquest against them (see below). In 19:12, the Levite is insistent that he will stay in Jebus lest he lodge "in a city of foreigners who are not of the children of Israel." Rather, he expresses his wish to press on and stay the night in Gibeah. Ironically, the inhabitants of Gibeah, who were of the children of Israel, commit the horrendous deeds that night, suggesting that perhaps the Levite and company would have been better off staying in a city of foreigners!

reference to the expected crying out of the Israelites to Yahweh for deliverance. Readers may easily overlook this fact, but the omission of this element of the cycle speaks volumes about the current degenerate and complacent state of Israel at that time (not to mention the grace of Yahweh in providing deliverance in spite of the people's complacency). Second, in the Jephthah cycle, Yahweh expresses that he will no longer save Israel (10:13), and he indicates that Samson will only *begin* to deliver the Israelites (13:5). Third, as the climax of the larger cycle, the Samson account is longer and includes significantly more detail than the other accounts, including a supernatural birth announcement. Finally, Samson himself represents the bottom of a consistent downward spiral in the lives of Israel's deliverers. His character throughout is anything but godly, and one gets the impression that God delivered Israel through Samson in spite of Samson's efforts and motivations. For these reasons and more, we can see how the broader contours of the narrative are already preparing the reader for the end section.

17:1–18:31: Micah's Shrine and the Danite Migration and Conquest

Chapters 17 and 18 break down into three episodes: (1) the story of Micah's image and shrine in 17:1–5; (2) the account of the installation of the Levite as Micah's priest in 17:7–13; and (3) the migration of the Danites in 18:1b–30. The first two sections are "expository background, concerning the time of events, their location, the personae, and routine information about the world of the figures."[394] They provide the necessary data for understanding the more extensive account of the Danites, consisting of four scenes. These episodes are structured around the refrain that appears in 17:6; 18:1; 19:1; and 21:25, a phrase that Sternberg notes "combines a segmentary with a unifying function."[395] Apart from the refrain, the narrator recounts these events very matter-of-factly, with little explicit evaluation (cf. Judg 2:20; 3:8; 10:7; also Num 12:9; 2 Sam 11:27). To add to this frustrating feature, the content of the text is often quite ambiguous, and expectations are often thwarted, so much so that at times commentators derive opposite meanings from the same material. Because of these features of the text, Polzin advised readers to apply the same evaluative criteria to the narrator that one would apply to the characters. He writes:

> The narrator, like one of his characters, might repeat so as to be better understood; yet sometimes these repetitions obscure rather than clarify. The

394. Amit, *Book of Judges*, 318.
395. Sternberg, *Poetics of Biblical Narrative*, 417.

> narrator, like one of his chief characters, may shift his point of view; yet the change in perspective may not incite insight but vertigo.[396]

Although the narrator's intention may be to incite confusion, as we follow the clues of the narrative, the negative judgment on the events of the end section is unmistakable.

Micah Establishes an Idolatrous Shrine (17:1–6)

The first episode concerns a certain Ephraimite named Micayehu.[397] The narrative opens with the statement, "And there was a man in the hill country of Ephraim and his name was Micayehu" (v. 1). The fact that this individual is from Ephraim may be cause for some alarm, based on the way that the Ephraimites/Ephraim have been portrayed elsewhere in Judges. In chapter 1, Ephraim failed to drive out the Canaanites and cohabited with them in the land (1:29), they nearly start a rash civil war in the Gideon cycle (8:1–3), and in the Jephthah cycle in fact do recklessly take up arms against Jephthah and the Gileadites and are slaughtered (12:1–6). Perhaps his pious-sounding name, "Who is like Yahweh?" may alleviate this alarm.[398] Surely parents who chose a name that expresses the incomparable nature of Yahweh would be pious and committed people of God, wouldn't they?[399] However, the narrative of these chapters was designed in such a way that what the reader expects to take place in a world occupied by the people of Yahweh is repeatedly reversed. The world projected throughout Judges and especially in the end section is a world-turned-upside-down, an "inverted world" where "actions are often ludicrous, absurd and self-defeating."[400] In this world Micayehu, as we will see, is undoubtedly a misnomer, because as the story unfolds, Micayehu turns out to be a thief, an idolater, and a cunning opportunist who is willing to exploit the name of Yahweh for his own benefit.

In 17:2 we are thrust into the midst of a troubling situation. Micayehu's first action is a jumbled confession about a sum of money he had apparently stolen from his mother. His confession proceeds something like this: "The eleven hundred units of silver that was taken from you, and about which you swore an oath – and also you said in my hearing – look, the silver is with me,

396. Polzin, *Moses*, 199.

397. In spite of most English translations, the narrator uses the name Micah only starting in v. 5.

398. See Boling, *Judges*, 255, who paraphrases מיכיהו/*mîkāyěhû* as "YHWH-the Incomparable."

399. Block, *Judges*, 478.

400. See Lasine, "Guest and Host," 37, 50.

I took it." Three features of this confession are worth noting. First, the Hebrew in this verse is untidy and awkward.[401] However, as Boling insightfully notes, "the narrator presents Micah on this embarrassing occasion as having difficulty forming his sentences."[402] Second, Micayehu's words represent a technique of "gradual exposure," whereby the revelation that he is the thief comes at the very end of the drawn-out confession: "silver that was taken . . . it is with me . . . *I* took it."[403] Third, his words clearly betray his motivation for confessing. He is not motivated by conscience or by his desire to repent of his lawlessness and disrespect toward his mother; rather, his primary motivation is to avoid the curse that his mother swore concerning the money, a curse that she uttered within earshot of Micayehu.

The sum that he stole (1100 pieces of silver) is a vast sum, the same amount of silver that the Philistine lords gave to Delilah for betraying Samson (16:5). Younger highlights how the exact sum of money in chapter 16 and again here exposes the fact that Mikayehu's betrayal is far worse than Delilah's betrayal: "In the Micah narrative, the money is stolen, not exchanged between consenting parties. Worse, Micah betrays the trust of blood-tie, of the mother-son kinship, not the betrayal of an ethnic enemy. And even worse, Micah's theft is not a business transaction for services rendered (as in the case of Delilah); it is nothing but the product of raw covetousness."[404] This is another example of Israel becoming its own worst enemy—this time in the institution of the family. The narrator does not indicate why he stole it, what he intends to do with it, and other details readers might desire. Clearly the fate of the stolen and returned silver is of much more importance for the purposes of the narrative.

The mother's curse is serious business and assumes terrible consequences for the one responsible for the theft.[405] His mother apparently perceives Micayehu's anxiety over the curse and immediately utters what appears to be a counter-curse: "Blessed be my son by Yahweh" (v. 2b). Again, the invocation of Yahweh seems promising on first glance. Yet, in a book where an innocent young woman becomes the victim of her father's rash oath (11:29–40) and where unthinkable atrocities take place as a result of the Israelites' impulsive oath (21:1–25), the easy reversal of this oath against Micayehu is unexpected (perhaps even suspect).

Micayehu returns the silver to his mother only when he is sufficiently assured that the curse had been annulled (17:3a). What the mother, by all ap-

401. The manuscripts and ancient versions support the MT in spite of the awkwardness; See Soggin, *Judges*, 265; Boling, *Judges*, 255.

402. Boling, *Judges*, 255.

403. For "gradual exposure," see Amit, *Book of Judges*, 324.

404. Younger, *Judges and Ruth*, 336.

405. Block, *Judges*, 479.

pearances a devoted worshiper of Yahweh, does next is utterly perplexing. She declares that she solemnly dedicates the 1100 pieces of silver to Yahweh so that Micayehu could make an idol (פסל/*pesel*) overlaid with molten metal (מסכה/*massēkâ*). The profound seriousness of this action is marked by the Hebrew practice of intensifying the main verb with a repetition of the same verb in the infinitive: "I devote with devotion," or "I consecrate with consecration" (i.e., I solemnly devote").[406] The end product of this devotion/consecration is an "idol overlaid with molten metal."[407]

What follows is rather confusing with money changing hands several times and with illegitimate objects being made and consecrated for worship (v. 4–5a).[408] Although she dedicated the whole sum of 1100 pieces of silver, only 200 goes to her intended purpose (to fashion an idol). The fact that the silversmith receives only 200 of the 1100 units of silver creates a gap in the reading.[409] Either the mother held back a substantial amount of the silver that she originally dedicated to Yahweh, or perhaps Micayehu ended up profiting from the repeated exchanges, or some other explanation. Amit notes that the "importance of such gaps lies in their very presence and exposure, because any attempt to fill them is likely to strengthen the dimension of irony and to present the heroes in a more negative light."[410] At the end of 17:4, the idol is set up in the house of Micayehu.

As if all of this isn't troubling enough, the narrator goes on to describe the further depths of the folly of this situation in verse 5. The first thing to note about 17:5 is that the narrator no longer refers to the protagonist as "Micayehu" but from this point in the story onward will refer to him by the shorter version "Micah." It is as though the narrator cannot tolerate the incongruity between his name and his character and reflects this by dropping the connection to Yah (i.e., Yahweh) in his name. The second thing to note is that Micah had a "shrine." Literally we could translate this as "a house of god" or more likely "a house of gods." In the context of Judges, this household shrine is reminiscent of the shrine in the household of Gideon's father (6:25–27). The narrator also

406. Block, *Judges*, 479 (see n. 18).

407. The Hebrew could give the impression of two items; hence the NIV translation: "a carved image and a cast idol." However, it seems more likely that the construction reflects a hendiadys, whereby the two terms connected by the conjunction express a single item; so Block, *Judges*, 480 n. 19, and Webb, *Book of Judges*, 422 n. 12.

408. Polzin, *Moses*, 197, notes that the ambiguity over what precisely was made contributes to a technique employed throughout chapters 17–18 in which name shifts take place. This technique blurs the details and contributes to the disorientating effect of these episodes.

409. See Sternberg, *Poetics of Biblical Narrative*, 186–229.

410. Amit, *Book of Judges*, 325.

reveals that in addition to the carved image that Micah set up here, there were also an ephod and תרפים/*tĕrāpîm* (i.e., household gods).[411] We are not told the origin of these cultic items, but the effect is to progressively reveal the depths of Micah's idolatry. Finally, the narrator indicates that Micah "ordained" one of his own sons to minister as a priest to oversee the worship in this idolatrous shrine.[412]

These opening verses of chapters 17–18—the beginning of the end section—raise more questions than they answer, and the narrator is eerily silent regarding what we should make of all of this . . . at least until 17:6. If we are utterly perplexed after reading Judg 17:1–5, the narrator has achieved one of the main objectives. Indeed this opening scene represents a topsy-turvy world. A cursed thief is blessed, money dedicated to Yahweh is used to make an idol, and those professing to serve God disobey his expressed will all the while thinking he will be honored by it.[413] If we had hoped that at the end of the book Israel would break out of the terrible cycle we have observed throughout the book, it is not looking promising. The narrator has also achieved another objective, explaining the origins of the idolatrous shrine, which will be key for the immediate unfolding story as well as for Israel's longer-term history, as we will see.

This episode closes and the next opens with the refrain in 17:6, "In those days there was no king in Israel, and everyone did what was right in his/her own eyes." This phrase is absolutely key. But what does it mean and how does it function in the context of these stories and in the overall purpose of the book? It is necessary to consider in detail this refrain before considering the episode concerning the wandering Levite.

This refrain appears in full here and in the very last verse of the book (21:25), and in a shortened version in 18:1 and 19:1, which puts an indelible stamp on the whole epilogue. Taken on its own, the phrase could be either positive or negative. However, the narrator's "objective" telling of the events, including reported speech, has masterfully drawn the reader into the narrative so that when one reaches the statement, "In those days," there is only one way to interpret it: without monarchy anarchy reigns.[414] And yet, it seems that the crisis in Israel "in those days" was not merely that they lacked a king but that

411. For a detailed discussion of the nature and function of these cultic items see Butler, *Judges*, 380–83.

412. Butler, *Judges*, 382, notes that outside the Mosaic/Aaronic narratives, the language of "ordaining" appears only here and in 1 Kgs 13:33 // 2 Chr 13:9: "these latter two in connection with Jeroboam consecrating 'illegitimate' priests . . . the Judges story in a unique fashion mirrors the sins of Jeroboam."

413. Contra Amit, *Book of Judges*, 334, who thinks that the cultic syncretism is a positive compromise as opposed to strictly pagan worship.

414. Amit, *Book of Judges*, 324.

they lacked a divine standard of morality. Micah and his mother violate no less than five of the ten commandments.[415] The refrain in the end-section seems to be the flipside of the refrain that starts each of the cycles (the Israelites "did evil in the eyes of Yahweh"; 3:7, 12; 4:1; 6:1; 10:6; 13:1). The point should be clear: the divine standard has been eclipsed in such a way that doing what is good in one's own eyes far outweighs resisting what is evil in Yahweh's eyes. As Wilson notes, the first formula "concerns moral action assessed in the eyes of Yahweh as evil," the second formula "concerns moral action assessed in the eyes of the Israelites as right. The contrast is striking."[416]

What does this have to do with kingship? In its context, the refrain seems to suggest that a king would sort out all the problems that these narratives in chapters 17–21 recount in painstaking detail. In fact, there is good reason to suppose that the narrator's argument for kingship is not only the solution to the problems presented in chapters 17–21, but that in line with this kind of overview ending, the "in those days" much more generally refers to the whole of the settlement period as depicted in the book of Judges. If this is correct (and I do think it is), then this refrain (along with 2:10) provides the vital clue to understanding the whole of Judges. I have argued in some detail elsewhere the minority position among commentators that the "no king in Israel" refrain is promoting in the first place Yahweh's kingship as the solution to the problem in the settlement period, and not the institution of monarchy.[417] The problem was not so much that Israel lacked a king but that they had rejected Yahweh's kingship and his rightful sovereignty over their lives.[418] The story of Micah's founding of an idolatrous shrine is but one example of the results of Israel's abandonment of their divine king. More examples follow.

The Wandering Levite Finds a Home and Micah Finds a Priest (17:7–13)

The story of the Levite (17:7–13) begins in much the same way as 17:1, including the same verbal form (*wayyiqṭōl* form of היה/*hāyâ*), a description of the individual (איש/*'îš* in 17:1 and נער/*naʿar* here), and an indication of locality, thus, "And there was a young man from Bethlehem of Judah, of the clan of Judah, and he was a Levite and he was a sojourner there." That this individual was a

415. McCann, *Judges*, 120.

416. Wilson, "As You Like It," 74.

417. See Beldman, *Completion of Judges*, 114–21.

418. See Wong, *Compositional Strategy*, 212–23, who argues that the "king" of the refrain refers to Yahweh, the divine king.

sojourner is not unusual since the Levites were not allotted land and lived with the other tribes on their allotments.[419] The man[420] sets out from Bethlehem "to sojourn in whatever [place] he could find," and he happens upon the "house" of Micah (v. 8). Notice the aimlessness of the Levite. In *Where Mortals Dwell: A Christian View of Place for Today*, Craig Bartholomew observes that according to the biblical witness,

> God has ordered creation in such a way that the whole earth is designed as a home for humankind. . . But the embodied nature of human beings means that our placidness is always local and particular; so too will be our primary responsibility for placemaking. Just as the first couple is called to tend to Eden, so we are called to tend to the respective places in which we have been put.[421]

The challenge of postfall human existence, as Bartholomew points out, is "to work hard at practicing placemaking in such a way that it takes place along the grain of God's order for creation, and thereby enhances the shalom of all the creation."[422] The inherent tension of Levitical life is that although Levites are called, as all Israelites are called, to manifest God's intention for human work and flourishing, they must do this without the benefit of having a place to call their own.

Of course, the Torah made provisions for this anomaly. Some Levites were especially consecrated for priestly service and others were meant to carry out their respective callings in cities embedded within the other tribal territories. Block points out that the language of 17:7 seems intentionally to parody Deut 18:6–9, which provides instructions for Levites who might leave the place of their dwelling.[423] The contrast between the instructions given in Deuteronomy and the actions of the Levite in Judg 17 is striking! He doesn't seek out a place that Yahweh chooses (the central shrine, i.e., the tabernacle/temple) but goes to whatever place he might find; he doesn't minister alongside other Levites but supplants the illegitimate priest (Micah's son) ministering at Micah's shrine; he doesn't minister in Yahweh's name but in Micah's name; and he doesn't receive the provision that

419. Num 35:1–8; Josh 21:1–42. This also likely explains the anomaly in v. 7 that he could be both a Levite and from the clan of Judah. Bethlehem in Judah is probably the place he was born and raised.

420. It is peculiar that the נער/*na'ar* ("boy, lad, youth") in v. 7 is האיש/*hā'îš* ("the man") in v. 8.

421. Bartholomew, *Where Mortals Dwell*, 245.

422. Bartholomew, *Where Mortals Dwell*, 245.

423. Block, *Judges*, 486.

Deut 18:1–5 stipulates but the accepts the terms that Micah sets.[424] We should not, therefore, be surprised that the Levite's service does not lead to the kind of enhancement of creation's shalom to which Bartholomew refers.

The dialogue that ensues in 17:9 explicitly reveals the mutual interest Micah and the Levite have in one another, even though the expositional material leading up to that point prepares the reader for the content of the dialogue. Verses 1–5 indicate that Micah has everything in his "house of gods" to fulfill his cultic needs (an ephod, a carved image, and household gods). However, necessity required him to ordain his own son as his priest rather than a bona fide Levite.[425] The narrator emphasizes not only the fact that the individual introduced in 17:7 is a Levite but also that he is a sojourner, that is, without a real home of his own, and longing for a place to settle. In other words, Micah needs a Levite priest and the Levite needs a home. Only the details need to be worked out in order to establish the Levite's residence at Beth-Elohim of Beth-Micah.

Amit suggests that the business-oriented dialogue between Micah and the Levite undermines the air of sanctity associated with the establishment of Micah's shrine.[426] When Micah asks about his origins (v. 9a), the Levite first indicates his Levitical status (in fact the first word out of his mouth is "Levite"; v. 9b). Moreover, in addition to indicating his place of origin in response to the query, the Levite mentions his search for a place to stay. He probably didn't realize that he had Micah at the word "Levite." Micah recognizes the instability of the Levite's situation and immediately capitalizes on the situation. With an imperative, he urges the Levite to dwell with him and offers him a privileged status ("father and priest"), an annual income ("10 units of silver"), and a provision for clothing and sustenance (v. 10). The terms of this arrangement are apparently agreeable to the Levite. The narrator reports that "the young man" (again הנער/*hanna'ar*) made his dwelling in Beth-Micah, and that he "became as Micah's son" (v. 11). The narrator also reports that Micah "consecrated" (literally, "filled [the] hand"[427]) him and he became Micah's priest (v. 12). The final verse of this account is like the punch line of a terrible joke. This verse (v. 13) records Micah's glee over the arrangement (not to mention the perversity of his intentions): "Now I know that Yahweh will be good to me because the Levite has become my priest!"

The circumstances of this account reiterate the fact that all is not well in

424. Block, *Judges*, 486–87.

425. That the lack of a Levitical priest is problematic according to Micah is implied by his declaration once he has secured the Levite's service (17:13).

426. Amit, *Book of Judges*, 326.

427. For this idiom as connoting ordination see Exod 32:29.

the land of Yahweh's people and give more evidence of a world-turned-upside-down. The first example of this inverted world is that the exact age and status of the Levite is impossible to determine. He is initially called "lad, boy, youth" in 17:7 but then is immediately referred to as a "man" in 17:8. Subsequently, he is again referred to as "the youth" in 17:11 and 12. To add to the confusion, Micah expresses his desire that the Levite become his "father" (אב/*'āb*) and priest, and although the status of priest suggests a higher social status and may carry with it paternal associations, Micah's choice of language regarding the Levite who was presumably younger than Micah strikes one as somewhat inappropriate. As if to confirm this intuition, the narrator notes that "the young man became as one of his sons" (v. 11).

The second example of the inverted world of the epilogue is the unquestioning readiness of the itinerant Levite to serve as a priest in a shrine devoted to illegitimate objects of worship. No sooner does Micah have the offer out of his mouth than, without verbal response, "the Levite goes in." The crisis in Israel that is reflected in these episodes is not so much that the people would resort to idol worship, but that not one of the protagonists makes any indication that there is "anything wrong with this type of idolatry."[428]

Finally, Micah's conduct in the affair is further evidence of an inverted world. His statement, "Now I know that Yahweh will be good to me because the Levite has become my priest," reveals his twisted intent. It shows that he was aware that he had violated protocol when he had installed his son as priest, indicating also that he is at least somewhat aware of traditional cultic practices. His misplaced confidence in his acquisition of a Levite to minister in the idol worship is dripping with irony. Ultimately, the statement reveals Micah's deepest, self-interested motivation. He is concerned to do what is right in his own eyes in order to secure personal happiness and prosperity from a god of his own making. For Micah 10 units of silver a year and clothing, room, and board (a fraction of the 1100 that was consecrated in v. 3) represent the price he is willing to put out in order to ensure God's blessing. How any one of God's people could imagine that such a situation would command Yahweh's blessing is baffling. Things are terribly wrong in Israel.

The Migration of Dan, the Levite, and Micah's Shrine (18:1–31)

The formula, "In those days there was no king in Israel," once again functions as a bridge between two sections; it serves as a negative comment on what pre-

428. Amit, *Book of Judges*, 328.

cedes it (Micah and the Levite's idolatrous scheming) and what follows it (the establishment of the shrine in the north). Yahweh's sovereignty over the life and affairs of the characters in these stories is clearly disregarded. What becomes clear is that the missing second line of the formula is certainly implied: "in those days everyone did what was right in his/her own eyes."

The first thing the narrator notes is that the Danites, quite like the Levite in the previous episode, were without a permanent home and seeking a place to dwell (v. 1b). In the account of the mop-up campaign in Judges 1:1–36, the Danites were unable to drive out the Amorites, who put the Danites on the defensive and forced them into the mountains (1:34–36).[429] This account at the beginning of the book is implicitly critical of the Danites for not being faithful in acquiring the land that was rightfully theirs. The narrator's comment here in 18:1 that the Danites were seeking a place because an allotment among the tribes had not fallen to them seems innocent enough, but in the light of 1:34–36 it is pregnant with disapproval. Their unfaithfulness in procuring their tribal allotment becomes the context for further bad behavior and unfaithfulness in this episode.

The chapter divides into two clear sections.[430] After setting the context of the story (v. 1), the first section recounts the Danite spy mission (vv. 2–10). The remainder of the chapter (vv. 11–31) recounts the Danite journey to and conquest of territory in the north. All the features of a typical spy/conquest story appear in this episode (vv. 2–31), but we will see that the way the story unfolds it is clearly a parody of the normal spy story.[431]

(1) The appointment of the spies (18:2)
(2) The sending of the spies with specific instructions (18:2)
(3) The report of the mission's execution (18:2b–7)
(4) The announcement of the spies' return and their report (18:8–10)
(5) The declaration that the land is a gift from Yahweh (18:10)
(6) The conclusion drawn from the spy report and the commencement of immigration/conquest (18:11–31)[432]

The lack of inheritance caused the Danites to search out the land to find a suitable place to dwell, and they send out a party of spies to accomplish

429. See also Deborah's song where she criticizes Dan for not joining the forces against the Canaanites. In the account of the division and allotment of land in Joshua, 19:47 seems to suggest that the "territory of the Danites was lost to them" (see NRSV, ESV, NJPS, etc.).

430. Webb, *Book of Judges*, 430.

431. See Bauer, "Judges 18," 37–47, who examines the use of the spy-story genre in Judg 18.

432. Bauer, "Judges 18," 38.

this (v. 2). A note about geography is necessary at this point, which will have a bearing on our understanding of the chronology of the book. The spies set out from Zorah and Eshtaol, which are towns in the region originally allotted to Dan (see Josh 19:41), sandwiched between Ephraim to the north and Judah to the south. In this chapter of Judges, the Danites migrate from this southern location to the furthest regions in the north. The revelation at the end of this chapter (ch. 18) that the Levite is Moses's grandson situates these events of the Danite migration very early in the settlement period. The Samson cycle, therefore, by virtue of the fact that it takes place in the territory allotted to Dan, took place even earlier than the events of chapter 18 because in that story the Danites (in this case Samson's family members) are still there in the south.[433] This is one major indicator that the events as they unfold in Judges do not (always) follow chronologically.

Verse 2 covers a lot of implied activity and time in short order. At the beginning of the verse the Danites choose and commission five men to spy and explore the land and by the end of the verse these Danites had packed their things, said their good-byes, and arrived at their first stop. This is where the story of Micah and the Levite and the story of the Danites converge, because their first stop is the house of Micah where the spies end up lodging.

In 18:3 the narrator backs up and informs readers that the familiar voice of the Levite is what attracted them to the house of Micah. That they recognize his voice implies that perhaps they had encountered him before, but the narrator is silent about the circumstances of their past encounter—perhaps in his own wandering for a place the Levite had sojourned in the regions of the Danites.[434] Whatever the case, it seems they are surprised that the bearer of this familiar voice should be found ministering at a shrine in Ephraim, prompting a series of questions: "Who brought you here? What are you doing in this place? What is there here for you?" (v. 3b).

Notice the solidarity that exists between the spies and the Levite: they belong to a wandering tribe and have no place of their own. The Levite, however, had found a place and a purpose. This solidarity may explain the interest of the spies in the Levite's current circumstances and may highlight their longing for a home.[435] A darker dimension of their solidarity is also implied. Despite what the Levite may have thought, he no doubt did have a home and had a God-given

433. E.g., Samson's family dwells in Zorah (13:2), the Spirit of Yahweh begins to work in Samson in Mahaneh-Dan between Zorah and Eshtaol (13:25).

434. Though see the suggestion that it wasn't this particular Levite's voice they recognized but an identifiable accent: Boling, *Judges*, 263; Younger, *Judges and Ruth*, 340.

435. Amit, *Book of Judges*, 328.

purpose, but for whatever reason was content to set out until he found himself as a priest in an idolatrous shrine. The Danites too had a tribal inheritance and had a God-given mandate to dwell there and fulfill their calling. In the Levite's destiny we may have a foreshadow of the destiny of the Danites—a dwelling and purpose that are outside of God's will.

The Levite's response in 18:4 is interesting because for the first time we clearly receive his interpretation of the events leading up to his ordination. The first part of his response is vague, "casual and flippant," but the second part of the response reveals how he understands the situation:[436] "Micah has done this and that for me—but he *has hired me* and I have become his priest" (emphasis added). In contrast to the narrator's description that Micah "*consecrated him* and he became his priest" (emphasis added), the Levite exposes his own understanding of what transpired: he regards his relationship to Micah as one of employee/employer and his role in Micah's house in business terms.[437] This seems to contrast Micah's expressed desire (17:10) that the Levite might become as a father to him (not to mention his reported status as like a son to Micah in 17:11). The Levite sees his priestly role as an opportunity for status and gainful employment. By framing his current situation as employment, the Levite might also be planting the seeds that he is open to promoting and advancing his occupational status if the right opportunity emerges.

A proper response to the Levite's explanation would be something like: "What are you doing ministering here at this idolatrous shrine, when you should be ministering with the other Levitical priests at the tabernacle?" However, at this point in Judges, it might come as no surprise that we can detect absolutely no sense of surprise or negative assessment on the part of the Danite spies . . . quite the opposite! Perhaps because they were impressed by the good fortunes of the "religious" man, the Danites, upon hearing of his status as priest, immediately ask the Levite to inquire of *ĕlohîm* as to the outcome of their mission (v. 5). The use of *ĕlohîm* rather than the personal name "Yahweh" may be significant, and perhaps in this context it should be translated in the plural: in Micah's "house of gods" (17:5) the Danites ask the priest to consult the gods. On the other hand, the use of *ĕlohîm* may just be the alternative for Yahweh, and the fact that the Danites think that God could be consulted by means of Micah's idolatrous shrine and priest then heightens the depravity of "those days." However we understand the request of the spies, it is more evidence of the infidelity of God's people.

Acting as "priest," the Levite instructs the Danites to go in peace, because

436. Quotation from Block, *Judges*, 497.

437. On this point see Webb, *Book of Judges*, 432–33.

"the way in which you are going is before the Yahweh" (v. 6).[438] The Levite's words here are quite ambiguous. Polzin notes that the preposition נכח/*nōkaḥ* (ranging from "opposite" to "in front of") could mean that the mission of the Danites is either agreeable or disagreeable to God. In other words, the Levite, an "arch- opportunist," chose his words carefully, tickling the ears of the Danites without being decisive either way.[439]

The Danite spies are reassured by this "word of Yahweh" and depart to Laish. In verse 7 the narrator recounts their initial impression of the people of Laish, emphasizing not only their state of peace, prosperity, and wealth but also their defenselessness and vulnerability.[440] The spies return and with one voice express their conviction that the land of Laish is a good land and would indeed be an easy target for the Danite army (vv. 9–10). With strong language the spies urge the Danites to move forward in the conquest of Laish. Their solidarity and resolve contrast sharply with the most famous spy report in Numbers where the twelve original spies are divided in their assessment of the Canaanite conquest (Num 13:25–33), and the Israelites end up suffering forty years of wandering for their lack of resolve.[441]

The response of the Danites again contrasts with the response of the Israelites to the report of the twelve tribes about to move into the promised land, which consists of a loud collective cry, weeping, complaining, and insurrection![442] The Danites are so persuaded by the report that immediately six hundred Danites gear up and set out for war (v. 11). Block notes that the party of six hundred seems small, and perhaps to this number might be added women and children. Apparently, this Danite party was significant enough that the place where they camped in Judah was renamed *Mahaneh-Dan* ("Camp of Dan"), one of a number of indications in these texts that these circumstances in this history of Israel had long-lasting implications.[443]

On their way north again, they come to the house of Micah where the five spies remember the shrine there and inform the six hundred warriors about it (specifically noting the existence of an ephod, household gods, and

438. Note the narrator's ironic use of "priest" to refer to the Levite.

439. Polzin, *Moses*, 198.

440. Polzin, *Moses*, 199, again identifies the deliberately ambiguous language used to describe the people of Laish. The verb בטח/*bāṭaḥ* can mean "confident" or "unsuspecting," and שקט/*šāqaṭ* can mean "peaceful" or "idle." The result, according to Polzin, is that choice of vocabulary deliberately obfuscates the characterization of Laish.

441. Block, *Judges*, 501.

442. Block, *Judges*, 501–2.

443. Webb, *Book of Judges*, 436.

the carved image). The original spies give the army the following enigmatic instruction: "Now consider what you should do" (v. 14). The text gives no explicit clue as to what the five had in mind; perhaps they were implying that they ought to turn in and have the priest inquire about the success of their campaign.[444] Apparently, the armed Danites understand precisely what the five spies had in mind, but the reader must wait until 18:17 to find out that the original intention was a heist.

Verses 16–18 pose a problem for commentators because the characters appear to jump from one location to another and because the narrator seems to report the theft more than once with what appears to be more than one possible perpetrator. However, the tension is alleviated in part when the last phrase is recognized as parenthetical. Thus:

> The six hundred men from the children of Dan who were girded with weapons of war were taking their stand at the entrance of the gate. Then the five men who had gone out to spy the land got up and entered there in order to take the idol, the ephod, the teraphim, and the molten image (by the way the priest was standing at the entrance to the gate with the six hundred men who were girded with weapons of war). These [i.e., the five spies] entered the house of Micah and took the idol, the ephod, the teraphim, and the molten images. And the priest said to them, "What are you doing?"

These verses leave no doubt that regardless of who did the actual deed, the whole company of Danites was culpable in the theft.

When the Levite asks what is going on (v. 18) the Danites reply brusquely with a demand for silence but also with an appeal to the Levite's ego (v. 19). Once again, the Levite receives a request to be "a father and a priest," with the added prestige of ministering to a whole tribe rather than a single household. The Levite's self-interest prevails, in fact "the heart of the priest was glad" over this fortunate turn of events, and he becomes an accomplice in the theft (v. 20): he himself takes the illegitimate cultic objects and joins the Danites.

As the company departs, they configure in a formation that anticipates an attack from behind (v. 21), no doubt expecting retaliation from Micah, the thief who had become the victim of thievery.[445] When Micah arrives with his own company (v. 22) the Danites mock him and his company with their falsely inno-

444. Amit, *Book of Judges*, 331; Webb, *Book of Judges*, 440.

445. Block, *Judges*, 509: "The young man who had first entered the picture as a thief finds himself the victim of grand larceny."

cent question (v. 23).[446] At this point Micah is a wreck and his pathetic protest reveals his true character: "My gods which I have made, you have taken, and the priest! And you have gone. What do I have left?" (v. 24a). Micah's confusion and incredulity (contrasted with his elation and surety in 17:13) are palpable. These are *his* gods (he made them!) and that is *his* priest. He is defined by the gods that he made, and without them he is nothing! How Micah could put such confidence in gods of his own making is more evidence of a world turned upside down. Micah's company is no match for the Danites and he is forced to return home empty-handed and dejected (v. 26).

At 18:27 the scene changes to the conquest of Laish. The migration of the Danites continues, but this time they are not empty-handed. After repeating (again!) the fact that the people of Laish were an undisturbed and unsuspecting people, the narrator reports that the Danites "struck them with the edge of the sword and burned the city with fire." Ironically, a tribe of Israel becomes the antagonist and the foreigners are found to be in need of a "deliverer" (v. 28a).[447] In the upside-down world portrayed by these chapters, the inhabitants of the foreign city of Laish are victims of the cruelty of the Danites—as Block notes, "the narrator keeps the reader's sympathies with these Canaanites."[448] Webb sees a deep irony here too, noting that things are not at all what they appear: "By conquering Laish, Dan has not contributed to Israel's conquest of Canaan at all, but to Canaan's conquest of Israel."[449] The Danites have already shown a propensity for Canaanite behavior, and their crowning achievement is the establishment of a place of their own to set up a society that is thoroughly Canaanite, at the center of which is an idolatrous shrine.

Verses 29–31 explain the significance of this whole account and are chock-full of noteworthy information. First, the Danites rebuild and rename Laish. Thus, the city of Dan is established and, by means of Micah's gods and his priest, becomes a central location in the north of Israel for idol worship. No doubt this shrine in Dan is linked to Jereboam's great abomination when he set up golden calves in the north—one in Bethel and one in Dan (1 Kgs 12:25–33).

Second, the narrator identifies the previously unnamed Levite as Jonathan the son of Gershom, the son of Moses.[450] According to the conventions of Old

446. Block, *Judges*, 507.

447. Admittedly, the verb used here for "deliverer" is a participle from the root נצל/*nāṣal* and not ישע/*yāšaʿ* that is used for the judges (3:9, 15, etc.). The verbs are clearly synonymous and are paralleled several times throughout the Old Testament (1 Chr. 16; Pss 7:1; 31:1; 33:16; 59:2; 71:2; 79:9; Jer 15:20; 42:11).

448. Block, *Judges*, 510.

449. Webb, *Book of Judges*, 447.

450. The superscripted nun in מ׳נשה/*Mĕnašše* in the MT is most likely an addition to a

Testament narrative, individuals are identified by name and ancestry when they are introduced into the narrative. Holding back the identity of the Levite until the end of the narrative is unusual.[451] Whenever deviations of conventions like this occur, they are almost always significant and are worth pondering. In the case of the Levite, the revelation of his identity provokes a profound sense of shock.[452] Most obviously, readers should be astounded that a grandson of the greatest moral, spiritual, and prophetic leader of Israel is ministering at an idolatrous shrine and implicated in such corrupt circumstances. Moreover, the reality that the Levite is a grandson of Moses situates the events of chapters 17–18 very early in the settlement period—just two generations from Moses and the events of the exodus, the Sinai covenant, and the wilderness wandering.[453] That the author would include in the end section events from early in the settlement period comes as quite a surprise. That surprise is compounded when we learn that the events in the following section (chs. 19–21) are also situated in this same early period (20:28). This chronological deviation that the identity of the Levite exposes may be incidental, but given that the events of chapters 19–21 are placed in the same generation, among other things, suggests that the author is doing something specific with this unusual temporal ordering of the whole book.[454] We will return to this feature of the book after we have considered the details of chapters 19–21.

Third, 18:30 indicates that the Levite and his progeny carried out the priestly function among the Danites until "the day of the captivity of the land." This reference to the captivity of the land, most likely a reference to the annexation of the Northern Kingdom by the Assyrian king Tiglath-pileser in the second half of the eighth century BC (2 Kgs 15:29), emphasizes that the events of Judg 17–18 are not insignificant events that took place according to

---

text that could no longer be altered in order to remove the association between Moses and the unscrupulous Levite. See Boling, *Judges*, 266.

451. For a fuller discussion of this feature see my discussion in Beldman, *Completion of Judges*, 131–32.

452. Both Block and Webb refer to the revelation of the Levite's identity as a "complete surprise" with Webb adding that it "has almost certainly been withheld until now precisely to achieve this effect"; Webb, *Book of Judges*, 448; Block, *Judges*, 510.

453. Of course, that "son," which in the context of genealogies can refer to descendant, may not be literal in the case of the Levite's ancestry is entirely possible. Webb, *Book of Judges*, 448, notes that Exodus does identify Moses as a Levite (6:16–20) and Gershom as a literal son of Moses (2:22), but he is less confident that Jonathan is a literal son of Gershom and is more likely a descendant. I'm inclined to think that literal son may be implied here, especially based on the reference in 20:28 to a grandson of Aaron. In fact, in that place in his commentary, Webb refers twice to Jonathan as the grandson of Moses (on page 486 in the main text and in n. 103).

454. I have explored the temporal ordering of Judges and its rhetorical significance in some detail in Beldman, *Completion of Judges*, 126–43.

mere happenstance; these events were detrimental to the life of the Israelites and had enduring effects in their history—from anarchy, through monarchy, to captivity.[455] Moreover, the combined reference to the shrine in Dan and the exile may subtly imply an association between the two (i.e., the shrine may have been part of the cause of the captivity of the land).

Finally, the reference to Shiloh is most significant. Shiloh is a town in the hill country of Ephraim, northeast of Bethel (see Judg 21:19). In the time of Joshua, the tabernacle of meeting was set up in Shiloh (Josh 18:1) and became the religious center in Israel (including the resting place of the ark of the covenant) until the time the ark was taken into battle and captured by the Philistines under the priestly leadership of Eli (1 Sam. 4:11). We are told that the Danites "established for themselves Micah's idol (which he had made), all the time that the house of God was at Shiloh" (v. 31). The illegitimate shrine of Micah's gods in Dan is here contrasted with the legitimate cultic center in Shiloh where the true worship of Yahweh took place.[456] Perhaps the reference to Shiloh is an even more subtle criticism of the Danites for marauding for a dwelling in the first place (which initially brought them into contact with Micah's idols). When the tabernacle was first erected in Shiloh (Josh 18:1–2), Joshua's first order of business was to allot an inheritance to seven landless tribes. Among those tribes was the tribe of Dan, which received seventeen cities along with the region near Joppa (19:40–48). If Dan had secured their tribal allotment, this idolatrous shrine that is contrasted with the true place of Yahweh's worship (Shiloh) may never have been established in the north. Webb observes that the storyteller masterfully ends chapters 17–18—both literally and symbolically—with "Shiloh."[457] "*The* house of God" was at Shiloh in the hill country of Ephraim, where this whole story began and where Micah set up "*a* house of god(s)." Webb notes:

> With one deft stroke [the author] has brought the narrative full circle, not just from the hill country of Ephraim, via Laish/Dan, back to the hill country of Ephraim, but from Micah's "house of gods," via its reincarnation in Dan, back to the *house of God* in Shiloh. And Shiloh, in the end, with its tabernacle housing the ark of the covenant and the ten words of Moses, becomes the final standpoint from which everything that has gone before is assessed. It is all "off-center," deviant, as idolatry always is.[458]

455. For the captivity, see Block, *Judges*, 513; Boling, *Judges*, 266; Chisholm, *Commentary on Judges and Ruth*, 462; Webb, *Book of Judges*, 449. That the events aren't happenstance, see Amit, *Book of Judges*, 333.

456. Schneider, *Judges*, 24[illegible].

457. Webb, *Book of Judges*, 450.

458. Webb, *Book of Judges*, 450.

Again, the crucial turn of events recounted here is simply more evidence that the people of Yahweh were not content to submit to his kingship and were determined to do what was right in their own eyes.

Uwe Bauer's research on the use of the spy-story genre in the context of a conquest account in Judg 18 seems to confirm the idea that the Danite migration and conquest was illegitimate from the outset.[459] On the one hand the spy-story genre is creatively "inverted," with the result that the conquest of Laish is clearly inappropriate. Although the items typical to a spy story appear in chapter 18, what is missing suggests that the genre is inverted.[460] First, a statement about Yahweh's gift of the land in question typically precedes the selection of the spies, but in Judg 18 this feature is missing. While the spies themselves make this claim, an independent confirmation is lacking. Second, the oracular support for the conquest that is typical of spy stories originates in Judg 18 from an unprincipled priest at an anti-Yahwistic site. The reliability of the young Levite's oracle is questionable at best. Finally, the inhabitants of the spied land are normally noted for their godlessness, brutality, lawlessness, and idolatry. The people of Laish, on the other hand, are not reported as having any of these characteristics, and in fact appear to be a peaceful, law-abiding community existing in security, and the Danites emerge in the story as characteristically godless, brutal, lawless, and idolatrous! Contrasting the Danite migration and conquest with the exodus and conquest cycle of the Israelites further highlights the illegitimacy of the Danite conquest of the north.[461] All of this amounts to the inappropriateness of the Danites' conquest campaign against Laish. The "anti-spy story" contributes further evidence to the topsy-turvy world of Judges.

19:1–21:25: The Atrocity at Gibeah and the Pan-Israelite War against Benjamin

The events of Micah and the Danites in the first part of the end section of Judges (chs. 17–18) are shocking and troubling. However, nothing quite prepares us

459. Bauer, "Judges 18," 37–47.

460. Bauer, "Judges 18," 38–39. What Bauer means by "inverted" is that the genre is used in an antinormative way. The function of a genre in such a case subverts a reader's expectations.

461. Malamat, "Danite Migration," 1–16. Malamat perceives a pattern of association between the migration and conquest campaign of the Danites and the pan-Israelite exodus from Egypt and conquest cycle, including ten harmonious elements. The conquest of the Danites is clearly wrong-headed precisely because of the way it differs from Israel's exodus and conquest campaign. Bauer successfully shows that the purpose of the association is to highlight the points of contrast (of which he identifies five) not the points of comparison; Bauer, "Judges 18," 42–44.

for what we encounter in the second part of the end section (chs. 19–21). The behavior of God's people is astoundingly bad, and in the context of Judges these narratives truly do represent the extreme depths of Israel's moral, social, and spiritual disintegration. The question that should be forefront in readers' minds is, of all the events from this time period, why did the author of Judges choose to end the book with these? What is it about these events that serves the purposes of the author?

Besides the bizarre nature of the events of chapters 19–21, another curiosity of these narratives is worth noting. With one notable exception, not a single individual in this long complex of stories is named.[462] This anonymity serves a number of purposes, but most importantly it universalizes the experience and actions of the characters:[463] "What better way to portray that every Levite, every father-in-law, every host, every single man within that society committed such barbaric atrocities 'from Dan to Beersheba' (20:1) than by allowing every perpetrator in the narrative to exist nameless?"[464] The one man doing right in his own eyes represents everyman doing right in his own eyes.[465]

Chapters 19–21 consist of three main narrative complexes that are linked together causally—one event involving two individuals (the estrangement of the Levite from his concubine) sets off a chain of events with terribly violent, wide-reaching, and national implications. This section unfolds as such. The first section (19:1–30) tells the story of the Levite and his concubine, which results in the tragic and brutal rape and murder of the latter. This section ends with the Levite's summons to the tribes of Israel to act. In the second section (20:1–48), the tribes decide to do something about the atrocity and this results in an all-out civil war in which the eleven tribes determined to completely annihilate the tribe of Benjamin. The final section (21:1–25) opens with the eleven tribes lamenting the fact that the tribe of Benjamin will soon pass out of existence (which, absurdly, was their goal in the first place), and the rest of this section recounts how they circumvent their vow to eliminate the tribe of Benjamin. The whole section and the whole book end with everyone returning to their inheritance and the full version of the "no king in Israel" refrain.

462. The exception is the priest in 20:28.

463. See Hudson, "Living in a Land of Epithets," 59–65.

464. Hudson, "Living in a Land of Epithets," 59. Cf. the 2018 Man Booker Prize–winning novel *Milkman* by Anna Burns, which tells the story of power, (sexual) exploitation, tribalism, religion, and fear—all without using proper names for the novel's characters.

465. My use of "man" here is deliberate, as the events in chs. 19–21 portray men perpetrating death and destruction, specifically at the expense of women.

Atrocity at Gibeah (19:1–30)

The final section of the book begins with a reminder that the unfolding events also took place in this chaotic time of kinglessness (v. 1). The appearance of the "no king in Israel" refrain already in 17:6 and 18:1 should prepare the reader here in 19:1 that what we are about to encounter will be further examples of lawlessness and anarchy.[466]

In this state of kinglessness, the narrator introduces us to the main characters and the "complication" that precipitates the unfolding narrative (vv. 1b–3). Strangely reminiscent of chapters 17–18, the primary characters are a wandering Levite and an individual (in this case the concubine[467]) from Bethlehem in Judah, and the initial location is the hill country of Ephraim.[468] There is no indication that the Levite introduced here ought to be associated with the Levite of the previous section (chs. 17–18), and yet the geographical information and the chronological proximity between the events in chapters 17–18 and chapters 19–21 may spark our imaginations. What if the Levite is one and the same person? What if Jonathan, grandson of Moses, was embroiled in both the establishment of the Danite shrine and the terrible events in Gibeah and the resulting civil war?[469] Whatever the case, this Levite, like Jonathan, is a self-serving opportunist.

The narrator introduces the "complication" in 19:2 as some kind of estrangement between the Levite and his concubine. However, the Hebrew here is difficult and how one translates the verb זנה/*zānâ* depends as much on interpretation as it does on the use of the verb here and elsewhere and a comparison with Semitic cognates and ancient versions. The translation "she played the part of a prostitute" seems unlikely to me and a more plausible rendering, based partly on the fact that the Levite initiates a mission of reconciliation with her, would be "she became angry with him."[470] Whatever the reason for her depar-

466. Webb, *Book of Judges*, 454.

467. As a concubine, this woman was of lower status than the Levite's assumed (but never mentioned) wife.

468. Webb, *Book of Judges*, 455.

469. This is, of course, purely speculation, and would probably require that the events of chs. 19–21 preceded those of chs. 17–18, but the chronology of events in the book as a whole does not follow sequentially so that in itself should not rule out the possibility. It is conceivable that before the events of chs. 17–18, the Levite who himself is associated with Bethlehem in Judah, met his concubine whose hometown is Bethlehem.

470. This is attested in the LXXA and supported by an Akkadian root-meaning of זנה/*zānâ*. See the thorough discussion in Butler, *Judges*, 418–19; and in Block, *Judges*, 523. Regardless of the cause of the estrangement, we should avoid understanding the fate of the concubine as retribution for her unfaithfulness to the Levite. What happens to her is evidence, according to the narrator, of

ture, the Levite goes after her (v. 3a), determined to win her back (literally, "to speak to her heart").

When the Levite finally does arrive at the house of his concubine's father, we might expect a tense or awkward scene involving the concubine and/or her father. At the very least we expect the Levite to speak those tender words to his concubine's heart. However, the narrator provides us with nothing of the exchange between the two or how they feel about the situation. In fact, from this point until the climax of the story, the concubine is pushed to the side, marginalized, and not acknowledged by the Levite or her father. At this early point in the story, the concubine simply brings the Levite into the house and the narrator focuses on the reaction of the concubine's father. For reasons not explained he is delighted at the Levite's arrival . . . the tension and awkwardness are yet to come.

Block notes that at this point the plot tension is resolved, reconciliation is complete.[471] Will the Levite and his concubine return home and live happily ever after? Of course, in Judges there are very few instances of happily ever after. Verses 4–9 introduce a plot complication. In these verses, the concubine's father presses upon the Levite absurdly excessive hospitality. After the initial offer (and acceptance) of three days of hospitality (v. 4), the father insists they stay the fourth morning (v. 5) and then evening (v. 6)—despite the Levite's effort to leave that evening (v. 7). The pattern begins again on the fifth day (v. 8) but toward the evening hour the Levite is restless, ready to depart. With one final and lengthy plea, the father tries to persuade them to stay until the morning of the sixth day (v. 9). With a sense of foreboding, he emphasizes how late in the day it is—the implication here is that it would not be wise or safe to begin a long journey late in the day. However, the Levite is unwilling to stay another minute. He packs his things, departs, and arrives near Jebus (v. 10). This episode of excessive hospitality on the part of the concubine's father serves at least two purposes. The more obvious is that it creates the circumstances wherein the Levite and his company require emergency lodgings because they set out so late in the day. However, the strange hospitality of the concubine's father will also contrast with the lack of hospitality among the Benjamites in Gibeah and then the twisted hospitality they receive from the wandering Ephraimite in Gibeah.

The Levite and company arrive at Gibeah in 19:15 but the intervening verses (vv. 10–14) afford the author the opportunity to expose with deep irony

---

the evils that are perpetrated when Yahweh's sovereignty is replaced with human autonomy (contra Webb, *Book of Judges*, 456; however, Webb admits [457] that the Levite's approach "suggests that she had not left without provocation").

471. Block, *Judges*, 524.

the distorted nature of these times. The narrator notes in 19:10 that, having left the house of the concubine's father, the Levite and his company "arrived opposite Jebus, (that is, Jerusalem)." In Judges, Jerusalem came up already in the conquest narrative (1:21) as the place that the Benjamites were not able to conquer.[472] The narrator makes the connection deliberately between the Jebus of 19:10 and Jerusalem of 1:21, highlighting the fact that had the tribe of Benjamin been faithful in driving the Jebusites out of Jebus/Jerusalem then the Levite and his company would have been approaching an Israelite town as the sun was setting (v. 11). This is ironic on multiple levels. The Levite expresses to his servant that he will by no means stop in "the city of foreigners, who do not belong to the sons of Israel; we will go on to Gibeah" (v. 12). This is ironic because it would not have been a city of foreigners had Benjamin obeyed Yahweh's command to drive out the Jebusites. As the narrative unfolds the irony goes deeper because, clearly, they would have been better off in a city of foreigners than in the Israelite city of Gibeah, whose inhabitants behave as badly as, if not worse than, the inhabitants of the worst foreign city in Israelite history (i.e., Sodom). In any case, they press on to Gibeah when the sun sets, and as darkness envelops them they settle in the city square because they could find no hospitality among their Benjamite kin who would be returning from their fields at that time of day (vv. 14–15).

The Levite does find pity and solidarity with an old man returning from his fieldwork (v. 16). Like the Levite, the old man is both from the hill country of Ephraim and a sojourner in a place he apparently does not belong. After explaining his situation, the Levite assures the old man that they have everything they need—the implication being that all they require is lodging.[473] Acting as the Benjamite residents should have, the old man not only offers a word of greeting ("Peace to you") but plays the part of the gracious host, providing for all their needs and even going so far as to feed the donkeys personally (vv. 20–21). He seems quite adamant that they should not stay in the square (v. 20b), and Block supposes that this conviction stems from his intimate knowledge of the kind of people who resided in Gibeah.[474]

The disaster of being without lodging for the night was averted by the kindness of the old Ephraimite man, but as they all settle into merry-making, evil incarnate comes knocking at the door (v. 22a). The narrator identifies them

472. The narrator indicates here in Judg 19 that Jebus and Jerusalem are one and the same place. It wasn't until later in Israel's history (several centuries later) that Jebus was renamed Jerusalem. This indicates that the author is writing to an audience that knows the place by the name Jerusalem but probably did not know that it was originally called Jebus. See Block, *Judges*, 528.

473. Webb, *Book of Judges*, 465.

474. Block, *Judges*, 532.

as "the men of the city," adding that these were "worthless men" or "men lacking honor."[475] They demand that the host release his male guest so that they may "know him" (v. 22b), a common euphemism in the Old Testament for sexual intimacy, which is clearly its use here. Block notes that three social/moral norms are in jeopardy here: "the law of hospitality, the proscription on intercourse outside of marriage, and proscription on homosexual intercourse."[476] Although the host urges the men of Gibeah against such evil acts, his reason ("for this man has come into my house") indicates that he is only concerned about the first of these three (v. 23). In fact, in a bizarre and horrifying twist, he will sacrifice his own virgin daughter (cf. Jephthah) and the Levite's concubine to preserve the honor of the Levite and his own honor as the Levite's host (v. 24)! The host will bring them out himself and they can "humiliate/afflict/do violence to"[477] (i.e., rape) the women, doing "what is good in [their] eyes." This is indeed a twisted sense of hospitality and would only be proposed as an acceptable alternative to homosexual rape in a world in which Yahweh's kingship has been abandoned for the sake of doing what is good in one's own eyes.

Realizing that the host's intervention was failing, the Levite acts, grabbing hold of his concubine and forcing her out the door, whereupon the men of Gibeah "knew her and abused her all night long until the morning, and they discarded her as dawn was breaking" (v. 25).[478] The narrator expresses only in vague terms the unspeakable horrors that the concubine endured during that tragic night, but somehow she survives. She drags herself to the door of the old Ephraimite and collapses until the morning fully dawned (v. 26).

The scene shifts in 19:27 to focus on the Levite. We might expect that he had an agonizing, guilt-tormented, and sleepless night. A coward might wait at the door till he heard that the mob had left and then attend to the abused concubine . . . not our Levite. Apparently, he threw his concubine to the wolves and then settled down for a good night's sleep. So chilling in its matter-of-fact telling, the story continues: the Levite gets up, opens the door to complete his journey, and discovers his concubine on the threshold of the house (v. 27). If this behavior isn't chilling enough, his response is most disturbing. Without a hint of sympathy or concern, he demands that she "get up," and when there is

475. The idiomatic phrase is more literally "men of the sons of *bĕliyyaʿal*." The Hebrew word בליעל/*bĕliyyaʿal* occurs over two dozen times in the Old Testament, often associated with people of ill moral repute—wicked, base, destructive, good-for-nothing. See Webb, *Book of Judges*, 466; Block, *Judges*, 535.

476. Block, *Judges*, 536.

477. Compare the use of this verb in the rape of Dinah (Gen 34:2).

478. Webb's translation of שׁלח/*šāˈaḥ* as "discard" seems particularly appropriate here; Webb, *Book of Judges*, 466.

no response, he heaves her unresponsive body onto a donkey and returns home (v. 28). The narrator no longer refers to the Levite as "her husband" (v. 3) but now as "her master," reflecting the reality of their relationship—she is his slave to be exploited as he sees fit.[479]

The journey from Gibeah to Bethlehem is inconsequential for the purposes of the narrative and we are told simply that "he arose and went to his place" (v. 28b). The conclusion of the story takes place in the intimacy of the Levite's home. There, the Levite callously carves up the concubine's body like nothing more than a slab of meat. Up to this point the narrator has not explicitly stated that she was dead, and we are left to wonder if in the end the Levite killed her himself.[480] The twelve pieces of her dismembered body are sent, presumably one piece each to the twelve tribes, as a summons to action (v. 29). This significance of this gruesome act may be clarified by a similar act by Saul in 1 Sam 11:7. There Saul slaughters and dismembers his yoke of oxen, sending the pieces of flesh throughout the territories of Israel and including a verbal warning: whoever does not heed his call to arms will end up like the oxen.[481] In this light, the concubine is indistinguishable from an animal carcass, to be divided and exploited.[482]

The Levite's call to action is extremely effective as it provokes "all the people of Israel" to convene (20:1), but the immediate reaction is one of shock and horror. The chapter ends with everyone who encountered the portions of the dismembered concubine expressing that "such a thing" was unprecedented in the history of God's people going all the way back to the exodus and that it requires action (v. 30).[483] Things have gotten completely out of control!

The events surrounding the Levite and his concubine, as we read on, precipitate more violence, more (sexual) exploitation, and more division, but

479. Webb, *Book of Judges*, 469–70.

480. According to the Levite's testimony in 20:5 she was dead before he dismembered her, but by that point in the story his trustworthiness is suspect.

481. The parallels between the Levite's dismemberment of the concubine and Saul's dismemberment of his team of oxen are too close to ignore, but whether the author of Judges was alluding to the incident in 1 Samuel or vice versa is debated. For the former see Block, *Judges*, 547 n. 282; for the latter see O'Connell, *Rhetoric*, 299–304.

482. In a chapter called "Mixed Menus: The Confusion of Food in Judges," MacDonald sees the connection between Saul's act with the oxen and the Levite's act with the concubine as part of a developing theme in Judges, namely, the collapse of natural and social boundaries (i.e., the natural boundaries between animals and humans as well as the social boundaries between food, sacrifice, killing, and sex); see MacDonald, *Not Bread Alone*, 100–133.

483. It may seem as though they are only referring to the division and sending out of the concubine's body, but we can probably assume that the Levite also included a message with the dismembered body pieces explaining what they meant, just as Saul did in 1 Sam 11:7.

it is worth pausing to take stock of this narrative. What is it about *these* events and how they unfold that serves the purpose of the author so well (presuming, as we should, that the author could have chosen a number of events from this time period to include in the end section of the book). First and most obviously, we have seen how these events give more evidence of the twisted, upside-down state of Israel and in fact provide some of the worst behavior we have encountered yet. In this regard, the exclamation of the people in 19:30 stands out as a clue for readers—"such a thing has never happened or been seen" since the exodus. The unprecedented horror of these events serves the author's purpose to show the depths of depravity that God's people are capable of when they desert their divine king and do whatever seems good in their eyes.

Second, these events ought to recall other events in the book of Judges that feature similar characters and relationships. For example, we might compare the Levite in chapter 19 with the Levite in chapters 17–18. The comparison provides more evidence of self-serving and despicable behavior from a member of a tribe who was meant to be set apart for special service to Yahweh and the people. Or we might compare the treatment of Jephthah's daughter with the fate of the concubine. Webb notes, "The concubine is the second woman to be 'sacrificed' by a man who should have been her protector."[484] The theme of hospitality in Judg 19 is a thread that weaves its way through Judges. For example, Gideon does not receive the hospitality from the Israelite cities of Succoth and Penuel that social norms would dictate; here in chapter 19, Israelite hospitality is demonstrated but in both cases it is twisted and has terrible consequences. Although we could unearth more examples like these, one final example bears consideration. The interrelationship between a woman, her husband, and her father is on display at the beginning of the book in a way that deliberately contrasts with the same kind of interrelationship here at the end.[485] In Judg 1:11–15, Caleb secures a worthy husband (Othniel) for his daughter Achsah, and, at the request of his daughter, Caleb blesses her and provides a good home with springs of water. The episode, as Block notes, is one "in which everyone (fathers and daughters, husbands and sons-in-law) functions with boldness and creativity but always respectful of the dignity and role of the other person in that socioeconomic environment."[486] The result is harmony and blessing. This contrasts sharply with the bizarre and damaging way that the Levite, the

484. Webb, *Book of Judges*, 472.

485. I have explored in some detail the "strategy of circularity" in the ending of Judges—that is, how events, circumstances, actions, etc., in the end of the book recall those that appear at the beginning. See Beldman, *Completion of Judges*, 84–107.

486. Block, *Judges*, 96.

concubine, and her father treat each other, with tragic consequences. The events in chapter 19, thus, resonate with themes and events throughout the book that serve the author's purpose in showing just how badly things were in this time of anarchy and (divine) kinglessness.

Finally, an absolutely vital clue to understanding the author's purpose in choosing to include the events of Judg 19 here is how these events echo with uncanny similarity the events of Lot's visit to Sodom in Gen 19. The verbal parallels between Gen 19 and Judg 19 are overwhelming.[487] Block insists that "there can be little doubt that the narrator was composing this text with Genesis 19 in mind and doing so intentionally that the reader might experience a sense of déjà vu."[488] Partly because of the despicable behavior of the residents of Sodom in Gen 19, the city of Sodom stands as a kind of archetype of evil and corruption. If you were to ask an Israelite of this time for some of the worst foreign cities in their history, Sodom would be right up at the top of the list. The implied message of Judg 19 is that a city in Israel has become worse than the worst foreign city in Israel's history. At least in Gen 19 the terrible atrocity was avoided, but not in Gibeah. There may not be a better set of events in the history of the settlement period than chapter 19 to show the utter depravity and canaanization of Israel! And yet, the story hasn't reached a conclusion, and we must read on.

War against Benjamin (20:1–48)

Judges 20 tells the story of the devastating civil war that results from the events of chapter 19. The chapter first gives the background and lead-up to the clash between Benjamin and the other eleven tribes (vv. 1–17) and then describes the multiple battles that ultimately conclude with the devastating defeat of the Benjamites (vv. 18–48). While the events of the civil war in chapter 20 are precipitated by the atrocity in Gibeah in chapter 19, the civil war itself gives rise to a new crisis, namely the extinction of Benjamin—a crisis that the Israelites deal with in chapter 21.

The narrative starts with an example, which is rare in Judges, of God's people showing unity, solidarity, and a common resolve to act. The opening verse gives an overwhelming sense not only of unity but completion: *all* the people, from *all* the territories, and they congregate as *a single* entity (v. 1).[489] In fact, the whole chapter seems to stress the comprehensive and collective action

487. See, e.g., Block, *Judges*, 533–34.

488. Block, *Judges*, 534.

489. "Dan to Bersheba" is a merism that expresses all the land from the northern to the southern reaches of the territories.

of the people of Israel, with the use of "all" in connection with the Israelites ("all the sons of Israel," "all the people of Israel," "all the tribes of Israel," "all the men of Israel") nine times in this chapter (vv. 1, 2, 7, 8, 10, 11, 26, 33, 34) and the people acting "as one man" three times (vv. 1, 8, 11). This seems to be in tension with the refrain that speaks of every "individual" (אִישׁ/*'îš*) doing right in his/her own eyes; however, as we will see even as a body, the Israelites act "as one man" doing what is right in his own eyes. While the narrator is emphasizing the unity and resolve of the assembly, Benjamin and at least one city in Gilead (21:1–9) were not present.

The people gather "before Yahweh at Mizpah" (v. 1b). This was a fitting gathering place for at least two reasons. First, it must have already been established as a kind of sanctuary or divine meeting place.[490] Second, Mizpah was appropriately located close by Gibeah, where the atrocity took place.[491] Here they gather to hear what has taken place in Gibeah, to take counsel, and to act. Verse 2 already hints at what the Israelite congregation has in mind, as we read that four hundred thousand sword-wielding foot soldiers were also present at Mizpah.

Appropriately, the assembly summons the Levite to give an account (v. 3b), and verses 4–7 are the Levite's carefully worded retelling of the events. His account conceals his responsibility in the events—for example, his rash decision to start the journey late in the day, his self-serving and cruel act of forcing his concubine out the door, his callous disposition upon discovering her lifeless body, and his command for her to get up. Also, he implies that the concubine died at the hands of the mob, but as Webb notes, his telling is "deceptively simple."[492] He doesn't actually say that the mob was responsible but deflects suspicion that he may have been the one who killed her in the end. Finally, the Levite subtly embellishes the account so as to heighten his audience's reaction.[493] He characterizes the men as the "rulers" of Gibeah (v. 5a) as opposed to "worthless men" mentioned in 19:22—this implies it wasn't just fringe citizens but those involved in governing the city. Moreover, he reports that their intention was to kill him (v. 5b) but that is not what the account in chapter 19 narrates. Thus, the Levite whitewashes and embellishes the events to deflect any suspicion about his own

490. Block, *Judges*, 551. This is based on the note that it was a place they met "before Yahweh," and also on the fact that later in Israel's history it features as a special meeting place for prayer, spiritual renewal, divine discernment, etc. (see 1 Sam 7:5–17; 10:17–27).

491. This Mizpah should be distinguished from another city of the same name that is featured in the Jephthah account (11:11).

492. Webb, *Book of Judges*, 475.

493. For the following, see Webb, *Book of Judges*, 475.

actions and to manipulate the assembly's reaction against Gibeah and Benjamin. From this point onward, the Levite disappears from the narrative altogether.

The Levite's report further unites the Israelites and swiftly resolves their will to "repay" Gibeah for the atrocity. The phrase "as one man" envelops 20:8–11, in which the Israelites prepare for war. The tribes enlist soldiers for the looming battle and allocate provisions for the standing army (v. 10). With singular determination, they decide not to rest until the residents of Gibeah pay for the outrage.

On first glance, the actions of the tribes in 20:12–13a seem promising. Seeking after justice, they send delegates to Benjamin to deal decisively with the terrible crime in Gibeah. After all, this atrocity needs to be answered. However, the way things unfold, the response of the tribes amounts to bloodthirsty revenge rather than a genuine sense of justice. Their initial action is to send delegates to the tribe of Benjamin, demanding that they give up the perpetrators so that the injustice can be made right (vv. 12–13a). The Benjamites will not hear the accusation against "their brothers" (v. 13b). They would rather risk civil war than give up the debased evildoers of Gibeah. The tension builds as Benjamin musters an army, including an elite squadron of left-handed, expert marksmen (vv. 15–16). Civil war is now inevitable as the Benjamite army deploys at Gibeah (v. 14). Even with this elite squadron, will the Benjamin army be any match for the four hundred thousand Israelite swordsmen?

We return to the question of whether the eleven tribes are acting out of a sense of justice or of revenge. An episode at the end of Joshua involving a conflict among the twelve tribes sheds light on this episode in Judg 20. In Josh 22:10–34, the Israelites level a complaint against the tribes east of the Jordan (Reuben, Gad, and half the tribe of Manasseh). The eastern tribes had made an altar that the other tribes felt was an affront to what they saw as the true worship of Yahweh at the tabernacle. Similar to the situation in Judg 20, the majority tribes gather an army to wage war against the eastern tribes, and they also send out delegates; but that is where the similarities stop. In the Joshua account, the delegation that the ten tribes sent included Phinehas the priest—the same priest who was ministering at the tabernacle during the events in Judg 20 (see 20:28)!—along with ten tribal chiefs (representatives of the ten tribes). Joshua 22 reports in detail the words that the delegates said to the eastern tribes: a clear description of their alleged crime, historical precedent for their wrong-doing, a genuine concern for their and the nation's safety and integrity, and an exhortation toward righteousness (Josh 22:16–20). On their part, the accused have the chance to give their perspective on the alleged wrong-doing (notice that the delegation of the eleven tribes in Judg 20 go throughout Benjamin but they do not go to or address Gibeah itself; see 20:12). The tribes east of the Jordan do give a long defense of their actions. In both the accusation and in the defense, each party invokes the name of Yahweh repeatedly and is concerned foremost with his reputation. The matter is concluded when the priest Phinehas and the other delegates absolve the eastern tribes of wrong-doing and war is averted. In fact, the whole process confirms to them that "Yahweh is in our midst" (Josh 22:31), ends with the delegates and the majority tribes determining that the justification of the eastern tribes was "good in their eyes" (vv. 30 and 33), and ultimately, causes the Israelites to "bless God" (v. 33).

This event at the end of Joshua exemplifies conflict resolution at a time when the Israelites were settling in the land. And yet it contrasts so sharply with how the eleven tribes (excluding Benjamin) attempt to deal with the outrage at Gibeah. Even without reading further we may suspect that things will not turn out well, and indeed the situation spirals desperately out of control in the ensuing narrative.

The rest of the chapter (vv. 12–48) is a long and detailed account of the various battles between the eleven tribes and the tribe of Benjamin. It is remarkable and not insignificant that in Judges, which includes many battles between Israel and the Canaanites, the greatest amount of space and description gets reserved for the devastating war in which Israelites battle against Israelites.[494] The battle reports are carefully structured into three sections and are marked by repetition: (1) 20:18–21, (2) 20:22–25, and (3) 20:26–48. Three times the eleven tribes inquire of Yahweh, three times Yahweh answers, and three times the eleven tribes attack the Benjamite forces. Only after being soundly defeated by the Benjamite forces twice are the eleven tribes victorious.

The campaign against the Benjamites begins almost exactly the same way that the book of Judges does; again we see at work the author's strategy of circularity, whereby events and circumstances at the end of the book recall incidents from the beginning of the book. The Israelites congregate at Bethel, inquire of Yahweh who should lead the campaign, this time against the Benjamites and not the Canaanites, and Yahweh elects Judah (v. 18). The narrator does not say how they determined Yahweh's will but it is reasonable to suppose that they cast lots or inquired by use of the Urim and Thummim (see Exod 28:30; 1 Sam 14:41). We might expect success, given that Yahweh has directed them in this way, so it is quite a surprise that Benjamin is victorious, killing twenty-two thousand Israelites (v. 21).

The very next day the Israelite army takes up battle formation and they inquire of Yahweh again, but before doing so they spend the day in lamentation "before the Yahweh" (v. 22–23a). Their initial defeat has caused them to lose

494. Webb, *Book of Judges*, 478; Block, *Judges*, 557.

their nerve, so rather than asking who should lead in the campaign against Benjamin, they ask if they should even go to battle again against the Benjamites, "their brothers" (v. 23b). Yahweh's response is simply: "Go up against them" (v. 23c). And once again, the forces of Benjamin soundly defeat them, slaughtering eighteen thousand swordsmen (v. 25).

The scenario plays out a third time, with some subtle differences. The narrator stresses the comprehensive nature of the gathering in Bethel this third time (v. 26a: "all the sons of Israel" and the "whole people/army").[495] In addition to weeping (which occurred after the first defeat), the Israelites fast and offer some of the prescribed sacrifices to Yahweh (v. 26). Block notes that "The reference to offerings is especially telling, suggesting that the Israelites may have finally come to realize that their covenant relationship with Yahweh is in doubt."[496] In all of this, the narrator brilliantly gives a sense of intensification after the second defeat—the people are desperate as they struggle to make sense of their lack of success. At this point they are questioning whether or not they should be engaged in this military campaign. When they inquire of Yahweh the third time, this indecision becomes apparent: "Should we yet again go up to battle . . . or should we stop?" (v. 28b). Essentially, they are saying: "Just give us the word, Yahweh, and we'll all go home."

For the *third* time, Yahweh tells them to proceed, but for the *first* time he assures them of success: "Go, for tomorrow I will give them into your hand" (v. 28c).[497] As we will see, Yahweh follows through on his promise, but it does raise a tricky question: Why does God direct the Israelites to engage in battle the first two times without success and then grant them success the third time? There may be any number of explanations for the change of outcome.[498] This seems like an example of God giving people over to their rebellious desires (in this case, Israel's unreasonable and unjust thirst for vengeance) while also setting boundaries. It's as though Yahweh is saying, "You want war, war you shall have!" Webb captures this well: "in this episode in which Israelites wage holy war on Israelites, Yahweh takes his place at the head of the assembly and distributes victory and defeat in such a way that the punishment of Benjamin by the other tribes is made the occasion for the whole of Israel to be chastised by Yahweh."[499] Similarly, Block states, "For once Yahweh has not operated in mercy. Justice is brutally exercised, but the criminals and their defenders are not the only ones

495. Webb, *Book of Judges*, 486.

496. Block, *Judges*, 560.

497. Notice the emergence of the "hand" motif, and how in this context Israelites are delivered "into the hand" of fellow Israelites.

498. For some of the options see Beldman, *Completion of Judges*, 88–90.

499. Webb, *Book of Judges*, 194.

who experience the loss."[500] Of course, this is a context where Yahweh's kingship is ignored, and people do what seems best to them, and in warfare in a context like this, everyone suffers loss.

To this point, I have set aside the note in 20:27b–28a about the ark of the covenant being there (in Bethel) and Aaron's grandson Phinehas ministering before the ark in those days. Although this note is parenthetical, it is by no means insignificant. Normally, the ark of the covenant belonged in the holiest place of the tabernacle. We can surmise from 18:31 that during this time period the tabernacle was set up in Shiloh, and yet the ark was at Bethel . . . why?[501] The Israelites no doubt brought the ark from Shiloh to Bethel as a "good luck charm" in the hopes of gaining success in the war against Benjamin.[502]

The note about Phinehas is also perplexing. We know from elsewhere in the Bible that Phinehas was a zealous defender of covenant fidelity (Num 25:6–13), a trusted leader (Num 31:6), and a wise judge and councilor (Josh 22:10–34). His role in the campaign against Benjamin and what he made of the circumstances will remain a mystery. One curiosity surrounding Phinehas's presence in the events of the civil war centers around chronology. Just like the events in chapters 17–18 that took place early in the period, with a grandson of Moses present, so the events of chapters 19–21 are also early, with a grandson of Aaron present. The appearance of these two Levitical first cousins is impossible to ignore. First, we are presented with the scandal of pedigree—how is it that the grandsons of Israel's preeminent political leader (Moses) and their preeminent religious leader (Aaron) could be embroiled in these twisted events? Second, we are presented with the scandal of chronology—how is it that events at the end of the book which narrate the worst behavior in the book could have happened so early in the period of the settlement? After all, Judges gives the impression of the gradual and steady degeneration of the Israelites during the postconquest period. Did the author make a mistake in introducing these events from early on in the period at the end of the book? We will return to this question at the end of our consideration of chapters 19–21, but the placement of these events at the end appears to cohere with a carefully planned rhetorical strategy.

The rest of the chapter (vv. 29–48) tells in some detail the final defeat of the Benjamite army and the ultimate decimation of the broader popula-

500. Block, *Judges*, 568.

501. That the tabernacle was in Shiloh is confirmed in 21:19, which references a yearly festival at Shiloh, presumably one of the festivals that the Israelites were commanded to keep in the Torah.

502. Block, *Judges*, 561; contra Webb, *Book of Judges*, 486, who thinks its presence here allows the Israelites to legitimately consult with Yahweh.

tion of the tribe of Benjamin. In comparison with the previous two battle reports (which essentially just summarize the defeat of the Israelite army), the third is rather extensive. This section may at first seem confusing and unnecessarily repetitive. It seems that the battle is told from (at least) two perspectives, first from the perspective of the eleven tribes (vv. 29–35) and then from the perspective of the Benjamites (vv. 36–41). In this third battle, the Israelites change their tactics. Rather than meeting the forces of Benjamin head on, they draw up battle lines but also set an ambush of soldiers. Emboldened by their previous success, the Benjamite forces are lured away from the city at which point the Israelite soldiers in hiding emerge. The carefully coordinated Israelite forces decimate the Benjamite army.[503] This section ends with a note about Yahweh's role in defeating Benjamin and the casualties they suffered (v. 35).

The perspective of the account shifts in 20:36 to give a sense of how the Benjamite forces experienced the defeat. We are told about the men in ambush entering the city of Gibeah and destroying it (v. 37), about the signal of fire that the Israelite forces predetermined for the men in ambush (vv. 38–39a), the Benjamites' sense of security with their initial success (v. 39b), and their feeling of dread as they watched the "whole city" go up in smoke (v. 40). The narrator notes their inner turmoil as they realize they are finished (v. 41).

Verses 42–47 describe the flight of the Benjamite army and how the Israelite army pursued and cut them down as they chased them. A mere six hundred men survived of the twenty-six-thousand-strong army of Benjamites (v. 47)—these survivors will be important for the conclusion of the story (ch. 21). Having defeated the Benjamite forces, the Israelite army turns their attention to the civilians of Benjamin, rampaging all the territories of Benjamin and leaving no survivors, whether human or beast. Yahweh had defeated the army of Benjamin (v. 35) and this scorched-earth, leave-no-survivors tactic goes beyond what is reasonable or divinely approved.

In this penultimate chapter in the book of Judges, we encounter holy war that clearly recalls the holy war waged against the Canaanites that started the book (ch. 1).[504] The comparison between the beginning and the end reveals the tragic irony—at the beginning the Israelites unite to obey Yahweh's command, wage holy war on Canaan and are unsuccessful; at the end, the Israelites unite to serve their own sense of vengeance, waging holy war on their own kin and are

503. The account notes that of the original 26,000 (v. 15), 25,100 men of Benjamin perished that day.

504. Commentators note how all the typical aspects of the holy war tradition are present in this narrative; see, e.g., Block, *Judges*, 567–68; Webb, *Book of Judges*, 494–95; Butler, *Judges*, 438.

largely successful. The events of chapter 20 do seem to exemplify the author's purpose to reveal the thorough canaanization of the people of Yahweh.[505]

Yahweh emerges in this chapter after several chapters of "absence." Judges 16:20 was the last time "Yahweh" was the subject of a verb, and there in a note about Yahweh leaving Samson.[506] In chapter 20 Yahweh speaks three times (vv. 18, 23, 28), two of which send the Israelite forces to defeat. The narrator reports Yahweh specifically acting only once, which is in 20:35: "Yahweh defeated Benjamin before Israel." Yahweh's ways are mysterious and difficult to understand, but it does appear that the nation is suffering because they have rejected his kingship. Justice has been terribly perverted and leads to further atrocity in the final chapter of the book.

Reconstruction after the War (21:1–25)

The final chapter of Judges occurs in the aftermath of the civil war. The events recounted here are tragic and absurd as the eleven tribes attempt to circumvent an oath they had made before the campaign against Benjamin. The terrible behavior of the Israelites is the author's final supporting evidence that this is a people who have rejected Yahweh's kingship and are doing what seems best to them (21:25).

The narrator starts with a flashback, providing a crucial piece of information that happened before the campaign against Benjamin. Unbeknown to the reader, the Israelite council at Mizpah (ch. 20) included a vow that upon pain of death they would not provide the Benjamites with wives (21:1). By making this vow before the war against Benjamin, they reveal just how hell-bent they are on eradicating the tribe of Benjamin. No doubt they expected to defeat the armies of Benjamin and then slaughter the Benjamite civilians, but anticipating the possibility of survivors, they ensured the eradication of Benjamin by preventing them from marrying and perpetuating the line of Benjamin.

If the narrator was reticent about informing readers about the vow before, chapter 21 makes up for it by repeating the vow three more times. In 21:1 the narrator provides the content of the vow. Verse 7 refers to it in the reported speech of the people as an oath that they had "sworn by/to Yahweh."[507] Finally, in 21:18, the narrator quotes the oath of the people as "cursed is the one who gives a wife to Benjamin." Just as Jephthah was unwilling to break his rash vow

505. Block, *Judges*, 568.

506. We may surmise that Yahweh acted to strengthen Samson after Samson's prayer, but the narrator is silent in that regard.

507. See Butler, *Judges*, 451, 452, who translates the phrase as "in the name of Yahweh."

and face the consequences, the Israelites too are unwilling and cook up not one, but two schemes to circumvent their vow.

Thus, in the wake of the near annihilation of Benjamin the vow emerges as a "fresh complication."[508] The people's response to the new reality is one of weeping and entreating Yahweh (vv. 2–3), which is deeply ironic because the last time they engaged in such activity it was because they were being defeated by the Benjamites and were pleading with God to give them victory over them. As the spoiled child, the Israelites cry when they don't get what they want and cry when they do get what they want! Their seemingly innocent question in 21:3 is telling. On the one hand, they ask the question as though it wasn't their intent from the beginning to eliminate Benjamin—which it was! On the other hand, their carefully chosen words lay the blame on Yahweh. Webb put it well: "The inquiry is less a request for information than an oblique form of protest, and an attempt by the inquirers (consciously or otherwise) to absolve themselves of responsibility."[509]

Clearly the people do not want an honest answer to their question but instead they want Yahweh to provide a solution to their predicament. Whereas he spoke three times in the previous chapter in response to Israel's requests, here Yahweh remains silent. Unable to accept Yahweh's silence, the people spend the next day erecting an altar and engaged in ritual activity, presumably to break Yahweh's silence.[510] But it is futile. They will have to rely on their own resources to reverse the curse—they will have to find a solution that seems right in their own eyes.

Verses 5–11 describe the assembly's attempt to find a solution to the extinction of Benjamin. It is difficult to follow the logic of the initial verses here (vv. 5–7), but this may, as Block suggests, be a reflection of the Israelites' own confusion and frustration in light of Yahweh's silence.[511] We are introduced to another vow in 21:5—apparently the Israelites swore an oath that any "tribe" that did not answer the call to arms against Benjamin would be put to death. The assembly determines that the city of Jabesh-gilead had failed to come. According to the vow of the assembly at Mizpah (ch. 20), Jabesh-gilead should be utterly destroyed. However, the assembly (at Bethel) decides that they will follow through on their vow to destroy Jabesh-gilead, including men, "women and children" (vv. 10b–11) . . . with one exception. Instead of killing all the inhabitants, the army should spare and bring back all female virgins; these would be given to the remnant of Benjamin as wives.

508. Webb, *Book of Judges*, 495.

509. Webb, *Book of Judges*, 496; cf. Block, *Judges*, 571.

510. Block, *Judges*, 571.

511. Block, *Judges*, 572.

This solution is deeply ironic. In order to circumvent one asinine vow, the Israelites are willing to fudge on another asinine vow, slaughtering a city that would have no part in the vengeful campaign against Benjamin and sparing the virgins of that city to perpetuate the line of the decimated tribe of Benjamin. Regardless, this seems like a good solution to all, and twelve thousand premier solders are commissioned and sent (vv. 10–11). They procure four hundred virgins (whose families and friends have presumably been slaughtered before their eyes) and bring them to Shiloh (v. 12). The narrator qualifies Shiloh as the place "which is in the land of Canaan," a curious note.[512] Webb supposes this "is a subtle reminder that, after all that has taken place in Judges, Israel still lives in an alien land."[513] Block, however, sees a rhetorical purpose in this: in referring to Shiloh as "in the land of Canaan" the narrator is making a judgment on the character and actions of the people in this place. In other words, Shiloh is Canaanite because the things that take place there are thoroughly Canaanite.[514]

Verse 13 demonstrates the Israelites acting once again as a unity: "the whole assembly" summons Benjamin; their intent is to "proclaim peace" (v. 13), although in this context it seems like a poor choice of phrases. The Benjamites, however, have "nothing to lose and everything to gain," and so they come and receive the "gift" (v. 14a–b).[515] Just when we may be hoping that this excruciating ordeal has come to an end, however bizarre and tragic that end is, a further complication emerges. The scheme is only partially "successful" as the campaign against Jabesh-gilead only provides wives for four hundred of the six hundred remaining Benjamites (v. 14c). We may be inclined to think that in 21:15 the narrator is laying the blame on Yahweh for the decimation of Benjamin: "because Yahweh had made a breach in the tribes of Israel." It seems more likely that this phrase is not the normative evaluation of the narrator but represents the perspective of the Israelites and constitutes the reason for their compassion—they felt sorry because *in their mind* Yahweh had created the breach.

Thus, this sordid affair is not over, and the narrative continues to limp along to its eventual end. This time the "elders" provide a solution (v. 16a), but first they rehearse the problem (vv. 16–18), which again seems quite redundant but serves to reiterate the absurdity of the circumstances. Their solution is even more outrageous than the first. Essentially, they recommend that the remaining Benjamite bachelors "catch" (v. 21) a wife among the virgins that come out to

512. Block, *Judges*, 576, observes that "this is the only place in the entire Old Testament where the designation 'land of Canaan' applies to the postconquest period."

513. Webb, *Book of Judges*, 501.

514. Block, *Judges*, 576–77.

515. Quotation from Block, *Judges*, 577.

dance at a yearly feast at Shiloh and then quickly escape back to their tribal territory in Benjamin. They had clearly thought through this plan as it is detailed and accounts for possible contingencies that may occur (vv. 19–22).

They identify the annual "feast of Yahweh at Shiloh" as a place where virgin wives could be had (v. 19a). From the note in 18:31, we know that the "house of God" was at Shiloh and can assume that this is the regular resting place of the tabernacle. The yearly feast of Yahweh no doubt refers to one of the major feasts stipulated in Deut. 16:1–17, namely, the Passover, the Feast of Weeks, or the Feast of Booths.[516] Given the fact that the Torah commands that all males make the annual pilgrimage to participate in these feasts, it's curious that the elders have to give detailed directions to the location of Shiloh (v. 19b).

The elders' solution shrewdly circumvents the vow. It gives immunity to the fathers of the "daughters of Shiloh"—because they did not willingly give their daughters to the remnant of Benjamin they will be free of guilt (v. 22). All the angles are covered. All parties are satisfied . . . but only if we ignore the interests of the young daughters of Shiloh. Not unlike the Levite's concubine with whom this whole affair started, the nameless two hundred daughters of Shiloh (not to mention the four hundred virgins of Jabesh-gilead) are merely pawns, commodities in a world that cares nothing for what is good for them.

The final verses bring the story to its conclusion and may strike the reader as deceptively detached. The Benjamites for their part did as they were instructed; they got their wives, returned to the devastated remains of their tribal territory and began the process of rebuilding and restoring their homes (v. 23). The other tribes also returned to "tribe and family," each to his inheritance (v. 24). The motif of returning to tribal territories in these final verses (vv. 23–24) further contributes to the author's strategy of circularity as it recalls almost the exact same phrase in 2:6.[517] In an article on endings in biblical literature, Isaac Gottlieb catalogues no less than ten biblical books and three psalms that end with the language/motif of return (שׁוּב/*šûb*).[518] The exemplary text is Ruth, which shares with Judges the fact that the motif of return appears at the beginning and the end. In Ruth, the returning at the end provides a deep sense of harmony, balance, and closure to the book.[519] This contrasts sharply with the end of Judges:

516. Block, *Judges*, 579.

517. On the strategy of circularity and the motif of return, see Beldman, *Completion of Judges*, 91–92.

518. Gottlieb, "*Sof Davar*," 218–19: Judg 21:23; Hos 14:8; Amos 9:14; Mic 7:19; Zeph 3:20; Mal 4:6; Job 42:10; Ruth 4:15; Lam 5:21; Eccl 12:7 and Pss 14:7; 53:6; 80:19.

519. Gottlieb, "*Sof Davar*," 220.

> The return of the Israelites to their homes at the end of Judges is not merely a return to the status quo. The events immediately preceding the note in 21:24 indicate that the thinned tribe of Benjamin would be returning to a devastated land to rebuild and eke out an existence after a close brush with extinction. The other tribes would also be returning to lands which they would coinhabit with Canaanites and also no doubt reflecting upon the atrocities they had perpetrated upon one of their own tribes.[520]

In Judges, therefore, the motif of returning and the circularity it evokes leave us with a sense of uneasiness and open-endedness.

As mentioned, the report of their return seems deceptively detached. Although the narrator may seem nonchalant in the reporting of the Israelites' return home, these statements are pregnant with criticism. That criticism is put to words in the final statement of the book, which is also the refrain that has punctuated the end section: "In those days there was no king in Israel. Everyone did what was right in his/her own eyes" (v. 25). This is a bold and clear reminder of the point the author has been trying to drill down and the hermeneutical key not only to these final chapters of Judges but to the book as a whole. These events make no sense at all unless they are understood as actions of a people whose hearts had grown cold to Yahweh—a people who had abandoned King Yahweh and his good purposes for them.

Retrospective Evaluation: A View of Judges from the End

Reflecting on the significance of the endings of stories, one literary theorist says, "We expect endings, much more than beginnings, to show what the story was about, what special effect was to be achieved."[521] René Girard maintains that the primary location of truth is at the conclusion of a narrative, evocatively referring to the ending as the "temple of truth."[522] We intuitively sense something of this in narrative forms like film, TV series, novels, and even children's storybooks. Endings draw all the threads together, often tying up loose ends, and bring completion to the whole. The truth of the narrative is incomplete or obscure until the very end.[523] Moreover, endings often require a reevaluation of a narrative's beginning and middle in light of the ending.

520. Beldman, *Completion of Judges*, 92.

521. Bonheim, *Narrative Modes*, 118.

522. Girard, *Deceit, Desire, and the Novel*, 307–8.

523. I have attempted to provide a detailed theoretical accounting of the significance of narratives in general in Beldman, *Completion of Judges*, esp. ch. 2.

All of this is true for literary endings in general and no less true in the case of the book of Judges. As we have seen and experienced, the ending of Judges (chs. 17–21) is by no means easy and it contains a number of peculiarities (to say the least!). How do these chapters bring the book to a close? What kind of ending is this? What is the author trying to achieve by ending the book this way? What special effect does the ending have on our understanding of Judges? Effectively, we want to consider what rhetorical "strategies of ending" the author has employed in the composition of the book. Having journeyed through the various twists and turns in the book, it's worth pausing to consider the book as a whole, now from the perspective of the ending.

The Strategy of Completion

The strategy of completion is the kind of ending we most typically come to expect at the end of a narrative. According to this strategy, the ending brings together the various strands of the narrative, often (but not always) bringing a sense of closure. In this way, readers can discern a logic to the ending—even with surprise endings elements that may have been obscure in the beginning and middle are illuminated in retrospect.[524]

We can discern the strategy of completion at work in Judges. Various themes and motifs that weave their way through Judg 1–16 find completion in the end section. At the broadest level, the thematic level, Judges displays this strategy at work. Many scholars and commentators who are in tune with the literary artistry of Judges maintain that from beginning to end Judges displays the progressive degeneration of the situation and character of Israel and Israel's leaders. In other words, as the book moves forward, Israel becomes more and more corrupt, the situations become more and more bizarre, Israel's saviors become more and more degenerate, and so on. Thus, by the time we get to the end section, Israel's behavior and character (morally, socially, religiously, etc.) reach an all-time low. Even though the events in chapters 17–21 are shocking and outrageous, we can discern a certain logic to this progression. Block refers to this degeneration as the canaanization of Israel, helpfully foregrounding the fact that they are being cast progressively in the image of the foreign nations around them.[525] This major

524. The now classic movie *The Sixth Sense* is masterful in this regard. It was nearly impossible to anticipate the surprise ending but the revelation at the end clarifies subtle clues throughout the film, so much so that we may be inclined to watch the film again afresh to discover, in retrospect, the clues that we may have missed in the course of the first viewing.

525. Block, *Judges*, 57–59.

theme of Judges is demonstrated in countless ways in more minor themes and motifs that run through the book and find their completion in chapters 17–21.[526]

Thus, we can clearly discern the strategy of completion at work in the ending of Judges. The purpose of this ending strategy is to display the worst behavior at the end. The effect is that Israel progressively gets worse and worse as the book spirals to its end. The *impression* this proffers is that over the course of time in the settlement period Israel becomes more corrupt and moves further away from their calling as the people of Yahweh. I stress that this is the *impression* that the book as a whole conveys because the strategy of completion is not the only ending strategy at work in Judges. As we carefully discern the thoughtfully crafted ending it becomes apparent that the progressive degeneration interpretation of Judges requires a significant reevaluation.

The Strategy of Circularity

At points in the commentary on chapters 17–21 I have identified actions, situations, and events in this end section that recall similar circumstances in the beginning of the book (1:1–3:6). The most obvious link between the beginning and end of Judges is the one between the pan-Israel war that starts the book and the pan-Israel war that ends it. In both cases the congregation gathers and asks Yahweh who should lead in war—"the methods of request that the Israelites employ, the questions they pose, and the answers they receive are in both cases identical."[527] However, this example of circularity exposes the irony of the situation at the end of the book. At the beginning they gathered to be obedient to Yahweh's command to drive the remaining nations from the land (even though they are increasingly unsuccessful); at the end they are gathered to fulfill their own sense of "justice" by wiping the tribe of Benjamin off the face of the planet (and they are nearly successful!). On its own, the campaign against Benjamin is a sad and troubling story, but the intertextual link with the similar circumstances at the beginning reveals a deeper level of corruption. The situation from beginning to end has been disturbingly inverted.

The two pan-Israel wars that frame the whole book are by no means the only example of circularity in the book. To that we could add the following:

526. The list includes the activity of Yahweh and the revelation of his word, the role and treatment of women, the motif of family relations, the internal relations between the Israelites, the making of oaths/vows, etc. For a full list and description of how this strategy plays out in these themes and motifs see Beldman, *Completion of Judges*, 78–83.

527. Beldman, *Completion of Judges*, 87.

tribes returning to their inheritances (2:6; and 21:24), Israel "weeping" (2:4; and 21:2), Israel's application of חרם/*ḥāram* (1:17; and 21:11) and "striking" towns/cities "with the edge of the sword" (1:8, 25; and 20:37, 48), spies and their missions (1:22–26; and 18:2–31), references to Jebus/Jerusalem (1:21; and 19:10–13), references to the leadership vacuum (1:1; 2:8, 21; and 17:6; 18:1; 19:1; 21:25), women riding on donkeys (1:14; and 19:28), human mutilation (1:6; and 19:29), arranged marriages (1:11–15; and 21:1–23), and innerfamily dynamics (1:11–15; and 17:1–5; and 19:1–10).

What is remarkable about this list is that almost all of these connections involve phrases, situations, actions, or references that only occur at the beginning and end and not at all in the core section of the book. Moreover, many of these links expose the same kind of degeneration from the situation as it occurs at the beginning and how it presents at the end. The overwhelming number of links between the beginning and end and their propensity to reveal an ironic reversal of situations suggest a rhetorical strategy at work in the end—what I refer to as the strategy of circularity.

I noted in the commentary on 18:30 and 20:28 that the references respectively to Jonathan (Moses's grandson) and Phinehas (Aaron's grandson) expose a deviation from sequential chronological order. We should acknowledge straightaway that the events in the two sections of the ending (chs. 17–18 and chs. 19–21) cohere with the ending strategies that we have already explored, namely, the strategy of completion (these events demonstrate the worst behavior and situations, a string of events that display progressively degenerate behavior throughout the book) and the strategy of circularity (these events recall events and situations recounted in the beginning of the book). This poses an important question to the careful observer: Did the author of Judges choose to recount these events at the end because they work well with these ending strategies and *in spite of* the chronological deviation they represent? Or does the chronological deviation itself serve a purpose in the author's ending strategy?

With regard to deviations in chronological ordering in biblical narrative, Amit notes, "The biblical story, which claims to be a historical narrative, is naturally bound to the chronological sequence, yet nevertheless, it contains some deviations from it, and they are always significant and functional."[528] There is good reason to believe that the deviation from chronological sequence at the end of Judges is functional and significant for the purposes of the book.[529] It

528. Amit, *Reading Biblical Narratives*, 110. For some examples see Beldman, *Completion of Judges*, 139–40.

529. For a full and detailed consideration of the chronology and temporal ordering of Judges see Beldman, *Completion of Judges*, 126–43.

seems like no mistake that both of the sections of the ending have a reference to the same generation and both connect these events to generations twice removed from Israel's preeminent political and religious leaders (Moses and Aaron respectively). Moreover, these references appear to reveal a carefully planned out design to connect the events of the end section right back to the beginning of the book—in fact right to 2:10. We recall that 2:10 is key to understanding Judges, as it clearly identifies the root of the problem in the settlement period, namely a generation that emerged after Joshua and the elders that outlived Joshua—that generation did not know Yahweh and all that he had done on behalf of Israel. Now here at the very end of the book, we have come full circle and the author has brought us right back temporally to the beginning.

If it is true, as I am convinced it is, that the author deliberately chose events that (1) showed some of the most terrible behavior we could imagine, and (2) happened early in the settlement period, then what does this achieve for the rhetorical thrust of the book? It's not at all unusual for narratives—both modern and ancient—to return at the end to events that happened early in the time period that the narrative covers. In the literary world, the technical term for this is *analepsis*. The literary theorist G. Genette describes analepsis as "any evocation after the fact of an event that took place earlier than that point in the story where we are at any given moment."[530] Analepsis is a kind of flashback and can serve any number of purposes.

The analepsis in Judges contributes to a frustrating sense of a lack of movement or goal in the book. The cyclical nature of the core section of the book (3:7–16:31) has prepared readers for this seemingly unbreakable cycle of sin/punishment/deliverance/peace, and the ending's return to the beginning reinforces the futility of Israel's behavior—there has been no development or movement forward at all! In this way, the analepsis in Judges contributes a new dimension to the strategy of circularity.

However, the analepsis also requires a reevaluation of the strategy of completion. If the author deliberately chose to narrate the events of chapters 17–21 because they are contemporaneous with the events of the beginning, then the widely accepted "progressive degeneration" interpretation of the book of Judges needs significant revision. From beginning to end, the author is indeed giving the impression that things are getting worse and worse. Just as we are sensing that the ending of Judges is meeting our expectations (i.e., narrating Israel at rock bottom), the rug gets pulled out from under us as we realize that these events happened early in the period. The references to the generation twice removed from Moses/Aaron in 18:30 and 20:28 are like a one-two punch—18:30

530. Genette, *Narrative Discourse*, 40

catches us off guard and sends us reeling and 20:28 puts us on the floor, dazed and confused.

The Strategy of Entrapment

The analepsis clearly contributes to the strategy of circularity as the end returns in a temporal way to the beginning of Judges. However, the sense of shock that the analepsis produces alerts us to a final ending strategy, namely, the strategy of entrapment. Having been trapped into thinking that Israel's deep corruption and rebellion at the end of Judges is the nadir of a steady and consistent decline *over the course of time*, the trap is sprung at the shocking revelation that these horrifying events took place early in the settlement period—in fact precisely at the time mentioned in 2:10. This is a brilliant rhetorical tool, but what does it achieve in the overall purpose of the book?

Once readers recover from the initial sense of shock, this revelation should prompt an all-important question: How is it that this remarkably depraved behavior could have emerged so early in Israel's settlement period? At this point we may search the end section for an answer, and that search will not be in vain, as the author provides all the clues necessary to unravel this mystery.

Two subjects emerge in the end section that on first reading might strike us as discordant when compared to the rest of the book, namely, kingship and cult. First,

> Although cultic matters arise at points previously in the narrative of Judges, the end section contains a concentration of circumstances and events which raise the issue of the cult in an unprecedented way. Here the reader gets exposure to several cultic locations (Dan, Mizpah, Bethel, and Shiloh) and a number of cultic practices (divine inquiry, lamentation, fasting, sacrifice, religious festival, etc.). Moreover, in the end section, the narrator introduces the reader of the book of Judges to a number of firsts with regard to the cult: the first mention of the sacred location of Shiloh, the first reference to the Ark of the Covenant, and the first time the Israelites "offered burnt offerings and peace offerings" (20:26; 21:4).[531]

This concerted effort to highlight cultic matters is the first clue to understanding how such bad behavior could have emerged so early in Israel's settlement period. Here at the end of the book we are alerted to what is missing throughout the book: properly observed worship. The covenant that Israel entered into

531. Beldman, *Completion of Judges*, 113.

with Yahweh, established at Sinai, and renewed on the plains of Moab, instituted practices and rhythms that would remind the Israelites of all that Yahweh had done for them—rescuing them from Egypt, giving them a new identity as a kingdom of priests and a holy nation, entering into covenant relationship with them, caring for them through the years of wilderness wandering, and conquering their enemies during the conquest period. Where in Judges do we see the people of Yahweh observing those essential identity-forming rites, customs and festivals?

Thus, matters of worship and cult emerge in the ending in a surprising way, but provide the first major clue to how Israel could have strayed so far so early in the settlement period. The second major clue is the surfacing of the idea of kingship. The "no king in Israel" refrain implicitly identifies the problem in the settlement period. By means of this refrain the author holds out the only real solution to the moral, social, and spiritual corruption of Israel that, at the end, we now realize takes root early on in the period.

On first glance, kingship may strike us as a bad solution to the problem we encounter on the pages of Judges. Over the course of Judges kingship, whether foreign or in the experiments with kingship under Gideon and his son Abimelech, only brings oppression, violence, and moral and spiritual corruption. Furthermore, the burden of the author throughout the book is to reveal that Israel's problem in the settlement period is not political but is rooted in their infidelity to Yahweh and his covenant. Thus, even though the repeated refrain that puts an indelible stamp on the end section and points to the author's central concern (this is what it's all about) identifies the lack of kingship as the key to understanding the settlement period, it requires thought and reflection as it seems in tension with the thrust of the rest of the book.

Not unlike the emphasis on cultic matters in the end section that requires a retrospective revaluation of the whole book, so the issue of kingship should prompt us to go back and rethink the whole of Judges to see how kingship offers the solution to the early corruption of Israel in the settlement period. As we do so we realize the tension is only apparent, as upon reflection it becomes clear that the refrain is primarily referring to Yahweh's kingship. In the commentary on Judg 8, we saw that Gideon hinted at Yahweh's reign in his mock rejection of the people's request to make him a dynastic monarch (8:22–23). Moreover, the reference to the "captivity of the land" in 18:30 suggests that the earliest dating of the authorship of Judges is after the Assyrian exile of the Northern Kingdom. As such, the original audience had observed and experienced the string of kings who had only intensified and institutionalized the kind of bad behavior we witness on the pages of Judges. Therefore, the history subsequent to the settlement period is some of the best evidence against kingship as a solution to the rebellious and corrupt behavior of Israel in the settlement period. Finally, the earliest and most authoritative commentary on the settlement period appears in 1 Sam 8:7–8. There Yahweh instructs Samuel to grant the Israelites their request for a king. His reason is most revealing: "they have not rejected you, but they have rejected me from being king over them. According to all the deeds that they have done, from the day I brought them up out of Egypt even to this day, forsaking me and serving other gods." This is key! The rejection of Yahweh as king is evident in all the actions of Israel from the exodus (i.e., their immoral and rebellious behavior) and in their deserting Yahweh and pledging allegiance to the Canaanite gods. Yahweh himself indicates that all the bad behavior in Judges boils down to this one crucial reality: they have rejected him as king. With regard to the only king that matters—the divine King—there was essentially no king in Israel. Political rulers and systems will come and go, but allegiance to King Yahweh is meant to provide the stable substructure of Israelite culture and society.

Robert O'Connell is helpful in navigating the apparent anomaly of the emergence of kingship and cult in the end section:

> First, how does the controlling purpose of the book . . . presented separately in Judges' prologue and superimposed in its body, relate to the monarchist refrain repeated in the double dénouement (17:6; 18:1; 19:1; 21:25)? Second, why do both the stories feature a Levite and finish with reference to Shiloh (18:31; 21:12–24) in spite of the fact that neither Levites nor Shiloh have been mentioned previously in Judges? Third, why is the ark of YHWH mentioned only in 20:27 and perhaps 18:30b despite the many "holy wars" of the book?[532]

O'Connell then identifies in these anomalies a literary strategy:

> This "dénouement," rather than unraveling the complications of the book's intriguing design, only entangles the reader with the need to make a reassessment of the first impression and binds upon the reader the conviction that he or she has been subjected to a *rhetorical strategy of entrapment*. . . . The introduction of these complications in chs. 17–21 invites the reader to reassess Judges' central section (3:7–16:31) to discern how it might cohere with a belated interest in both kingship and cult center. This rhetorical strategy, by which the compiler/redactor withheld essential information until the dénouement, seems to have been designed to entrap the reader into a

532. O'Connell, *Rhetoric*, 6.

premature assessment of Judges' hero stories so as to invite a retroactive reassessment of the book's characters (if not of the reader's perceptions of leadership in Israel). From a rhetorical perspective, it may be the "incongruity" of Judges' thematic concerns that offers the best clue to its overall strategy.[533]

Summary and Conclusion

We started this section with the sentiments of the literary theorists Bonheim and Ginette, namely, that endings reveal what a story is all about, what the author is trying to accomplish, and that endings are the preeminent location of truth in a narrative. It should be clear by now that the ending of Judges is sophisticated and meaning-full! The ending of Judges reveals what it's all about and the purpose driving the author. Over the course of the book, readers get the sense of the steady deterioration of Israel. In a sense, we are tricked into thinking that this decline happens over the course of time. When we reach the end, which displays the most terrible behavior in the book, we are brought right back to the beginning of the book—a jolting reality that confuses and disorients. We look to the end to provide the key to understanding how Israel could have strayed so far from their calling so early in the settlement period. The author then identifies that key: Israel had rejected Yahweh as king and suffers from a kind of social amnesia because they were not observing the practices that the Torah established to remind them of who they are because of what Yahweh had done for them in the past. This message resonates deeply for audiences dealing with the devastation of exile, struggling with the reality of returning to a decimated postexilic Palestine, or grappling with the daily struggle of living consistently before the face of God in the twenty-first century.

533. O'Connell, *Rhetoric*, 6–7 (emphasis added).

Theological Reflection

Judges and Biblical Theology

Theological interpretation emerges from a deep conviction that in and through Scripture God speaks, and I'm convinced that in and through Scripture he speaks with a unified voice.[1] This is not to deny the variety and diversity of types of literature in the Bible nor the different historical contexts addressed by the biblical authors, which called for a range of instructional material. The Bible, as Christopher Wright notes, is not like a river with a single channel, "It is rather a complex mixture of all kinds of smaller narratives, many of them rather self-contained, with all kinds of other material embedded within them—more like a great delta. But there is clearly a direction, a flow."[2]

Thus, "In the economy of theological interpretation, biblical theology is the practice that helps readers of Scripture to grasp God's Word particularly in terms of its unity," and it does so "on the basis of terms and categories derived from the Bible itself."[3] At the broadest level, biblical theology should attend to the narrative shape of the whole Bible—from Eden to the new Jerusalem, from creation to new creation. Central to the task of biblical theology is the relationship between the Old Testament and the New Testament. While biblical theology rightly emphasizes the unity from Old to New Testament, we ought to acknowledge the radicality of the "Christ event," which gives shape to and freshly illuminates the Old Testament.[4] As a result, the Christ event and the

1. See Beldman and Swales, "Biblical Theology and Theological Interpretation," 149–50.

2. Wright, *Mission of God*, 64.

3. Beldman and Swales, "Biblical Theology and Theological Interpretation," 149–50.

4. The "Christ event" is a shorthand way of referring to the birth, ministry, death, resurrection, and ascension of Jesus the Messiah.

New Testament's interpretation of it require a reinterpretation of the Old Testament, and yet this should not short-circuit a careful attentiveness to listening to the Old Testament on its own terms. Brevard Childs is helpful in this regard as he insists that biblical theology should start with the discrete witness of the Old Testament and the New Testament and then broaden out to reflect theologically on the whole canon.[5]

This section on Judges and biblical theology follows this approach. As mentioned in the introduction, we can only properly hear the message of Judges when we situate it first within the story of God's dealing with his people in the biblical story. This section starts by doing just that. We will then explore how Judges was crafted in light of certain texts and traditions of the Old Testament (narrowing in on the Sinai covenant, Deuteronomy, and Joshua) and how subsequent Old Testament texts used and understood Judges and/or the settlement period. Finally, the use of Judges in the New Testament will receive due attention.

Judges and the Grand Narrative of Scripture

Central to the book of Judges is the intimate relationship and interaction between Yahweh and the twelve tribes of Israel. It assumes the foundational stories and traditions, which include the story of the exodus, the Sinai covenant, the wilderness wandering, and the conquest, but stretches further in history to Yahweh's covenant relationship with Abraham, Isaac, and Jacob.[6] That these foundation stories are in the background of Judges is apparent in Judg 2:10, which sets the context of the book in the midst of generations who had forgotten these identity-shaping stories.

In fact, when we turn the pages of our Bibles to Judges, we ought to be impressed with the significance of the moment in history in which the Israelites find themselves. Immediately preceding Judges—both chronologically and in terms of the ordering of the books of the Old Testament—is the book of Joshua, and the ending of Joshua provides an important clue to understanding the pivotal function of Judges. Anticipating his own death, Joshua addresses the Israelites and expresses the importance of that particular moment. He notes, "You know with all your hearts and all your souls, all of you, that not a single word has failed of all the good words that Yahweh your God promised con-

5. Childs, *Biblical Theology of the Old and New Testaments*, 78.

6. The following is a reiteration of the work I have done on Judges and the biblical story in Beldman, *Deserting the King*, 12–24.

cerning you. All have come to pass for you. Not a single word of them has failed" (Josh 23:14). Joshua goes on to warn them and to inspire them—just as Yahweh has been faithful to all his promises, the people should be faithful to Yahweh, serving him alone and forsaking the culture and practices of the Canaanite environment. The final chapter of Joshua consists of a typical covenant renewal ceremony, to which we will return, but for now it is important to note Joshua's emphasis on Yahweh fulfilling *all the words or promises*. What is Joshua referring to here?

Of course, Yahweh had made many promises to his people over the course of history, but the root of them all goes back at least to Gen 12:1–3. There Yahweh summons Abraham to leave everything that would, in the ancient world, have provided security, stability, and prosperity. The promises to Abraham amount to the following: (1) Yahweh would give Abraham numerous descendants so that his descendants would become a great nation, (2) Yahweh would establish a relationship of mutual blessing between Yahweh and Abraham's descendants (and the nations), and (3) Yahweh would give his descendants a land of their own.[7] Yahweh's purpose in blessing Abraham and his descendants in this way becomes apparent in the fourth and climactic promise in Gen 12:1–3, namely, the blessing of all the nations of the earth. I'm convinced that the three basic aspects of the promises to Abraham (a great and numerous nation, relationship of mutual blessing, and land) are subordinate to and facilitate Abraham and his descendants in fulfilling this calling to bless all nations.[8] In any case, this vital aspect of the calling of Abraham emerges repeatedly as God establishes and reaffirms the covenant with Abraham and his descendants (see Gen 18:17–19; 22:15–18; 26:3–4; 28:13–14). In Gal 3:8, Paul goes so far as to say that the blessing of the nations here in Gen 12:3 communicates to Abraham the essence of the gospel.

Yahweh's calling of Abraham is foundational for the unfolding Old Testament story and we will see how it drives the story forward. However, in order to grasp fully how the calling of Abraham, and especially the blessing of the nations, constitute the gospel, we need to look back to Gen 1–11. In Gen 1–2 the world is established as the good, harmonious place that God intended it to be. At the very center of creation are the human creatures, made in the very image of God and *blessed by him* to cultivate and care for the creation.

7. See Clines, *Theme of the Pentateuch*, 30, who summarizes these as (1) posterity, (2) divine-human relationship, and (3) land.

8. Goheen, *Light to the Nations*, 31–32, refers to the identity of Abraham and his descendants (and by implication all God's people of all times) as a "*so-that* people." He writes, "Abraham, his family, and the nation that will issue from him are chosen to participate in God's mission: to enjoy God's redemptive blessing and to walk in the way of the Lord *so that* the nations might participate in that blessing" (32).

They are in perfect relationship with God, with each other, and with the creation. And yet, in a tragic act of defiance, the human subjects rebelled against their Creator-King, casting the world into chaos. God's perfect world, which was characterized by harmony, integrity, vitality, and blessing, would now be marked by confusion, fear, death, and curse. In Gen 4–11 sin and rebellion get unleashed in the world and even though God responds with mercy, the results are devastating. What will reverse the curse of human rebellion? Is there any hope for blessing?[9]

The calling of Abraham constitutes God's response to the curse and rebellion of Gen 3–11, providing hope for restoration. The five-fold repetition of cursing in Gen 3–11 (3:14, 17; 4:11; 5:29; 9:25) is replaced with a five-fold repetition of blessing to Abraham, his descendants, and all nations (12:2 [2x], 3 [3x]), indicating that blessing will overcome the curse. Instead of humans making a name for themselves (11:4), Yahweh would make Abraham's name great (12:2). Instead of nations being corrupted, at odds with each other, and destroyed, all nations would be unified in Yahweh's blessing through Abraham (12:3). In other words, Yahweh's calling of Abraham would somehow restore the order and integrity of creation that was lost because of the fall. This is the gospel!

Thus, the calling of Abraham looks back and responds to the chaos that was unleashed because of human rebellion, but it also anticipates and gives shape to the unfolding Old Testament story. As Wenham notes, "It looks forward to the later patriarchs and beyond them to the nation of Israel and the Davidic monarchy, the great nation that will inherit the land of Canaan."[10] David Clines has shown that the three elements of the promise to Abraham (posterity, divine-human relationship, and land) are bound up in the theme of the Pentateuch. Thus, "The theme of the Pentateuch is the partial fulfillment . . . of the promise to or blessing of the patriarchs."[11]

Although the three elements of the promise to Abraham and their partial fulfillment thread through the whole of the Pentateuch, each are dominant in different parts of the first five books of the Bible.

In Genesis the seemingly impossible promise of Abraham fathering a great nation with many descendants dominates as Sarah's barrenness and other challenges stand in the way of this promise. Although at the end of Genesis Abraham's descendants total only seventy individuals (Gen 46:27), when we

9. In naming his son, Noah's father expresses something of the longing for a return to the way the world ought to be: "Out of the ground that Yahweh has cursed this one shall bring us relief from our work and from the painful toil of our hands" (Gen 5:29).

10. Wenham, *Genesis 1–15*, 281.

11. Clines, *Theme of the Pentateuch*, 30.

turn the page to Exodus a number of generations have passed, and they are great and numerous. The narrator in Exodus seems especially keen to emphasize that this element of the promise to Abraham has been fulfilled. John Durham translates Exod 1:7 as: "But the sons of Israel were fertile, and so they became a teeming swarm. Indeed, they became so many they were a strength to be reckoned with by their numbers alone. The land was simply filled with them."[12] The purpose, according to Durham, is to emphasize the miraculous growth of the seventy who had settled in Egypt to this teeming swarm only a few generations later—an act of divine blessing in fulfillment to his promises to Abraham![13]

The increase of Abraham's descendants into a great nation foregrounds the problem regarding the other two elements of the promise to Abraham, and indeed the reality of their great numbers becomes the catalyst for Yahweh fulfilling them. After all, Abraham's descendants are slaves to a ruthless master, Pharaoh, and they are dwelling in a foreign land. Thus, the second element of the promise becomes dominant on the pages of Exodus and Leviticus as (1) Yahweh faces off against Pharaoh over who has a rightful claim on the people of Israel and (2) having proved his claim on Israel by defeating Pharaoh, Yahweh forges his relationship with Israel at Sinai. The Sinai covenant is constituted on Yahweh's redemption of Israel from Egypt (Exod 19:4), and as a result Israel emerges with a new identity: as Yahweh's special treasure they are called to be a kingdom of priests and a holy nation (Exod 19:5–6). These two vital aspects of Israel's identity perfectly capture Yahweh's original calling to Abraham. As a holy nation, the people are called to be distinct from the nations—their way of being would run counter to the culture and religion of the Canaanite nations that they would go in to possess. As a priestly kingdom, they would mediate the blessing of Yahweh to the surrounding nations. These dimensions of their identity would hold each other in tension as Israel would be in and among the nations, but would exist for the sake of the nations. All the terms and conditions of the Sinai covenant amount to a manifesto for a priestly kingdom and a holy nation—they set the terms for a relationship of mutual blessing.

Finally, the promise of the land becomes dominant in Numbers and Deuteronomy. Sadly, because of their fear and rebellion, the promise of the land is deferred. They do not enter the land, and by the time we reach the end of Deuteronomy, the people are gazing out over the promised land and have received further instruction on how they should live as Yahweh's people in the land, for the sake of the nations.

12. Durham, *Exodus*, 2.
13. Durham, *Exodus*, 5.

So far, we have seen that the theme of the Pentateuch is the partial fulfillment of the promises to the patriarchs, promises that consist of a great and numerous nation, a relationship of mutual blessing, and land, and we have seen how that theme weaves its way through the pages of the Pentateuch. Moreover, these promises are God's response to the sin and chaos that resulted from the fall—the promises and calling of Abraham are meant to fulfill God's original purpose for humanity and the creation, now in a postfall world. As we move beyond the Pentateuch, this theme, with the associated promises, continues to drive the story forward.

In Joshua, Israel continues as a great nation. The relationship of mutual blessing forged at Sinai remains in question: Will Israel fulfill their calling to be a kingdom of priests and a holy nation committed to Yahweh and his covenant with them? To that point, they had proven themselves to be a stiff-necked and rebellious people. While that question remains paramount, Joshua focuses on the third element of the promise to Abraham, namely the land. Joshua recounts the Israelite conquest of the land:[14]

> Yahweh goes before the 12 Israelite tribes and helps them take possession of the land. Joshua 13–21 recounts in painstaking detail the parceling out of the land and the territorial boundaries for each of the tribes. Why all of these repetitive details? The amount of space devoted to the parceling out of the land is an indication of its significance: The final promise God made to Abraham is now fulfilled.[15]

This brings us back to where we started: Joshua announcing to the twelve tribes that Yahweh had fulfilled all of the promises, not one of them having failed (Josh 23:14). This emphatic statement about Yahweh's unswerving faithfulness to the promises he made to Abraham, and the subsequent covenant renewal ceremony in Josh 24 are absolutely key for understanding Judges. Joshua assembled all the people at Shechem, and after rehearsing all that Yahweh had done for them—from the calling of Abraham to the conquest of Canaan—he summons the people to choose between pledging allegiance to Yahweh and his covenant, and being loyal to the gods of the Canaanites and serving them. No less than three times the Israelites pledge their loyalty to Yahweh and declare, "We will serve Yahweh" (Josh 24:18, 21, and 24).

14. An important and thorny issue is how Israel's calling to bless the nations relates to the conquest of Canaan. The two seem mutually exclusive as subjugating and/or driving the Canaanite nations from their homes seems like anything but a blessing. We will return to this question below.

15. Beldman, *Deserting the King*, 17.

The significance of this moment should not be missed! All the promises that Yahweh made to Abraham have been accomplished and the people of God are collectively committed to serving him. With the words "We will serve Yahweh" echoing in our ears and with a keen sense of anticipation, we turn the page to the book of Judges. We anticipate encountering great things! This significant moment in Israel's history is sure to spawn great blessing not only for Israel, but also for the nations, and the kingdom of God is sure to advance in great leaps and bounds! Seen in this light, in this context, what we do encounter in the book of Judges is all the more tragic. Not only do the Israelites utterly (and quickly) fail at being a distinct nation that exists for the sake of the nations, they become in every way like the Canaanite nations, which, it turns out, is not only very bad for the Israelites, but also has drastic consequences for the nations they are called to bless.

In the Old Testament story subsequent to Judges, the people persist in their idolatry and covenant disloyalty. The new political regime of monarchy provides no solution to their rebellion, and on the whole the kings promote and institutionalize the bad behavior that Judges puts on display. In spite of the warnings of the prophets the people and their leaders persist in their infidelity, and as a result the kingdom is divided, then Assyria defeats and exiles the Northern Kingdom, and finally Judah suffers the same fate at the hands of the Babylonians.

The experience of exile brings a new and shocking reality, especially when interpreted in light of those promises Yahweh made to Abraham. Israel is no longer a great nation but one that is conquered, divided, and decimated. Israel is no longer in the land, but dwells in a foreign land under foreign rule. What about the relationship of mutual blessing? That seems no more than a hopeless ideal of ancient history. And yet hope does exist beyond exile. Yahweh most certainly has not given up on his plans to restore the order of creation, nor Israel's role in that plan. He will yet bless all the nations of the earth through his people. It's as though Yahweh strips back the promised blessings that he made to Abraham to expose with crystal clarity his purpose for making the promises (i.e., the blessing of the nations).

Nowhere is this clearer than in the message Yahweh gives to the exiles through the prophet Jeremiah. Essentially, Yahweh instructs the exiles to get comfortable in Babylon—build houses, marry off their sons and daughters, and increase in numbers and multiply (Jer 29:5–7). Is Yahweh just adding insult to injury? What purpose could this possibly serve? Yahweh goes on to make his purpose crystal clear: "Seek the *shalom* of the city where I have sent you into exile and pray to Yahweh on its behalf, for in its *shalom* you will find your *shalom*" (v. 7). *Shalom* is a rich Hebrew word that signifies wholeness, integrity, harmony, and peace—it's the way God intended his world to be. As a message devoid of context, this message seems downright mean? How could Yahweh instruct the exiles to seek the blessing and shalom of the foreign nations that had taken away or destroyed everything that gave them meaning and hope? However, from the vantage point of Yahweh's history with Israel going back to the promises made to Abraham, this message makes perfect sense. It's as though Yahweh is saying:

> In the past, I promised to make you a great nation, to give you a land of your own, and to establish my relationship of blessing with you, but those were merely means to an end: so that you could bless the nations. You didn't fulfill your calling to be a channel of blessing with all the promises in place. Now that all the promises of blessing have been stripped back, start acting as a kingdom of priests because in seeking the shalom of your sworn enemies you will find shalom![16]

Yahweh's message, therefore, is perfectly logical when understood in light of the calling of Abraham, the covenants with the patriarchs, the Sinai covenant, and so on. He is reminding them of their central calling—to bless the nations—and summoning them to carry out that calling, now in the context of exile.

During this time the poets and other prophets also drive this message home, reminding God's people who they are and to what Yahweh has called them to be. Goheen notes, "Israel's identity and self-understanding, its role and its calling in the midst of the nations, are constantly celebrated and nourished by its liturgy . . . the worship of the psalms reminds Israel of the universal horizon of its calling—for the sake of the nations."[17] Goheen calls attention to the opening lines of Ps 67 that, intriguingly, assume that God's blessing of his people is the instrument of salvation for the nations![18]

> May God be gracious to us and bless us
> 	and make his face shine on us—
> *so that* your ways may be known on the earth,
> 	your salvation among all nations.
> 	May all the peoples praise you, God;
> 	May all the peoples praise you.

16. Beldman, *Deserting the King*, 20.

17. Goheen, *Light to the Nations*, 57–58. Goheen references W. Creighton Marlowe who refers to the Psalms as the "music of missions," Mark Boda who calls the Psalter a "missional collection," and George Peters who identifies in the Psalter over 175 references to the nations of the world (58).

18. Goheen, *Light to the Nations*, 58.

Again, Jeremiah announces that a return to Yahweh and covenant faithfulness on the part of God's people will result in the nations invoking Yahweh's blessing (Jer 4:1–2). Isaiah foresees a day when Egypt, Assyria, and Israel together will constitute his people, worshiping him and blessing the earth (Isa 19:23–25). Yahweh will restore the remnant of Israel and reconstitute them as "a light to the nations, so that my salvation may reach to the ends of the earth" (Isa 49:5–6). Similarly, Ezekiel sees a future in which Israel no longer profanes the name of Yahweh among the nations but will be gathered, cleaned, and used by Yahweh to make his name known to the nations (Ezek 36:22–38), and Zechariah speaks of many nations being bound to Yahweh as his people (Zech 2:10–11), and the nations who were once enemies will make pilgrimage to Jerusalem, worshiping Yahweh and participating in the Feast of Booths (14:16).

Sadly, on the whole this message does not penetrate into the core of the exiles and returnees. Although we get glimpses of shalom and blessing emanating from the people of God into the darkness (e.g., Daniel), these are the exception and not the rule. The exiles return and rebuild, but over the course of the centuries leading up to Jesus, rather than taking up their calling as a channel of blessing they become increasingly inward focused, sectarian, and nationalistic.

> By the time a baby boy is born to an unlikely couple from an insignificant town in the Roman province of Judea, however, God's people had developed an intense longing for Yahweh to return, for freedom, for political independence, for shalom. Ironically, their vision was too small for the Redeemer who was born in a stable in Bethlehem. Jesus' vision of the kingdom was not reduced to a parcel of land in Palestine but included the whole cosmos. His vision for the people of God was not reduced to a single ethnicity but included all nations, tribes, and tongues. And the means of accomplishing his cosmic kingdom was not a sword but a cross—not military might but humility, sacrifice, and service.[19]

The kingdom that Jesus came announcing and that was accomplished through his death and resurrection is one in which all are invited to participate. Jesus reminds us that God's purposes were not for Israel as an end in itself—it never was—but was a means to worldwide blessing and renewal. This kingdom of blessing will come in its fullness when Jesus will return and establish the new creation. The nations and their kings will journey to the new Jerusalem and the "glory and honor of the nations" will be brought into the city (Rev 21:24–26) by way of twelve gates, inscribed with the twelve tribes of Israel (Rev 21:12–14).

19. Beldman, *Deserting the King*, 22.

There the nations will walk by the light of the Lord God almighty (Rev 21:24) and find healing in the tree of life, with its twelve kinds of fruit (Rev 22:2). Until that day the people of God are commissioned to continue Jesus's mission, which, at its core, was the mission of Israel—bless the nations, seek the shalom of the surrounding city and culture, exist as a foretaste of the coming kingdom.

This recounting of the history of Yahweh's dealings with his people may seem rather arduous and perhaps wide of the mark, which after all is the book of Judges. The point, however, has been to understand that Judges does not stand alone, that it is part of a much bigger story of redemption. Situating Judges within the larger biblical drama brings into relief the significance of this chapter in Israel's history. Of course, in the narratives prior to Judges, Israel does figure as a persistently rebellious people, but in the lead up to Judges it's as though the stars are aligned for God's kingdom to advance and his purposes to be fulfilled in ways that are arguably unprecedented. And yet they fail so rapidly and so profoundly. At this crucial fork in the road that holds so much potential, God's people choose the way of rebellion, curse, and death.

Understanding Judges in light of the biblical story helps us to see the overwhelming sense of tragedy and lost opportunity, but it also serves a number of other purposes. It reveals to us that God is playing the long game. Even the profoundly bad behavior we witness in Judges will not foil God's plan for universal blessing, and he patiently persists even in the face of human rebellion. Furthermore, situating Judges in the grand biblical narrative also helps twenty-first-century readers attune our ears to rightly hear the powerful and surprisingly relevant message of Judges for today. The story of Judges is part of the universal story of God—it is our story. Judges resonates through the centuries and speaks to us about the true character of God, the calling of his people, the powerful allure of idolatry, the tragic and far-reaching results of forsaking the divine King, and so much more. We will have the opportunity to reflect on these things in the pages below.

Judges and the Old Testament

So far in this section on Judges and biblical theology, I have attempted to provide a sketch of the unifying narrative that gives shape to the whole Bible and place Judges within that narrative. The aim in this section on Judges and the Old Testament is twofold. On the one hand, we want to explore how Old Testament theology, traditions, and texts provide the foundation or substructure for understanding Judges. We have already done some of this work by connecting Judges to the creation and fall narratives, the patriarchal promises, and so on.

The aim is not to repeat that; however, some fleshing out is necessary to fully hear and understand the message of Judges. So we will focus on the backdrop of (1) the Sinai covenant, (2) Deuteronomy and (3) Joshua for the narrative of Judges. On the other hand, we want to see how Judges and/or the settlement period features in the subsequent Old Testament historical accounts, in the psalms, and in the prophets. This too should provide helpful insights into understanding the book of Judges.

Judges and the Sinai Covenant

In the introduction of his 1975 commentary in the Anchor Bible series, Boling has an intriguing little section which he titled "Heaven and Earth: Yahweh's Kingdom."[20] In that section he acknowledges the intense scholarly activity analyzing ancient Near Eastern vassal treaty documents between conquering kings and the subjugated people and comparing them with Israel's early narrative forms. Boling notes that the research in this area

> has shown that the Sinai covenant . . . casts Yahweh in the role of Suzerain, Great King, King of kings, so that every man confessing faith in Yahweh becomes thereby a citizen of Israel and one of Yahweh's freed kings. In other words, Israel is the nucleus of the earthly half of the kingdom of Yahweh.[21]

Boling goes on to describe how the laws of the Sinai covenant provided the legal policy and structure for the realm of King Yahweh, and how the blessings and curses would provide motivation (both positive and negative) for loyal citizenship in Yahweh's kingdom.

Boling admits that the covenant form as such remains in the background of Judges, and yet it functions significantly in all sorts of ways throughout the book, as he shows. He ends the section noting, "Somewhere in the middle, between the stylized depiction of Joshua's success and the candid portrayal of David's success, we are to apprehend the judges stories as stemming from the daily reality of ancient Israel's struggle for survival in Canaan—a struggle for survival as Yahweh's very real historical kingdom."[22]

The kingdom of Yahweh/God is one of the major themes in biblical theology. There is no question that the kingdom of God/heaven dominates New

20. Boling, *Judges*, 24–29.
21. Boling, *Judges*, 24.
22. Boling, *Judges*, 29.

Testament theology, especially in the Synoptic Gospels, where it features as *the* dominant theme in Jesus's ministry. However, even in the Old Testament the kingdom of God is preeminent.[23] As mentioned in the previous section, God's people are reborn at Sinai as a priestly kingdom and a holy nation (Exod 19:6), and the stipulations of the Sinai covenant set before them a counter-cultural way of being in the world, lived under the kingship of Yahweh. No realm of Israelite life was outside of Yahweh's reign. The laws pertaining to agriculture, land, and even architecture were a reminder that every square inch of their lives is within the orb of Yahweh's kingship. The ritual laws pertaining to sacrifice, holy days, Sabbaths, and Jubilee imply that every waking hour is subject to Yahweh's reign. Laws touching on family and kinship relations, sexuality, social justice, governance, and jurisprudence demonstrate that social, economic, political, and judicial order was to be governed by the principles of the kingdom of Yahweh. All of life is all for Yahweh.

If Boling is right, and I believe he is, that we are to understand Judges as Israel's struggle to manifest the earthly reality of Yahweh's kingdom and the Sinai covenant as the structuring principle for that reality, then the tragedy of Judges comes into full relief. The problem that dogs the people of God in Judges is not merely moral or spiritual. Israel's rejection of Yahweh as king and their allegiance to the Canaanite gods sets the trajectory for a full orbed social (dis)order that is thoroughly Canaanite and counter to the principles and practices of the kingdom of Yahweh. Of course, the Israelites in Judges display immoral behavior and twisted religious practices, but these are symptoms along with political and social corruption that are rooted in a commitment to another king, another kingdom. The Sinai covenant remains in the background of Judges, but no less provides the basic ideal against which we must compare the reality of Judges.

Judges and Deuteronomy

The publication in 1943 of Martin Noth's *Überlieferungsgeschichtliche Studien* (later published in English as *The Deuteronomistic History*) was a watershed moment in the study of Judges and the complex of books consisting of Joshua,

23. Recent Old Testament scholarship has borne this out. In Gen 1 God features as the creator-king and humans, created in the image of God, are cast as his viceregents; see Middleton, *Liberating Image*, 70–74. The most recent trend in the study of Psalms examines the editorial shaping of the Psalter as a whole, and the consensus is that the psalms of the nineties, which emphasize Yahweh's kingship, are at the very center of the psalter; see McCann, *Psalms as Torah*; Mays, *Psalms*. In the prophetic literature, not least the apocalyptic literature, the theme of Yahweh's reign is key.

Judges, 1 and 2 Samuel, and 1 and 2 Kings.[24] In a nutshell, Noth maintained that the narrative running from Joshua to Kings is a unified literary composition (the Deuteronomistic History), the result of a single author (whom he called the Deuteronomist). Because the language, themes, and theology of Deuteronomy seem to dominate Joshua–Kings, Noth did not think that it was originally integral to the Pentateuch but was rather composed as a programmatic introduction to the Deuteronomistic History. With regard to Judges, Noth's work has been so influential that, as Butler notes, since its publication, "the great majority of scholars have begun discussion of the composition of Judges by speaking of the Deuteronomistic Historian's final editorial shaping and interpretation of Judges, along with Joshua, Samuel, and Kings."[25]

The purpose of bringing up Noth's work is not to suggest that the Deuteronomistic History theory is the final word on the composition of Judges. In fact, since its publication there seems no end to scholarly revisions and modifications to the theory, and more recent scholars have dispensed with the theory altogether.[26] Rather, the point where the Deuteronomistic History theory is instructive for our purposes is in the foundational role that Deuteronomy plays in understanding Judges. Whatever the precise nature of their compositional relationship might be, it seems difficult to deny that Deuteronomy shaped the author of Judges' understanding and interpretation of the settlement period.[27] The indebtedness of Judges to Deuteronomy, as Webb notes, "is universally recognized."[28]

In what ways can we see the influence of Deuteronomy on Judges? Deuteronomy, of course, is a reiteration and exposition of Israel's covenant relationship with Yahweh on the plains of Moab as the people gazed out into the promised land. As they are about to enter Canaan, Moses's sermons urge God's people not to forget who they are in light of what Yahweh has done. He holds

24. Noth, *Überlieferungsgeschichtliche Studien*; in English: *Deuteronomistic History*.

25. Butler, *Judges*, xlv.

26. For a brief summary of Noth's work and subsequent revisions see Beldman, *Completion of Judges*, 12–14. My own work on Judges, particularly in my doctoral work (published as *Completion of Judges*), has made me skeptical of Noth's Deuteronomistic History theory and the subsequent modifications. My view aligns with the conclusion of Block, who notes, "Although the Book of Judges contains numerous ideological and literary links with the rest of the books in Noth's so-called Deuteronomistic History, the evidence seems convincing that this is an independent literary composition, written in light of the authentically Mosaic theology of Deuteronomy and Joshua. The theory of a separate literary work is reinforced by the independent literary integrity of the Book of Judges itself"; Block, *Judges*, 49.

27. See the detailed study of pentateuchal allusions in Judges: Ross, "People Heeds Not Scripture."

28. Webb, *Book of Judges*, 53.

out to them two ways—one is the way of covenant fidelity, which leads to blessing and life, and the other is the way of covenant rebellion, which leads to curse and death. Divine election, redemption, covenant faithfulness expressed in Torah obedience, and the consequences of covenant rebellion are themes that dominate Deuteronomy.

We see these themes clearly in Judges in key passages where Yahweh reminds the people of his past works on their behalf and confronts them with their disobedience (2:1–5; 6:7–10; 10:11–14). The interpretive framework introduced in Judg 3:11–23 and that structures (with some variation) the cycle of Judges resonates with Deuteronomy (cf. Deut 4:25; 9:18; 17:2; 31:29). Moreover, the curses for covenant disobedience that Deut 28 catalogs are realized on the pages of Judges as Israel is subjugated under foreign rule, their crops and livestock are ravaged and pillaged by their enemies, children are carried away, wives are ravaged, and so on. As Webb puts it, "In Judges Israel experiences God's presence and sovereignty over its affairs as either blessing (peace in the land) or curse (oppression at the hands of enemies), very much as Moses warned it would."[29]

Finally, it is worth noting that commentators often discern within Deuteronomy a strict, mechanistic retribution theology, which they then perceive being imposed on Judges. Webb offers a helpful corrective in this regard.

> The stark alternatives put to Israel in Deuteronomy 30:11–20 give voice to the truth that Israel has real choices to make, and those choices will have real consequences: blessing or curse, life or death. In that sense Israel could expect to get what it deserved. But to depict this in a mechanistic way, as though everything in Judges can be understood in terms of a rigid principle of retribution or reward, would not do justice to either the book of Judges itself, or the book of Deuteronomy.[30]

Webb goes on to explain another fundamental reality that shines through in both Deuteronomy and Judges, namely, that the foundation of Yahweh's relationship with Israel is not Israel's obedience but Yahweh's electing love. The theology of both Deuteronomy and Judges is not retribution theology, but "It is a theology of conflict in which both parties suffer, and in which Israel survives only because Yahweh does not give up on her and simply walk away."[31]

29. Webb, *Book of Judges*, 53.
30. Webb, *Book of Judges*, 53–54.
31. Webb, *Book of Judges*, 54.

Judges and Joshua

We saw above in the overview of the biblical story that in light of the words of Joshua, and Israel's thrice-repeated commitment to Yahweh at the end of the book of Joshua, Judges emerges as a terrible disappointment in the unfolding plot of the biblical story. However, there is more to say about the relationship between Joshua and Judges than just the logic of the continuing story. The overwhelming evidence suggests that Joshua and Judges are not merely neighbors but also unmistakable if not odd bedfellows in the canon of Scripture.

We might start by simply observing how both books begin and how they end. Joshua begins with the words "After the death of Moses the servant of Yahweh, Yahweh said to Joshua, the son of Nun, Moses's official" and Judges with the words "After the death of Joshua, the people inquired of Yahweh." At the end of Joshua, immediately after the covenant renewal ceremony at Shechem, we read "So Joshua sent the people away, each to his inheritance" (24:28).[32] At the end of Judges, after convening to find a solution to the problem of the lack of wives for Benjamin, first the Benjamites return to their inheritance (21:23) and then the rest of the Israelites "departed from there at that time, each to his tribe and family, and they went from there, each to his inheritance" (21:24). The similarities are obvious, and on that basis alone we have enough to assume some kind of literary dependence. However, the subtle but unmistakable differences provide a clue to understanding their dynamic relationship. In Josh 1:1 the transition of leadership from Moses to Joshua is obvious. Contrasting this with Judg 1:1 exposes the unmistakable leadership vacuum—there is no successor to Joshua after his death. A comparison of Josh 24:28 and Judg 21:24 only underscores this point. At the end of Joshua, the Israelites have a leader to send them to their tribal inheritances, whereas in Judges the assembly simply disbands and departs to their tribal inheritances. The opening and closing lines of Joshua and Judges are obviously connected, but the differences foreground something deeper and more significant at work.

Butler has explored in depth the relationship between Joshua and Judges, and, having written substantial commentaries on both Joshua and Judges, he is probably better positioned to evaluate authoritatively this relationship than anyone else.[33] I will not attempt to rehearse all his arguments here, and leave the details to the keen reader to pursue, but his basic premise, which he works out

32. There follows from this a short epilogue on the life, legacy and death of Joshua, part of which, incidentally, appears verbatim in Judg 2:6–9.

33. For the relationship, see Butler, *Judges*, lvii–lxiv. His two commentaries, which appear in the Word Biblical Commentary Series, are Butler, *Joshua*; Butler, *Judges*.

in painstaking detail, is that "the content, themes, and structure of the Judges narrative together reflect a conscious effort to reverse the content, themes, and structure of the Joshua narrative."[34] After explaining on multiple levels how this great reversal works out on the pages of Judges, Butler concludes

> Thus, just as Judges consciously began the story in midstream with the death of Joshua, so it ends the story unfinished, pointing forward to a type of king it knows not. In so doing it has dissembled the structure of Joshua, destroyed the unity Joshua created, ransacked the cultic loyalty Joshua renewed, and ignored the Mosaic law Joshua so carefully followed and taught. Everything Joshua created, politically, literarily, theologically, religiously, and geographically, Judges has done away with.[35]

Butler's analysis and conclusions demonstrate that Judges was deliberately written in the light of the book of Joshua, such that to rightly hear the message of Judges, with all of its nuance, we must listen to it not so much in harmony as in discordance with Joshua.

Another important insight emerging in comparing Joshua and Judges that Butler does not really explore is the underlying view of history at work in the two books. Joshua is driven by a distinct telos: the wandering and homeless Israelites cross the Jordan at the beginning of the book and eventually settle in their tribal inheritance at the end of the book. The underlying view of history is that history is linear. As we have seen, Judges portrays a distinct sense of aimlessness in the settlement period. The book is dominated by a cyclical view of history, which is evident not only on the micro level (the level of the cycle of judges) but also on the macro level (the circularity of the end section of Judges). It's enough to say here that attention to the nature of history undergirding Judges suggests that sin and rebellion in some sense impedes the forward march of history.

So far in our consideration of Judges and the Old Testament, we have looked back to some of the foundational texts and traditions that have shaped the composition of Judges and are thus vital for a proper understanding of Judges: the Sinai covenant, Deuteronomy, and Joshua.[36] We will now turn our attention on the ways that succeeding Old Testament historians, poets, and prophets refer to Judges and/or the settlement period.

34. Butler, *Judges*, lviii.

35. Butler, *Judges*, lxiii–lxiv.

36. Again, Genesis—both the universal history of Gen 1–11 and the patriarchal narratives of Gen 12–50—is no less significant for understanding Judges. However, since the section "Judges and the Grand Narrative of Scripture" covered these in some detail, it is not necessary to include that in this section.

Judges in the Old Testament Historical Narratives

Direct references to the book of Judges are rare in the Old Testament.[37] By Groves's count only twelve references to Judges appear in the Old Testament, and even among these references it is not at all clear that the book of Judges is the source.[38] Rather, the Old Testament historians, prophets, or poets draw on historical events, individuals, or the settlement period as a whole. It's possible that they are utilizing Judges as a source, but it's also possible they are drawing on other historical annals or oral history in making these references. On the whole, these references to the settlement period reflect the same negative evaluation that we find in Judges.[39]

The opening line of Ruth sets the events of the book "in the days when the judges ruled" (1:1), but the book makes no mention of the events and situation of the settlement period. Allusions to the settlement period generally, and to events and people in Judges specifically, do appear in the books of Samuel. I have highlighted how Israel's request for a king in 1 Sam 8:5 prompts an evaluation by Yahweh of Israel's history, including in a general way the settlement period, as the history of Israel's rejection of Yahweh's kingship (vv. 7–8). In Samuel's farewell address, Samuel gets more specific. He interprets the problem of the settlement period as one of collective social amnesia: The Israelites "forgot Yahweh their God" (1 Sam 12:9). He then goes on to recount the history in such a way that it sounds similar to the cyclical framework of Judges, mentioning the foreign oppression of Sisera and the king of Moab that comes at the hand of Yahweh, the crying out of the Israelites, and Yahweh's sending of Jerubbaal (i.e., Gideon), Barak, and Jephthah, who brought deliverance and safety (vv. 9–11). David's commander Joab is clearly aware of the specifics of Abimelech's death (Judg 9:53–54), mentioning the woman who dropped the millstone on him from the wall of the city (2 Sam 11:21) as a historical precedent for the dangers of getting too close to the city wall in siege warfare.

Elsewhere in the historical narratives, Nehemiah narrates a sweeping overview of the judges period, evaluating the period negatively in similar language to what we find in Judges (Neh 9:26–31). Nehemiah prefaces his evaluation of the

37. For the following, I am indebted to helpful work of collating the various references to Judges in the Bible by Block, *Judges*, 26–27; and Groves, "Judges," 410.

38. Groves, "Judges," 410.

39. Groves, "Judges," 410, holds that "there is one positive allusion to the period of the judges (Isa. 1:26), where Isaiah sees the future Zion, purified of sin, as a time of the restoration of judges 'as in the days of old.'" However, it is not at all clear that this vision that Isaiah receives is implying a positive evaluation of the judges period (or even that this is most certainly a reference to the settlement period).

settlement period with an account of the mighty works of Yahweh in fulfilling the Abrahamic promises (vv. 22–25), but then goes on to recount the persistent disobedience and rebellion of God's people. Nehemiah makes mention of Yahweh giving them over to their enemies, the Israelites crying out for deliverance, the saviors that Yahweh sent to bring them deliverance, and the resulting rest they experienced. Thus, the cyclical nature of the settlement period is highlighted, and he even specifically references Yahweh's Spirit through the prophets warning the people (v. 30). Nehemiah attributes the rebellion of the people to their abandoning the Torah (vv. 26, 29). The section closes by highlighting Yahweh's patient and merciful persistence with Israel in that he did not utterly destroy or forsake them (v. 31). This overview of the settlement period is a helpful and apt evaluative summary of this chapter in Israel's history.

Judges in the Old Testament Prophets

Block notes that in the prophets, "only Isaiah and Hosea allude to this premonarchic period."[40] Twice Isaiah makes reference to Yahweh's defeat of Midian (Isa 9:4; 10:26; cf. Judg 7:19–25), the latter specifically mentioning the victory at the "Rock of Oreb" (Judg 17:25). The prophet Hosea twice identifies the outrage at Gibeah (Judg 19) as an instance of deep corruption prompting Yahweh's judgment (Hos 9:9; 10:9).

Judges in the Psalms

The psalmists at times put Israel's history to verse and so, as we would expect, the settlement period does feature in these poetic retellings of the past. But once again, the references to Judges are few in the Psalter. Block notes that Ps 68:7–14 is reminiscent of parts of the Song of Deborah (Judg 5), and indeed the similar imagery and language is hard to miss.[41] The emphasis in this psalm is on Yahweh's defeat of Israel's enemies during the judges period.

Psalm 78 is a lengthy psalm that recounts in poetic form the history of Israel. Intriguingly, the purpose of the psalm is stated up front: "to tell the coming generation the glorious deeds of Yahweh and his might, the wonders that he has done" (v. 4; cf. Judg 2:10). The psalmist includes the settlement period in his sweeping overview of Israel's history. Although short on specific details, Ps 78 characterizes the period of the settlement as one in which Israel rebelled,

40. Block, *Judges*, 27.
41. Block, *Judges*, 27.

provoked Yahweh to anger, and incurred the punishment of foreign oppression, but also experienced his deliverance.

Psalm 83, on the other hand, does have specific references to the events that feature in Judges. A psalm of lament, Ps 83 implores Yahweh to act against the enemies as he did to Israel's enemies in the settlement period: Midian (v. 9a; cf. Judg 7:19–25), Sisera and Jabin (v. 9b; cf. Judg 4:15–24), Oreb and Zeeb (v. 11a; cf. Judg 7:25), and Zebah and Zalmunna (v. 11b; cf. Judg 8:4–21). The purpose of the references to the judges period in this psalm is to draw on Yahweh's pattern of deliverance in the past as a precedent for deliverance in the present.

Psalm 106, similar to Ps 68, provides a broad sketch of Israel's history. The psalm mixes elements of praise and lament, and it appears from verse 47 that the psalmist and his community are experiencing foreign captivity—he therefore praises Yahweh for his steadfastness in the mighty deeds of the past and looks for deliverance for the present (vv. 1–5; 47). Verses 34–46 recount in generalities the settlement period, and once again the psalmist highlights the persistent rebellion and idolatry of the people in this period (specifically mentioning child sacrifice), the anger of Yahweh inciting him to deliver them over to foreign enemies, their crying out, and Yahweh's repeated salvation of Israel.

In this survey it is apparent that the settlement period is part of the historical consciousness of some of the authors of the Old Testament, even if it does not feature largely in the Old Testament literature. Moreover, we cannot determine for certain whether the book of Judges per se was the specific source or whether the Old Testament historians, poets, and prophets were drawing from other sources. From the references to this period that we do find, it is instructive to observe how the authors regarded the era of the judges: it is a period dominated by Israel's persistent rebellion and covenant infidelity and by Yahweh's persistent mercy and covenant faithfulness. Block sums it up well: "the period of the judges is consistently viewed negatively, as a time of intense apostasy. But there is also the consistent recognition of Yahweh who, in his grace, raises up saviors to rescue the oppressed from their enemies."[42]

Judges in the New Testament

If references to the settlement period are rare in the Old Testament, they are even scarcer in the New Testament. Block and Webb perceive veiled allusions to the blessing of Jael in the Song of Deborah (Judg 5:24) in the blessing of Mary in Luke 1:42 and also to Samson's birth announcement in that of John

42. Block, *Judges*, 68.

the Baptist (Luke 1:15) and Jesus (Matt 2:23).[43] Furthermore, Block holds that John the Baptist features in Luke as a "Samson-like Nazirite" (Luke 1:15).[44] An allusion, veiled or otherwise, seems to imply an intentional connection between events and it is not clear in these cases that this kind of intentionality is at work.

Paul's exhortation in the Antioch synagogue recounts Israel's history from God's election of the patriarchs to the death and resurrection of Jesus (Acts 13:16–41), the climax of his message coming at these words: "We bring you the good news that what God promised to the fathers, this he has fulfilled to us their children by raising Jesus" (vv. 32–33). In this historical overview, Paul is aware of the settlement period when he makes mention of God providing judges (v. 20), though he offers no evaluation.

By far the most significant, and perhaps puzzling, consideration of the settlement period appears in Heb 11.[45] Having surveyed the faith of figures like Abel, Enoch, Noah, Abraham, Sarah, Isaac, Jacob, Joseph, and Moses, and the faith of the Israelites in crossing the Red Sea and conquering the land (Heb 11:4–31), the author of Hebrews specifically highlights four judges:

> And what more shall I say? For time would fail me to tell of Gideon, Barak, Samson, Jephthah, of David and Samuel and the prophets—who through faith conquered kingdoms, enforced justice, obtained promises, stopped the mouths of lions, quenched the power of fire, escaped the edge of the sword, were made strong out of weakness, became mighty in war, put foreign enemies to flight. (Heb 11:32–34)

The inclusion of Gideon, Barak, Samson, and Jephthah among the so-called "heroes of the faith" may stop us in our tracks! The author of Hebrews' interpretation of these individuals seems so fundamentally at odds with the interpretation of Judges in this commentary—is it possible that we have misunderstood Judges (or at least the four judges that Hebrews mentions)? Surely Othniel, Deborah, or even Ehud would have been better candidates for the purposes of Heb 11 than Gideon, Barak, Samson, and Jephthah. What are we to make of this? Is it possible to reconcile the interpretation of these judges with what we find in the book of Judges?

First, we must acknowledge the different purposes at work in the composition of Heb 11 and the book of Judges. Whereas the purpose of Judges is to demonstrate the moral, social, and spiritual corruption of Israel in the settle-

43. Webb, *Book of Judges*, 55; Block, *Judges*, 69–70.

44. Block, *Judges*, 69–70.

45. I have dealt specifically with the challenges of Heb 11 and the interpretation of Judges in Beldman, *Deserting the King*, 90–93, and what follows draws on those reflections.

ment period as a result of their rejection of Yahweh's kingship, Heb 11 aims to highlight the faith of individuals from Israel's past, faith that the author of Hebrews defines specifically as "the assurance of things hoped for, the conviction of things not seen" (Heb 11:1). The emphasis in Hebrews, therefore, is on those characteristics of past individuals that serve the aim of the author.

Being intimately acquainted with the history and traditions of the Old Testament, the author of Hebrews knew that the people figured in Heb 11 were not paragons of virtue: for example, Abraham, Sarah, Jacob, and Moses "doubted Yahweh's promises, took action to secure the promises in ungodly ways, or circumvented God's will through disobedience."[46] And yet these flawed individuals also provide examples of faith and insofar as they do so, they provide inspiration for the present. The interpretation of past individuals in Heb 11 is not unlike what we find in the books of Chronicles. There the chronicler, fully aware of the shortcomings of David and Solomon, nevertheless portrays the very best aspects of their leadership so as to encourage and motivate the Chronicler's audience.[47] We should regard the inclusion of the four judges in Heb 11 similarly. This is not a fanciful reinterpretation of Gideon, Barak, Samson, and Jephthah, but rather a deliberate highlighting of their more positive aspects.

Second, two clues in Heb 11:32–34 itself provide some clarity on this issue. First, if indeed it is true, as many suppose, that Hebrews originated as a sermon, the note about time not permitting the opportunity to tell about Gideon, Barak, and the others is curious.[48] Based on a careful reading of Judges, much more time and nuance would be required to elucidate how Gideon, Barak, Samson and Jephthah qualify as exemplars of faith. Their stories are complex, and perhaps the author of Hebrews is acknowledging the complexity. Second, the author is specific in identifying their demonstrations of faith in verses 33–34. We can certainly affirm with Hebrews that

> Despite all his fears and foibles, Gideon did destroy the altar to Baal (6:25–28) and put the enemy to flight with an army of 300 (7:1–23). His faith may have been weak, but he was a man of faith. And for all his shortcomings, Samson did stop the mouth of a lion (14:6), escape the edge of the sword (throughout the Samson narratives), and was made strong in his moment of weakness (16:28–30). Hesitant Barak and manipulative Jephthah led armies that did indeed conquer mighty kingdoms (4:10, 14–16; 11:32–33).[49]

46. Beldman, *Deserting the King*, 52.

47. Block, *Judges*, 70.

48. For Hebrews originating as a sermon, see the discussion in Lane, *Hebrews 1–8*, lxx–lxxv.

49. Beldman, *Deserting the King*, 52.

In these ways, we should have no difficulty affirming how Heb 11 commends these individuals as people of faith. Thus, there is no contradiction between Judges and Heb 11. Moreover, we should avoid the temptation to use Heb 11 to short-circuit a careful reading of Judges. As Webb helpfully notes,

> None of this means that the book of Judges cannot be allowed to speak for itself, or that we must whitewash the judges and turn them into paragons of virtue and models in all respects for Christian behavior. That would be to overlook the obviously flawed character of the judges. . . . In short, it would be bad exegesis, and bad exegesis cannot be a foundation for good biblical theology.[50]

Conclusion

Scripture is a wonderful symphony, with various movements and variations. In this section on Judges and biblical theology we have attuned our ears to hear Judges particularly as it resonates throughout the Bible. We have seen how Judges itself is a variation of themes and motifs that precede it in the canon and also how its own uniqueness has given rise to further resonances in the rest of the Old and New Testaments. As the previous quotation from Webb highlights, good biblical theology needs to be founded on good exegesis. In turn, good biblical theology provides a solid foundation for good systematic theology.[51] The exegetical work and theological reflection in the commentary section and this foray into biblical theology should, I trust, provide a sure footing for reflecting on what Judges might contribute to systematic theology.

Judges and Systematic Theology

Judges, of course, is not a book of systematic theology. Systematic theology is the discipline that carefully identifies, abstracts, collates, and organizes various foci from the biblical texts and articulates them for today. The very best systematic theology is no less biblical than biblical theology, but where the two differ

50. Webb, *Book of Judges*, 57.

51. This is not to say that the relationship between biblical exegesis, biblical theology, and systematic theology is unidirectional. The basic truths of orthodox Christianity have been captured in the creeds, which are systematic theology (however brief). The articles of faith found in these creeds about God the Father, Jesus, the Holy Spirit, the church, etc., provide the orb within which theological interpretation (including practices like exegesis and biblical theology) of the Bible takes place.

is that whereas biblical theology aims to articulate the unity of Scripture on the basis of terms and categories derived from the Bible itself, systematic theology involves abstraction and can draw on categories from outside Scripture (e.g., philosophy). In the practice of systematic theology, biblical texts are the raw material for formulating doctrinal statements (i.e., teachings) that help believers navigate the truths concerning God (the Father, Son, and Spirit), the human person, creation, salvation, sin, and the list goes on.

This is not to say that systematic theology bypasses sound biblical exegesis. An accusation that sometimes gets leveled at systematic theologians is that they exploit select biblical texts as mere proof-texts in support of a given doctrine. Done properly, systematic theology ought to engage deeply with the variegated texture and contextual nature of the biblical data in formulating doctrine. In his monumental twelve-volume *Church Dogmatics*, Karl Barth, the preeminent systematic theologian of the twentieth century, exemplifies the best kind of deep engagement with Scripture for the purposes of doctrine.[52] Alongside his doctrinal formulations are sections in which he practices meaningful exegesis at great length and with remarkable sophistication. Moreover, the best systematic theology should reflect on the whole counsel of God in Scripture and avoid the temptation to focus only on the New Testament, or on sections of the Bible (e.g., the New Testament epistles) or authors (e.g., Paul) that the theologian may regard as best suited to the task of systematic theology. Systematic theology should be biblical not only in the sense that it draws on biblical texts but also in the sense that it reflects as much as is possible the Bible in its totality.

As mentioned, Judges is not systematic theology; it is narrative. Moreover, with regard to many of the heads of doctrine it has very little to offer.[53] As Lindsay Wilson notes, "not every book of the Bible will speak to every issue in theology."[54] And yet, Judges is a rich book for theological reflection, as I hope we have seen so far. The purpose of this section, therefore, is to explore the ways that Judges illumines systematic theology. No doubt Judges will reinforce the typical teachings of systematic theology, deepening our appreciation of the church's doctrine. We will also see, however, that Judges will nuance, and in some cases challenge and critique some aspects of systematic theology. For example, some articulations of divine impassibility would need to be carefully

52. Barth, *Church Dogmatics*.

53. Cf. Wilson's commentary on Job in the Two Horizons series. There he notes, "In a number of areas of systematic theology we would expect the book of Job to have little impact. It does not speak of ecclesiology, sacraments, the person and work of Jesus, election, pneumatology, or ecclesiology" (Wilson, *Job*, 332).

54. Wilson, *Job*, 332.

nuanced on the basis of a close reading of Judges (or for that matter other Old Testament narratives).

In the history of the practice of systematic theology, Judges has not featured as a dominant source for doctrine, but this is, in my mind, to the detriment of the discipline. On the basis of Scripture indices, the major works of systematic theology very rarely turn specifically to Judges in support of doctrinal formulation, and where references do appear they are often insignificant passing references (i.e., proof texts) that are removed from the purposes of Judges.[55] John Calvin's *Institutes of the Christian Religion* contains thirty references to Judges in only eleven sections, and Charles Hodge's three-volume *Systematic Theology* only nine. Judges appears six times in the Scripture index of Wolfhart Pannenberg's three-volume *Systematic Theology* and only twice in Emil Brunner's *Dogmatics* (also three volumes). Herman Bavinck's four-volume *Reformed Dogmatics* refers to judges a total of seventy-three times, whereas Barth's fourteen volumes only refer specifically to Judges thirty-four times. More recently, the Scripture index of John Frame's twelve-hundred-page *Systematic Theology* features twenty-four references to Judges, and Wayne Grudem's popular-level one-volume *Systematic Theology* doesn't contain a single reference to Judges in the Scripture index.[56] This is not to say that the works of systematic theology are not informed by Judges at a more intuitive level; after all, specific scriptural references are only one tool theologians use in formulating doctrine. Moreover, the broad scope of systematic theology requires a degree of human limitations—systematic theologians cannot gain expertise in all areas of the Bible. These limitations foreground the vital importance of a genuine dialogue between biblical theology and systematic theology (and biblical exegesis and biblical theology for that matter).

What follows does not attempt to exhaustively reflect on the contribution of Judges to systematic theology. Rather, I have attempted to identify and discuss areas of theology that are dominant in Judges and deserve consideration, theological teachings in Judges that have been neglected in typical systematic treatments, and/or instances where a theological reading of Judges requires a reevaluation of typical doctrinal formulations. To that end, the following will consider Judges and (1) the doctrine of God, (2) the doctrine of the Holy Spirit, (3) the doctrine of sin, (4) the doctrine of divine providence, and (5) political theology. Again, the aim in this section is to explore how Judges illuminates the discipline of systematic theology.

55. For the full references of the following works of systematic theology consult the bibliography.

56. However, I did discover specific references to Judges in Grudem's work that apparently did not appear in the Scripture reference index.

Judges and the Doctrine of God

God stands out as the main character of Judges, speaking, acting, and propelling history forward. God's purpose for a certain kind of world and a certain kind of people is always just below the surface and at times comes to the fore on the pages of Judges. The book is about God from start to finish. The opening line (1:1) sets the context as one in which no fixed human leader is present but in which Yahweh is king and his subjects consult him as such. The closing line speaks (for the fourth and final time, albeit in veiled terms) of a context in which his subjects no longer acknowledge Yahweh's kingship or live according to his rule (though he is no less present even in these circumstances). There was a king in Israel and then there was no king in Israel. A proper discussion of the doctrine of God in light of Judges must be filtered through his character as king and his kingdom purposes.

Systematic theology often begins with the knowledge of God, and more specifically with the incomprehensibility of God in his essence. This is not to say that humans can have no knowledge of God—God reveals himself in various ways and most fully in Scripture and in the person and work of Jesus the Messiah—but our knowledge will always be in part and incomplete. Descriptions and propositional statements about the character of God are rare in Judges. Two means of God's revelation of himself that theologians draw on are significant in Judges. The first is Scripture's use of names for God and the second is God's action in history.

God's names reveal something of his character, and so a focus on the use of divine names in Judges contributes to theology. In Judges, God is most often referred to by his personal name, Yahweh, which highlights his covenantal and thereby kingly nature. This divine name appears a grand total of 175 times in 137 verses, most often by the narrator but also by Yahweh's messengers and at times by the judges, minor characters, or by the assembly of Israel (the latter only in ch. 21). Intriguingly, often when human characters invoke God's personal name it is either for self-serving reasons or reflects a blatant misunderstanding of whom it is they are invoking (e.g., Gideon's disingenuous statement about Yahweh ruling over Israel, Jephthah's vow to offer to Yahweh whatever comes out of his house, Samson's prayer to Yahweh for vengeance for his two eyes, Micah's mother's dedication of the silver to Yahweh and fashioning of idolatrous items, Micah's certainty that Yahweh will bless him because of his shrine and Levite priest, the Levite Jonathan's sketchy assurance that the Danites' conquest is under the purview of Yahweh). According to the narrator, the covenant God (including all the associated back history) is the prime mover during the settlement period, even if the human characters have lost touch with his nature. The titles "Yahweh Elohim," "Yahweh Elohim of Israel," and "the Elohim of Israel," which appear throughout the book, also emphasize the covenantal character of God in Judges.

The divine name Elohim on its own appears approximately three dozen times in the book. This is a more generic name for God, and in Old Testament theology can evoke God's character as Creator. This use is certainly attested in Judges as in Elohim manipulating the dew in Gideon's tests regarding the fleece (6:40), Elohim splitting the rock to provide water to quench Samson's thirst (15:19), and perhaps also in Jotham's parable in which Elohim benefits from the oil that the olive tree produces (9:9) and the wine that the grapevines produce (9:13). Understandably, foreigners use Elohim in reference to God (Adoni-Bezek in 1:7 and the Midianite soldier in 7:14); less understandable and perhaps suspicious are the places in Judges where Israelite characters use Elohim when we might expect Yahweh to be the more appropriate name; for example, Gideon speaking to Elohim in 6:36–40, the use of Elohim in the narrative of Samson's birth announcement (ch. 13), and the Danites' inquiry of Elohim about their planned conquest of Laish (18:5). The shift in the use of divine names in the Old Testament can often serve a rhetorical function, and by virtue of the fact that Elohim can be translated as either "God" or "gods" depending on the context (both uses are attested throughout Judges), one wonders if the use of Elohim at certain points in Judges may reflect a confusion on the part of the human characters about precisely who it is they are conversing with/evoking.

Gideon invokes God as Adonai ("master") three times, although twice before he recognized his true identity (6:15, 16, 22), as do Manoah (13:8) and Samson (16:28). Jephthah uses the title "Judge" for God (11:27). Moreover, human names in Judges provide a window into God's character, even though in some cases they represent misnomers: Joshua ("Yahweh-Is-Salvation"), Gideon's father Joash ("Yahweh-Is-Strong"), Jotham ("Yahweh-Is-Perfect"), Jair ("Yahweh-Gives-Light"), Micayehu ("Yahweh-the-Incomparable"), Jonathan ("Yahweh-Has-Given"), and Eleazar ("El/God-Has-Helped"). These human names provide a window into the character of God. An intriguing insight with regard to divine names emerges when Manoah asks the divine messenger/Yahweh his name (13:17). The messenger, apparently the mouthpiece of Yahweh, responds: "Why do you ask my name? It is wonderful/incomprehensible" (v. 18). In reference to this verse, Bavinck notes, "Although he reveals himself in his names, no name is adequate to the purpose. He is nameless; his name is a name of wonder."[57]

Indeed in Judges, much more adequate to the purposes of discerning the

57. Bavinck, *Reformed Dogmatics*, 1:34.

character of God (his revelation) are his words and especially his actions. Here a composite, detailed, and sometimes perplexing theology emerges.

What divine attributes or characteristics feature in Judges? A good many divine attributes appear, and chief among them are God's covenantal judgment and his covenantal compassion. God is both judge and savior. In this regard, Lee Roy Martin notes that the cycle of judges with its various elements boils down to two movements: (1) the rebellion of the Israelites and God's punishment, and (2) Israel's cry of distress and God's salvation. He notes, "The uniting of these two movements into one recurring cycle registers the theological tension between the justice of God and the mercy of God (cf. Exod 34:6–7)."[58]

Readers of Judges have sometimes found it difficult to hold onto the theological tension that Martin identifies, and my suspicion is that one's theological framework may tend to silence either the aspects of God's justice or of his mercy. For example, a neo-Marcionite tendency that is present in much contemporary Christianity sees the God of the Old Testament as full of wrath and judgment and devoid of the grace and mercy that characterizes the God of the New Testament, revealed ultimately in Jesus. An unnuanced and unbalanced reading of Judges might confirm this caricature. On the other hand, with every good intention, some readers might tend to highlight the longsuffering mercy of God toward Israel in Judges while at the same time downplaying God's repeated judgment against the Israelites for their rebellion.

In Judges, Yahweh is judge, the arbiter of covenant fidelity and executioner of divine justice. He repeatedly punishes the iniquity of his rebellious people, and also exacts retribution on individuals (e.g., 9:56–57; cf. 1:7). The people's infidelity arouses Yahweh's anger, and he brings about the curses of the covenant. And yet the God of the covenant is moved to compassion as a result of the cry of his people (2:18)—Yahweh's mercy prevents the people from self-destruction and utter annihilation.

Thus, the unity, consistency, and complexity of God's character that systematic theology aims to articulate are on full display in Judges. Yahweh's character in Judges displays the God so poignantly revealed to Moses in Exod 34:6–7, as well as the purpose and work of Jesus, who embodied both divine justice and divine mercy. The reality of the judges cycle, as the commentary bore out, is that the Israelites crying out as a result of Yahweh's punishment does not constitute genuine repentance; consequently, Yahweh's acts of deliverance, by means of the judges/deliverers, do represent the mercy of God.

Yahweh displays an overwhelming unity of purpose in Judges, and, thus, the book contributes to the concept of God's immutability. Systematic

58. Martin, "Power to Save!?," 23.

theology's articulation of divine immutability does not mitigate the reality that God responds and even at times changes his mind in specific circumstances. The immutability of God has to do, as Bavinck notes, with his existence and being, his will and purposes.[59] Bavinck nevertheless warns that God's immutability "should not be confused with monotonous sameness or rigid immobility. Scripture itself leads us in describing God in the most manifold relations to all his creatures. While immutable in himself, he nevertheless, as it were, lives the life of his creatures and participates in all their changing states."[60] The repeated cycle demonstrates God's unswerving and unrelenting purpose for Israel to be the people he has called them to be. Moreover, Israel's negative encounters with foreign nations, however difficult those may be to contemporary readers, are consequences for covenant rebellion that Yahweh had promised would occur (Deut 28). And yet, Yahweh is moved to compassion, and responds in light of changing circumstances, in each case according to his unchangeable character and will.

God's providence, a key doctrine in systematic theology, is indelibly stamped on every page of Judges. According to divine providence, God orders and maintains all things at all times.[61] By no means the god of the deists, Yahweh is deeply involved in the lives and affairs of the people, not least in the political realm. Foreign nations do Yahweh's bidding. He repeatedly raises up deliverers. Yahweh's Spirit is active in Judges, inspiring heroic and redemptive deeds. Although he is most active in human affairs, God also intervenes in creation, at times upsetting the natural order of things, as in the fleecing incident (6:36–40), the miraculous sending of fire to consume the offerings of Gideon (6:21) and of Samson's parents (13:20), and the splitting open of the rock to provide water for Samson (15:19). At Yahweh's command circumstances are thrown into chaos, and by his will the land experiences rest. Of course, the doctrine of divine providence needs to be carefully balanced by the notion of human responsibility, a theological tension that is present in Judges.

Although the Hebrew word for holy (קדוש/*qādôš*) does not appear in Judges, the book assumes the concept of Yahweh's holiness. God's holiness is fully on display at points in the book, not least in the theophanic moments that literally instill the fear of God in Gideon (6:21–23) and Manoah and his wife (13:20–23). The consuming otherness of God may be the reason he sends messengers throughout the book, because, as Yahweh said to Moses, "A human

59. Bavinck, *Reformed Dogmatics*, 2:153.

60. Bavinck, *Reformed Dogmatics*, 2:158.

61. See the discussion in Bavinck, *Reformed Dogmatics*, 2:374–80.

cannot see me and live" (Exod 33:20). God's holiness sets him apart from the gods of the nations that make a regular appearance in Judges. His holiness is the root of his righteous anger in the face of Israel's covenant rebellion; thus, Bavinck notes, "When Israel breaks his covenant, desecrates his name, and violates his laws, it is precisely God's holiness that incites him to mete out punishment. His holiness demands that Israel be holy."[62] And yet, Bavinck also maintains that God's holiness is intricately bound to his repeated deliverance of Israel: "His holiness does not permit him to let Israel perish. As the Holy One, he is the creator, redeemer, and king of Israel."[63]

Yahweh's holiness suggests his transcendence that is evident in Judges, but so too is his immanence. This is manifest in the many and varied ways that God intervenes in the circumstances of history but also in the surprising number of times, embedded in the narratives, that Yahweh speaks and/or explicitly makes his will known. He does this by a number of means. Sometimes the text simply states that Yahweh spoke, and in these cases perhaps the individuals received an audible voice (Gideon: 6:25–26; 7:2–7, 9–11; and the Israelites: 10:10–14). Yahweh makes his will known four times in the two pan-Israel battles, perhaps by means of the Urim and Thummim (1:2; 20:18, 23, 28). He speaks once through the voice of a prophet (6:7–10), and four times by means of the messenger/angel of Yahweh (to all Israel: 2:1–3; to Gideon: 6:11–24; and twice to Samson's parents: 13:3–5, 11–18).

In all these ways, and more besides, Judges makes a positive contribution to the doctrine of God. One final note on Judges' contribution to the doctrine of God is worth mentioning. There are places in the book where Yahweh's will is shrouded in mystery. Chief among them is the introduction to the cycle of Jephthah. This is the singular place in the judges cycle where the Israelites specifically acknowledge their sin, put away their idols, and "served Yahweh" (10:10, 15–16). In that instance, in spite of their confession and act of repentance, Yahweh explicitly determines *not* to save them (vv. 11–14). What's more, the narrative makes it clear that Jephthah is not Yahweh's choice, and yet Yahweh's Spirit empowers Jephthah (11:29) and Yahweh delivered the Ammonites into Jephthah's hand (v. 32). Granted, Jephthah sacrifices his daughter and slaughters forty-two thousand Ephraimites, and the land decidedly does not experience rest in this cycle, but Yahweh's actions in this context are perplexing. In the other cases, Israel's crying out is one of distress and not repentance and still Yahweh saves; in this case the crying out is accompanied by confession and acts of apparent contrition and Yahweh determines not to save (although he

62. Bavinck, *Reformed Dogmatics*, 2:220.
63. Bavinck, *Reformed Dogmatics*, 2:220.

does provide at least a degree of deliverance).[64] This does represent something of a theological conundrum that is not easy to reconcile. Of course, this is an exception in the book and perhaps we should not draw too much from the exception, but it should give us pause. Similarly, Yahweh's verbal assent to sending the pan-Israelite army against the Benjamites to be defeated twice and then a third time granting victory is also mysterious. I offered an explanation for this perplexing turn of events in the commentary, but we must acknowledge in our theological formulations that although we can affirm and know many things about God, he is still God and we are humans. We can never plumb the depths of his character or understand all the dimensions of his mysterious will. He is the God "who gives life to all things . . . the blessed and only Sovereign, the King of kings and Lord of lords, who alone has immortality, who dwells in unapproachable light, whom no one has ever seen or can see" (1 Tim 6:13–16).

Judges and the Doctrine of the Holy Spirit

Perhaps for many contemporary Christians drawing on the New Testament, the work of the Holy Spirit is most obviously associated with special gifts like speaking in tongues, healing, and prophecy. The New Testament also emphasizes the role of the Spirit in producing personal faith and conversion (regeneration), in equipping Christians for holy living (sanctification), in contributing to the production of Scripture (inspiration), and in aiding in discerning the will of God, especially as it is revealed in the Bible (illumination).

In the Old Testament, the Spirit is said to have empowered David at his anointing, equipping him for his office as king (1 Sam 16:13), and Bezalel, endowing him with "ability and intelligence, with knowledge and all craftsmanship" to build the tabernacle and the various articles associated with it (Exod 35:30–35) and to instruct others to help with the task (35:34). The Spirit also prompts some Old Testament figures to prophesy (Balaam: Num 24:2; Saul and his messengers: 1 Sam 10:6, 10; 19:20–24; Ezekiel: Ezek 11:5; Micah: Mic 3:8, etc.) and gives wisdom for making good judgments (Num 11:17, 25–26).

The Spirit plays a role a number of times in the book of Judges, empowering the likes of Othniel, Gideon, Jephthah, and Samson.[65] The phrase "the

64. I hesitate to use the word repentance to describe Israel's words and actions here. This may well be a case of Israel doing the right thing (confessing and putting away the idols) for the wrong reasons (to alleviate their distress, but not to commit themselves to the service of King Yahweh).

65. In a number of studies, Martin has done significant work on the Spirit in Judges; see his dissertation: "Unheard Voice of God," now published as Martin, *The Unheard Voice: A Pentecostal Hearing of the Book of Judges*; see also, Martin, "Power to Save!?," 21–50.

Spirit of Yahweh" (רוח יהוה/*rûaḥ YHWH*) occurs seven times in the book (3:10; 6:34; 11:29; 13:25; 14:6, 19; 15:14), and as Martin notes, Judges is the first canonical record of the specific phrase "Spirit of Yahweh."[66] The Hebrew word רוח/*rûaḥ* has a broad range of meaning, including but not limited to "breath," "wind," "spirit," "air," and "disposition."[67] Context is a determining factor in how we ought to understand the Spirit in Judges.

That the author of Judges provides no explanation or definition of the Spirit of Yahweh is not insignificant and suggests that the audience would have understood the concept.[68] According to Martin, "part of the conceptual fabric of the book's theology of salvation" is the role of the Spirit in the exodus narrative to effect salvation.[69] According to Dale Moody, "the primacy of the exodus in Israel's faith promoted *ruach* as the metaphor for God's direct action in nature and history."[70] Additionally, the background to the notion of the Spirit of Yahweh in Judges is the Israelite narrative tradition in which the Spirit is associated with sustaining human life (Gen 6:3), and providing special discernment (Gen 41:38), skill for craftsmanship (Exod 28:3; 31:3; 35:31), prophetic utterance (Num 11:25; 24:2), and leadership ability (Num 27:18; Deut 34:9).[71] Thus, in addition to the "wind" that effects salvation, the "Spirit" is associated with the "untamable gift of the energizing presence of Yahweh."[72] In this way, Israel's God was unique among the ancient Near Eastern gods, who may control the "wind" (רוח/*rûaḥ*) but do not possess a "spirit" (רוח/*rûaḥ*).[73]

I cannot but wonder if the audience of Judges would also have been aware of the prophecies regarding the role of God's Spirit in the future, though this would depend on the date of the composition of Judges in relation to that of the prophecies. Joel looked forward to the great day of Yahweh in which Yahweh's Spirit would unite and empower all of God's people (Joel 2:28–29). Moreover, Isaiah prophesied of the coming arrival of the messiah who would be filled with Yahweh's Spirit—this Spirit-filled son of Jesse would bring judgment, gather

66. Martin, "Power to Save!?," 21.

67. Martin, "Power to Save!?," 25.

68. Martin, "Power to Save!?," 25.

69. Martin, "Power to Save!?," 25; Yahweh influences an east "wind" to bring about the locust plague (Exod 10:13) and a west "wind" to stop it (10:19), and Yahweh's manipulation of the east "wind" allows the Israelites to cross the Red Sea on dry ground, while drowning Pharaoh and his armies (14:21), which is celebrated in the Song of Moses (15:8, 10). It is significant to note, in this regard, the comprehensive scope of salvation—the Spirit's role is not reduced to individual faith and salvation.

70. Cited in Martin, "Power to Save!?," 25–26.

71. Martin, "Power to Save!?," 26.

72. Martin, "Power to Save!?," 26.

73. See Martin, "Power to Save!?," 26, and the associated references.

the twelve tribes of Israel and establish peace (Isa 11; 42:1–4). This messiah will acknowledge the Spirit's indwelling, announce good news, and proclaim Yahweh's Jubilee (Isa 61:1–2). Finally, when they encountered the stirring of Yahweh's Spirit in Judges, the original audience of Judges may have heard resonances with Ezekiel, who was told to prophesy to the house of Israel that for the sake of his own name, which they had profaned before the nations, Yahweh would gather and unite the scattered tribes, cleanse and renew them, put his Spirit within them so that they would keep his commandments, and create great flourishing when there was previously only desolation (Ezek 36:22–38). Of course, those who lived during the exile and beyond who were aware of these prophecies were still longing for this *Spirit*ual revolution, but perhaps when they read Judges they could see glimpses, small foretastes of what would come in the day of Yahweh.

Thus, the background for Judges' understanding of the Spirit of Yahweh likely derives from the association between "wind" and the exodus, and the presence of Yahweh by means of the gift of his "Spirit" to individuals and groups for a particular purpose. Later prophecies may also have resonated with readers of Judges. How then do we see the Spirit of Yahweh working in Judges and what does this contribute to the understanding of the Spirit in general? Martin's thorough research on the role of the Spirit in Judges leads him to conclude that although the Spirit of Yahweh has a unique and dynamic role in each of the contexts that it appears, "the Spirit of Yahweh in Judges functions primarily as the dynamic presence of Yahweh that compels and empowers the judge to effectuate Yahweh's salvation of his covenant people."[74]

This role of the Spirit in bringing about Yahweh's salvation of his people is demonstrated most clearly in Othniel—the Spirit comes upon him, he wages war, and he liberates Israel from the oppressive Mesopotamian regime (3:10). In the case of Gideon, the Spirit emboldens Gideon and empowers him to unite a coalition army (6:34–35), and although the victory is delayed there is no question that Yahweh's presence through his Spirit grants the victory to Gideon and his three hundred soldiers. The Spirit also comes upon Jephthah, inspiring his journey to the enemy battle lines (11:29), and though the Spirit does not prevent Jephthah from making his terrible vow to Yahweh, he does defeat the Ammonite armies. Martin notes that Gideon and Jephthah demonstrate that the endowment of Yahweh's Spirit to achieve salvation can produce an enduring confidence that is self-serving and opposed to God's will.[75]

The Spirit's role in the life of Samson is even more complex. According

74. Martin, "Power to Save!?," 22.

75. Martin, "Power to Save!?," 40.

to Martin, a key to understanding the limited effect of the Spirit in the Samson cycle is (1) Yahweh's previous determination in the Jephthah cycle not to save Israel again (10:13), and (2) the specific note in the Samson cycle that Yahweh through Samson will only begin to save Israel from the Philistines (13:5).[76] The role of the Spirit in Samson, therefore, is not to save Israel but, it seems, to act against the Philistines and to save Samson. In this way, the role of the Spirit in the Samson cycle is circumscribed and somewhat anomalous in the broader context.[77]

What then can we say about the contribution of Judges to the doctrine of the Holy Spirit? Judges confirms doctrinal formulations that highlight the Spirit as the very presence of God with his people. Judges also supports the role of the Spirit in bringing about salvation and renewal, though in Judges the efficacy of that salvation is felt in the community (i.e., the nation of Israel). Specifically in the case of Gideon, but also perhaps implied in that of Othniel and Jephthah, the Spirit unites the people of God in solidarity so that they are resolved to battle the oppressors. The Spirit preserves God's people from certain ruin, liberates, and initiates "new beginnings."[78] In these ways, Judges may serve as a reminder of the broad scope of the Spirit's role in the lives of God's people and the comprehensive extent of the Spirit's salvation.

Judges and the Doctrine of Sin

The doctrine of sin as it is articulated in systematic theology naturally centers around the origin and nature of sin. One expects to find detailed expositions on original sin and its implications, the various lexical terms for sin in Scripture, and the extent to which sin is a violation of the divine moral law. What does Judges contribute to the doctrine of sin? Sin is clearly a driving force in the narratives of Judges. However, Judges does not attempt to explain the origins of sin, except insofar as the corruption of Israel in the settlement period is rooted in a failure of previous generations to pass on the stories and tradition of Yahweh and his redemptive works on behalf of Israel (2:10); but that is not in view in the discussions of original sin. The various Hebrew terms that provide a composite picture of sin are almost completely absent from the narratives of Judges.[79] And while it is by no means false to say that Judges assumes that sin

76. Martin, "Power to Save!?," 48.
77. Martin, "Power to Save!?," 48–49.
78. Martin, "Power to Save!?," 50.
79. See the helpful summary in Bavinck, *Reformed Dogmatics*, 3:129.

is a violation of moral law, it seems that the book is at pains to demonstrate that the problem of sin goes much deeper than that and it spreads much wider.

It should go without saying that Judges does not provide a full-orbed doctrine of sin, just as it does not provide a comprehensive doctrine of God, or the Holy Spirit, or many other subjects. In fact, the locus of attention with regard to sin in Judges is on the sin of the people of God, and the book has little to say about sin as it relates to the nations.[80] Even though Judges' contribution to the doctrine of sin is necessarily circumscribed, it does illumine the foundational nature of sin and its consequences—and is instructive for today.

Sin, according to Judges, is an orientation that arises out of allegiance to foreign gods (and thus, disloyalty to Yahweh and his covenant) and manifests itself in far-reaching (i.e., religiously, morally, socially, politically) corrupt behavior. By far the most typical way Judges expresses this is by means of the phrase Israel "did what was evil in the eyes of Yahweh" (2:11; 3:7, 12; 4:1; 6:1; 10:6; 13:1). This phrase appears a number of times in the Pentateuch, including Deuteronomy where doing "evil in the eyes of Yahweh" is intricately bound up with the worship of false gods (Deut. 4:25; 9:18; 17:2–3). This link is clearly made throughout Judges as the phrase is often followed immediately by clarifying statements: Israel "did what was evil in the eyes of Yahweh. . ."

> and served the Baals, and they abandoned Yahweh, the God of their fathers. . . . They went after other gods, from among the gods of the peoples who were around them, and bowed down to them. . . . They abandoned Yahweh and served the Baals and Ashtaroth (2:11–13).
>
> They forgot Yahweh their God and served the Baals and Asheroth (3:7).
>
> and served the Baals and the Ashtaroth, the gods of Syria, the gods of Sidon, the gods of Moab, the gods of the Ammonites, and the gods of the Philistines. And they forsook Yahweh and did not serve him (10:6).

The point cannot and should not be missed that "doing evil in the eyes of Yahweh" is tantamount to divine treason. The repetition of the phrase (and

80. In this regard, we might consider the case of the foreign king Adoni-bezek who, at least according to his own evaluation of his circumstances, considered the severing of his thumbs and big toes as divine retribution (Judg 1:7). Moreover, God himself indicated that Israel's conquest of Canaan was (at least in part) a consequence of the sin of the nations (Gen 15:13–16; Deut 9:5). However, the conquest of Canaan is cast more in terms of Israel's disobedience in respect to Yahweh's instruction than Canaan's iniquity, even if perhaps the latter is assumed (as it seems to be in Judg 14:4, which speaks of Yahweh's hidden agenda to oppose the Philistines).

associated explanations) and their strategic structural placement in the book are such that it is not an exaggeration to say that the book of Judges is all about where Israel's allegiance lies—with Yahweh or with the foreign deities.

Thus, "doing evil in the eyes of Yahweh" amounts to disloyalty to Yahweh and loyalty and service to foreign gods. This is confirmed in the one place where the Hebrew verb "to sin" (חטא/*ḥāṭā'*) is used in association with Israel. In Judg 10:10 the Israelites confess, "We have sinned against you [Yahweh], because we have forsaken our God and have served the Baals" (cf. v. 15), and Yahweh confirms their assessment (v. 13). Here the association between sin and disloyalty to Yahweh could not be clearer.

It is worth clarifying that we never encounter Israelites (individually or collectively) denying Yahweh's existence or alternatively acknowledging his existence but then consciously rejecting his divine authority. Instead, we have plenty of examples of a syncretistic blending of Israelite and Canaanite "religion." This religious syncretism is quite evident at a number of places, not least in the example of Gideon's patriarchal household and in Gideon himself. Gideon's father maintained a shrine to Baal and Ashtoreth (6:25–32) and yet his father must have passed down something of the tradition and history of Israel because Gideon recalls some of them (6:13). Gideon himself rightly acknowledges the rule of Yahweh but then immediately fashions an idol and sets up a shrine that "all Israel whored after" and that "became a snare to Gideon and to his family." When it comes to dividing divine loyalties, like father, like son. Indeed, according to the pervasive polytheistic cognitive environment of the ancient Near East, paying homage to Yahweh and also serving the local deities would be the most natural thing for the Israelites to do. And yet, Yahweh was unique among the gods of the nations and by virtue of his special relationship with them and his redemptive and preserving deeds on their behalf, Israel was called to be a unique people. Accordingly, there was to be no division of loyalties—service to foreign gods is implicitly a rejection of Yahweh.

At its root, then, sin is a disposition in the hearts of the people of God, and not specific acts that transgress a moral code. That is not to say that actions and behavior are irrelevant. In fact, this disposition of disloyalty to Yahweh *manifests itself in* actions that transgress Yahweh's will. This becomes most clear in Judges by means of the words of Yahweh (through his messenger and prophet) and clarifying statements by the narrator. In 2:1–2a Yahweh recalls his own oath never to break covenant and that his people should not covenant with the Canaanites, but rather should break down their altars. Contrary to this, Yahweh says, "You have not obeyed my voice. What is this you have done?" (v. 2b). Similarly, in the announcement of the cycle in 2:11–23, the narrator quotes Yahweh as saying he will not drive the Canaanites out, "Because this people has transgressed my covenant that I commanded their fathers and have not obeyed my voice" (2:20). In that context, the narrator contrasts the disobedient generations of the settlement period with their ancestors, "who had obeyed the commandments of Yahweh" (v. 17). Rather they "whored after" foreign gods and "bowed down" to them (vv. 17, 19a); "They did not abandon their practices or their stubborn ways" (v. 19b). Again, the prophet in 6:7–10 accuses the people of disobedience (v. 10). In these cases, the disposition of loyalty/disloyalty is connected to or, perhaps better, *made evident in* acts of obedience/disobedience.

What are these acts of disobedience/sins? In the contexts mentioned above, idol worship seems most obviously to be in mind. The specific reference to covenant-breaking and disobeying Yahweh's commandments could be any number of offenses and may be intentionally broad, the details of which are filled out in the unfolding narratives. Indeed, the subsequent stories in Judges display in high resolution the kinds of behavior (i.e., sin) that result from disloyalty to Yahweh and allegiance to the Canaanite deities.

The sins of Israel in Judges include not obeying Yahweh's command to drive out the nations. This is a context-specific command for Israel at that time, and we do not get the sense that once the land of Canaan is under their control that they would have continued the conquest further in the Fertile Crescent and beyond. In the Gideon cycle, the men of Gideon's town were so zealous for Baal that they were willing to murder anyone who dared to sabotage the Baal shrine. Although Gideon's father dissuades them from it, we get a hint of what radical allegiance to Baal could yield. Gideon's demonstration of a "Canaanite" style of tyrannical and megalomaniacal leadership arguably emerges out of a commitment to Canaanite religion and is certainly at odds with Yahweh's Torah concerning leaders (particularly kings in Deut 17:14–20). The same could be said for his son Abimelech's experiment with kingship, which involved Abimelech murdering his seventy brothers and ruthlessly eliminating any other resistance to his absolute authority. Presumed loyalty to Canaanite deities prompted Jephthah to make a foolish vow consistent with Canaanite child sacrifice rites and to follow through on that vow; this loyalty is also manifest in Jephthah's slaughter of forty-two thousand Ephraimites as a result of a personal slight. Samson does what is right in his own eyes (14:3, 7), which at times amounts to doing what is evil in Yahweh's eyes. His repeated liaisons with foreign women are a direct violation of Yahweh's instruction (Deut 7:3–4), and he disregards his Nazirite status, defiling not only himself but also his parents. Micah steals, dishonors his mother, and is complicit in idolatry. The Danites in Judg 18 are thieving mercenaries, and while disobedience leaves them homeless, they ruthlessly annihilate a peaceful and vulnerable people outside the promised land. In chapters 19–21 the seeds of sin that are rooted in allegiance to the Canaanite gods come into full bloom, resulting in rape, cowardice, false testimony, distorted judicial proceedings, ruthless revenge, foolish vows, exploitation of women, and so on.

In the context of the sins of Micah and the Danites, of the atrocity of Gibeah and the resulting disasters (chs. 17–21), the refrain "doing evil in the eyes of Yahweh" gives way to people "doing right in their own eyes." The moral standard has shifted from divine to human, and the resulting moral relativism leads to chaos. As I have argued throughout this commentary, the people (individually and collectively) doing what seems good in their own eyes is bound up with their rejection of Yahweh as king ("There was no king in Israel"), so again these narratives underscore the connection between divine allegiance and sin.

So far, we have seen how sin is rooted in allegiance to foreign gods, which gives rise to the many and varied ways that the people of God violate his will. The consequences of sin in Judges are also worth considering. The stranglehold of sin not only creates a context of widespread immorality, but also produces an environment of uncertainty, division, oppression (economic and other), fear, suspicion, false hospitality, cowardice, and familial and social brokenness. Sin is like a cancer that literally sucks the life out of its host. Not content to be confined or limited, sin, once taken root, spreads in such a way that it saps the energy and life that feeds cells and organs. The result is that the cancer (sin) thrives and grows while the host environment of the cancer deteriorates and eventually dies.

Too often Christians tend to individualize sin and contain it to the realm of personal "morality." Judges is not ignorant of personal sin and it takes that seriously, but it also faces squarely corporate, institutional, and national sin. As we saw in the introduction, idolatry and sin cannot be contained, and their toxicity is pervasive in all spheres of life. Moreover, individual sin like that of Gibeah can lead to national sin and disaster. Even in the broader culture we hear statements like, we should not impose our own moral standard on others—if it's not hurting others then people should live and behave however they see fit. Again, Judges confronts us with the stark reality that sin has far-reaching and unforeseen consequences. Even seemingly victimless offenses cannot easily be circumscribed or contained—sin is like that.

In this fallen world, allegiance to God and King Jesus does not guarantee life and flourishing this side of eternity, but disloyalty that breeds sin will only in the long run produce disharmony, fear, oppression, misery, death—all those things that are opposed to life and flourishing. Accordingly, Judges' full-orbed instruction on sin also implies something about the doctrine of salvation. Along with the thrust of the biblical story, Judges communicates (albeit as a subtext) a longing for deliverance that extends as wide and as deep as the pervasive spread of sin. Judges provides a stark and sobering picture of sin and its consequences, and thus stands as a vital source for a multidimensional doctrine of sin, but also implies a cosmic redemption that heals the ills of human immorality, institutional corruption, economic oppression, and societal breakdown—thus, it stands as a vital source for a multidimensional doctrine of salvation.

Judges and the Doctrine of Providence

The consideration of divine providence is a good example of the task of systematic theology, and we touched on God's providence above in considering Judges and the doctrine of God. Although the word "providence" does not occur in Scripture, the pervasive sense of God's providence exists on almost every page of the Bible. Accordingly, providence as such is an abstraction. Bavinck notes, "Scripture does not use the abstract word 'providence'. . . . Instead, it depicts the activity itself in a most splendid and vital way and exhibits it to us in history. Scripture in its totality is itself the book of God's providence."[81] Bavinck refers favorably to the Heidelberg Catechism, which he thinks captures beautifully the notion of God's providence as "the almighty and ever present power of God by which he upholds, as with his hand, heaven and earth and all creatures and so rules them that . . . all things, in fact, come to us, not by chance but from his fatherly hand" (Lord's Day 10, Q&A 27).[82] Bavinck himself defines providence as "God's active will ruling all things and includes preservation, concurrence, and government."[83] The terms preservation and government in Bavinck's definition should be self-evident; by "concurrence" Bavinck means to clarify the intricate relationship between the primary cause (God) and secondary causes (creatures), and to hold the tension between God's benevolent sovereignty and creaturely (particularly human) responsibility.[84] Thus,

> wood burns and it is God alone who makes it burn, yet the burning process may not be formally attributed to God but must be attributed to the wood as subject. Human persons speak, act, and believe, and it is God alone who supplies to a sinner all the vitality and strength he or she needs for the commission of a sin. Nevertheless the subject and author of the sin is not God but the human being. In this manner Scripture draws the lines within which the reconciliation of God's sovereignty and human freedom has to be sought.

81. Bavinck, *Reformed Dogmatics*, 2:595.
82. Bavinck, *Reformed Dogmatics*, 2:604.
83. Bavinck, *Reformed Dogmatics*, 2:591.
84. Bavinck, *Reformed Dogmatics*, 2:615.

One may perceive at work in Bavinck's attempt to hold together both God's sovereignty and human responsibility clever theological gymnastics that twist and contort two irreconcilable ideas so that they cohere. On the contrary, on display here is the very heart of responsible systematic theology that allows the full counsel of Scripture to inform doctrine without flattening the tensions that we face in the teachings of Scripture.

If Scripture, as Bavinck holds, is the book of God's providence, then Judges is a vital chapter in that book. In reflecting on the doctrine of divine providence in light of Judges, we perceive the dynamic relationship between systematic theology and scriptural interpretation. Of course, systematic theology must draw on biblical teaching for doctrinal formulation, and Judges stands out as a testimony to God's providence. However, the best biblical doctrine should also illuminate what we encounter on the pages of Scripture, as it does in the case of Judges. The doctrine of providence can help us understand the tension in Judges between God's judgment on the one hand and his mercy on the other. The notion of concurrence just mentioned can help us make sense of perplexities in Judges like, for example, how Yahweh can work out his purposes in and through the mixed motivations and intentions of people like Gideon, Jephthah, and Samson, and also use the oppressive regimes of Mesopotamia, Moab, Midian, Philistia, and other ones, and yet hold them accountable for their oppression.

Bavinck is careful to explain that the three dimensions of God's providence (preservation, concurrence, and government) are not divisible, but are integrally connected at all times, and the dynamic relationship between the three is definitely evident in Judges.[85] According to God's ultimate redemptive purposes, Israel would be an agent of restoration and blessing in a broken and sinful world. But they are "free agents," as it were, and they manifest an astounding propensity to live contrary to their divine calling. In fact, their way of existence during the settlement period would have certainly resulted in self-destruction, annihilation from external forces and/or assimilation—but whatever the case may have been, the preserving hand of divine providence prevents the people of God from eventual nonexistence. According to the notion of concurrence, Yahweh works in and through the agency of the imperial designs of the Canaanite (and other) nations to motivate Israel to covenant faithfulness, and he works in and through the mixed motivations of the Israelites themselves to preserve and deliver them. Although Yahweh's ultimate goal is full restoration and blessing, he does bring about moments of temporary and limited peace and rest even in the midst of chaos. In all of this, his governing hand is evident. I

85. Bavinck, *Reformed Dogmatics*, 2:605.

have been at pains to explain how the root cause of all the disorder in Judges is Israel's rejection of God as king; however, their rejection of his rule does not for a moment mitigate his effective, providential governance—humanly speaking it complicates Yahweh's sovereign rule but does not in any way diminish it.

This has implications for a nuanced view of history. In discussions of the philosophy of history, scholars have noted that the Hebrew Scriptures have a linear view of history that is unique in ancient cultures.[86] The Christian canon only serves to confirm this linear view of history. God's providence is ultimately moving history toward the return of Jesus and the establishment of the new creation. As a chapter in the book of God's providence, Judges, it seems, does not substantially advance God's redemptive purposes. History is cyclical in Judges, moving around in circles rather than in a line forward. Not only is this evident in the six-fold pattern of the cycle, but is also emphasized by the end section, which loops back to the beginning of the settlement period. The effect is an overwhelming sense of aimlessness and a complete lack of goal in the history of the settlement period. This does not contradict the biblical view of history as linear; however, it does demonstrate the powerful effects of human rebellion in the economy of divine providence. Again, human agency cannot thwart the purposes of God—that much is evident throughout Scripture, not least Judges—but it can, at least in certain times and circumstances, induce the kind of death spiral we encounter in Judges.

The doctrine of providence in light of Judges can speak powerfully today. We can draw comfort from the fact that God is moving history forward, that his plan of redemption that was accomplished in Jesus and awaits its final consummation upon his return cannot be prevented. Moreover, we can be inspired by Yahweh's use of broken vessels that accomplished his will. However, we ought also to be sobered by the powerful force of human rebellion that, apart from divine providence, would certainly lead to self-destruction.

Judges and Political Theology

Judges is not often leveraged as a significant source for constructive political theology. On the one hand, this is understandable since by and large the behavior, institutions, and governance models found in Judges are cast as antinormative. For this reason, articulating a constructive political theology from Judges is complicated. On the other hand, political matters permeate the book. The title of the book is drawn from a political office. From the opening line to the

86. See, e.g., Bebbington, *Patterns in History*, 44–48.

closing line, Judges is cast in the context of a leadership vacuum. Moreover, Israel emerges in the settlement period as a nation, and a central concern of Judges is what kind of nation and society Israel is constructing.

In Judges scholarship, a certain aspect of the political dimension of the book has received sustained attention, especially in the last century. This attention focuses on the extent to which Judges displays a promonarchy agenda or more specifically a pro-David/anti-Saul agenda. Many scholars perceive Judges to be a substantive piece of political propaganda in support of the Davidic dynasty.[87] Other scholars have resisted this interpretation of Judges. Susan Niditch, for example, maintains (rightly in my opinion) that "There is no consistent, heavy-handed polemics in Judges, pro- or anti-monarchic. . . . The book of Judges offers a complex and ambivalent view of kingship that acknowledges its role in Israelite polity without endorsing it or propagandizing in favor of monarchy."[88] Block regards the increasingly fashionable trend that casts Judges as political propaganda in support of Davidic monarchy as misguided—according to Block, Judges is "a prophetic book, not a political tractate."[89]

Somewhat understandably, the political dimension of Judges as it features in biblical scholarship is descriptive. The same can be said about the one book-length treatment of Judges and politics of which I am aware. John C. Yoder's book *Power and Politics in the Book of Judges: Men and Women of Valor* is a sophisticated study of "the variety of strategies the men and women of valor [in Judges] used to gain and consolidate power."[90] Yoder's focus is on *describing* the political culture of Israel in the settlement period.[91] On the basis of Judges, what, if anything, can be said constructively about politics and governance, about the use of violent force, about international relations and diplomacy, and so on?

The Jewish scholar Yoram Hazony has been engaged in pioneering work on the political philosophy and theology of the Hebrew Bible. His article "Does the Bible Have a Political Teaching?" provides a helpful entryway into the discussion of Judges and political theology. In it he maintains that "the central historical narrative of the Hebrew Bible (beginning in Genesis and ending

87. The most detailed and sustained argument along these lines is found in O'Connell, *Rhetoric*.

88. Niditch, "Judges, Kingship and Political Ethics," 70.

89. Block, *Judges*, 57–58. A danger that we should avoid is that of making a dichotomy between prophetic and political. Biblical prophecy, after all, is often quite political.

90. Yoder, *Power and Politics*, xii.

91. Yoder, *Power and Politics*, 3; the goal of the book, according to Yoder, is to provide a "detailed *description* of the internal dynamics of the patron-client relationship . . . [and] an in-depth analysis of political culture, the set of underlying values that shape all political behavior" (emphasis added).

with the book of Kings) was composed with an eye to advancing a consistent political theory."[92] Out of this complex of narratives emerges the political ideal of a limited state governed by an Israelite monarch who is not elevated above "his brothers" (Deut 17:20) and who maintains "the way that is good and right" (1 Sam 12:23). This limited state is the *via media* between the oppressive and boundless power of the imperial state common in the ancient Near East (typified by Egypt in the biblical narratives) and its opposite, namely political anarchy (represented by Israel in Judges). The exodus, in part, is an indictment against imperial statehood and its inevitable injustices. Hazony notes that the exodus from Egypt elicited a hope among the Israelites to return to the condition of anarchic liberty that existed during the time of the patriarchs.[93] However, anarchy is not the Bible's political ideal, and Judges teaches why:

> As much as the narrative evidences sympathy for the dream of an anarchic order, its verdict is not for anarchy. It is for a state. And the reason is simple: anarchy just doesn't work out as one might have hoped. Indeed, the entire book of Judges is one long indictment of anarchy, making it the pivot on which the political teaching of the Hebrew Bible turns.[94]

Hazony expertly describes how the composite parts of the book demonstrate the inadequacy of political anarchy.[95] The rhetorical capstone of the book, the atrocity at Gibeah and its consequences (chs. 19–21), teaches a clear lesson

> that while enslavement to the Egyptian state was an evil of unfathomable proportions, so too is anarchy in which "every man did that which was right in his own eyes." For what happened in Benjamin could as easily happen anywhere—or everywhere. No obstacle remained to prevent all of Israel from descending to the level of Sodom. And Sodom, of course, was judged so perverse that it was destroyed from the face of the earth.[96]

The biblical answer to the political ills of the settlement period, according to Hazony, is a nation-state under the leadership of a king, and this comes at the unanimous request of all Israel (1 Sam 8:4–6). Despite this populous demand, Hazony notes that this is not the social-contract state of early-modern political

92. Hazony, "Does the Bible Have a Political Teaching?," 137.
93. Hazony, "Does the Bible Have a Political Teaching?," 143.
94. Hazony, "Does the Bible Have a Political Teaching?," 144.
95. Hazony, "Does the Bible Have a Political Teaching?," 144–50.
96. Hazony, "Does the Bible Have a Political Teaching?," 150.

theory, but establishes the biblical state as an agreement between the people and God (the latter portrayed as a reluctant party).[97] The legitimacy of the state derives not merely from the consent of the people (who have already evidenced a propensity to sanction evil), but more importantly from a standard of rule established by God. This standard puts obvious limitations on the state, as articulated in the "Law of the King" in Deut 17:14–20, and sets the biblical state in contradistinction to the imperial states of the ancient Near East. As Hazony notes, "If we are to state this simply, the Law of the King was set against the life of the imperial state. Instead, it proposes what we might today call a *limited state*: one headed by a king whose life is not consumed in the unending quest for ever greater power."[98]

Hazony proceeds to show how Solomon undermined this ideal limited state. In sum,

> Solomon hoarded wives, gold, and chariots. It was his wives and gold that brought about the establishment of idolatry in the land. It was the taxation and servitude that brought resentment and rebellion. It was the arrogance of a ruler whose "head was lifted above his brothers" [contra Deut 17:20] that brought precipitous decline to a kingdom that only a few years earlier had been the envy of all mankind.[99]

Despite Solomon's failure, which had serious political implications, Hazony still holds that the limited state is *the* political ideal according to the Hebrew Bible:

> In the political theory advanced by the Hebrew Bible, there is such an alternative [between the imperial state and anarchy]. If one wishes for political betterment, there is no choice but to establish a state. Yet this state cannot be unlimited in principle . . . one must have rulers who understand that virtue emerges from limitation of the state.[100]

Hazony's reflection on the political teaching as it emerges from the Hebrew Bible's core narrative is creative and insightful. To understand properly

97. Hazony, "Does the Bible Have a Political Teaching?," 152.

98. Hazony, "Does the Bible Have a Political Teaching?," 154. Hazony also highlights the clear geographical circumscription of the Israelite state. "Taken together, the Law of the King, the limitation of Israel's borders generally, and the proscription of conquest on Israel's eastern border in particular, afford a clear understanding that Israel is to be a state different from its neighbors in that it is to be limited in its aspirations—perhaps the first state in the world to have been limited in its might by decree of its own God" (155).

99. Hazony, "Does the Bible Have a Political Teaching?," 159–60.

100. Hazony, "Does the Bible Have a Political Teaching?," 161.

the political teaching of Judges requires situating the book (and its political teachings) in the broader narrative. In this narrative, the changing political landscape of the Israelites demands development and evolution in their understanding of governance and the state. In asking "What kind of political system did Israel have and what can we learn from it?" Wright notes that we must confront the historical nature of the revelation of God with regard to political theology.[101] Wright aims to take seriously Oliver O'Donovan's warning:

> If political theologians are to treat ancient Israel's political tradition as normative, they must observe the discipline of treating it as *history*. They may not plunder the Old Testament as though it were so much raw material to be consumed, in any order and in any variety of proportions, in the manufacture of their own theological artefact. They are dealing with a disclosure which took form in a succession of political developments, each one of which has to be weighed and interpreted in light of what preceded and followed it.[102]

Hazony is adept at this drawing out with clarity and sophistication the historical evolution of political affairs in Genesis–Kings.[103] However, a few niggling issues, in my mind, require some further clarity.

Hazony observes that the political order of anarchy was the "hope" and "dream" (dare we say ideal) of the Israelites as they emerged from the tyranny of imperial Egypt.[104] I question whether "anarchy" is the best term to describe the order of rule for the people of God anytime in the Old Testament. "Anarchy" seems to imply the absence of authority and the freedom of the individual—this is clearly not the ideal according to the biblical witness.

Moreover, even if we grant that the limited state emerges as the ideal because of the failure of so-called "anarchy" during the settlement period, why should we continue to regard the limited state as the biblical ideal after its own failure in Solomon (and beyond)? From the time Israel left Egypt, throughout the settlement period, and their establishment as a united (and then divided) kingdom, the evolution of Israel demanded evolving political models. The failure

101. Wright, *Old Testament Ethics for the People of God*, 219.

102. O'Donovan, *Desire of the Nations*, 27 (emphasis original). Cf. Nugent's appreciation for Yoder's Old Testament narration and its significance for social ethics; Nugent, "Politics of YHWH," 91.

103. Unfortunately, in the end he does seem to fall prey to O'Donovan's warning, as he does not consider the significance of the exilic and postexilic experience for the Hebrew Bible's political teaching—this is the second of my "niggling issues" (see below).

104. Hazony, "Does the Bible Have a Political Teaching?," 142–43.

of "anarchy" and the failure of a limited state manifest a common denominator, which amounts to a failure to remain faithful to Yahweh and heed his instruction. "Anarchy" could have succeeded (at least for a time) just as a limited state could have succeeded had Israel remained loyal to King Yahweh. Even the foundational text for a limited state, the Law of the King (Deut 17:14–20), strikes me as provisional and not inevitable. One gets the sense that Yahweh is permitting monarchy but setting the necessary boundaries on it, not setting out the ideal political model—it's as though Yahweh is saying, "If it's a king you want, okay go ahead and crown a king, but this is who he should be, and this is how he should rule." Wright makes this point: "The law in Deuteronomy refers to 'the king the Lord your God chooses,' but only as a secondary, limiting, condition to a situation brought about by the people's desire: 'Let us set a king over us.'"[105] This seems a far cry from promoting the ideal. In a reflection on the weekly Torah reading (in this case on the Law of the King in Deut 17), Jonathan Sacks makes the bold statement, "There is no subject on which the Torah is more ambivalent than the issue of monarchy in particular, and politics in general."[106]

The changing circumstances and history of Israel required that they hold loosely to any political model. The ambivalence with regard to monarchy that Niditch perceives in Judges arguably reflects a similar ambivalence in Scripture toward a *variety of legitimate* political models. Commenting on Judges, Susanne Gillmayr-Bucher maintains, "The king is not a reliable solution per se, but if a king is able to implement the cultic and ethical requirements of the law, then a king offers a solution."[107] It would seem that the political teaching of the Old Testament is that God's people can live and thrive under a number of political models, and that they show an incredible propensity to distort good, God-given political models in ways that undermine the "kingdom" principles and purposes of King Yahweh.

This relates to the second issue that requires clarification with regard to Hazony's survey of the political teaching of the Hebrew Bible. What do the texts beyond the Old Testament's central narrative (Genesis through Kings) contribute to political theology? Hazony identifies four pivotal moments in this complex of narratives that elucidate the Hebrew Bible's political teaching: (1) the exodus from Egypt (the imperial state), (2) the concubine in Gibeah (anarchy), (3) the founding of the Israelite state (limited state), and (4) the division of the kingdom (failure of the limited state). Circumscribed in this way, the government of God's people comes full circle, from foreign tyranny to

105. Wright, *Old Testament Ethics for the People of God*, 230.
106. Sacks, "Shoftim: On the Limits of Power."
107. Gillmayr-Bucher, "Memories Laid to Rest," 128.

homegrown tyranny. However, what does the exilic and postexilic experience have to contribute to the Bible's political teaching?

Here we might consider something along the lines of the *political model of the dispersion*, which entails both participation in and subversion of foreign imperial order, but clearly for the sake of the flourishing of all people. Jeremiah's prophetic letter to the exiles urges them to get comfortable in Babylon and engage in culture-making that ultimately seeks the shalom of the place where they find themselves (Jer 29:1–14), and yet in a "massive tirade" describes in vivid and disturbing language the comprehensive judgment that would come upon Babylon for its wickedness (chs. 50–51).[108] Daniel and his friends typify this political theology as they are trained and contribute meaningfully to the political life of Babylon and Persia, and yet boldly defy the idolatry and injustice of the empire. Moreover, the apocalyptic visions of Daniel subvert the overreach of the oppressive political regimes, which will eventually result in their demise. Wright sums up well the political model of the dispersion at work in Daniel: on the one hand, "Daniel's doctrine of the divine appointment of human authority did not make him a passive pawn, giving uncritical obedience to the particular authority under which he lived"; on the other hand, "Daniel's doctrine of the satanic influence on human powers did not make him withdraw as an escapist from political involvement."[109] Other examples, like Nehemiah and Esther, confirm this approach of *participation* and *subversion*. This politics of the dispersion is particularly important for Christian political theology that emerges in the context of Second Temple Judaism and is captured in Jesus's teaching, give to Caesar what is Caesar's and to God what is God's (Matt 22:21; Mark 12:17; Luke 20:25). Jesus's vision of the kingdom of God, which is already present but not yet present in its fullness, involves participation and subversion in earthly political affairs. Paul reminds the Philippian church that their citizenship is in heaven (Phil 3:20) and their allegiance is to Jesus, whom all people will confess as Lord (2:10–11; a treasonous statement in the Roman Empire if there ever was one), and yet he urges the church in this letter and elsewhere to shine the light of the gospel of the kingdom into the recesses of their private and public lives, even if it ends in execution as political criminals. Similarly, Peter draws on the historic call of Israel to be a royal priesthood and a holy nation (1 Pet 2:9; Exod 19:6) and urges the "elect *of the dispersion* in Pontus, Galatia, Cappadocia, Asia, and Bithynia" (1:1, emphasis added) on the basis of Leviticus to "be holy as I am holy" (1:13–2:12), but their character as a people set apart should not prevent them from being subject "to every human institution" (emperor, governors, etc.;

108. Quotation from Wright, *Old Testament Ethics for the People of God*, 242.

109. Wright, *Old Testament Ethics for the People of God*, 247.

2:13–17). Thus, the political model of the dispersion involves both subversion and participation and is reflected in the New Testament's political theology.

A political state, limited or otherwise, is not at the core of the Bible's political teaching. Rather a community undividedly loyal to God and his kingdom must necessarily involve political engagement in whatever context God's people find themselves. The political model of "anarchy" failed in the settlement period not because "anarchy" is intrinsically faulty, but because the people built a society and institutions on the basis of the Canaanite "sacred order." The results are catastrophic.

What does all of this contribute to Christian political theology for today? In the history of Western Civilization, Christendom looms large and provides countless examples of Lord Acton's famous adage "absolute power corrupts absolutely." It seems power as an end in itself, and not the witness to the principles and character of Jesus and his kingdom, became the driving force. Judges should teach us that in the wake of Christian imperialism, which at times brought oppression and bondage, "anarchy" will not necessarily provide freedom and flourishing. As Christians living in twenty-first-century Western culture, we seem far removed from the Christendom of the past, and probably have the most to learn from the political model of the dispersion. An absolute commitment to Jesus as citizens of the kingdom of God will inevitably put us at odds with the culture and its political structures, and yet should motivate us to deep engagement in the affairs (political and other) of our culture as agents of salt and light (Matt 5:13–16).

Conclusion

Although Judges is a complicated book, it also stands as a rich resource for the discipline of systematic theology. We have explored how Judges illuminates five doctrinal areas of systematic theology. It should be clear that theological exegesis and biblical theological reflection are vital elements in discerning the contribution of Judges to systematic theology. The combination of all three (theological exegesis, biblical theology, and systematic theology) situates us well for drawing out some specific ways that the teaching of Judges speaks to contemporary readers and their situations.

Judges for Today

So far in this commentary we have encountered many examples of the enduring testimony of Judges for today. Judges presents contemporary readers of faith with many theological principles and practical applications, but also some less palatable material (e.g., violence and the treatment of women). This final section will afford an opportunity to draw out in concentration the major teachings of the book for today, and also confront head-on some of the challenges of hearing Judges today as Scripture. To say that Judges is the most challenging and thus the most neglected book of the Old Testament would be an exaggeration, but it is probably close to the top of the list. However, the resurgence of expository preaching and the growing appreciation for the Bible as a grand narrative from beginning to end have contributed to a growing interest in some Christian traditions for parts of the Old Testament that have been neglected. Anecdotally, I have heard of several churches that have done series of sermons on Judges from beginning to end.[110] Commentaries written specifically for pastors and specialized studies on Judges for the laity seem to suggest an interest in the teaching of Judges for today.[111]

A word about methods of application is necessary. In some circles one can find heated debates over whether or not we should moralize the stories of the Bible. Moralizing often involves taking a biblical character or situation and drawing moral application, either positively or negatively. According to this approach contemporary readers may be urged to be like David who slew the giant Goliath—accordingly we should identify those "Goliaths" in our life (i.e., a certain temptation like anger or situation like unemployment) and no matter how insurmountable they may seem we ought to overcome them in the strength of God. Others argue that this is a distortion of the purpose of the Bible and advocate a typological approach. Using the same example, this approach would highlight the fact that David is Yahweh's anointed (messiah) and a type of Christ; accordingly, it would be wrong to identify with David as we should be identifying with the cowardly soldiers on the sidelines who are unable and unwilling to save themselves and instead benefit from the saving work of the Messiah. This typological approach that discerns patterns in the way God relates to his people is generally speaking a more responsible approach to biblical interpretation. However, as long as we are aware of what we are doing, moralizing may have its place. For example, it would be entirely appropriate to consider, in light of Jephthah's sacrifice of his daughter, the ways in our current context we have "sacrificed" our children on account of our own ambition for power or self-

110. E.g., several years ago, I was asked to do a training session on Judges for a team of pastors in a network of churches in Phoenix called Redemption. Simultaneously, over the course of seven weeks in ten locations in Phoenix, pastors opened up the riches of Judges for their audiences.

111. E.g., McCann, *Judges*; Keller, *Judges for You*; Goldingay, *Joshua, Judges, and Ruth for Everyone*; Biddle, *Reading Judges*; Stone, *Judges*; Beldman, *Deserting the King*.

promotion. Moreover, some ways of practicing typological interpretation can also deaden the full message of biblical texts. Again anecdotally, I have perceived an overemphasis on the judges/deliverers as types of Christ and, by virtue of their imperfections and the limited scope of their salvation, leaving us longing for the true Deliverer. There is truth here in this kind of reading of Judges backward from the perspective of the New Testament, but in my opinion, there is a danger in moving too quickly to a typological/christological reading of Judges in this way. The danger is that we fail to take seriously Israel's very real calling in a very real context to live out the reality of Yahweh's kingdom for the sake of the nations, which may dampen the impact of Judges for our own kingdom calling . . . after all Jesus did it for us! Judges is a valuable resource and a sober warning for redeemed people trying to live with integrity before the face of God. The following will try to draw that out. This section will first tackle the thorny issue of violence and then the treatment of women in Judges, on the basis that these challenging aspects of the book sometimes prevent modern-day readers from taking the book seriously as a source of instruction. Following that we will consider some of the key ways that Judges speaks to issues and situations today.

Violence in Judges

One of the most challenging and, if we're honest, repugnant dimensions of Judges for contemporary readers of faith is the violence that appears on almost every page of the book. Christians are followers of Jesus, and Jesus it seems preached and embodied nonviolence and an attitude of love for enemies. Don't Jesus's teaching and example contradict what we find in Judges? Furthermore, if the ultimate goal of God's calling of Abraham/Israel is to bless all nations, don't Israel's conquest and further military engagement with the Canaanites in the settlement period stand at odds with the goal of their calling? Finally, can people of faith in the twenty-first century with integrity draw ethical teachings from a book that depicts such morally offensive behavior as sibling murder, child sacrifice, gang rape, dismemberment, kidnap, and forced marriage? These are very serious matters with which Christians need to wrestle. They also require careful teasing out so that the real issues get separated out from the apparent issues—and the violence of Judges does confront us with real issues. While we may never gain an entirely satisfactory answer to all of our questions, careful consideration can help us better understand the violence we encounter in Judges.[112]

112. The following is aided by the work I have already published on this topic in Beldman, *Deserting the King*, 70–80.

Theological interpretation emerges from a place of faith—a deep-seated trust in the God who created a good world that humans twist in all sorts of ways and in the God who is at work healing and redeeming in the midst of brokenness. This trust ought not cause readers of faith to avoid the challenging parts of Scripture, but to confront them honestly and humbly. This honest and humble attitude is reflected in Wright when he confesses,

> There is something about this part of our Bible that I have to include in my basket of things I don't understand about God and his ways. I find myself thinking, "God, I wish you had found some other way to work out your plans." There are days I wish this narrative were not in the Bible at all (usually after I've faced another barrage of questions about it), though I know it is wrong to wish that in relation to Scripture. God knew what he was doing—in the events themselves and in the record of them that he has given us. But it is still hard.[113]

All Violence Is Alien to God's Creation

The proper starting place for any discussion of violence (in Judges or elsewhere) is that violence is antinormative—any and all violence runs counter to God's creational intention for the world. Genesis 1–2 picture for us a world of overwhelming integrity, harmony, beauty, and goodness. Everything is as it should be. Genesis 3 provides the origins of violence and misery that result from the rebellion of our first parents Adam and Eve. It is interesting that the desire for human autonomy (doing what is right in one's own eyes) in Gen 3 spawned in Gen 4–11 fratricide (Cain murdering Abel; Gen 4:8), prideful ambition and vengeance (4:23–24), comprehensive wickedness and the inclination to do evil continually (6:5), pervasive violence (6:13), and idolatrous city-building as the crowning achievement of human autonomy (11:1–9). The parallels between Gen 4–11 and the behavior and inclinations of Israel in Judges are hard to miss! God's intention for a world of *shalom* was spoiled by sin; the death and resurrection of Jesus broke the curse and secured a future creation without the devastating consequences of sin. So the violence we encounter in Judges is alien to God's good creation and ought to be seen in light of the fall; furthermore, Israel was called to create a society that kept sin and violence at bay and promoted shalom and justice. For both of these reasons our intuitive reaction to the violence of Judges is justified!

113. Wright, *God I Don't Understand*, 86.

The Violence of the Canaanite Conquest

Warfare is one dominating form of violence that appears in Judges. Webb helpfully categorizes the warfare in Judges into three basic types: "wars of conquest and occupation in the introduction (1:1–3:6), wars of liberation in the main central section (3:7–16:31), and civil war in the epilogue (chs. 17–21)."[114] Of these three, the most challenging for contemporary readers is the first, the divinely sanctioned wholesale slaughter of the Canaanites. Whether we like it or not, this aspect of Judges (particularly ch. 1 and Joshua) will at some point confront contemporary people of faith who engage in evangelism or apologetics, and it has been a favorite target of proponents of the recent New Atheism.[115] Webb's sober honesty echoes that of Wright and should be reflective in any engagement with this difficult issue:

> There definitely is a problem here, and it may be that nothing can be said that will ever entirely dispel the unease we feel about it. Furthermore, any response which ignores or downplays the immense human suffering involved in order to find a tidy theological solution will be inadequate and grossly insensitive. But a response which is entirely determined by our feelings will also be inadequate. Part of the challenge of being a Christian is to bring our thoughts and feelings under the discipline of scriptural teaching.[116]

Granting that we may never have a fully satisfactory explanation of the conquest of Canaan, how can we allow scriptural teaching on the matter to hold our thoughts and emotions in check? I offer the following points to that end.

The conquest of Canaan was a one-time, limited event in the history of God's redemption plan. Although God did command the conquest of Canaan, it was limited temporally and geographically. Thus,

> Conquest was not a pattern that Yahweh set for his people; their identity was not as a conquering nation. Yahweh's holy nation and priestly kingdom was not meant to be an ever-expanding empire like that of Alexander the Great or Genghis Khan. From the beginning, the period of conquest always had an intended expiration date, and in reality the conquest only lasted

114. Webb, *Book of Judges*, 59. He also notes the wars of subjugation against Israel and the number of violent hostilities among the various tribes.

115. E.g., see Dawkins, *God Delusion*; Hitchens, *God Is Not Great*.

116. Webb, *Book of Judges*, 51. Webb's treatment of the issue of violence is worth consulting (59–67); he also includes a helpful roundup of resources on the subject (59 n. 134).

> about a generation or two (predominantly Joshua's generation with perhaps some spillover into the generation after Joshua). Of course, Israel would be engaged in warfare in the time after the conquest, but much of that is either defensive or else flatly condemned as the activity of power-hungry and land-hungry kings.[117]

Moreover, even before the Israelites journeyed to the promised land, Yahweh set clear geographic boundaries to the conquest, indicating that he bestowed certain territories to other nations that are out of bounds for the Israelites (Deut 2:3–22).

Once settled into the land, Israel was to cease from military expansion and live out their calling as a priestly kingdom and holy nation. Had they consistently fulfilled their calling we would expect Yahweh's kingdom to spread, not by military expansion, but by the incorporation of foreign nations into the kingdom of Yahweh to live under his rule and experience his blessing. Understood in this way in the economy of God's redemption plan, the conquest was a limited but necessary "evil," so to speak.

The conquest of Canaan was in part judgment on the Canaanite nations. Again, we want to allow Scripture to inform our understanding of the conquest, and in understanding it as judgment we need to articulate this carefully and avoid being glib. In being guided by Scripture on this point we should avoid the temptation to vilify all the Canaanites in a way that goes beyond what the texts teach us. Moreover, we should not think that the Israelites deserved the land because they were so righteous and the Canaanites were so wicked. However,

> The conquest is not an evil perpetrated against an upright nation; rather, it constitutes Yahweh's righteous judgment on a people who committed wickedness. We may be tempted to paint the Canaanites as the worst kind of moral monsters history has ever seen, but likely they weren't, and not all Canaanites would have participated in their most heinous acts (e.g., child sacrifice). However, their wickedness—both in terms of their false religion and their distorted conduct—is well documented in Scripture (e.g., Lev 18:24–25; 20:22–24; Deut 9:5; 12:29–31; 18:9–14).[118]

And the iniquity of the Canaanites had been accumulating for generations. Although God promised to give Abraham the land, he also clarifies that only after four generations, when their wickedness had reached its full measure would

117. Beldman, *Deserting the King*, 76.
118. Beldman, *Deserting the King*, 78.

Abraham's descendants inherit the land (Gen 15:13–16). In other words, God would tolerate the Canaanite wickedness for a time (some four hundred years) but a day of reckoning and judgment would come. Furthermore, on the plains of Moab Yahweh makes crystal clear that the Israelites would receive the land not because of their own righteousness but because of the wickedness of the nations who dwell there (Deut 9:5). Thus, the conquest in part represents God's righteous judgment on the Canaanites for their wickedness.

The Conquest as Instruction for Today

It should go without saying that Christians today are not commanded to engage in the kind of violent holy war as ancient Israel was in the conquest. To be sure, Christians as much as the ancient Israelites are engaged in battle. The New Testament frequently uses the language of warfare. What Paul writes to the church in Ephesus is as true for the Israelites as it is for us today: our battle, which requires the full armor of God, is not with flesh and blood but with spiritual forces (Eph 6:10–20). The Canaanite people as such were not the problem, but the Canaanite worldview that gave rise to cultural principles and practices is the target of Yahweh's holy war. Again, to draw on Rieff's conceptualization,[119] the wickedness that permeated the social order of the Canaanites emerged out of the sacred order of the Canaanite religion. That was the most significant impediment to the advancement of Yahweh's kingdom of blessing. As a political entity, the Israelites were commanded to eradicate the Canaanites to make way for Yahweh's kingdom to take root in the heart of the Fertile Crescent. As difficult as that might be for contemporary readers to stomach—and it is still difficult—its instruction has enduring value.

The people of God are not a political organization as the ancient Israelites were and as such we are not called to engage in military conquest. However, Yahweh's willingness to wipe out whole nations because of the powerful allure of the cultural expression of Canaanite religion should be a sober warning for us today regarding the danger of syncretism. Paul's letter to the Corinthians is instructive in this regard. It is no accident that he zeroes in on the cultural ideals of power, wisdom, and love. The Greco-Roman context generally prized strength and knowledge, and Corinth in particularly, with its temple to Aphrodite, prized "love," but Paul urges the Corinthian church to reimagine these cultural ideals in light of Christ. Jesus's death, viewed by the culture as the epitome of weakness and folly, was true power and true wisdom (1 Cor 1:18–31),

119. Rieff, *My Life among the Deathworks*, 2.

and the way of love that he embodied was humble and selfless, counter to the cultural ideal of love, which was really nothing more than self-seeking and self-promoting (1 Cor 13:1–13). The Corinthian church had to "eradicate" those cultural idolatries and embody a countercultural way of being that manifested Jesus and his kingdom. The cultures we live in are not neutral, and our calling as Jesus-followers cannot be limited to a sphere of "personal religion"—that would be to capitulate to the spirit of our age. Although we are not called to take up arms literally, we are in the midst of a very real battle.

Violence in Judges is a Consequence of Israel's Rebellion

The conquest of Canaan is not the only violence that the book of Judges depicts. What are we to make of the other manifestations of violence in the book? If we bracket for a moment the violence of conquest (Judg 1), all of the violence in Judges is a result of Israel's failure and sin. Their failure to obey Yahweh's command to drive out the Canaanite nations results in the Canaanite culture becoming a snare to the Israelites. Whereas their covenant faithfulness could have created a context of generosity toward and blessing of the nations, their evil-doing puts them at odds with the Canaanite nations. From a human perspective, God's use of foreign oppression seems an ill-fitting punishment for Israel's failure to be a priestly kingdom and holy nation that exists for the sake of the foreign nations, especially since their deliverance results in the defeat of their foreign oppressors. We might at this point resonate with Wright's sentiments above, wishing that God had found some other way to work out his plans, but this is part of his plan, rooted in the curses of the covenant in Deut 28. We may not like it, but we have to acknowledge that the root cause of the violence exchanged between Israel and the nations in Judges is Israel's unfaithfulness. This reality should cause us to reflect on how our own allegiances are divided between Jesus and the cultural idolatries of our day and consider the ways that our unfaithfulness to our calling has prevented us from being a blessing to the "nations" around us.

Furthermore, when violence occurs in Judges (and elsewhere in the Bible for that matter) it is not necessarily endorsed. The narrator does seem to endorse (reluctantly?) the brutal and violent demise of Eglon and Sisera.[120] However, much of the violence in Judges, especially perpetrated by Israelites against Israelites in Judges, is senseless and offensive, even from the perspective of the narrator (and thus God). Our sensibilities are correct when we are offended by

120. I suggest reluctantly because, again, the only reason Moab and Midian were at odds with Israel was their evil-doing ways and the resulting divine displeasure and punishment.

Abimelech's slaughter of his brothers, Jephthah's sacrifice of his daughter and his massacre of the Ephraimites, the men of Gibeah's violent sexual assault of the Levite's concubine, and so on. Violence of this kind should not be practiced by subjects of the kingdom of Yahweh. It is wrong and there is no excusing it. McCann captures this well, "In short, the book of Judges is not a commendation of violence but rather a condemnation of it. It reminds its readers that when God's justice, righteousness, and peace are not established for all, then violence is the natural result."[121]

Judges' Instruction on Violence for Today

Understood in this way, Judges' treatment of violence provides timely instruction for contemporary people of faith. Our time and culture are no less violent than those of ancient Israel.[122] On the one hand, we live in a culture that celebrates and consumes violence in film, video games, and sport. On the other hand, we lament the violence that plagues our city streets, hides behind the closed doors of our homes, enters our schools and claims our children, feeds on racism and other forms of prejudice, wreaks havoc on the global political stage, and dominates our media coverage. Violence breeds violence and creates a culture of fear and anxiety; the cycle seems unbreakable. As valuable and worthwhile as they are, anger management seminars, violence awareness, counseling, and diplomatic peace talks cannot eradicate the violence that plagues a society like ours in which everyone does what is right in their own eyes. And like Israel in the settlement period, any hope for change must begin with the people of God, radically committed to the divine king and unswervingly motivated to live out his kingdom principles. Therefore, the violence in Judges should not drive contemporary readers of faith away from the book but should cause us to search out the vital instruction that Judges has to offer people living in a culture of fear and violence.

The Treatment of Women in Judges

Another potential stumbling block to taking Judges seriously as instruction for today is the book's treatment of women. In fact, this is a broader discussion

121. McCann, *Judges*, 21.

122. McCann, *Judges*, 20–21. McCann's succinct section on violence and vengeance in Judges is helpful and I am indebted to it.

in which the Old and New Testament are viewed as archaic and steeped in the patriarchy of their contexts. There is no denying that the Bible (Judges included) is the product of patriarchal cultures and that its teachings reflect and speak into that aspect of the ancient Near Eastern and Greco-Roman contexts—theological interpretation of the Bible for today must take this seriously. However, while the Bible reflects and, in some cases, reinforces patriarchal ideals, we can also detect ways that biblical teachings undermine those ideals in a manner that is countercultural in the ancient Near East. A consideration of the role of women in the Bible should be carefully balanced and work hard to understand the patriarchal context out of which it emerged and only then to draw appropriate application.

Among the books of the Old Testament, the concentration of women characters—both major and minor, Israelite and foreign—in Judges is unique. Susan Ackerman notes the "remarkable assembly of women and the multitude of roles they play in the book of Judges."[123] Webb indicates that women in Judges "are not stereotyped as either good or bad, passive or active, wise or foolish, but are shown as exhibiting the same basic traits of character and capacities for good or ill as men are."[124]

Admittedly, Judges reflects the patriarchal perspective of the ancient Near East in several places. For example, the Levite's concubine seeks refuge in her father's house after a falling out with her husband. Jephthah's daughter passively submits to the consequences of her father's terrible vow. That the council assumes that the fathers and brothers of the Shiloh virgins would be offended at their forced marriage, reflects patriarchal ideals. We can detect a patriarchal chauvinism underlying Deborah's verdict that Sisera would be delivered into the hand of a woman because of Barak's hesitancy to lead. The arranged marriage of Achsah seems to reduce her to a reward for bravery; however, it reflects Caleb's desire to secure a heroic and faithful husband for his daughter in a context in which arranged marriages were the norm.

The portrayal of a few of the women may elicit some of the deepest emotional responses in readers; for example, Jephthah's daughter, the Levite's concubine, Sisera's mother, and perhaps (though more subtly) Samson's mother.[125] In Judges, women feature as leaders, deliverers, and celebrated heroes (Deborah, Jael, and the woman of Thebez who dropped the millstone on Abimelech's head); in one case a foreign woman is the villain (Delilah) and in another an Israelite woman is a corrupt idolater (Micah's mother). Achsah who is char-

123. Ackerman, *Warrior, Dancer, Seductress, Queen*, 6, cited in McCann, *Judges*, 22.

124. Webb, *Book of Judges*, 58.

125. Webb, *Book of Judges*, 58.

acterized by dignity, integrity, and assertiveness is a kind of paradigmatic female figure, a standard for understanding the other women in Judges and their situations.

Sadly, but in line with the rhetorical purpose of the book, most women in Judges are exploited and victimized. In these cases, the violence against women is by no means normalized or excused on the basis of the patriarchal culture but is the result of Israel's canaanization. On the whole, the sympathy and dignity afforded to women in Judges tend to run counter to patriarchal ideals of the ancient world.[126] The bottom line regarding the exploitation of women in Judges is that, as McCann puts it, "Judges serves as a call to repentance for injustices and abuses that result from unbridled self-assertion/idolatry—injustices and abuses that, then and now, often most directly affect women."[127]

The Enduring Testimony of Judges for Today

> *God is dead! God remains dead! And we have killed him! How can we console ourselves, the murderers of all murderers! The holiest and mightiest thing the world has ever possessed has bled to death under our knives: who will wipe this blood from us? With what water could we clean ourselves? What festivals of atonement, what holy games will we have to invent for ourselves? Is the magnitude of this deed not too great for us? Do we not ourselves have to become gods merely to appear worthy of it? There was never a greater deed—and whoever is born after us will on account of this deed belong to a higher history than all history up to now!. . . What then are these churches now if not the tombs and sepulchers of God?*
>
> —Friedrich Nietzsche, "The Madman"

The desire for human autonomy and freedom from the rule of God is an age-old desire and, according to the biblical witness, is the root of all the sin and brokenness in the world. Moreover, this age-old desire motivates God's people in the settlement period. To hear properly the powerful message of Judges for today requires taking stock of the current cultural context in which we find ourselves.

126. The book of Ruth is a profound story centering around two women in the settlement period. For an insightful treatment of Ruth that understands Ruth and Naomi as subverting the patriarchal system in a way that brings life and flourishing beyond the two female characters, see James, *Finding God at the Margins*.

127. McCann, *Judges*, 23.

The chickens of modern individualism and secularism in the West—which is grounded in the root assumption of individual autonomy—have certainly come home to roost, and the results are troubling and surprising. And we should not think for a moment that Christian communities are immune to the spirit of our age. Peering into the book of Judges we find in Israel's corruption and syncretism a mirror of our own corruption and syncretism.

Idolatry and Autonomy in Judges

In Judges, Israel in the settlement period is pictured with vividness as a people not content to live under the rule of the Creator of the world and their Redeemer. One might detect a contradiction in this regard. On the one hand, Judges portrays Israel as thoroughly canaanized, abandoning Yahweh and serving the Canaanite gods. On the other hand, Judges seems burdened to make the point that the Israelites conducted themselves as autonomous (implicitly through their actions in the narratives and explicitly in the refrain of chs. 17–21: "everyone did what was right in his/her own eyes"). In the heart of this apparent contradiction is a subtle but key insight: Israel's rejection of Yahweh's rule is not fundamentally an exchange of one divine rule (the rule of Yahweh) for another divine rule (the rule of one Canaanite god or another); rather, their allegiance to the foreign deities (and thus disloyalty to Yahweh) exposes their fundamental drive to chart their own course, realize their own destiny, and set the standard for their own conduct apart from God. Idolatry and autonomy, thus, are intricately intertwined, two sides of the same coin.

That Israel's service to foreign gods is bound up with a desire for human autonomy should not be surprising for at least two reasons. First, if we recall the contours of ancient Near Eastern religion, the rationale for allegiance to the gods was not the character of the gods (e.g., their goodness, trustworthiness, benevolence, or whatever) but was the interest of the human worshiper (the prosperity, stability, security, etc. that the gods could provide). In other words, the Israelites worshiped the local deities to gain a sense of control over their own flourishing. Probably the best, albeit ironic, example of this is Micah's sentiments after he established his shrine and employed the Levite as priest: "Now I know that Yahweh will prosper me" (17:13).

Second, that the allegiance to foreign gods is bound up with a desire for autonomy should not be surprising given the nature of the Canaanite gods as themselves independent, selfish, and self-serving. Consequently, the Israelites reflect the image of the Canaanite gods, existing for themselves and to further their own comfort and stability. To be sure, Israel's service to the Canaanite gods did influence Israel's moral and social norms, but at root here is the quest for human autonomy. This historical reality exposes a universal truth, namely, the quest for human autonomy does not bring freedom but results in bondage and oppression.

Idolatry and Autonomy in Modern Western Culture

What time is it in our culture? This is a key question for all humans and is especially vital to Christians who are called to witness to the kingdom of God in faithful and relevant ways in our own cultural contexts. Rieff contends that cultures of the modern West reflect the third of three dominating world cultures. Whereas the so-called first and second world cultures (generally associated with pagan polytheistic cultures motivated by a sense of fate and monotheistic cultures motivated by faith respectively) emerged out of a transcendent sacred order, third world cultures "sever the connection between sacred order and social order, limiting the 'real' world to the visible and locating moral authority in the self. Similarly, whereas each of the first two worlds sought to construct identity *vertically* from above, our third world rejects the vertical in favor of constructing identity *horizontally* from below."[128] The result of such cultures is ultimately nihilism (everything is meaningless), and the destructive products of such cultures Rieff calls "deathworks." Instead of leading to abundant life, our current culture will ultimately self-destruct, and the signs of this are all around us. Our leading culture-makers, according to Rieff, are "virtuosi of de-creation."[129]

Thus, for Rieff, the problem of modern cultures is autonomy. As we have already seen, idolatry is intricately bound together with autonomy. The idols of modern Western culture are no longer wood and stone, but they are fundamentally no different than the gods that ensnared Israel. What is an idol in its essence? Crouch maintains "it just has to offer transcendent benefits and demand ultimate allegiance."[130] Crouch uses addiction as an example of the universal pattern of idolatry.[131] It starts with an essentially good, created thing, that creates in humans a transcendent expectation—the promise of becoming like god. Initially and in the short term (the "success phase"), the "idol" delivers on its promise (it provides escape, power, freedom, control, focus, or

128. Ashford, "Theological Sickness unto Death," 37 (emphasis original).
129. Rieff, *My Life Among the Deathworks*, 4.
130. Crouch, *Playing God*, 56.
131. Crouch, *Playing God*, 56–64.

some other sense of transcendence) with relatively little cost. At some point all idols become less effective and more unpredictable, in what Crouch calls the "intermediate stage." Remarkably, when the rewards of idolatry become less consistent is precisely the time when "idols consolidate their control over the worshiper."[132] The worshiper becomes *more* committed and *more* enslaved to the idol when the "benefit" of transcendence is less frequent or predictable. Finally, the "terminal stage" of idolatry occurs when "the idol ceases entirely to deliver but exacts its full demands for unwavering worship."[133] Whether the idolatry of substance addiction, pornography, gambling, or a host of other forms of idolatry, the idol's demands are comprehensive, and the cost leaves the worshiper isolated, alienated, enslaved, and fragmented. Crouch's example of addiction is on the level of the individual, but what about communal or cultural idolatry?

The idolatry of secular culture is, arguably, in terminal stage. In a recent book examining our current cultural moment, Patrick Deneen considers the failure of what he calls "liberalism."[134] By "liberalism" he does not mean a political doctrine but a spirit of liberal autonomy that undergirds both conservative and progressive political ideology.[135] To be sure, liberalism is rooted in those very good creational ideals of human dignity, freedom from oppression, and the common good. Initially, the ideals of liberalism delivered on their promises with relatively little cost (the casualties of the guillotine notwithstanding!). As liberalism increasingly failed to deliver on the promise of a utopian society, we have generally witnessed increased allegiance to its ideals and not less. According to Chief Rabbi Jonathan Sacks, the notion of "society" playing out today is

> an aggregate of individuals pursuing private interests, coming together temporarily and contractually, leaving the state to resolve their conflicts on value-neutral grounds. The key words in this new scheme are not moral rules and duty but *autonomy* and *rights*. The key principle of both morality and politics is that we should be free to act as we please so long as we do not harm others.[136]

132. Crouch, *Playing God*, 58.

133. Crouch, *Playing God*, 63.

134. E.g., see Deneen, *Why Liberalism Failed*. Cf. Lilla, *Stillborn God*.

135. Cf. Koyzis, *Political Visions and Illusions*, 37: "Most of the modern ideologies are members of the same religious family. . . . In some fashion each makes humanity into a god."

136. Sacks, *Faith in the Future*, 11 (emphasis original). Sacks holds that the original ideals of liberal democracy (from Locke to Jefferson and beyond) have been eclipsed by the inspiration of Nietzche (morally) and John Stuart Mill (politically). I'm not sure to what extent he would agree that we have witnessed an increasing commitment to the ideals of liberalism.

What are the results? Today the deathworks of society's commitment to human autonomy and freedom are all around us. Sacks notes that

> the human cost of this new dispensation has proved very high indeed in terms of fragile relationships, broken marriages, confused and uncared-for children, growing inequalities, rising crime, self-reinforcing circles of deprivation, a decline in civility and a weakening of the civic bond. The strong survive, as they always did. But that was not the prophetic test of a just and compassionate society, nor can it be ours if anything of that older morality persists, if we are moved by the plight of poverty in the midst of affluence, if we see too many wasted lives and wonder what kind of world we are creating for our children.[137]

If we shift focus from society to the individual the picture does not improve. Sacks notes, "the new individualism narrows the horizons of human happiness. . . . A straight road leads from individualism to cynicism and despair."[138]

Just over two decades after Sacks wrote those words the situation is bleaker yet. Despite the many good things that we enjoy as a result of modernism, technology and the proliferation of information have left us isolated, distracted, and confused. Teen suicide is at an all-time high, and abortion continues at alarming rates.[139] Contemporary halls of power and economic institutions are places of astounding corruption. Although reporters have never been unbiased, the news media conglomerates are polarized, to the extent that we no longer expect fair and balanced reporting. Healthcare and education are in crisis. Although racism has always existed, it seems the current context is giving impetus to new levels of xenophobia, racial hatred, and violence. Underground sexual exploitation is as strong as ever and is giving rise to human trafficking, but exploitation is increasingly being exposed (e.g., the "Me Too" movement) in the very halls of power and other cultural institutions (e.g., not least in the world of entertainment). The divide between the rich and the poor seems ever-increasing, and national and personal debt is at an all-time high. Modern industrialism has contributed to a global environmental crisis. In a surprising twist, modern "liberalism" is giving rise to forms of autocratic rule and an increasing surveillance culture in which individual freedom is being forfeited for a semblance of security and stability.[140]

137. Sacks, *Faith in the Future*, 11–12.

138. Sacks, *Faith in the Future*, 12.

139. According to the Centers for Disease Control and Prevention, abortion rates are on the decline, but still over 630,000 abortions were reported in 2015.

140. Deneen, *Why Liberalism Failed*, 180–82.

Moreover, nationalism is on the rise. The utopian dream of human autonomy is more like a nightmare from which we cannot awake.

Sacks recognized this nightmare. In the introduction to Sacks's *Faith in the Future*, Clifford Longley acknowledges the great potential of modern democracies and market-based economic systems but identifies the shadow side of these systems:

> They put power in the hands of individuals, so that they can live their lives more nearly as they choose, but they offer no guidance as to the choices themselves: which goods and services to buy, which policies to support. This maximization of personal autonomy could become very dangerous, once it is perceived as an end in itself. The libertarian dream, as Dr Sacks recognizes, could quickly become a nightmare. It is morally bankrupt. Human freedom is only a benefit once we know *what freedom is for*.[141]

Some twenty-plus years later, it would be more appropriate to say that the maximization of personal autonomy *has become* very dangerous, and the libertarian dream *has become* a nightmare.

B. Goudzwaard and Craig Bartholomew identify a number of puzzling paradoxes of our modern context, including the paradox of poverty, time, care, employment, and the environment.[142] In the current age, it would seem we have the significant resources and technology needed to eradicate poverty, free up more time for rest and leisure, provide better care (health and other kinds), create more jobs, and improve the environment. However, modernization has not only failed to provide the solution to these societal crises but has compounded the problems.

In the midst of this death spiral of liberal autonomy, countercultural movements are afoot. In the late twentieth century and the twenty-first century, religion has inexplicitly (it seems) made a major comeback. Local markets are emerging, craft is making a comeback, alternative forms of education are being explored, and countercultural communities are popping up. Individuals and communities are reimagining "liberty after liberalism."[143] Although these are troubling times, the prognosis is not all bad. However, how do we live with integrity as disciples of Jesus in the current context?

It would be naïve to think that Christian individuals and communities are immune to the spirit of the modern age. On the one hand, we have by and

141. Longley, introduction to Sacks, *Faith in the Future*, xiii (emphasis added).

142. Goudzwaard and Bartholomew, *Beyond the Modern Age*, 91–94.

143. This is from the title of the conclusion of Deneen, *Why Liberalism Failed*, ch. 8.

large bought into the lie of secularism that religion belongs to the personal and private sphere and should be kept out of the public realm. On the other hand, rather than stand as a distinct, countercultural community for the sake of the culture, we have aped many of the principles and practices of the wider culture. This is not good for us and it certainly provides no benefit for the culture in which we are called to be salt and light. It is beyond the scope of this book to provide an answer to the vast problems of modern Western society; however, it is entirely appropriate—necessary even—to consider what Judges has to contribute to the pressing needs of our day and to our calling as Christians in the midst of this broken world.

Hearing Judges Today

Judges stands as a testimony that genuine human freedom that leads to flourishing exists within boundaries and in relationship with God. Judges makes this point negatively, by portraying a people called to undivided allegiance to Yahweh and to a distinct vocation for the sake of the nations, who in reality sought a way that seemed right in their own eyes, leading to comprehensive (spiritual, moral, and social) failure. Andreas Köstenberger and Michael Kruger note that whereas the idea of everyone doing what is right in his/her own eyes stands as an indictment over the days of the judges, in our culture this is "celebrated as the ultimate expression of truly enlightened humanity."[144] The misery of our culture exposes the cracks in the foundation of human autonomy and relativism, and Judges shines a light on those cracks.

Judges, like all of Scripture, is public truth and its teachings about what it means to be human, what is the nature of reality and society, and so on, are relevant in a universal way. However, the focus of Judges' teaching is on and for the people of God (though with obvious implications for the nations). This commentary has repeatedly exposed how the chaos of the settlement period stems from the root of disloyalty to Yahweh as the divine king, and we have seen the consequences of this disloyalty in example after example in the book. How is it that the people of God shifted so drastically from one generation that professed unequivocally and repeatedly, "We will serve Yahweh" (Josh 24:18, 21, 24), to another generation and their descendants who "abandoned Yahweh" and "served" the gods of the nations (Judg 2:11–13, etc.)?

The clue, of course, is provided in Judg 2:10: "There arose another generation after them who did not know Yahweh or the work that he had done for

144. Köstenberger and Kruger, *Heresy of Orthodoxy*, 15.

Israel." So much is packed into this brief sentence. In short, the people of God had abandoned the story of a good and personal God who created the world with humans as the crown of creation, of a world cast into sin because of human rebellion, and of Yahweh choosing their ancestor Abraham to display his good purposes for the world now fractured by sin. They had abandoned that story to live out of another story. The statement implies that they had not recounted the stories of Abraham, Isaac, and Jacob, of Yahweh's defeat of Pharaoh and his covenant at Sinai, of Yahweh's protection and providence in the wilderness, and his presence in the conquest. It implies that they had not performed the many rituals—in the morning and evening of each day, every week, every month, every year, every seven years, and every fifty years—that would actualize those great events in Israel's past for future generations. It implies that they had not sung the songs of Yahweh's great victory and care on behalf of their ancestors. To be sure, there is a sense in Judges that the people were cognitively aware of their heritage, that they performed at least some of the rituals, and perhaps had a vague awareness of the songs of their tradition. However, they were not living as active participants in these stories. These stories, rituals, and songs were not functioning as proper and powerful "liturgies" that would capture their imagination, form their identity, shape their desires, and attune them to the world.[145] The "cultural liturgies" of Canaan proved to be far more alluring, twisting the desires of the people of God and shaping their conception of the good life.

Herein lies a profound message for the Christian church today. The powerful idols of individualism, consumerism, and secularism are shaping generations of people who identify as Christians and it is tainting their Christian witness. Köstenberger and Kruger note that these idols are not just out there in the culture, but in and among us: "Even in churches and houses of worship, what people are looking for is a variety of options, and if they don't like what they see, they take their business—or worship—elsewhere."[146] With remarkable clarity, John Carroll, self-admittedly not a Christian, fingers the problem: "The waning of Christianity as practiced in the West is easy to explain. The Christian churches have comprehensively failed in their one central task—to retell their foundation story in a way that might speak to the times."[147] Is this a fair assessment of modern Christianity? It is fair if by "telling the story" we include not only the verbal expression but also a consistent indwelling of the biblical story. This bears out if we evaluate modern Christianity through the prism of story, ritual, and song.

145. See Smith, *Desiring the Kingdom*, 25.

146. Köstenberger and Kruger, *Heresy of Orthodoxy*, 15.

147. Carroll, *Existential Jesus*, 7.

Preaching and evangelism are two key ways that Christians tell the gospel story, and while these practices are alive and well in some traditions, they can also be distorted. Sermons fail to tell the foundational story if they are reduced to heart-warming anecdotes or self-help guides, and they only tell part of the story (albeit an important part) if they focus solely on institutional corruption and social inequalities. Moreover, the full scope of the gospel's comprehensive message of salvation is all too often reduced to personal salvation and an otherworldly focus on heaven as the ultimate destination. Thus, telling the gospel story can either be avoided or truncated. In either case, it leads to a distorted witness in the world.

In terms of ritual, Evangelical Christianity is in some sense thriving, but it often exhibits an antiritual bias in favor of spontaneity and individualistic emotional response. The infrequent practice of the Eucharist in some churches is a symptom of this antiritualism. In traditions where ritual is valued, there is a danger that rituals become empty and meaningless. The church and individual Christians need powerful, vibrant, and relevant rituals that reinforce a sense of Christian identity and shape kingdom desires.

Moreover, the powerful songs that have the potential to inspire and shape the worshiper can in contemporary worship be trite and lack depth, or in more traditional worship sometimes be cast in language and melodies that are difficult for modern Christians to connect with, let alone be inspired by. For example, the range of human experience and emotion that we find in Israel's worship book, the Psalter, which Calvin referred to as an "anatomy of all parts of the soul," has been drastically reduced or distorted.[148]

This is not to say that the state of contemporary Christianity is all bad. Evidence exists in some Christian circles of a recovery of the Bible as the grand story of God's cosmic redemption plan, and Christian communities are learning to tell and live out this story in all its fullness. Some churches and individuals are retrieving the practices and rhythms of the church's tradition and putting them to use in meaningful ways. Furthermore, contemporary hymn-writers and worship-song composers are tapping the riches of Scripture and putting them to beautiful and inspiring melodies for today. A recovery of the Psalms, even the psalms of lament, as a source for authentic Christian worship is taking place, although perhaps it is still in the early days.

All of this points to another truth that Judges has to offer contemporary Christianity as a whole with regard to the tribalism and fragmentation of Christianity. The twelve tribes that, as a whole, made up the people of God in the settlement period were diverse, with evidence of strengths and gifts, and

148. Cited in Mays, "Calvin's Commentary on the Psalms," 200.

also weaknesses. The tribe of Benjamin included in its fold seven hundred expert marksmen, the Levites contributed to the nation its priestly functionaries, the Ephraimites seemed somewhat at the margins and based on Judg 12:6, the Ephraimites and Gileadites varied in their pronunciation of certain words. Other differences no doubt existed depending on regional distinctiveness and other factors. And yet together they were called to be a kingdom of priests and a holy nation, by no means flattening out their tribal distinctives but directing those to a common goal and a common calling. The diversity of the Christian church today, evidenced by the countless denominations, is not necessarily negative as such, but it can negatively affect the church's witness when it leads to isolationism, fragmentation, and balkanization. What Christian unity looks like in the proliferation of denominations is difficult to say, but we need each other. We especially need to listen to and learn from each other in such a way that we maximize the strengths of each tradition and make up for one another's weaknesses, for the sake of our witness to the world. Jesus's high-priestly prayer in John 17 singles out the vital importance of the unity of believers for the sake of our witness (see esp. vv. 21–23).

While there are some promising signs in contemporary Christianity, we should by no means underestimate the powerful idols of our times. Just like God's people during the settlement period, the church needs to acknowledge the extent to which we have divided our allegiances. We may expend all our energy doing battle with the enemy without, while ignoring the enemy within. Israel could have contributed to the solution, but by abandoning Yahweh and serving the Baals they had capitulated on their calling and become part of the problem. It will not do to go to church on Sunday and sing the praises of Jesus, while pursuing the "American dream" the other six days of the week, with negative implications not only for ourselves, but for our families, local and global communities, and the planet. An undivided commitment to Jesus as Lord should not result in a quietist retreat from the public square but in a full engagement *as followers of Jesus* into politics, the arts, business, economics, urban planning, creation care, and so on. The powerful allure of idolatry in the settlement period that influenced a people's desire for their own good should be a warning for the people of God today.

Judges, concerned as it is with leadership, is also instructive for today. Three places in the book portray the people seeking for themselves/electing a leader (Gideon in 8:22, Abimelech in 9:1–3, and Jephthah 11:1–11). In each case, they desire leadership that would overcome their wrongly identified problem (i.e., political instability stemming from the lack of strong, enduring leadership). Like the Israelites who showed a preference for leaders like Jephthah and the later Gideon who used excessive force to battle the external enemies, we demonstrate a preference for the flashy and powerful leadership qualities that our culture prizes, rather than the courageous, servant leadership of the early Gideon who exposed and dismantled the enemy within the gates. If there's one thing we learn from Gideon it is that messing with people's idols is an unpopular and potentially life-threatening business! Are our leaders inspiring and equipping us toward a more faithful, undivided witness to the power of the gospel, or are they inadvertently setting up idols in our midst that all of God's people "whore after" (8:27, 33), or themselves sacrificing family and other God-given gifts to further their own ends (11:39).

Perhaps surprisingly, Judges is a book for our times. If we have eyes to see and ears to hear, it exposes the idols in our midst that compromise our way of being in the world. It holds out hope for breaking the cycle of violence, misery, and despair for a people committed to Jesus and his kingdom—that his kingdom may come, and his will be done on earth and among his people for the sake of the world, as it is in heaven.

Bibliography

Ackerman, Susan. *Warrior, Dancer, Seductress, Queen: Women in Judges and Biblical Israel.* ABRL. New York: Doubleday, 1998.

Albright, W. F. "The Ancient Near East and the Religion of Israel." *JBL* 59 (1940): 85–112.

Alter, Robert. *Ancient Israel: The Former Prophets; Joshua, Judges, Samuel, and Kings; A Translation with Commentary*. New York: Norton., 2013.

———. *The Art of Biblical Narrative*. New York: Basic Books, 1981.

Amit, Yaira. *The Book of Judges: The Art of Editing*. Translated by Jonathan Chipman. BibInt 38. Leiden: Brill, 1999.

———. "Endings—Especially Reversal Endings." *Scriptura* 87 (2004): 213–26.

———. *Reading Biblical Narratives: Literary Criticism and the Hebrew Bible*. Minneapolis: Fortress, 2001.

Anderson, Bernhard W. *Understanding the Old Testament.* Englewood Cliffs, NJ: Prentice-Hall, 1957.

Ashford, Bruce R. "A Theological Sickness unto Death: Philip Rieff's Prophetic Analysis of Our Secular Age." *Themelios* 43 (2018): 34–44.

Baker, David W. "Scribes as Transmitters of Tradition." Pages 65–77 in *Faith, Tradition, and History: Old Testament Historiography in Its Near Eastern Context*. Edited by Alan R. Millard, James K. Hoffmeier, and David W. Baker. Winona Lake, IN: Eisenbrauns, 1994.

Barry, John D., ed. *Lexham Bible Dictionary*. Bellingham, WA: Lexham, 2016.

Barth, Karl. *Church Dogmatics*. 14 vols. Translated by G. W. Bromiley and Thomas F. Torrance. Edinburgh: T&T Clark, 1960–1977.

Bartholomew, Craig G. *Where Mortals Dwell: A Christian View of Place for Today*. Grand Rapids: Baker Academic, 2011.

Bauer, Uwe F. W. "Judges 18 as an Anti-Spy Story in the Context of an Anti-Conquest Story: The Creative Usage of Literary Genres." *JSOT* 88 (2000): 37–47.

Bavinck, Herman. *Reformed Dogmatics* 4 vols. Edited by John Bolt. Translated by John Vriend. Grand Rapids: Baker Academic, 2003–2008.

Bebbington, David. *Patterns in History: A Christian Perspective on Historical Thought*. Vancouver: Regent College Publishing, 1990.

Beck, John A. "Gideon, Dew and the Narrative-Geographical Shaping of Judges 6:33–40." *BSac* 165 (2008): 28–38.

Beldman, David J. H. *The Completion of Judges: Strategies of Ending in Judges 17–21*. Siphrut 21. Winona Lake, IN: Eisenbrauns, 2017.

———. *Deserting the King: The Book of Judges*. Transformative Word Series. Bellingham, WA: Lexham, 2017.

———. "Literary Approaches and Old Testament Interpretation." Pages 67–95 in *Hearing the Old Testament: Listening for God's Address*. Edited by Craig G. Bartholomew and David J. H. Beldman. Grand Rapids: Eerdmans, 2012.

Beldman, David J. H., and Jonathan Swales. "Biblical Theology and Theological Interpretation." Pages 149–70 in *A Manifesto for Theological Interpretation*. Edited by Craig G. Bartholomew and Heath A. Thomas. Grand Rapids: Baker Academic, 2016.

Benedict, Philip. "Religion and Politics in Europe, 1500–1700." Pages 155–76 in *Religion und Gewalt: Konflikte, Rituale, Deutungen (1500–1800)*. Edited by Kaspar von Greyerz and Kim Seibenhüner. Veröffentlichungen des Max-Planck-Instituts für Geschichte 215. Göttingen: Vandenhoeck & Ruprecht, 2006.

Biddle, Mark E. *Reading Judges: A Literary and Theological Commentary*. Macon: Smyth & Helwys, 2012.

Block, Daniel I. *Judges, Ruth*. NAC 6. Nashville: Broadman & Holman, 1999.

———. "The Period of the Judges: Religious Disintegration under Tribal Rule." Pages 39–57 in *Israel's Apostasy and Restoration: Essays in Honor of Roland K. Harrison*. Edited by Avraham Gileadi. Grand Rapids: Baker, 1988.

———. "Will the Real Gideon Please Stand Up? Narrative Style and Intention in Judges 6–9." *JETS* 40 (1997): 353–66.

Bluedorn, Wolfgang. *Yahweh Versus Baalism: A Theological Reading of the Gideon Abimelech Narrative*. JSOTSup 329. Sheffield: Sheffield Academic, 2001.

Boling, Robert G. *Judges: A New Translation with Introduction and Commentary*. AB 6A. Garden City, NY: Doubleday, 1975.

Bonheim, Helmut. *The Narrative Modes: Techniques of the Short Story*. Cambridge: Brewer, 1982.

Brettler, Marc Zvi. *The Book of Judges*. OTR. New York: Routledge, 2002.

Brunner, Emil. *Dogmatics*. 3 vols. Translated by Olive Wyon. London: Lutterworth, 1952–1966.

Burns, Anna. *Milkman*. London: Faber & Faber, 2018.

Butler, Trent C. *Joshua*. WBC 7. Dallas: Word, 1998.

———. *Judges*. WBC 8. Nashville: Nelson, 2009.

Byrd, James P. *Sacred Scripture, Sacred War: The Bible and the American Revolution*. Oxford: Oxford University Press, 2013.

Calvin, John. *Institutes of the Christian Religion*. 2 vols. Edited by John T. McNeill. Translated by Ford Lewis Battles. LCC. Louisville: Westminster John Knox, 2011.

Carroll, John. *The Existential Jesus*. Berkeley: Counterpoint, 2007.

Cassel, Paulus. *The Book of Judges*. Translated by P. H. Steenstra. New York: Scribners, 1871.

Childs, Brevard S. *Biblical Theology of the Old and New Testaments: Theological Reflection on the Christian Bible*. Minneapolis: Fortress, 1993.

Chisholm, Robert B., Jr. *A Commentary on Judges and Ruth*. Kregel Exegetical Library. Grand Rapids: Kregel, 2013.

———. "Identity Crisis: Assessing Samson's Birth and Career." *BSac* 166 (2009): 147–62.

———. "What's Wrong with This Picture? Stylistic Variation as a Rhetorical Technique in Judges." *JSOT* 34 (2009): 171–82.

———. "Yahweh Versus the Canaanite Gods: Polemic in Judges and 1Samuel 1–7." *BSac* 164 (2007): 165–80.

Christianson, E. S. "A Fistful of Shekels: Scrutinizing Ehud's Entertaining Violence (Judges 3:12–30)." *BibInt* 11 (2003): 53–78.

Clines, David J. A. *The Theme of the Pentateuch*. JSOTSup 10. Sheffield: Sheffield Academic, 1978.

Crawford, Timothy. "Reading Samson with the Dead." *PRSt* 35 (2008): 223–36.

Crouch, Andy. *Playing God: Redeeming the Gift of Power*. Downers Grove, IL: InterVarsity Press, 2013.

Culp, A. J. *Puzzling Portraits: Seeing the Old Testament's Confusing Characters as Ethical Models*. Eugene, OR: Wipf & Stock, 2013.

Cundall, Arthur E. "Judges." Pages 7–215 in *Judges and Ruth: An Introduction and Commentary*. TOTC. Downers Grove, IL: InterVarsity Press, 1968.

Dawkins, Richard. *The God Delusion*. London: Bantam, 2006.

Deneen, Patrick J. *Why Liberalism Failed*. Politics and Culture. New Haven: Yale University Press, 2018.

Durham, John I. *Exodus*. WBC 3. Dallas: Word, 1998.

Echols, Charles L. "The Eclipse of God in the Song of Deborah (Judges 5)." *TynBul* 56 (2005): 149–52.

———. *"Tell Me, O Muse": The Song of Deborah (Judges 5) in the Light of Heroic Poetry*. LHBOTS 487. London: T&T Clark, 2008.

Elwell, Walter A., and Barry J. Beitzel. "Angel of the Lord." Page 90 in vol. 1 of *Baker Encyclopedia of the Bible*. Edited by Walter A. Elwell. Grand Rapids: Baker, 1988.

Emmrich, Martin. "The Symbolism of the Lion and the Bees: Another Ironic Twist in the Samson Cycle." *JETS* 44 (2001): 67–74.

Endris, Vince. "Yahweh versus Baal: A Narrative-Critical Reading of the Gideon/Abimelech Narrative." *JSOT* 33 (2008): 173–95.

Exum, J. Cheryl. "The Centre Cannot Hold: Thematic and Textual Instabilities in Judges." *CBQ* 52 (1990): 410–31.

———. *Fragmented Women: Feminist (Sub)versions of Biblical Narratives*. JSOTSup 163. Sheffield: JSOT Press, 1993.

Fishbane, Michael A. *Biblical Interpretation in Ancient Israel*. Oxford: Oxford University Press, 1985.

Frame, John M. *Systematic Theology: An Introduction to Christian Belief*. Phillipsburg, NJ: P&R Publishing, 2013.

Frolov, Serge. *Judges*. FOTL 6B. Grand Rapids: Eerdmans, 2013.

Fuchs, Andreas. "Assyria at War: Strategy and Conduct." Pages 380–401 in *The Oxford Handbook of Cuneiform Culture*. Edited by Karen Radner and Eleanor Robson. Oxford: Oxford University Press, 2011.

Genette, G. *Narrative Discourse: An Essay in Method*. Ithaca, NY: Cornell University Press, 1983.

Gillmayr-Bucher, Susanne. "Memories Laid to Rest: The Book of Judges in the Persian Period." Pages 115–32 in *Deuteronomy–Kings as Emerging Authoritative Books: A Conversation*. Edited by Diana V. Edelman. ANEM 6. Atlanta: SBL Press, 2014.

Girard, René. *Deceit, Desire, and the Novel: Self and Other in Literary Structure*. Translated by Yvonne Freccero. Baltimore: Johns Hopkins University Press, 1965.

Goheen, Michael W. *A Light to the Nations: The Missional Church and the Biblical Story*. Grand Rapids: Baker Academic, 2011.

Golden, Jonathan M. *Ancient Canaan and Israel: New Perspectives*. Understanding Ancient Civilizations. Santa Barbara: ABC-CLIO, 2004.

Goldingay, John. *Joshua, Judges, and Ruth for Everyone*. Louisville: Westminster John Knox, 2011.

Gooding, David W. "The Composition of the Book of Judges." *ErIsr* 16 (1982): 70*–79*.

Gottlieb, Isaac B. "*Sof Davar*: Biblical Endings." *Proof* 11 (1991): 213–24.

Goudzwaard, B., and Craig G. Bartholomew. *Beyond the Modern Age: An Archaeology of Contemporary Culture*. Downers Grove, IL: InterVarsity Press, 2017.

Greenstein, Edward L. "The Riddle of Samson." *Proof* 1 (1981): 237–60.

Grossman, David. *Lion's Honey: The Myth of Samson*. Toronto: Knopf Canada, 2005.

Groves, J. Alan. "Judges, Book of." Pages 410–15 in *Dictionary for Theological Interpretation of the Bible*. Edited by Kevin J. Vanhoozer, Craig G. Bartholomew, Daniel J. Treier, and N. T. Wright. Grand Rapids: Baker Academic, 2005.

Grudem, Wayne A. *Systematic Theology: An Introduction to Biblical Doctrine*. Grand Rapids: Zondervan, 1994.

Gunn, David M. *Judges*. Blackwell Bible Commentaries. Oxford: Blackwell, 2005.

———. "Judges." Pages 89–103 in *The Oxford Handbook of the Reception History of the Bible*. Edited by Michael Lieb, Emma Mason, and Jonathan Roberts. Oxford: Oxford University Press, 2011.

Hackett, Jo Ann A. "Violence and Women's Lives in the Book of Judges." *Int* 58 (2004): 356–64.

Hartley, John E. *Leviticus*. WBC 4. Dallas: Word, 1999.

Hauser, Alan J. "Judging Judges Scholarship." Pages 431–44 in *Interested Readers: Essays on the Hebrew Bible in Honor of David J. A. Clines*. Edited by James K. Aitken, Jeremy M. S. Clines, and Cristl M. Maier. Atlanta: SBL Press, 2013.

———. "Unity and Diversity in Early Israel before Samuel." *JETS* 22 (1979): 289–303.

Hazony, Yoram. "Does the Bible Have a Political Teaching?" *Hebraic Political Studies* 1 (2006): 137–61.

Herzberg, Bruce. "Deborah and Moses." *JSOT* 38 (2013): 15–33.

Hitchens, Christopher. *God Is Not Great: How Religion Poisons Everything*. New York: Twelve, 2007.

Hodge, Charles. *Systematic Theology*. 3 vols. Grand Rapids: Eerdmans, 1970.

Holland, Glenn S. *Gods in the Desert: Religions of the Ancient Near East*. New York: Rowman & Littlefield, 2009.

Hoyt, JoAnna. "Reassessing Repentance in Judges." *BSac* 169 (2012): 143–58.

Hudson, Don Michael. "Living in a Land of Epithets: Anonymity in Judges 19–21." *JSOT* 62 (1994): 49–66.

James, Carolyn C. *Finding God in the Margins: The Book of Ruth*. Transformative Word Series. Bellingham, WA: Lexham, 2018.

Janzen, David. "Why the Deuteronomist Told about the Sacrifice of Jephthah's Daughter." *JSOT* 29 (2005): 339–57.

Jenkins, G. "Commentary on Judges: Patristic and Medieval Sources." Pages 231–48 in *A Companion to Peter Martyr Vermigli*. Edited by Torrance Kirby, Emidio Campi, and Frank A. James III. Leiden: Brill, 2009.

Johnson, Benjamin J. M. "What Type of Son Is Samson? Reading Judges 13 as a Biblical Type-Scene." *JETS* 53 (2010): 269–86.

Jonquière, Tessel M. "Of Valour and Strength: The Samson Cycle in Josephus' Work: *Jewish Antiquities* 5.276–317." Pages 119–23 in *Samson: Hero or Fool? The Many Faces of Samson*. Edited by Erik Eynikel and Tobias Nicklas. TBN 17. Leiden: Brill, 2014.

Jordan, James B. *Judges: A Practical and Theological Commentary*. Eugene, OR: Wipf & Stock, 1999.

Keil, Carl F., and Franz Delitzsch. *Commentary on the Old Testament,* Vol. 2: *The Pentateuch*. Translated by James Martin. Peabody, MA: Hendrickson, 1996.

Keller, Timothy. *Judges for You*. New York: Good Book Company, 2013.

Klein, Lillian R. *The Triumph of Irony in the Book of Judges*. JSOTSup 68. Sheffield: Almond Press, 1988.

Köstenberger, Andreas J., and Michael J. Kruger. *The Heresy of Orthodoxy: How Contemporary Culture's Fascination with Diversity Has Reshaped Our Understanding of Early Christianity*. Nottingham: Apollos, 2010.

Koyzis, David T. *Political Visions and Illusions: A Survey and Christian Critique of Contemporary Ideologies*. Downers Grove, IL: InterVarsity Press, 2003.

Landers, Solomon. "Did Jephthah Kill His Daughter?" *BR* 7 (1991): 28–31.

Lane, William L. *Hebrews 1–8*. WBC 47A. Waco, TX: Word, 1991.

Lasine, Stuart. "Guest and Host in Judges 19: Lot's Hospitality in an Inverted World." *JSOT* 29 (1984): 37–59.

Lilla, Mark. *The Stillborn God: Religion, Politics, and the Modern West*. New York: Vintage, 2008.

Longley, Clifford. Introduction to *Faith in the Future*, by Jonathan Sacks, x–xiv. London: Darton, Longman & Todd, 1995.

MacDonald, Nathan. *Not Bread Alone: The Uses of Food in the Old Testament*. Oxford: Oxford University Press, 2008.

Malamat, Abraham. "The Danite Migration and the Pan-Israelite Exodus-Conquest: A Biblical Narrative Pattern." *Bib* 51 (1970): 1–16.

Martin, Lee Roy. "Power to Save!? The Role of the Spirit of the Lord in the Book of Judges." *JPT* 16 (2008): 21–50.

———. "The Unheard Voice of God: A Pentecostal Hearing of the Book of Judges." PhD diss., University of South Africa, 2006.

———. *The Unheard Voice: A Pentecostal Hearing of the Book of Judges*. JPTSup 32. Blandford Forum: Deo, 2008.

Mayfield, Tyler. "Accounts of Deborah." *CurBR* 7 (2009): 306–35.

Mays, James L. "Calvin's Commentary on the Psalms: The Preface as Introduction." Pages 195–204 in *John Calvin and the Church: A Prism of Reform*. Edited by Timothy George. Louisville: Westminster John Knox, 1990.

———. *Psalms*. IBC. Louisville: Westminster John Knox, 2011.

McCann, J. Clinton, Jr. *Judges*. IBC. Louisville: John Knox, 2002.

———. *A Theological Introduction to the Psalms: The Psalms as Torah*. Nashville: Abingdon, 1993.

Merrill, Eugene H. *Deuteronomy*. NAC 4. Nashville: Broadman & Holman, 1994.

Middleton, J. Richard. *The Liberating Image: The* Imago Dei *in Genesis 1*. Grand Rapids: Brazos, 2005.

Miller, Paul. "Moral Formation and the Book of Judges." *EvQ* 75 (2003): 99–115.
Moore, George Foot. *A Critical and Exegetical Commentary on Judges*. ICC. Edinburgh: T&T Clark, 1949.
Morgenstern, Mira. "Strangeness, Violence, and the Establishment of Nationhood in Rousseau." *Eighteenth-Century Studies* 41 (2008): 359–81.
Muilenburg, James. "Form Criticism and Beyond." *JBL* 88 (1969): 1–18.
Newsom, Carol A., Sharon H. Ringe, and Jacqueline E. Lapsley, eds. *Women's Bible Commentary: Revised and Updated*. Louisville: Westminster John Knox, 2012.
Niditch, Susan. *Judges: A Commentary*. OTL. Louisville: Westminster John Knox, 2008.
———. "Judges, Kingship and Political Ethics: A Challenge to the Conventional Wisdom." Pages 59–70 in *Thus Says the Lord: Essays on the Former and Latter Prophets in Honor of Robert R. Wilson*. Edited by John J. Ahn and Stephen L Cook. LHBOTS 502. New York: T&T Clark, 2009.
Nietzsche, Friedrich. "The Madman." Pages 181–82 in *The Gay Science: With a Prelude in Rhymes and an Appendix of Songs*. Translated by Walter Kaufmann. New York: Random House, 1974.
Nikolsky, Ronit. "Rabbinic Discourse about Samson: Continuity and Change between the Tannaitic Culture to the Amoraic." Pages 101–18 in *Samson: Hero or Fool? The Many Faces of Samson*. Edited by Erik Eynikel and Tobias Nicklas. TBN 17. Leiden: Brill, 2014.
Noth, Martin. *The Deuteronomistic History*. Translated by David Orton. JSOTSup 15. Sheffield: JSOT Press, 1981.
———. *Überlieferungsgeschichtliche Studien*. Halle: Niemeyer, 1943.
Nugent, John C. "The Politics of YHWH: John Howard Yoder's Old Testament Narration and Its Implications for Social Ethics." *Journal for Religious Ethics* 39 (2011): 71–99.
Nyquist, Mary. "The Plight of Buchanan's Jephtha: Sacrifice, Sovereignty, and Paternal Power." *Comparative Literature* 60 (2008): 331–54.
O'Connell, Robert H. *The Rhetoric of the Book of Judges*. VTSup 63. Leiden: Brill, 1996.
O'Donovan, Oliver. *Desire of the Nations: Rediscovering the Roots of Political Theology*. Cambridge: Cambridge University Press, 1996.
Ogden, Graham S. "Jotham's Fable: Its Structure and Function in Judges 9." *BT* 46 (1995): 301–8.
———. "The Special Features of a Story: A Study of Judges 3.12–20." *BT* 42 (1991): 408–14.
Pannenberg, Wolfhart. *Systematic Theology*. Translated by G. W. Bromiley. 3 vols. Grand Rapids: Eerdmans, 1991–1998.
Polzin, Robert. *Moses and the Deuteronomist: A Literary Study of the Deuteronomic History; Part One; Deuteronomy, Joshua, Judges*. New York: Seabury, 1980.
Reis, Pamela T. "Spoiled Child: A Fresh Look at Jephthah's Daughter." *Prooftexts* 17 (1997): 279–98.
Rieff, Philip. *My Life Among the Deathworks: Illustrations of the Aesthetics of Authority*. Charlottesville: University of Virginia Press, 2006.
Robertson, John F. "The Social and Economic Organization of Ancient Mesopotamian Temples." Pages 443–54 in vol. 1 of *Civilizations of the Ancient Near East*. Edited by Jack M. Sasson. New York: Scribner, 1995.
Ross, Jillian L. "A People Heeds Not Scripture: A Poetics of Pentateuchal Allusions in the Book of Judges." PhD diss., Trinity Evangelical Divinity School, 2015.

Rowley, Matthew P. "Godly Violence: Military Providentialism in the Puritan Atlantic World, 1636–1676." PhD diss., University of Leicester, 2018.

Ryan, Roger. *Judges*. OTR. Sheffield: Sheffield Phoenix, 2007.

Sacks, Jonathan. *Faith in the Future*. London: Darton, Longman & Todd, 1995.

———. "Shoftim: On the Limits of Power." *Covenant & Conversation* (blog). August 16, 2007. http://rabbisacks.org/shoftim-5767-on-the-limits-of-power

Sasson, Jack M. *Judges 1–12: A New Translation with Introduction and Commentary*. AB 6D. New Haven: Yale University Press, 2014.

Schneider, Tammi. *Judges*. Berit Olam. Collegeville, MN: Liturgical Press, 2000.

Schöpflin, Karin. "Jotham's Speech and Fable as Prophetic Comment on Abimelech's Story: The Genesis of Judges 9." *SJOT* 18 (2004): 3–22.

———. "Samson in European Literature: Some Examples from English, French and German Poetry." Pages 177–96 in *Samson: Hero or Fool? The Many Faces of Samson*. Edited by Erik Eynikel and Tobias Nicklas. TBN 17. Leiden: Brill, 2014.

Sixth Sense, The. Written and directed by M. Night Shyamalan. Hollywood Pictures; Spyglass Entertainment, 1999.

Smith, Barbara Herrnstein. *Poetic Closure: A Study of How Poems End*. Chicago: University of Chicago Press, 1968.

Smith, James K. A. *Desiring the Kingdom: Worship, Worldview, and Cultural Formation*. Grand Rapids: Baker Academic, 2011.

Smith, Michael J. "The Failure of the Family in Judges, Part 1: Jephthah." *BSac* 162 (2005): 279–98.

Soggin, J. Alberto. *Judges: A Commentary*. OTL. Philadelphia: Westminster, 1981.

Spronk, Klaas. "The Looks of a Hero: Some Aspects of Samson in Fine Arts." Pages 197–209 in *Samson: Hero or Fool? The Many Faces of Samson*. Edited by Erik Eynikel and Tobias Nicklas. TBN 17. Leiden: Brill, 2014.

Sternberg, Meir. *The Poetics of Biblical Narrative: Ideological Literature and the Drama of Reading*. ISBL. Bloomington: Indiana University Press, 1987.

Stone, Lawson G. *Judges*. Cornerstone Biblical Commentary. Carol Stream, IL: Tyndale House, 2012.

Stump, Eleonore. "Samson and Self-Destroying Evil." Pages 199–217 in *Philosophers and the Jewish Bible*. Edited by Charles Harry Manekin and Robert Eisen. STJHC 17. Bethesda, MD: University Press of Maryland, 2008.

Sypherd, Wilbur O. *Jephthah and His Daughter: A Study in Comparative Literature*. Wilmington: University of Delaware, 1948.

Taylor, Marion Ann, and Christiana de Groot, eds. *Women of War, Women of Woe: Joshua and Judges through the Eyes of Nineteenth-Century Female Biblical Interpreters*. Grand Rapids: Eerdmans, 2016.

Thompson, John L. "Preaching Texts of Terror in the Book of Judges: How Does the History of Interpretation Help?" *CTJ* 37 (2002): 49–61.

———. *Reading the Bible with the Dead: What You Can Learn from the History of Exegesis That You Can't Learn from Exegesis Alone*. Grand Rapids: Eerdmans, 2007.

Turner, Laurence A. *Announcements of Plot in Genesis*. JSOTSup 96. Sheffield: JSOT Press, 1990.

Walton, John H. *Ancient Near Eastern Thought and the Old Testament: Introducing the Conceptual World of the Hebrew Bible*. Grand Rapids: Baker Academic, 2006.

Walton, John H., Victor H. Matthews, and Mark W. Chavalas. *The IVP Bible Background Commentary: Old Testament*. Downers Grove, IL: InterVarsity Press, 2000.

Webb, Barry G. *The Book of the Judges: An Integrated Reading*. JSOTSup 46. Sheffield: JSOT Press, 1987.

———. *The Book of Judges*. NICOT. Grand Rapids: Eerdmans, 2012.

Wenham, Gordon J. *Genesis 1–15*. WBC 1. Dallas: Word, 1998.

———. *Story as Torah: Reading the Old Testament Ethically*. Grand Rapids: Baker Academic, 2000.

Wilson, Lindsay. *Job*. THOTC. Grand Rapids: Eerdmans, 2015.

Wilson, Michael K. "'As You Like It': The Idolatry of Micah and the Danites (Judges 17–18)." *RTR* 54 (1995): 73–85.

Wong, Gregory T. K. *Compositional Strategy of the Book of Judges: An Inductive, Rhetorical Study*. VTSup 111. Leiden: Brill, 2006.

———. "Song of Deborah as Polemic." *Bib* 88 (2007): 1–22.

Wright, Christopher J. H. *The God I Don't Understand: Reflections on Tough Questions of Faith*. Grand Rapids: Zondervan, 2008.

———. *The Mission of God: Unlocking the Bible's Grand Narrative*. Downers Grove, IL: InterVarsity Press, 2006.

———. *Old Testament Ethics for the People of God*. Downers Grove, IL: InterVarsity Press, 2004.

Yee, Gale A. "By the Hand of a Woman: The Metaphor of the Woman Warrior in Judges 4." *Semeia* 61 (1993): 110–12.

Yoder, John C. *Power and Politics in the Book of Judges: Men and Women of Valor*. Minneapolis: Fortress, 2015.

Younger, K. Lawson, Jr. "Judges 1 in Its Near Eastern Literary Context." Pages 207–27 in *Faith, Tradition, History: Essays on Old Testament Historiography in Its Near Eastern Context*. Edited by Alan R. Millard, James K. Hoffmeier and David W. Baker. Winona Lake, IN: Eisenbrauns, 1994.

———. *Judges and Ruth*. NIVAC. Grand Rapids: Zondervan, 2002.

Author Index

Scripture Index